TEACHER'S RESOURCE MANUAL

ONE NATION MANY PEOPLE

VOLUME ONE

THE UNITED STATES TO 1900

VOLUME TWO

THE UNITED STATES SINCE 1876

GLOBE FEARON
Educational Publisher
Paramus, New Jersey

Executive Editor: Stephen Lewin
Senior Editor: Francie Holder
Editor: Kirsten Richert
Editorial Assistant: Mindy DePalma
Educational Consultant: Deborah Parks
Production Manager: Penny Gibson
Senior Production Editor: Linda Greenberg
Production Editor: Alan Dalgleish
Art Director: Nancy Sharkey
Senior Product Manager: Elmer Ildefonso
Book Design: Carol Anson
Electronic Page Production: Impressions
Photo Research: Jenifer Hixson
Cover Design: Richard Puder Design

ISBN: 0-835-90804-6

Printed in the United States of America
1 2 3 4 5 6 7 8 9 10 99 98 97 96 95 94

GLOBE FEARON
EDUCATIONAL PUBLISHER
PARAMUS, NEW JERSEY

Paramount Publishing

CONTENTS

▶INTRODUCING *ONE NATION,*
▶*MANY PEOPLE*

A Program That Puts American History Within the Grasp of All Students

One Nation, Many People is a comprehensive American history program designed for students reading below grade level. Unlike other such programs, it is neither a watered-down version of a detail-crammed, on-level text; nor is it an elementary school text with inappropriate text and illustrations for older students.

Six major features distinguish ***One Nation, Many People*** from other text programs designed for students reading below level.

LINKS THE PAST TO THE STUDENTS' PRESENT AND THEIR FUTURE

One Nation, Many People is based on three important principles:

(1) American history is an exciting and dramatic story. All students can be caught up in the story if the material is presented with the drama that it deserves.

(2) Students today need to know the relevance of history to their lives. That relevance exists; it requires only some effort and imagination to bring it out.

(3) The authors of ***One Nation, Many People*** believe that students learn best what is a part of their social and cultural experiences. Learning about one's cultural roots enhances the potential of students. Hence, the authors have put a great emphasis on the infusion of multicultural content into ***One Nation, Many People.***

EMPHASIZES OUR MULTICULTURAL PAST

One Nation, Many People provides the first truly inclusive approach to American history. It tells the history of all Americans, emphasizing the underrepresented roles of women, African Americans, Latinos, Asians, and Native Americans.

No other program has such an in-depth treatment of people of color and of women. This multicultural content is not an afterthought presented in sidebars that are not central to the content. Multicultural history is an integral part of the content and concepts taught in the text. ***One Nation, Many People*** treats in detail numerous multicultural themes of our history that are barely mentioned in traditional programs. For example, here are some of the themes treated in the period prior to the Civil War:

- The multicultural nature of the American colonies
- The development of an advanced Latino culture at a time when the colonies were little more than rude settlements hugging the Atlantic coast
- The major role of freed African Americans in the Middle Colonies
- Legal, political, and military efforts by Native Americans to prevent their ejection from lands east of the Mississippi River
- Efforts by Latinos in the Mexican borderlands to preserve their rights after the United States' takeover of these lands following the U.S.-Mexican War
- The struggle by enslaved African Americans to preserve their families and their culture

MEETS THE SPECIAL LEARNING NEEDS OF TODAY'S AMERICAN HISTORY CLASSROOM

The authors and editors of ***One Nation, Many People*** recognize that the very nature of the American classroom has changed in recent years. To meet these new needs, they have created new approaches to the presentation of content.

One Nation, Many People has a straightforward writing style. It does not use idioms or colloquialisms. It eschews complicated sentence structure. It does not have confusing flashbacks of content. This straightforward style is particularly appropriate for ESL students and for students who have a limited proficiency with the English language.

In addition, every chapter of ***One Nation, Many People*** has a variety of devices that aid in learning: for example, the directed-reading question at the beginning of the chapter, and classroom-tested ideas for cooperative/collaborative activities at the end of the chapter. Every chapter has extensive support for student learning, in the form of chapter and section reading focus questions, **Looking at Key Terms, Looking at Key Words** (a vocabulary preview), and the **Study Hint**. Furthermore, the two books are illustrated with age-appropriate photos and artwork selected from the period being studied. There are no elementary school-type drawings that the older student will find condescending.

PRESENTS A STORY RICHLY TOLD, YET EASY TO READ

Telling the story of our nation's history should be exciting, yet easy to read. ***One Nation, Many People*** presents a dramatic human story that points out the significance for our times. It is filled with the drama and color necessary to involve all students. The profusion of human interest elements gives a "You Are There" quality to the narrative.

However, ***One Nation, Many People*** is easy to read and understand because it written in a way that students can comprehend. The many easy-to-understand illustrations, charts, maps, and timelines enhance mastery.

Color and drama are important. But students require content. ***One Nation, Many People*** has the substance that your students need. It is never just a collection of stories. Rather, it provides students with a framework for understanding our history. It has the comprehensive history that will help your students succeed. This comprehensive content helps ESL/LEP student learn about American culture. It provides the background of traditional American institutions such as Thanksgiving or the Fourth of July.

GIVES STUDENTS THE TOOLS TO ASSURE LEARNING

Five key learning aids help your students organize the chapter content.

- Chapter and section titles are complete sentences to facilitate outlining and prereading.
- Chapters and sections begin with a question that poses the main idea.
- ***Looking at Key Terms*** previews important people, events, places, documents, and laws.
- ***Looking at Key Words*** defines the vocabulary words introduced in the section.
- The ***Study Hint*** helps students become active learners rather than passive readers.

Every chapter has a **Timeline** located on the second spread of the chapter. This timeline provides students with the opportunity to preview and organize the content.

Chapters end with a variety of elements geared for lower-level and ESL/LEP students. **Chapter Key Ideas** offers students a summary of what they have learned. **Reviewing the Chapter** presents vocabulary, recall, comprehension, and skills questions. Then it has a number of brief writing activities, including an activity titled **What Would You Have Done?** This activity puts the student in the position of making concrete and personal decisions about real historical events. Each chapter review has **Working Together** that presents two cooperative learning activities. These are brief activities that can be accomplished within the confines of a classroom and within the time frame of one class session. These activities, whether taken individually or as a whole, are particularly useful for students whose progress has been limited and for ESL and LEP students. Finally, a **Past to Present** activity invites students to discover the relationship of U.S. history to their lives today.

DESIGNED FOR HETEROGENEOUS CLASSES WITH ESL AND LEP STUDENTS

One Nation, Many People is uniquely designed for use with heterogeneous groupings of students, especially those classrooms that have significant numbers of students whose proficiency with the English language is limited, or who are ESL students. Each lesson provides a parallel lesson plan to enable teachers to meet the needs of students with a variety of proficiencies. The lessons begin with common goals for all students in the class. Then they branch off into activities appropriate for your mainstream student and activities that are within the grasp of your ESL and LEP students. Finally, a section entitled **Pulling It All Together** allows the teacher to have students from the different groups share the outcomes of their activities. Each of the separate activities is supported by worksheets appropriate to the level of English proficiency. All lessons contain a teaching tip about ESL/LEP methods, classroom management, or an interesting technique to enhance classroom activities. In addition, a two-page section presents ongoing activities, some for ESL/LEP students and others for all students, that tie together chapters, units, and more. Some are skills related; others offer opportunities to extend and enrich student learning. These activities can be used as opportunities for alternative assessment.

An interdisciplinary handbook presents ways to integrate other disciplines into the teaching of history. The ***Teacher's Resource Manual*** includes a discussion of language arts in social studies and continues with four **Writing Workshops** that walk students through the writing process as they learn to write about history. Guides, entitled **Writing Workshop Evaluations,** are included to help assess student writing. A two-page chart entitled **Using Maps with *One Nation, Many People*** provided suggestions for emphasizing the five themes of geography in teaching American history. This is followed by outline maps of the world and the Americas, and by two maps of the United States and the Eastern seaboard.

Finally, the ***Teacher's Resource Manual*** provides a traditional testing program. Both unit and chapter tests are included. All tests go beyond recall to have students write essays and interpret and evaluate history.

TEACHING STRATEGIES FOR ESL/LEP STUDENTS

Although the thought of teaching social studies in a language diverse classroom may seem overwhelming at first, it is comforting to realize that techniques for teaching ESL/LEP students are simply good teaching techniques that are directed toward students' special needs. (The ESL/LEP population includes students for whom English is a second language as well as native English speakers with limited proficiency). With an awareness of those needs and what works for students, teachers can easily adapt their instructional styles to language-diverse classrooms.

LESSON PLANS

Students with survival skills in English are ready to learn in that language. They can learn the concepts in the context areas as they develop scholastic and communicative language skills. To help them succeed, it is important to develop content-driven, activity-based lessons at the appropriate grade level and appropriate stage of language-skills development. Lesson plans created with the following components, developed in sheltered English classrooms, meet the needs of ESL/LEP students and lead to their success:

1. **Lesson Theme/Topic**—organizes the thinking needed to learn concepts.
2. **Key Concepts**—focus the learning process on the main reason for studying the particular theme or topic. Concepts also organize the learning process.
3. **Essential Vocabulary**—consists of the terms that are required to learn the key concepts of the lesson. Learning the vocabulary can begin to build the background necessary for understanding the material. A vocabulary activity can also be incorporated into the next section.
4. **Set**—reveals if students have the background knowledge required for the lesson. If not, the teacher builds this background knowledge. This phase requires interaction between the teacher and the class.
5. **Input**—includes all the activities the teacher does with students either in groups or as a class to provide the facts they need to start the learning process. Activities may result from the text, realia, audiovisual materials, and so on.
6. **Guided Practice**—creates interaction among groups of students and the text, the targeted vocabulary, one another, and the teacher to practice their growing knowledge of the concepts of the lesson. At this point, the teacher must monitor student progress and adjust the lesson accordingly.
7. **Follow-Up Activities**—include independent activities in which students practice the skills they have developed throughout the lesson. These provide an opportunity for the teacher to do formative evaluation, to ascertain if the students are ready for their final evaluation, and if they meet the objectives of the lesson. Writing exercises promote word and concept retention.
8. **Evaluation**—sets up demonstrations of mastery of the concepts. Evaluation activities need not be dependent on language. They may include such activities as making a collage and role playing. However, they can be language-based such as developing semantic maps or outlines or using previously developed semantic maps or outlines to write essays. The method of evaluation should match the stage of language development of the students and must hold them accountable for the academic concepts to be learned.

STRATEGIES

Among effective strategies to consider when developing and presenting lessons for ESL/LEP students are the following:

- **Modeling**—visual or auditory examples used to explain what is expected
- **Contextual Clues**—use of realia, pantomime, gestures, and connection of the familiar with the unknown; act out meaning when possible.
- **Built-in Redundancy**—repetition, paraphrasing, restatement, and use of

synonyms

- **Age Appropriateness**—tasks reasonably difficult for the age of the students
- **Humor**—spontaneous and planned humor to lower anxiety level and increase chances for success
- **Equal Status Activities**—two-way cooperative interactions between and among learners such as peer tutoring, inclusion of student interests and experiences, and crosscultural activities.
- **Cooperative/Collaborative Activities**—structured techniques with positive interdependence and individual accountability

ACTIVITIES AND TECHNIQUES

Experienced social studies teachers working with ESL/LEP students have some suggestions that may be helpful to first-time teachers of language-diverse students. They recommend that students have a good dictionary. Often these teachers plan simple questions to get students involved. ESL-LEP teachers provide basic word lists to be learned and memorized for automatic recognition and mark the key words in each lesson. They provide an outline of the main ideas and simplify English to increase students' comprehension. ESL/LEP teachers involve students in meaningful interaction. The focus is on meaning rather than on form.

Teachers might consider these additional activities as they implement the ESL/LEP strategies:

- Summarize a paragraph or two, perhaps in the primary language. Then, have students translate to English, using a dictionary.
- Paraphrase a paragraph or primary source.
- In small groups, have students role play dialogues or events in history with a student who is more proficient in English.
- Have students make illustrated timelines.
- Have students create visual displays—collages, posters, bulletin board displays, and so forth.
- Write down each of the people, places, or events in a particular era of history on a series of cards. In small groups, have students make connections among the cards or arrange them in chronological order.
- Write out each sentence of a three-to-five sentence paragraph on separate index cards. In small groups, have ESL/LEP students arrange sentences in the order that makes the most sense. Ask them to explain why.
- Whenever possible, relate incidents in history or characters in history to student experiences in their primary languages or cultures. For example, after studying the American Revolution, discuss the significance of the Fourth of July. Ask students: How is Independence Day celebrated in your community?
- Have students listen to a taped version of a paragraph, speech, or primary source. Ask them to write words they are not familiar with. Explain new vocabulary and replay the tape until students understand.
- Reproduce a "cloze" version of a paragraph—with fill-ins every fifth word.
- Ask students to choose the sentence that explains the main idea of a paragraph or choose one or two sentences that support the main idea.
- Create picture cards for vocabulary terms.
- Practice tenses by making predictions. For example: What do you think the U.S. government will do about the rebellion in Texas?
- In small groups, have students play 20 Questions or Who Am I.

Developing lessons using the lesson plan format explained above and implementing the strategies and techniques presented here will help students focus on the essential material in a lesson and also help teachers keep track of what students are learning. Focusing on the essentials enables both teacher and student to work on developing content-area concepts and specific language skills that help students succeed.

Unit Strategies and On-Going Activities

The lesson plans in Volumes 1 and 2 of the Teacher's Resource Manual for *One Nation, Many People* offers two approaches for teaching each chapter. Set side by side, you can see at a glance two methods for individualizing instruction to meet the special learning needs of your students. Below are a series of on-going projects that can be done individually or in groups. You can use these activities to bridge the chapters in a unit or the units in a volume.

ESL

Word-a-Day Calendar Post a large calendar on the bulletin board. Start or end each class by asking students to record at least one new word that they have learned for the day. At periodical intervals, such as at the end of a unit or at the end of the month, review these words by playing a game of pictionary. Assign teams of students to illustrate the words in each of the weeks covered on the calendar. Challenge other teams to guess the word. As an extension, have students define and spell the word correctly. (Tip: Students can keep their own individual word-a-day calendars in their notebooks.)

ESL

Class Reference Books As an on-going study tool, students can design any one of these three reference books: a biographical dictionary, a gazetteer, a class dictionary. To help students get started, you might place three-ring notebooks divided by alphabetical tabs at the front of the class room. At the end of every chapter, encourage students to develop lists of people, places, or terms that caught their attention. Have them write a brief description or definition for each item on a separate sheet of loose-leaf paper. At the end of the entry, students should record the page in the text where each item can be found. Students should then place their entries alphabetically in the appropriate reference book.

Class Timelines To help students link chapters chronologically, request that volunteers set up timelines for each unit. (Dates appear in parentheses at the end of each chapter title.) Have students use sheets of butcher paper or connected strips of computer paper to develop wall-size timelines. Timelines should be divided into appropriate intervals for the unit of study. Also encourage students to leave enough room on their timelines for illustrations or written entries. Select "class historians" on a rotating basis to record entries on the timeline on a daily or weekly basis. Periodic review of the timeline will help students identify patterns of change, predict trends, and/or spot cause-and-effect relationships.

ESL

Peer Teaching As a cooperative learning activity, you might assign teams of students to teach or review parts of chapters or units. Suggest that students prepare at least one handout and/or one visual aid. Tell the "teachers" to create a short in-class assignment for students to do. They should also write several questions for use in a self-evaluation test at the end of the chapter or unit.

Freewriting About History Periodically have students identify major topics studied in a block of chapters or units. (Chapter and section titles provide obvious clues.) Next, tell students to pick one of these topics. Set a time limit of three to five minutes, and have students write nonstop about this topic. (ESL/LEP students can write in their primary language or in a mix of English and non-English.) If students have a block, suggest that they keep writing "I have a block" until it breaks—it usually does. Tell students that the trick in freewriting is to keep writing so that creative ideas have a chance to come out on paper.

When students are done, instruct them to review their writing to identify important or new ideas on the topic. With the class as a whole, list these ideas in sentence form on the chalkboard. (ESL/LEP students should first translate their sentences into English.) Encourage students to arrange these sentences into paragraphs, adding transition sentences as needed.

As a variation of this activity, you might have students try freewriting on a computer. In this case, tell them to darken the screen so that they do not stop to read the results. When they are done, have them print out their freewriting for review.

History Log Whenever you assign a chapter, you might request an individual or group of students to imagine they are one of the actors in the chapter. Direct them to write a series of personal observations about special events or developments mentioned in this chapter. Whenever possible, entries should be tagged by dates. Students should take turns performing this task until the end of the unit. Then request volunteers to read the entries aloud. Have students guess the identity of the historical person who wrote each set of observations. As an extension, you might distribute the entries for peer editing. Have students underline selections of entries that they think are well-written. Also encourage them to make corrections or suggest changes that would improve the writing.

Library Field Trip Although your students may have been in a library on many occasions, you might want to upgrade their library skills by preparing "field trips" in which students use a variety of reference materials to look up information on select topics in each unit. You can organize the field trip something like a scavenger hunt in which students must track down information in a variety of reference sources, such as atlases, encyclopedias, card catalogues, special collections (such as record or tape collections), periodical indices, and so forth. For example, if you are studying the civil rights movement, you might have students collect the following items:

- A handwritten copy of entries in *The Reader's Guide to Periodical Literature* on the 1954 Supreme Court decision on *Brown v. Board of Education of Topeka, Kansas.* (If possible, they should try to get a get a photocopy or microfilm printout of one of the articles.)
- A handwritten copy of a subject or title entry in the card catalogue on the civil rights movement and a copy of the book cited.
- A biography of Dr. Martin Luther King, Jr.
- Notes from an encyclopedia entry on Dr. Martin Luther King, Jr.
- A recording of a civil rights song or a copy of the lyrics.
- A children's book on the civil rights movement. (That may mean going into a different section or room in the library)

After setting up one field trip/scavenger hunt as a model, you might request volunteers who will take turns preparing other field trips. After each field trip, have students present their findings and report how they found each item.

Student Portfolios To help students monitor their own progress, set up individual portfolios in a file cabinet in the classroom. Have them include completed work in the portfolios on a chapter-by-chapter basis. Also encourage students to set study and learning goals at the start of each unit and to evaluate their success in reaching these goals at the end of each unit. To help students accomplish this task, you might distribute the following self-assessment sheets.

Unit-Opening Assessment

Study Goals for This Unit's Study
1.

2.

3.

How I Might Achieve These Goals
1.

2.

3.

Unit-Closing Assessment

Goals Achieved
1.

2.

3.

Problems Encountered
1.

2.

3.

Unexpected Successes
1.

2.

3.

Ideas for New Goals
1.

2.

3.

CHAPTER 1: The United States Is a Diverse Nation.

Opening It Up

MOTIVATING: With students, define the term *diverse*. Then conduct two brainstorming sessions: one in which students name examples of human/cultural diversity and one in which students name examples of physical/geographic diversity in the United States. (Save responses for the "Sharing" activity.)

SETTING UP: Special materials include a recent almanac, sheets of newsprint or poster board, and colored pencils, inks, or tempera paints. For photographs of geographic regions in the United States and Canada, see March/April 1994 special issue of *Sierra* entitled "21 Ecoregions." Teacher's manual resources include Chapter 1 answer key (p. 267), Chapter 1 Test (p. 95) and Chapter 1 Activity sheet (p. 167).

TEACHING TIP

This chapter highlights diversity. If you have students who have recently arrived from other countries, encourage them to bring in items that illustrate their culture(s). If any students have lived in different regions in the United States, have them bring in photographs showing differences in physical landscape, climate, and so on.

Teaching It Two Ways

LEARNING OBJECTIVES

- To understand that the United States is diverse in many ways
- To explain why the United States is called "a multicultural nation"
- To explain the link between geography and history
- To name six regions that make up the United States

TO INTERPRET STATISTICS

Have students look up the following data in a recent almanac, such as *The World Almanac* or *The Universal Almanac:* (1) the makeup of the U.S. population regarding race and Latino origin and (2) the percentage of growth since 1980. Have students show their findings in the form of a table. Ask: *Which two groups form the largest percentage of our population?* (whites and African Americans) *Which groups showed the biggest increase since 1980?* (Asians and people of Latino origin) Next, distribute copies of the Chapter 1 Activity Sheet. After students have finished the sheet, have them write a sentence explaining how immigration has made our nation more diverse since 1980.

TO IDENTIFY REGIONS:

Call on students to look up the term *region* in the dictionary. Then have them write a definition. ESL/LEP students can write the definition in their primary language and then translate it into English. Next, set up six groups of students and assign each group one of the six regions in the text. Then tell students to illustrate the characteristics of each region on a piece of newsprint or poster board. (Pictures can also be found in the special issue of *Sierra,* in illustrated encyclopedias, or in travel guides.) When students are finished, have them write a sentence in their primary language and/or English explaining how physical geography has made our country more diverse.

Putting It All Together

SHARING: Call on volunteers to read their sentences aloud. Recall the brainstorming sessions. Ask: *Which examples of human diversity in the United States can be traced to immigration? Which examples of physical geographic diversity can be tied to a specific region or regions?*

ASSESSING: Have students list some of the ways in which the United States is diverse. Encourage students to illustrate each item.

PAST TO PRESENT: Write the name "First Americans" on the chalkboard. Challenge students to identify who the first immigrants might have been. Ask: *Based on what you know about physical geography, why might these people develop different ways of life as they spread across the land?*

CHAPTER 2: The First Americans Develop Great Cultures.

Opening It Up

MOTIVATING: Open with this story: In the 1500s, the diversity of people on Caribbean islands and in present-day Mexico and Central America startled the Spanish priest Bartolomé de las Casas. He wrote: "This could not happen except by the passage of many years. . . . [T]here is not a great argument that people on these islands and continent are very ancient." Ask students to guess when the first people might have arrived in the Americas.

SETTING UP: Prepare copies of the Maidu legend in the activity below. Teacher's manual resources include Chapter 2 answer key (p. 267), Chapter 2 Test (p. 96), and Chapter 2 Activity Sheet (p. 168).

TEACHING TIP

Storytellers played an important role in traditional Native American societies. Their tales wove the generations together. Ask volunteers to find a Native American story to retell to the class. A highly readable source is *Native American Stories,* by Mohawk storyteller Joseph Bruchac.

Teaching It Two Ways

LEARNING OBJECTIVES

- To explain how the first Americans came to North America
- To describe different Native American cultures
- To identify the accomplishments of the great Native American empires

TO INTERPRET ORAL HISTORY

Distribute copies of this Maidu legend:

For a long time everyone spoke the same language. . . [But then] people began to speak in different tongues. Kulsu [the Creator], . . . could speak all the languages, so he called his people together and told them the names of the animals in their own language, taught them to get food, and gave them laws and rituals. Then he sent each people to a different place to live.

Ask students what the myth explains. (origins of diverse ways of life) Tell them to find information in the text that describes what life was like "when everyone spoke the same language." Have students use this data to write a legend that begins: "Long, Long ago, when all things were new."

TO MAKE COMPARISONS

Tell students that the word *compare* means "to look for similarities and differences." To practice this skill, have students compare their social studies class with their science or math class. Ask: *How are the two classes alike? How are they different?* Then tell students that Chapter 2 gives them the chance to compare Native American ways of life. To help students make these comparisons, hand out copies of the Chapter 2 Activity Sheet. When students have completed the activity, ask them for similarities among two or more groups. (Similarities might include the groups that practiced hunting or farming.) Then ask: *What aspect of life made each group different from other peoples?*

Putting It All Together

SHARING: Ask volunteers to read their legends about the first Americans. Then, using an opaque projector, show some of the sketches that compare the ways of life that developed over the centuries. Now reread the Maidu legend for the whole class. Why do students think historians sometimes study legends for clues about early people?

ASSESSING: Have students design a cause-and-effect chart showing the reasons that the first Americans became more diverse. Causes might include: end of the Ice Age, settling in diverse environments, and so on.

PAST TO PRESENT: Have students imagine that it is October 12th—the day on which people traditionally celebrate Christopher Columbus's "discovery" of the Americas. Have students draw a political cartoon that challenges the idea that a European was the first person to find the continents of North and South America.

CHAPTER 3: The Spanish Reach the Americas.

Opening It Up

MOTIVATING: Ask students to imagine that the United States is recruiting members of a space expedition that will explore a solar system beyond our own. Discuss the characteristics that students think crew members should possess. Ask: *If you had the chance, would you sign up for the expedition? Why or why not?* Use student comments to lead into a discussion of European voyages of exploration.

SETTING UP: Make copies of the outline map of the world on page 253. You might also bring historical atlases to class. Teacher manual resources include Chapter 3 answer key (p. 267), Chapter 3 Test (p. 97) and Chapter 3 Activity Sheet (p. 169).

TEACHING TIP

The Activity Sheet for this chapter introduces students to primary sources. Tell students that primary sources can be either written or visual. They must, however, be created by someone who actually witnessed or experienced an event. Then have students find examples of primary sources in Chapter 3.

Teaching It Two Ways

LEARNING OBJECTIVES

- To state why Europeans tried to find new routes to Asia
- To explain how Columbus's voyage changed world history
- To describe how the Spanish settlement of Hispanola affected Native Americans

TO SHOW MOVEMENT ON A MAP

Have groups of students locate places named in Chapter 3 on an outline map of the world. (As a tip, tell students that the Holy Land lies in what is now Israel. Mention also that the Vikings sailed from Scandinavia to Greenland and Newfoundland.) Direct students to draw arrows showing the direction of travel out of Europe. (You might refer students to the historical atlas.) Ask how these voyages expanded the European view of the world.

Next, assign the Activity Sheet. After students have completed the assignment, ask: *How does this exercise show that Europeans still had a lot to learn about lands on the other side of the Atlantic?* (Refer students to the discussion of Native American cultures in Chapter 2.)

TO WRITE HEADLINES

Working in groups, have students identify the various journeys that led Europeans beyond their borders. Then challenge students to write two headlines for each journey. The first headline should state the purpose of the journey as it began. The second headline should announce the outcome of the journey. Students may write the headlines in their primary language and then translate them into English. (If you have any Spanish-speaking students, you might encourage them to expand their Spanish headlines on Columbus into broadsheets that might have been posted in Palos, Spain. Hang these in the classroom.)

Putting It All Together

SHARING: Using an opaque projector, show to the class one of the completed route maps. Challenge students to match the headlines with the correct routes. Ask: *Which of the journeys do you think fulfilled the Europeans' original purposes?*

ASSESSING: Have students draw a before-and-after poster showing the effect of Spanish arrival on Native Americans on Hispaniola. The pictures should reflect the changes mentioned in the text.

PAST TO PRESENT: Tell students that the Tainos who lived on Puerto Rico called their island *Borinquen.* Then read aloud the following lyrics from the national song of Puerto Rico: "When Columbus arrived / Filled with admiration, he exclaimed: Oh! Oh! Oh! / This is the beautiful land / I'm looking for / It's Borinquen, the daughter/daughter of the sea and sun." Ask students what these lyrics say about how Puerto Ricans see their heritage. (a blend of Taino and European influences)

CHAPTER 4: Three Great Cultures Meet in the Americas.

Opening It Up

MOTIVATING: Write the following questions on the chalkboard: (1) *Who* is the chapter about? (2) *Where* do these people meet? (3) *When* do they meet? Then tell students that they can find answers to all three questions in the chapter title and the chapter-opening question. Ask: *What do you think this chapter will be about?*

SETTING UP: Make a recording of the selection in the LEP activity, or select a student reader who will act as a resource person. Teacher's manual resources include Chapter 4 answer key (p. 267), Chapter 4 Test (p. 98), Chapter 4 Activity Sheet (p. 170), and Unit 1 Test (p. 83).

TEACHING TIP

Students can direct their own reading through use of the six questions used by reporters: *Who? When? Where? What? Why? How?* They can turn any titles or heads in this book into questions by using these words. Have them practice in Chapter 4.

Teaching It Two Ways

LEARNING OBJECTIVES

- To explain how Spain conquered peoples in the Caribbean
- To name the accomplishments of the great West African empires
- To describe the fall of the Aztec empire

TO MAKE COMPARISONS

Have small groups of students make charts comparing the Spanish empire, West African empires, and the Aztec empire. Column heads might include: location, key cities, basis of economy, sources of labor, religion, military advantages, and so on. Ask students how the empires differed and how they were alike.

Then assign the Activity Sheet for this chapter. After students have finished, have them draw arrows from the African kingdoms into the Atlantic. Tell students to write "slave trade" on the arrows. Ask: *Why might this trade have weakened the West African empires? Why might it have strengthened the Spanish empire?*

ESL TO ILLUSTRATE A POEM

Play a tape recording of the following Aztec verses on the fall of Tenochtitlan.

How can we save our homes, my people?
The Aztec are deserting the city:
The city is in flames, and all
is darkness and destruction.
Weep, my people:
know that with these disasters
we have lost the Mexican nation.

Tell students to visualize the scene described. (Replay the tape as often as necessary.) Then have them draw this scene, using a style similar to the art on text page 38.

Putting It All Together

SHARING: Ask volunteers to report on how the rise of the Spanish empire affected empires and kingdoms in West Africa and in present-day Mexico. To show the emotional effect of this clash, have other students present pictures illustrating the fall of Tehochtitlan.

ASSESSING: To evaluate the effect of the Spanish conquest, have students write a description of life in Hispaniola from the following points of view: (a) the owner of an *encomienda,* (b) a Native American assigned to the *encomienda,* (c) an enslaved African on a sugar plantation. Accounts should reflect the data in the text.

PAST TO PRESENT: Tell students that one fifth of the Africans carried across the Atlantic as slaves came from Muslim areas. Although Islam did not survive the slave experience, a number of African Americans converted to Islam during the civil-rights movement. Ask students to speculate on the reasons that African Americans might have for viewing Islam as a part of their heritage.

CHAPTER 5: Latino Culture Develops.

Opening It Up

MOTIVATING: Explain that a bronze plaque in Mexico City marks the site of the Aztec surrender. The plaque reads in part: "It was neither a triumph nor a defeat: It was the painful birth of the *mestizo* nation that is Mexico today." Direct students to look up the term *mestizo* in the Glossary. Ask: *What do the words on the plaque tell you about the culture that developed in New Spain?*

SETTING UP: Special materials include strips of computer paper, poster board, and colored pencils, felt-tipped pens, or tempera paints. Teacher's manual resources include Chapter 5 answer key (p. 267), Chapter 5 Test (p. 99), and Chapter 5 Activity Sheet (p. 171).

TEACHING TIP

In classes with mixed English-proficient and LEP students, two-way cooperation and tutoring is important. Create situations in which LEP students can be the "teachers." A good equalizing activity is to have LEP students create picture flash cards to test the knowledge of their classmates.

Teaching It Two Ways

LEARNING OBJECTIVES

- To describe life in Mexico City
- To trace the area known as the Spanish borderlands
- To explain why Spanish priests set up missions
- To list Spanish, Native American, and African contributions to Latino culture

TO PLOT DATES ON A TIMELINE

Direct small groups of students to identify key dates mentioned in the chapter. Then have students plot and write captions for these dates along a timeline. (Strips of computer paper work well for this activity.) Remind students that timelines should be divided into regular, easy-to-read intervals. Encourage students to illustrate some of the events listed on their timelines. If possible, appoint a resource person from each group to check the school library for additional events. (Suggest that students check the card catalog or encyclopedia for places mentioned in the chapter.)

TO CATEGORIZE INFORMATION

Have students identify examples of Spanish, African, and Native American contributions to Latino culture. Remind students to check the chapter's pictures for ideas. Have students organize these examples into the appropriate categories. Next, direct students to use poster board to design flash cards illustrating these contributions. On the back of each flash card, students should write group responsible for the contribution. If your library has a copy of the book *Seeds of Change* by the Smithsonian Institute, have students look through the pictures for additional examples.

Putting It All Together

SHARING: Post the completed timelines. Call on volunteers to state what Spain had accomplished from 1500 to 1700. Then jumble up the flash cards. Have students identify each contribution as Spanish, African, or Native American. Use these exercises to answer the chapter-opening question on page 42.

ASSESSING: Assign the Chapter 5 Activity sheet. Then, using information in Section 1, have students complete these "cloze" sentences: "The sweat of ______ and ______ fueled the silver trade. But the wealth flowed into the pockets of the ________________."

PAST TO PRESENT: Compare the map on page 00 of the text with a political map of the United States. Ask: *What present-day states were influenced by the Latino culture that took root in lands held by Spain in the 1500s and 1600s?*

CHAPTER 6: The English Launch Colonies in North America.

Opening It Up

MOTIVATING: Tell students that the scene now shifts to the Atlantic coast of North America. Locate this area on a wall map of the United States. Mention that the first English settlers in what is now Massachusetts described the land as "a hideous wilderness." Ask: *How might Native Americans have seen this same land?* Then ask students to look for reasons the English came to North America.

SETTING UP: Prepare copies of the extract in the activity below. Teacher's manual resources include Chapter 6 answer key (p. 267), Chapter 6 Test (p. 100), and Chapter 6 Activity Sheet (p. 172).

TEACHING TIP

History chronicles the passage of time. You might make sure LEP students understand common English time terms. Examples include *decade, century, age, era, A.D., B.C., B.P.* You might also go over terms that signal sequences, such as *before, after, during, meanwhile,* etc.

Teaching It Two Ways

LEARNING OBJECTIVES

- To understand the conflict between democracy and slavery
- To state reasons that the English came to North America
- To cite milestones in self-government

TO INTERPRET A HISTORIC DOCUMENT

Distribute copies of the following selection from the Mayflower Compact:

Having undertaken, for the glory of God, and the spreading of the Christian faith . . . a voyage to plant the first colony in the northern part of Virginia, we do . . . solemnly . . . join ourselves together as a group of citizens . . . And we agree to enact . . . such just and equal laws . . . as shall be most proper for the general good of the colony. To these we promise all due . . . obedience."

Ask students to rewrite this document in everyday language. Then have them write a sentence stating the purpose of the compact.

TO UNDERSTAND CHRONOLOGY

Remind students that graphs provide handy tools for organizing statistics. Then tell them that there are two tools for organizing dates: the timeline and the chronology. Explain that a timeline is sometimes called an "interval graph." This is because it divides a range of dates into regular intervals, or units. A chronology places events in sequence, or in order. Ask: *Which tool do you think is most helpful in organizing events over a long period? Which tool would help you estimate time spans most quickly?* To practice using a chronology, have teams of students complete the Activity Sheet for Chapter 6.

Putting It All Together

SHARING: Use an opaque projector to show a completed chronology. Then call on students to read their revisions of the Mayflower Compact. Explore the reasons this document was a milestone in self-government. Referring to chronology, ask when the Mayflower Compact was written. Ask: *What other milestones in self-government can you identify?*

ASSESSING: Using the opaque projector, show illustrations of events on the various chronologies. Challenge students to guess which event is depicted.

PAST TO PRESENT: Conduct a brainstorming session in which students identify the freedoms that Americans enjoy today. List these on the chalkboard. Then have students name those freedoms that had their roots in colonial Virginia or colonial New England. (You might save this list for further evaluation at the end of Chapter 7, which covers the rest of the colonies.)

CHAPTER 7: People from Many Lands Settle in the English Colonies.

Opening It Up

MOTIVATING: Review the line graph on page 55 of Chapter 6. Ask: *What pattern of change can you identify?* (growth of the African American population) *What difference existed between the northern and southern colonies?* (many more African Americans in the South) *Do you think this difference will continue? Why or why not?* (yes; because it has continued for 90 years) Tell students that Chapter 7 explores other ways in which the colonies differed.

SETTING UP: Prepare copies of the outline map of the 13 colonies on page 251. Teacher's manual resources include Chapter 7 answer key (p. 267), Chapter 7 Test (p. 101), and Chapter 7 Activity Sheet (p. 173).

TEACHING TIP

Challenge students to become word detectives. Instead of just looking up a word's meaning, encourage them to track down its roots. Whenever students find a word (e.g., *ketchup*—China) that has slipped into English from another language, have them post it on the bulletin board.

Teaching It Two Ways

LEARNING OBJECTIVES

- To cite reasons that people from other countries came to the English colonies.
- To name the Southern Colonies.
- To describe how the three sets of colonies differed from one another.

TO IDENTIFY DIVERSITY

Tell students that in 1744 a doctor from Maryland visited Philadelphia. He wrote:

I dined at a tavern with a very mixed company of different nations and religions. There were Scots, English, Dutch, Germans, and Irish. There were Roman Catholics, Church [of England] men, Presbyterians, Quakers, . . . Moravians, . . . and one Jew."

Ask students to identify the types of diversity mentioned by the doctor. (national and religious diversity) Then have students complete the chart suggested on page 62 of the text. On a separate sheet of paper, have them list other examples of diversity that existed in the colonies.

TO DRAW AN ILLUSTRATED MAP

Distribute copies of the outline map of the 13 colonies. Tell students to use the map on page 00 of the text as a guide to outline each of the three regions in three colors on the blank map. Then, based on information in the text, have students add illustrations that show some of the unique features of each region. (Ships and whales might be drawn off the New England coast. A tobacco plantation might be drawn in the South. School buildings might dot New England. Swedish log cabins might be scattered in New Jersey or Delaware.) If any students request more illustration space, suggest that they use an opaque projector to trace the outline map onto poster board.

Putting It All Together

SHARING: Have members from each group present their charts and maps. Ask students to name two characteristics that they think made each region unique. Then assign the Activity Sheet for this chapter. Ask: *What trait did all the colonies share?* (a growing population) Encourage students to name other shared traits.

ASSESSING: Write the following incomplete sentence on the chalkboard: "The 13 Colonies were diverse because __________." Challenge students to think of as many ways as possible to complete it.

PAST TO PRESENT: Suggest that interested students use an almanac to compile a list of facts that illustrate religious diversity in the United States today. Have students present their findings in a series of statements that begin with the words "Did you know that" and end with a question mark.

CHAPTER 8: The People of the 13 Colonies Become Americans.

Opening It Up

MOTIVATING: Tell students that in 1760 a British minister named Andrew Burnaby said of the colonies: "Fire and water are not more . . . different. In short, . . . [if] left to themselves there would soon be a civil war from one end of the continent to the other." Ask volunteers to recall examples of how the colonies differed. Then explain that Chapter 8 explores some of the ideas and practices that helped unite the colonists into one people.

SETTING UP: Prepare copies of the incomplete letter in the activity below. Teacher's manual resources include Chapter 8 answer key (p. 268), Chapter 8 Test (p. 102), and Chapter 8 Activity Sheet (p. 174).

TEACHING TIP

The "Cloze" technique is an easy tool for promoting and/or assessing reading comprehension. Write or copy a selection, omitting key words randomly. Do not cut proper names or technical terms. Have students fill in the blank spaces so that the passage makes sense. (See the Chapter 8 Activity Sheet.)

Teaching It Two Ways

LEARNING OBJECTIVES

- To list some of the responsibilities and jobs of colonial women
- To describe the horrors of the Middle Passage
- To name some of the beliefs that colonists shared

TO WRITE A LETTER

Distribute copies of the following incomplete letter written by Eliza Lucas to in 1742.

My Dearest Friend,
Won't you laugh at me if I tell you I am so busy in providing for posterity [the future] that I hardly allow myself time to eat or sleep. I . . . am making a large plantation of oaks which I look upon as my own property whether my father gives me the land or not. . . . I have no doubt this will prove a valuable commodity [product]. . . .

Instruct students to complete the letter. The remaining paragraphs should capture more of the activities of Eliza Lucas and colonial women in general.

TO INTERPRET A DIAGRAM

Distribute copies of the Activity Sheet. Tell students to imagine they are one of the enslaved Africans packed onto the platform pictured in View D. Then slowly read aloud these words by Olaudah Equiano (Gustavus Vasa):

I was soon put under the decks. . . . With the awful smell and crying, I became . . . sick. . . . [T]he ship was so crowded that each barely had enough room to turn. . . . I began to hope [death] would put an end to my miseries.

Ask: *What does Equiano tell you about how a slave ship smelled, sounded, looked, or felt?* (Reread the passage or allow students to take turns reading it aloud.) Tell students to keep this information in mind as they complete the Activity Sheet.

Putting It All Together

SHARING: Have students read aloud their letters or reports (no. 5 on the Activity Sheet). Then request volunteers complete each of these sentences: "To be a woman in colonial times meant ________." "To be an enslaved African in colonial times meant __________."

ASSESSING: Assign students to design a poster entitled "The Ties that Bind." Using words and pictures, have students illustrate some of the beliefs that were turning the colonists into Americans.

PAST TO PRESENT: Have interested students read the 1st Amendment to the Constitution. Ask them to prepare an oral report in which they connect this amendment to the trial of John Peter Zenger. In an open discussion, challenge students to assess the role of a free press in preserving our democracy.

CHAPTER 9: The French Set Up Colonies in North America.

Opening It Up

MOTIVATING: In Chapter 9, the number of political actors in North America increases. Refer students to the map on page 78 of the text, and ask them to compare European land claims. Ask: *Which nation held the most territory? Do you think that conflicts between the British and French were inevitable? If so, where might these conflicts erupt?*

SETTING UP: Prepare copies of the physical map on page 249 of this guide. Arrange also to have a historical atlas available. Teacher's manual resources include Chapter 9 answer key (p. 268), Chapter 9 Test (p. 103), Chapter 9 Activity Sheet (p. 175), and Unit 2 Test (p. 84).

TEACHING TIP

Graphic organizers, such as the one in the Activity Sheet for this chapter, help ESL/ LEP students represent information and identify relationships. When students become familiar with graphic organizers, they can turn them into prewriting activities or study tools for testtaking.

Teaching It Two Ways

LEARNING OBJECTIVES

- To trace French explorations in North America
- To describe the economy of New France
- To cite causes and effects of the French and Indian War

TO TRACE ROUTES ON A MAP

Distribute copies of the physical map on page 249 of this guide. Have students compile a list of place names mentioned in this chapter. Then have them locate each of these places on the outline map. Based on descriptions in the text, have students use arrows to show the routes of French explorers. Suggest that they use a historical atlas to check these routes. (The Table of Contents and/or Index will help students to locate a map of French exploration of North America.) Tell students to design a symbol to indicate the sites of battles between the French and British. Have them use different colors to distinguish victories by each side.

TO UNDERSTAND CAUSE AND EFFECT

Distribute copies of the Activity Sheet for this chapter. To make sure students understand the difference between cause and effect, ask volunteers to name a recent change in their lives. Ask: *Why did this change occur?* (cause) *What has happened as a result of this change?* (effect) Then have students use information in Section 3 to fill out the graphic organizer. To get students started, you might tell them that they can find at least one cause in the first paragraph of Section 3 (French and British rivalries in Europe).

Putting It All Together

SHARING: Use an opaque projector to show one of the completed maps. Relate French exploration to French land claims. Then focus on battle sites. Ask students to use their graphic organizers to name the causes of these battles. Based on the "effect" boxes, have students point to lands lost by France as a result of the war.

ASSESSMENT: Assign students to develop a chart comparing New France to the British colonies. Column heads might include "Population Size," "Trade/Farming," "Government," "Relations with Native Americans."

PAST TO PRESENT: Tell students that history is filled with "what ifs." As an example, have students consider this scenario: *If France had won the French and Indian War, how might the history of the United States be different?*

CHAPTER 10: The British Tighten Their Control.

Opening It Up

MOTIVATING: Refer students to the map of the triangular trade routes on page 72 of Chapter 8. Ask: *What evidence proves that the colonies traded with other countries besides Britain? Suppose the British tried to restrict this trade. How might the colonists react?* Tell students they will learn the answer in Chapter 10.

SETTING UP: Prepare copies of the news story in the activity below. Create blank cause-and-effect graphic organizers similar to the one in the Chapter 9 Activity Sheet. Teacher's manual resources include Chapter 10 answer key (p. 268), Chapter 10 Test (p. 104), and Chapter 10 Activity Sheet (p. 176).

TEACHING TIP

Encourage students to create stories about the past by organizing a "storytelling bee." Have students form a circle. Then have one person compose the opening line. Ask each person in the circle to add new parts. If possible, tape-record the storytelling bee so that students can listen to their oral tale.

Teaching It Two Ways

LEARNING OBJECTIVES

- To list the reasons that the British tried to curb westward settlement
- To name the taxes passed by the British in the 1760s
- To describe the colonial response to these taxes

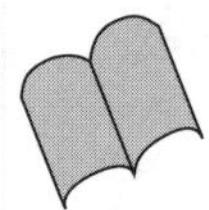

TO INTERPRET A TABLE

Distribute copies of this news story:

BOSTON, June 23, 1765—A colonist cannot make a button, a horseshoe, nor a hobnail, but some snooty ironmonger [a dealer in iron goods] or respectable buttonmaker in Britain shall bawl [cry] . . . that [he's being] cheated and robbed by the . . . Americans.

Discuss what this story shows about how the British viewed colonial manufacturing. Based on the text, ask in what other ways did the British felt "cheated and robbed" by the colonists. Assign the Activity Sheet for this chapter. Have students write a short paragraph describing British economic goals in 1765.

TO INCREASE ORAL FLUENCY

Distribute copies of the blank cause-and-effect graphic organizers. Direct students to use these tools to analyze the causes and effects of the Stamp Act of 1765. Once students have completed these notes, conduct a storytelling bee in which they describe the outcry over taxes. (See Teaching Tips.) To help students get started, read the following lines into a tape recorder: "In 1765, the colonists were awfully mad. The British had just passed a new tax called the Stamp Act." Then pass the tape recorder from student to student. Have each one add some new lines to the story. (You might repeat this activity with the Proclamation of 1763.)

Putting It All Together

SHARING: Based on the news story and the Chapter 10 Activity Sheet, have students list the goals of British economic policy in 1765. Then play the tape-recorded story about the Stamp Act. Ask: *Which of these goals does the story illustrate?*

ASSESSING: Assign students to create a two-column chart entitled "British Colonial Policies, 1763-1766." The two columns should read: "British Actions" and "Colonial Responses." Charts should present key laws and protests mentioned in the text.

PAST TO PRESENT: Ask students to design a poster entitled "Taxes, Taxes, and More Taxes." Tell them to list or illustrate the types of taxes that Americans pay today (income taxes, sales taxes, school taxes, property taxes, etc.). Ask students to discuss some of the ways in which people can protest taxes that they do not agree with.

CHAPTER 11: The Colonists Fight Back.

Opening It Up

MOTIVATING: Inform students that in 1774 members of the Virginia assembly invited members of other assemblies to a meeting in Philadelphia. The invitation said: "Tis time to consult upon the present state of the colonies and the miseries in which they are in." Have students guess what these "miseries" might have been.

SETTING UP: Prepare copies of the poem below. Have a map of the United States available. Teacher's manual resources include Chapter 11 answer key (p. 268), Chapter 11 Test (p. 105), Chapter 11 Activity Sheet (p. 245), and reproducible map of the United States (p. 177).

TEACHING TIP

ESL/LEP students profit from visual aids. Before assigning a chapter, skim the pages for potentially troublesome words. Write these words and their definitions on a transparency. Project these words on a screen so that students can easily refer to them as they read.

Teaching It Two Ways

LEARNING OBJECTIVES

- To list ways in which colonists protested taxes
- To explain why the Boston Massacre is important to U.S. history
- To name events that led to the Continental Congress

TO INTERPRET A POEM

Distribute copies of the following poem written by a Daughter of Liberty:

Let the Daughters of Liberty, nobly arise,
And tho' we've no Voice, but a negative here,
The use of the Taxables, let us forebear.
Stand firmly resolved and bid Britain to see,
Rather than Freedom, we'll part with our Tea."

Ask: *What is the poem about?* (protesting British taxes) *What did the poet mean when she said "we've no Voice."* (Women couldn't vote.) *What power did women have?* (power to boycott taxable goods) *Which law was she protesting?* (Tea Act) Next, assign groups of students poems to write describing other events in the chapter. Caution them not to name the event.

TO DETERMINE DISTANCE

Refer students to a map of the United States. Locate the scale, and explain how it works. Then have students calculate the distance between various colonial cities, such as Boston and Savannah, Charleston and New York, Philadelphia and Jamestown. Use this exercise to point out that most colonists had little contact with each other. Then direct students to the term *Committee of Correspondence* on page 97. Ask students how these committees helped colonists to get to know each other. To help students to appreciate how the protest of British laws pulled colonists together, assign the Chapter 11 Activity Sheet.

Putting It All Together

SHARING: Read aloud the poems created by students and ask the rest of the class to guess the event described. Arrange the "postcards" designed/written in the Activity Sheet in a bulletin board display called "Learning About America."

ASSESSING: Assign volunteers to choose several people in this chapter. Make sure that they understand the importance of each person. Have these students take turns sitting in front of the class. Challenge the remaining students to ask a series of yes-or-no questions aimed at discovering the identity of each "mystery person." If students fail to name a person, have the volunteers pantomime clues.

PAST TO PRESENT: Today historic markers guide visitors to Boston on a tour of historic sites from the Revolution. One site is the scene of the Boston Massacre. Instruct students to write an inscription for the marker they would place there.

CHAPTER 12: The American Revolution Is Launched.

Opening It Up

MOTIVATING: When King George III learned of the colonial response to the Intolerable Acts, he exploded: “The die is cast. The colonists must triumph or submit.” Repeat this story to students. Explore the meaning of the expression “the die is cast.” (The game has started; there’s no turning back.) Ask: *Which choice do you think the colonists will make in the next round of play—to triumph or submit? Which events from Chapter 11 support your answer?*

SETTING UP: Prepare copies of the selection below. Teacher’s resources include Chapter 12 answer key (p. 268), Chapter 12 Test (p. 106), and Chapter 12 Activity Sheet (p. 178).

TEACHING TIP

To find the main idea in a paragraph, have students remember two questions: *What is the general subject of the paragraph? What main point does the paragraph make about the subject?* When students find a sentence or combination of sentences that answer these questions, they have found the main idea.

Teaching It Two Ways
LEARNING OBJECTIVES

- To explain the importance of the battles of Lexington and Concord
- To name events leading to the call for independence
- To list actions taken by the Second Continental Congress

TO IDENTIFY THE MAIN IDEA

Distribute copies of Patrick Henry’s March 1775 speech. Tell students to circle the sentence or sentences that express the main idea of the speech. Then have them underline details that Henry uses to support this idea.

There is no longer any room for hope. If we wish to be free, . . . we must fight! . . . Gentlemen may cry, peace, peace; but there is no peace. The war is already begun! The next gale [wind] that sweeps from the North will bring to our ears the clash of resounding arms! Our brethren [brothers] are already in the field! . . . Is life so dear or peace so sweet as to be purchased at the price of chains and slavery? Forbid it, Almighty God—I know not what course others may take; but as for me, give me liberty, or give me death!”

TO SUMMARIZE CHRONOLOGICAL INFORMATION

Remind students that a chronology shows the order in which events occurred. By organizing events into a chronology (or a timeline), it becomes easier to identify patterns or changes over time. With this background in mind, have students complete the chronology on the Chapter 13 Activity Sheet. Before students write their summary sentences at the bottom of the activity sheet, ask them to compare events listed on the chronology. Ask: *What similarities or differences can you spot?* (One common thread is fighting between the colonists and British. Another common thread is the talk of independence.) Write students’ answers on the chalkboard. Tell students to use these notes to help them with their summary sentences.

Putting It All Together

SHARING: Ask a student to do a dramatic reading of Patrick Henry’s speech. Then show one of the completed chronologies. Ask: *Which of Henry’s predictions came true?* (“the clash of resounding arms” in the North) *How long did it take to happen?* (about one month)

ASSESSING: Assign students to write headlines capturing the importance of each of the events listed in the completed chronology on the Activity Sheet.

PAST TO PRESENT: To underscore the revolutionary nature of events mentioned in this chapter, have students imagine similar events in a U.S. commonwealth or possession today. (Examples might include Puerto Rico, Guam, American Samoa, Virgin Islands.)

CHAPTER 13: The Americans Declare Their Independence.

Opening It Up

MOTIVATING: Independence was a serious matter. Tell students that during the debate about independence, Benjamin Franklin remarked: "We must all hang together, or most assuredly we will hang separately." Ask students to explain what Franklin meant. Then write the word *treason* on the chalkboard. Refer students to the definition on page 110 of the text. Ask students to name *treasonous* acts already taken by the colonists.

SETTING UP: Each activity calls for students to make charts. The Sharing section involves a debate. Teacher's manual resources include Chapter 13 answer key (p. 268), Chapter 13 Test (p. 107), and Chapter 13 Activity Sheet (p. 179).

TEACHING TIP

"Know thine enemy" is good advice in a debate. Have teams of debaters brainstorm both pro and con arguments. They should pick their arguments based on the strongest points that the other side might offer. Tell students to prioritize their arguments, saving the "knockout punch" for last.

Teaching It Two Ways

LEARNING OBJECTIVES

- To cite reasons that the colonists declared independence
- To describe the four parts of the Declaration of Independence
- To discuss responses to the Declaration

TO IDENTIFY POINTS OF VIEW

Tell students that the Declaration of Independence divided the colonists. Benjamin Franklin, for example, supported independence. His son William joined the British. To illustrate some of the factors that influenced decisions, have students draw and complete the chart below. Encourage students to think beyond the textbook. If they had been alive in 1776, what ideas or events would have mattered most to them?

	Reasons for Independence	Reasons Against Independence
Colonists of European Ancestry		
African Americans		

TO ORGANIZE INFORMATION ON A CHART

Copy the following graphic organizer on the chalkboard or an overhead transparency. Ask students to copy this diagram onto notebook paper or on poster board. Working in small groups, have them fill in items.

The Declaration of Independence

Purpose of Document:______________________

____

Main Points

Part 1	Part 2	Part 3	Part 4

Putting It All Together

SHARING: Challenge students to debate the following topic. Resolved: That the colonists should declare their independence. Make sure that the debate teams include students who have completed each chart. (Charts will provide background data for the debate.) To organize arguments, have students complete the Chapter 13 Activity Sheet.

ASSESSING: After students have completed their debate, tell them to imagine that it is 1776. Have them write a letter to a European friend describing the different opinions about independence in the colonies.

PAST TO PRESENT: Call on a volunteer to describe how people celebrate the 4th of July. Then request ESL/LEP students to describe important national holidays in their country of origin.

CHAPTER 14: The Colonists Fight for Independence.

Opening It Up

MOTIVATING: Read aloud the first two paragraphs of Section 1. Ask: *What advantage did the British have in this early battle?* (many more troops) *Suppose you were a British officer. What would you predict about the outcome of the Revolution?* (probably an easy victory) Tell students that Chapter 14 shows how the Americans seized victory away from the British.

SETTING UP: Bring in strips of computer paper or newsprint for a timeline. Also prepare copies of the reading in the ESL/LEP activity. Teacher's manual resources include Chapter 14 answer key (p. 269), Chapter 14 Test (p. 108), Chapter 14 Activity Sheet (p. 180), and Unit 3 Test (p. 85).

TEACHING TIP

Designing commemorative stamps gives students a chance to illustrate the importance of an event or individual in visual form. The Chapter 14 Activity Sheet calls for such a stamp. Have students collect commemorative stamps for an ongoing bulletin-board display called "Who's Who at the Post Office."

Teaching It Two Ways

LEARNING OBJECTIVES

- To compare American and British advantages and disadvantages at the start of the war
- To list key events leading from the battle of Saratoga to the battle of Yorktown
- To describe how Americans won allies from other nations

TO ORGANIZE EVENTS ON A TIMELINE

To understand the reasons for Spain's siding with the Americans, have students plot the following events on a timeline: **1762:** France gives Louisiana to Spain in wars against Britain. Britain seizes Havana, Cuba, from Spain. **1763:** In the treaty ending the French and Indian War, Britain returns Havana and takes Florida from Spain. **1776:** Colonists sign the Declaration of Independence. France and Spain begin raising money for the United States. **1778:** France forms an alliance with the United States. **1779:** Spain declares war on Britain. Bernardo de Galvez marches on West Florida. **1781:** The Spanish capture Pensacola, Florida.

TO COMPARE ACCOMPLISHMENTS

Distribute copies of the following selection from a letter by the Marquis de Lafayette to his wife.

I will now tell you about this country. . . . Simplicity of manners, kindness, and love of country and of liberty, and a delightful equality are found everywhere. . . . My sympathy [is] with these people. . . . [There is great] similarity between their mode [way] of thinking and my own . . . love of liberty and glory.

Ask students why Lafayette joined the Americans. To assess the sacrifices that Lafayette and others made in defense of liberty, assign students to complete the Chapter 14 Activity Sheet.

Putting It All Together

SHARING: Display the completed timelines. Ask students to write a sentence explaining the reasons that Spain might have sided with the Americans. Ask: *How did Spain benefit from the American victory?* Next, have students consider each of the people on the Chapter 14 Activity Sheet. Discuss why and how each of these people became involved.

ASSESSING: Ask students to analyze key battles of the Revolution in a chart. Column heads should include "Name of Battle," "Outcome," "Reasons for Outcome," "Results of Battle."

PAST TO PRESENT: Have students compare the map of North America in 1783 (p. 122) with the map of North America in 1750 (p. 78). How had power shifted? Ask: *Do you think the United States would be content with its new lands? Why or why not?*

CHAPTER 15: A New Government Is Formed.

Opening It Up

MOTIVATING: In 1781, a British clergyman named Josiah Tucker predicted: "The Americans will have no Center of Union among them. . . . [W]hen the power and Government of England are finally removed, . . . their fate will be—A DISUNITED PEOPLE, till the End of Time." Ask students what Tucker said would happen to the 13 states after the war. (They'd have no central government to unite them.) Explain that Chapter 15 shows how Americans proved Tucker wrong.

SETTING UP: Teacher's manual resources include Chapter 15 answer key (p. 269), Chapter 15 Test (p. 109), and Chapter 15 Activity Sheet (p. 181).

TEACHING TIP

Successful ESL/LEP strategies tap students as resources for information on their native countries. Encourage students to talk to relatives about government in their homelands. Have students share their findings. Then ask the class to compare U.S. ideas on government with ideas in other nations.

Teaching It Two Ways

LEARNING OBJECTIVES

- To explain the provisions of the Constitution
- To present the pros and cons of adopting the constitution
- To recognize the limitations of the Constitution

TO WRITE A SPEECH

When Mercy Otis Warren learned of the new Constitution, she remarked: "Not one legislature in the United States had any idea when they sent delegates to the convention at Philadelphia that it would destroy their state governments." To find out what Warren meant, have students list the powers of state governments under the Articles of Confederation. Ask: *How would the Constitution change these powers?* With this in mind, have teams take the parts of Federalists or Anti-Federalists and write speeches defending or attacking the new Constitution. To help students take notes, suggest that they draw graphic organizers similar to the one in the Chapter 14 Activity Sheet.

TO DESIGN A POSTER

Have students list arguments for and against the Constitution. Then assign each of the arguments to teams of students. Direct them to design posters illustrating the various arguments. Encourage students to get their message across through a combination of pictures and words. (For example, a poster favoring the Constitution might show a U.S. map breaking apart. A slogan might say: "United or Dis-United States—It's Up to You." A poster opposing the Constitution might show a picture of a smiling king or queen holding the Constitution. This slogan might say: "And I Thought You Didn't Love Me.")

Putting It All Together

SHARING: Call on the students who wrote speeches to deliver them aloud. Tell the rest of the class to hold up pro or con posters as soon as they recognize the position of the speech maker. Next, assign the Chapter 15 Activity Sheet. Based on these exercises, ask students to identify the three states in which their various speeches or posters might have had the most appeal.

ASSESSING: Challenge students to draw a political cartoon that views the Constitution through the eyes of an African American. The cartoon should focus on the limits of liberty.

PAST TO PRESENT: Explain that American fears of a strong executive continued into the 20th century. Assign students the 20th Amendment to read. Ask: *How does this amendment restrict the power of the President?* (limited the President to two terms) Have volunteers research the identity of the only President to be elected four times. (FDR)

CHAPTER 16: The Constitution Is the Foundation of Our Government.

Opening It Up

MOTIVATING: Read aloud these words from the Preamble to the Constitution: "We the people of the United States, in Order to form a more perfect Union, establish . . . this Constitution." Review what was "imperfect" about the Articles of Confederation. Then have students figure out the age of the Constitution. (Subtract 1787 from the current date.) Explain that Chapter 16 takes a look at the world's oldest written plan of government.

SETTING UP: Prepare copies of the 14th Amendment (see below). Teacher's manual resources include: Chapter 16 answer key (p. 269), Chapter 16 Test (p. 110), and Chapter 16 Activity Sheet (p. 182).

TEACHING TIP

Venn diagrams, or Euler circles, show the relationships between or among classes. The chart in the Chapter 16 Activity Sheet is modeled after an "overlapping Venn diagram." It compares two classes—federal and state powers—to show distinct and shared traits.

Teaching It Two Ways

LEARNING OBJECTIVES

- To list the powers of Congress, the President, and the Supreme Court
- To explain the system of checks and balances
- To name liberties protected by the Bill of Rights

TO INTERPRET AN AMENDMENT

Distribute copies of the following adaptation of the 14th Amendment.

1. All persons born or naturalized in the United States . . . are citizens of the United States and of the State in which they reside. 2. No State shall make or enforce any law which shall . . . deprive any person of life, liberty, or property, without due process or law, 3. nor [may a State] deny to any person . . . equal protection of the law.

Tell students to circle all difficult words. Have them look up each word in the dictionary. Then have students summarize in their own words the rights guaranteed by each numbered statement.

TO ILLUSTRATES AMENDMENTS

Have students make a list of the amendments in the Bill of Rights. (pp. 139–141) Under each amendment, have students summarize its most important points. Then direct students to design a poster illustrating some of the liberties protected by these amendments. For a past-to-present link, suggest that students look through magazines or newspapers for pictures that show how these amendments touch our lives today. Students with an interest in photography might take their own pictures. (A photo of a news stand illustrates freedom of press. A photo of a church, synagogue, or mosque shows freedom of religion.)

Putting It All Together

SHARING: Have students share their summaries of the 14th Amendment. Ask the class how these provisions were used in the case of *Brown* v. *Board of Education Topeka* (volume 2, pp. 176–177). Next, display student posters. Ask what freedoms or liberties are illustrated in each. Then have students complete this sentence: Amendments to the Constitution have made our government more perfect by ______.

ASSESSING: Have volunteers make flash cards naming various government functions listed in Chapter 16. Hold up these cards, and challenge students to identify the governmental branch that carries out each task.

PAST TO PRESENT: Our federal system of government touches students' everyday lives in many ways. To show students how the Constitution makes sure that no branch of government exercises too much control over people, assign the Chapter 16 Activity Sheet.

CHAPTER 17: The New Government Begins to Work.

Opening It Up

MOTIVATING: Write the following words from Washington's First Inaugural Address on the chalkboard: "The . . . fire of liberty is . . . staked to the experiment entrusted to the American people." Ask: *What did Washington mean by the word experiment?* (government by the people) *What did he imply would happen if the experiment failed?* (The fire of liberty would go out.) Point out that Chapter 17 traces the steps taken by Washington and others to ensure that the experiment succeeded.

SETTING UP: Teacher's manual resources include Chapter 17 answer key (p. 269), Chapter 17 Test (p. 111), and Chapter 17 Activity Sheet (p. 183).

TEACHING TIP

News stories are a creative way to describe past events. Familiarize students with the main parts of a news story: *headline* (identifies the topic), *dateline* (sets the place and time), *byline* (names the reporter), and *lead* (opens the story; it's a quick summary of the story or a "hook" to grab reader attention).

Teaching It Two Ways

LEARNING OBJECTIVES

- To list precedents set by George Washington
- To explain reasons for the rise of political parties
- To describe provisions of the 12th Amendment

TO WRITE A MEMO

Copy the following chart headings on the chalkboard or an overhead transparency.

Washington's Ideas on Government

Term	Precedents Set	Advice Offered

Have students complete the chart. Based on this chart, have students compose a memo that Washington might have written to his successor, John Adams. In it, Washington offers tips on how best to serve the nation.

TO WRITE A NEWS STORY

Assign the Chapter 17 Activity Sheet. Ask for volunteers to read aloud the eyewitness account. Ask: *Why was the number 13 so significant?* (represented the 13 colonies and original states) Point out the presence of a Spanish ship. Ask: *What does this tell you about relations between the U.S. and Spain?* (that they were friendly) Focus on the use of the term *Excellency*. Point out that this word is applied to people of unusually high honor or position. Ask: *What does this word choice tell you about the author's opinion of Washington?* With this background in mind, have students take notes for their news story. (See Teaching Tip for an explanation of the parts of a news story.)

Putting It All Together

SHARING: Photocopy news stories for distribution to the class. (You make take the part of a news hawker, saying, "Read All About It: Washington Arrives in New York.") Ask students to describe the way in which Americans viewed Washington. Next, hand out copies of the memos. Identify tips offered by Washington to Adams. Discuss whether Adams followed any of this advice. Ask which tips, if any, are followed by Presidents today.

ASSESSING: Assign students campaign speeches to write for a Federalist or a Democratic-Republican candidate for the House. Read these speeches aloud and have students guess the candidate's political party.

PAST TO PRESENT: Review Washington's ideas on foreign policy. Then ask students to clip articles showing how the nation's attitude toward foreign policy has changed.

CHAPTER 18: Jefferson Strengthens the Nation.

Opening It Up

MOTIVATING: Copy the following definition on an overhead transparency: *expand,* a verb meaning "to spread out" or "to make greater in size." Tell students that this is what happened to the United States in the first half of the 1800s: It expanded. Refer them to the maps on pages 152 and 155. Ask: *In what direction did the nation expand in the years 1800–1814?* (westward)

SETTING UP: Prepare copies of the quotations below. Bring in poster board, felt-tipped pens, and tempera paints for the ESL/LEP activity. Teacher's manual resources include Chapter 18 answer key (p. 269), Chapter 18 Test (p. 112), and Chapter 18 Activity Sheet (p. 184).

TEACHING TIP

One way to infuse cultural diversity into history lessons is to ask students to view past events through the eyes of various cultural groups. This will help you to relate historical perspectives to student diversity. The technique also develops empathy for the cultural experiences of others.

Teaching It Two Ways

LEARNING OBJECTIVES

- To explain how the United States organized territories in the West
- To list reasons that the United States bought the Louisiana Territory
- To describe how the War of 1812 affected the nation's identity

TO DEVELOP EMPATHY

Distribute copies of the following quotations.

At first the white men ask for land sufficient for a wigwam; now, nothing will satisfy them but the whole of our hunting grounds. (Tecumseh)

On the . . . day Louisiana was given to the United States, the French and Spanish [were] . . . deeply moved. [They] barely held back their . . . tears. (French official)

Ask students to identify groups affected by western expansion of the United States. (Native Americans, Spanish, French) Then have students compose poems expressing the losses that each of these groups felt.

TO DESIGN ILLUSTRATED MAPS

Using an opaque projector, have students copy the map entitled "The Louisiana Purchase" onto poster board. Then have them tell the story of the Lewis and Clark expedition in the form of map illustrations. Encourage students to visualize some of the scenes described on pages 154-155 of the text. Remind them to highlight the contributions of York and Sacajawea. When students are done, direct them to choose one of the scenes depicted on the map. Make sure all scenes are selected. Have them describe this scene in the form of a diary entry, like those written by Lewis and Clark. Tape these entries on the map next to the correct illustrations.

Putting It All Together

SHARING: Post the completed map in the front of the classroom. Ask how the Louisiana Purchase increased the size of the United States. Have students speculate on how people in the 13 states might have viewed this growth. Then use the student poems to explore how people in the west saw this same expansion. Ask students to cite reasons for these different points of view.

ASSESSING: Ask students to list the causes and effects of the War of 1812. Then tell them to rank the causes and effects in order of importance. Students should be prepared to defend their choices.

PAST TO PRESENT: To illustrate the importance of historical events such as the War of 1812 and U.S. life today, have students complete the Chapter 18 Activity Sheet. When students have finished, discuss their answers. Ask: *When do we hear "The Star-Spangled Banner" today? Why?*

CHAPTER 19: The North and South Take Different Paths.

Opening It Up

MOTIVATING: Ask students if they have heard of Abraham Lincoln. Explore student knowledge. Then tell students that in the late 1850s Lincoln said: "A House divided against itself cannot stand." Refer students to the chapter title. Ask: *To what "house" was Lincoln referring?* (the United States) Explain that this chapter explores the widening division between North and South.

SETTING UP: Prepare copies of the poems in the activity below. Teacher's manual resources include Chapter 19 answer key (p. 270), Chapter 19 Test (p. 113), and Chapter 19 Activity Sheet (p. 185).

TEACHING TIP

An important goal in teaching ESL/LEP students is to increase their oral fluency. Create situations in which students read aloud. Allow students to practice reading in a one-on-one situation with a classmate. This allows them to try out new words or to ask another student to pronounce it.

Teaching It Two Ways

LEARNING OBJECTIVES

- To trace the growth of factories in New England
- To explain the connection between invention of the cotton gin and the growth of slavery
- To name ways by which enslaved African Americans survived slavery

TO MAKE COMPARISONS

Distribute copies of these poems by women factory workers for students to compare.

I. Despite of toil we all agree
Or out of the mills, or in,
Dependent on others we ne'er will be
So long as we're able to spin.

II. Oh! Isn't it a pity that such a pretty girl as I
Should be sent to the factory to pine away and die?
Oh! I cannot be a slave,
I will not be a slave,
For I'm so fond of liberty
That I cannot be a slave.

Ask: *How does each worker view factory life?* Have the students capture these responses in letters.

ESL TO INTERPRET POETRY

Ask students to envision slavery through the eyes of this six year old: "My brothers and sisters were bid off first, . . . while my mother, paralyzed with grief, held me by the hand. . . . Her turn came and . . . then I was offered."

Based on this description of an auction, have students finish this sentence: "To be a slave meant_________." Next, distribute copies of the Chapter 19 Activity Sheet. Go over the vocabulary list. Spend some time on pronunciation. For example, read the poem aloud to illustrate rhyme. Find out if students want any of the words repeated. Then, as the Activity Sheet suggests, have students team up with other classmates.

Putting It All Together

SHARING: Ask volunteers to read the poems by the two women factory workers. Ask: *How did each see her job?* (One saw it as the key to independence, the other saw it as slavery.) Explore the reasons for the differences. (Wages freed women from their families or husbands. Low wages and low hours made women slaves to machines.) Now have a volunteer read aloud George R. Allen's poem. Ask; *How did a slave's life differ from even the most miserable factory worker's?* (A slave was not free.)

ASSESSING: Ask students to design a poster entitled: "Inventions That Split the Nation." Instruct them to show how the cotton gin and factory drove apart the North and South.

PAST TO PRESENT: Spirituals are a U.S. invention, born in the slave cabins of the South. Ask students to locate recordings of spirituals in their library. Use these songs to explore the importance of religion to enslaved African Americans.

CHAPTER 20: Americans Move West.

Opening It Up

MOTIVATING: Refer students to the three maps in this chapter. Ask: *In what direction is most of the movement?* (west) Then repeat these song lyrics from a tune sung by some Georgians in the 1830s. "All I ask in this creation / Is a . . . big plantation / Way up yonder / In the Cherokee nation." Ask: *What do these lyrics tell you about the reason that the Cherokee headed west?* Explain that Chapter 20 will explore why groups of people moved during the 1840s and 1850s.

SETTING UP: Copy the quotes in Assessing. Teacher's manual resources include Chapter 20 answer key (p.270), Chapter 20 Test (p. 114) and Chapter 20 Activity Sheet (p. 186).

TEACHING TIP

Social Studies classes provide a chance to explore such American ideals as a belief in liberty, equality, and government by consent. Despite the diversity of the United States, a shared belief in these ideals has historically united the American people. Chapter 20 explores some of these ideals.

Teaching It Two Ways

LEARNING OBJECTIVES

- To explain how canals, roads, and trails encouraged growth
- To describe the growth of democracy in the West
- To discuss the forced migration of Native Americans out of the Southeast

TO INTERPRET A MAP

Refer students to the map entitled "Trails West." Have them locate the Oregon Trail. Ask: *Where did the trail start?* (Independence, Missouri) *Where did it end?* (in the Oregon Territory near present-day Portland) Challenge students to use the scale to estimate the distance traveled. Ask: *What geographic barrier did travelers have to overcome?* (Rocky Mountains) *How did travelers cut through this barrier?* (at the South Pass) Then distribute copies of the Chapter 20 Activity Sheet.

TO INTERPRET A MAP

Refer students to the map entitled "Native Americans Forced to Indian Territory." Have small groups answer these questions: 1. What five Native American nations lived in the Southeast? 2. In what states were their lands? 3. Where were they forced to move? 4. In 1828, the government sent the Cherokee this letter: "The United States [wants] to secure to the Cherokee Nation . . . a permanent home . . . which shall . . . remain theirs forever." Would you have believed this promise? Why or why not?

Putting It Together

SHARING: Call on students to report on reasons the pioneers and the Cherokee moved west. Ask: *How did the experiences of the pioneers and Cherokee differ?* (Pioneers moved onto good land of their own free will. The Cherokee were forced off good land and onto a reservation.)

ASSESSING: Explain that the pioneers and Cherokee shared something in common: a belief in written plans of government. Distribute these quotations:

We had proceeded only a few days . . . when . . . we pitched our tents for the purpose of enacting a code of laws." (diary entry, Oregon pioneer)

We, the people . . . do hereby . . . agree to form ourselves into one body politic under the . . . title of the Cherokee Nation." (call for a constitution by Sequoyah)

As they work in small groups, challenge students to draw up a set of proposals for each new plan of government. (For ideas, refer to Chapter 16.)

PAST TO PRESENT: Ask students to locate a map of interstate highways in a road atlas of the United States such as the *Rand McNally Road Atlas*. Ask them to write a paragraph linking transportation to national unity.

CHAPTER 21: Cultures Clash in the Southwest.

Opening It Up

MOTIVATING: In 1829, a Mexican general in the borderlands warned: "The North Americans have conquered whatever territory adjoins them. In less than half a century, they have become masters of extensive colonies that formerly belonged to Spain and France." Ask students what the general implies will happen to the borderlands. Tell students that they will find out if he was right in Chapter 21.

SETTING UP: Activities require an overhead transparency of the table below and a wall map of the United States. Teacher manual resources include Chapter 21 answer key (p. 270), Chapter 21 Test (p. 115), Unit 4 Test (p. 86), and Chapter 21 Activity Sheet (p. 187).

TEACHING TIP

Built-in redundancy is an effective strategy for developing ESL/LEP lessons. Seeing or using similar language more than once promotes recall or language patterning. Repetition helps ESL/LEP students begin to process information more quickly, promoting a feeling of mastery.

Teaching It Two Ways

LEARNING OBJECTIVES

- To list causes of the Texas Revolt
- To identify the causes and effects of the war between Mexico and the United States
- To explain how the Gold Rush affected California
- To describe the new way of life that developed in what became the U.S. Southwest

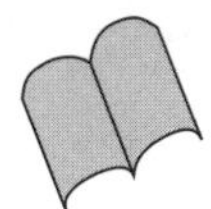

TO TRANSLATE MAP INFORMATION INTO A TABLE

Show students an overhead transparency of the table below. Ask them to copy it onto paper. Have students fill in the missing data.

Territory	Date	How Acquired	From Whom
Original 13 States	1783	Treaty of Paris	Britain
Louisiana Territory			
West Florida			
East Florida			
Texas			
Oregon Territory	1849	Oregon Treaty	Britain
Mexican Cession			
Gadsden Purchase			

TO ORGANIZE HISTORICAL INFORMATION

Display a wall map of the United States at the front of the classroom. Then refer students to the maps of the Texas Revolt and the war between Mexico and the United States on pages 178 and 180. Ask them to make a list of the present-day states affected by the conflict. Use this exercise to remind students that all of these states once belonged to Spain and later Mexico. To find out how these lands came into U.S. hands, assign students the Chapter 21 Activity Sheet. (Students can take notes in their native language and then write them in English on the two charts.)

Putting It All Together

SHARING: Have members from each group present their completed tables and charts. Encourage students to compare information on the Texas Revolt and the Mexican War. Ask: *What similarities and differences can you identify in the two conflicts?* Ask: *How has the United States obtained most of its territory? Was it through peaceful acquisition or by acts of war?*

ASSESSING: Ask for volunteers to prepare a skit in which a *tejano, californio,* and a Latino from New Mexico describe how they became U.S. citizens. The skit should include mention of any rights lost or gained. If you have any Spanish-speaking students, they might tell their stories in Spanish with a classmate translating the tales for the rest of the class.

PAST TO PRESENT: Have students list ways in which the *tejanos, californios,* and *nuevomexianos* have enriched U.S. culture. Encourage them to research additional examples. Have students present their findings on posters.

CHAPTER 22: Immigrants Flock to the United States.

Opening It Up

MOTIVATING: In 1848, roads leading to ports in Europe were jammed with people. One observer remarked: "It is a sad sight to see these long files of carts that meet you every mile, carrying the whole property of the poor, who are about to cross the Atlantic." Ask: *Where was this mass of people headed?* (the U.S.) The story of these Forty-Eighters is in this chapter.

SETTING UP: Prepare copies of the tables below. Teacher's manual resources include Chapter 22 answer key (p. 270), Chapter 22 Test (p. 116), and Chapter 22 Activity Sheet (p. 188).

TEACHING TIP

When possible, tie U.S. history to events in other nations to provide a global perspective more suited to the diverse backgrounds of students. An example is the Teaching It activity that shows the effect of Irish immigration to the United States upon the population of Ireland.

Teaching It Two Ways

LEARNING OBJECTIVES

- To give the reasons that the Irish and Germans left their homelands in the mid-1800s
- To give the reasons that the Chinese traveled to the United States
- To describe the prejudice faced by immigrants

TO ANALYZE CAUSE-AND-EFFECT RELATIONSHIPS

Distribute copies of the table below. Then have students answer: *How many Irish immigrants came to the United States during the years shown? In what two decades was immigration the highest? How did this immigration affect Ireland?*

Years	Irish Immigration to U.S.	Year	Population in Ireland
1831–1840	207,381	1841	8,196,597
1841–1850	780,719	1851	6,574,278
1851–1860	914,119	1861	5,888,564
1861–1870	435,778	1871	5,412,377
1871–1880	436,871	1881	5,174,836
1881–1890	655,481	1891	4,704,750
1891-1900	388,416	1901	4,456,546

TO ORGANIZE INFORMATION ON A CHART

Distribute copies of the table below:

Group	Push Factors	Pull Factors
Irish		
Germans		
Chinese		

Using information in the book, ask students to list conditions that "pushed " each of these groups out their native countries and "pulled" them into the United States.

Putting It All Together

SHARING: Ask students to read their paragraphs on Irish immigration aloud. Ask them to explore the possible negative effects of a large-scale movement of people out of a nation. (loss of labor, talent, etc.) To understand why such movements occurred in the mid-1800s, show a completed push-and-pull chart. Then assign the Chapter 22 Activity Sheet. Ask students what the letter reveals about the way in which immigration affected the U.S.

ASSESSING: Read this 1854 statement by the Know-Nothing Party: "America for the Americans, we say. And why not? . . . Haven't they developed it, as only Americans could, into a mighty nation." Challenge students to attack this statement by listing achievements of immigrants.

PAST TO PRESENT: Using a recent almanac, have students identify the largest groups of immigrants coming to the United States today. Ask students how immigration patterns have changed since the mid-1800s.

CHAPTER 23: Women Fight for Reform.

Opening It Up

MOTIVATING: A well-known saying in the 1800s declared, "A woman's name should appear in print but twice: when she marries and when she dies." Ask students how women might respond if they heard this statement today. Use students' comments to point out that such remarks outraged a handful of outspoken women in the mid-1800s. Their support of women's rights won them the name of "feminists." Refer students to the definition of this term on page 195.

SETTING UP: The ESL/LEP activity requires materials for making posters. Teacher's manual resources include Chapter 23 answer key (p. 270), Chapter 23 Test (p. 117), and Chapter 23 Activity Sheet (p. 189).

TEACHING TIP

Explain that some words evoke emotional responses because of the positive or negative associations acquired over time. An example is the word *feminist*. Explore images called up by this word. Then ask students to think of other examples of "loaded words," or words that have emotional impact.

Teaching It Two Ways

LEARNING OBJECTIVES

- To identify the goals of the women's rights movement
- To list advances made by women in the mid-1800s
- To name some of the other reform movements backed by women

TO DEVLOP AN ARGUMENT

Tell students that in 1853 a group of men tried to block Susan B. Anthony from addressing an audience on the subject of women's rights. They accused her of trying to turn their wives into "Susan B's," a negative name given to feminists of the time. Anthony responded: "It seems to me, gentlemen, that none of you quite comprehend the cause of women." Read this statement slowly and have students copy it on a sheet of paper. Using information in the text, ask students to develop an argument that Anthony might have used to explain that cause. Tell students to be prepared to deliver their arguments to the class in a speech.

TO DESIGN POSTERS

Have students identify the various reform movements mentioned in the text. (women's rights movement, abolition movement, crusade to help the mentally ill, temperance movement, public education movement, crusade for women's education) Then ask students to list the goals of each movement or crusade. Divide students into small groups and have them create posters that capture the goals of each movement. Challenge students to get their message across without using any words. Students can use illustrations, political cartoons, symbols, or magazine pictures.

Putting It All Together

SHARING: Hold up each poster created by students, and ask the rest of the class to identify the movement depicted. Then call on members to role-play Susan B. Anthony's "None of you quite comprehend" speech while adding their own arguments. Tell the rest of the class to take notes on the arguments offered by Anthony. Ask: *Which two arguments do you think are the most forceful? Why?*

ASSESSING: Assign the Chapter 23 Activity Sheet. When students are done, have them write a paragraph explaining the link between women's colleges, such as Mount Holyoke, and the advancement of women's rights.

PAST TO PRESENT: Tell students that March is women's history month. Have them design commemorative stamps that the federal government might issue next March to honor women mentioned in this chapter. Interested students can send their ideas to this address: Postmaster General, U.S. Postal Service, 1333 H. St. NW, Washington, D.C. 20268.

CHAPTER 24: The Fight Against Slavery Gains Ground.

Opening It Up

MOTIVATING: On July 4, 1852, former slave Frederick Douglass told a white audience: "This Fourth of July is *yours,* not *mine.* . . . What, to the American slave, is your Fourth of July? . . . To him the holiday is a fake." Ask: *What was Douglass criticizing?* (celebrating liberty in a land that allowed slavery) Explain that in Chapter 24 students will meet other people who upset American consciences.

SETTING UP: Provide poster board or strips of paper for storyboards. Teacher's manual resources include Chapter 24 answer key (p. 271), Chapter 24 Test (p. 118), and Chapter 24 Activity Sheet (p. 190).

TEACHING TIP

Define *propaganda:* "a planned attempt to promote an idea, product, etc." Point out that propaganda is neither good nor bad. It is a technique aimed at influencing the opinions of others. Have students bring in advertisements that use propaganda. You can use these ads as a springboard.

Teaching It Two Ways

LEARNING OBJECTIVES

- To identify ways in which the abolitionists opposed slavery
- To explain how the Underground Railroad worked
- To name leading African American abolitionists

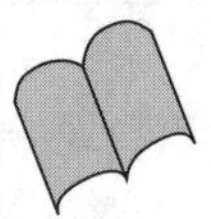

TO INTERPRET A POLITICAL ADVERTISEMENT

Go over the definition of propaganda (see Teaching Tips). Then tell them that there are two types of propaganda: concealed propaganda and revealed propaganda. Concealed propaganda tries to influence people secretly. (An example might be a staged photograph of a political candidate.) Revealed propaganda makes no effort to disguise its message. (Almost all advertising is revealed propaganda.) Distribute copies of the activity sheet. Ask: *What type of propaganda is this advertisement?* (revealed) *What does Garrison want readers to do?* (oppose slavery) Say: *Abolitionists would see this as positive propaganda. How would a slaveholder view it?* (as negative) *Why?* (threatened to undermine slavery)

TO USE HISTORICAL IMAGINATION

Go over the biblical story of Moses. Then tell students that enslaved African Americans called Harriet Tubman the "Moses of Her People." Ask students to explain the reasons for this nickname. Next, challenge students to imagine that they are enslaved African Americans living on a plantation outside Baltimore, Maryland. One dark night, the words of a spiritual awaken them. "Go down, Moses, / Way down in Egypt's land. / Let my people go." This is Harriet Tubman's way of saying she has come to lead another "freedom train" north. Using strips of computer paper, have students design storyboards depicting their flight out of bondage. (Remind students that storyboards are like the frames in a film.)

Putting It All Together

SHARING: Post the completed Activity Sheets on the bulletin board and the storyboards on classroom walls. Have students examine each other's work. Then ask how Garrison and Tubman worked to end slavery. List students' answers on the chalkboard. Then have them add other methods of resistance mentioned in the text.

ASSESSING: Have students create advertisements encouraging people to join the abolitionist movement. Ads might be geared to the students' own age group. (Children and young people did in fact take part in the abolitionist movement.)

PAST TO PRESENT: Today the Mother Bethel African Methodist Episcopal Church is a national landmark. Have interested students write for information on the church to: Mother Bethel AME Church, 419 South Sixth Street, Philadelphia, PA 19147.

CHAPTER 25: Slavery Divides the Nation.

Opening It Up

MOTIVATING: Write the word *sectional* on the chalkboard. Then have a volunteer look up and read aloud a definition of this word from a class dictionary (characteristic of a given section, district, or region). Then refer students to the map entitled "Slavery in the United States, 1850–1854" on page 214. Ask students to explain why slavery was a *sectional* issue. Then point out that Chapter 25 traces the way in which slavery split the United States apart.

SETTING UP: Bring in computer paper for a timeline. Prepare for the mock trial in Assessing. Teacher's manual resources include Chapter 25 answer key (p. 271), Chapter 25 Test (p. 119), and Chapter 25 Activity Sheet (p. 191).

TEACHING TIP

Scripted role-playing provide an opportunity for ESL/LEP students to create and practice dialogues with English-proficient students. Students should begin by writing dialogues for role-playing. They should then rehearse these dialogues by reading them aloud or by recording them on tape.

Teaching It Two Ways

LEARNING OBJECTIVES

- To list reasons for the spread of slavery
- To explain why compromise over slavery failed
- To describe how the Dred Scott Decision and John Brown's Raid split the nation

TO WRITE HEADLINES

Write the following list of events or acts on the chalkboard or an overhead transparency: *Compromise of 1850, Fugitive Slave Act of 1850, Return of Anthony Burns to the South (1854), Passage of Kansas Nebraska Act (1854), Bleeding Kansas (1856), Dred Scott Decision (1857), Raid on Harpers Ferry (1859).* Assign half of the students to write headlines about each of these items that might have run in a Southern newspaper. The other half should write headlines that might have run in a Northern newspaper.

TO DESIGN ILLUSTRATED TIMELINES

Have students use a long strip of computer paper to create the illustrated timeline suggested on page 00 of the text. Tell them that the timeline should include all of the items listed for the activity. Additional entries might include the *Missouri Request for Statehood (1819), Missouri Compromise (1820), War with Mexico (1846–1848), Splits in the Two Major Parties (1848).* Have students push together desks to work on the timeline. When they are done, post the completed timeline on the wall.

Putting It All Together

SHARING: Direct students to tape their completed headlines above the appropriate events and illustrations on the timeline. Have students study these events. For each set of headlines: have students complete this sentence: "The [name of event/act] increased sectional conflict by ________."

ASSESSING: Assign the Activity Sheet for this chapter. Next, have groups of students prepare scripted skits for mock trials of John Brown. Roles should include the defending attorney, prosecuting attorney, judge, John Brown, and several witnesses for each side. (The defending attorney might call former enslaved African Americans. The prosecuting attorney might call eyewitnesses to the violence.) Remind students that Brown broke a federal law. As each group presents its skit, have the rest of the class act as the jury. At the end of the skits, poll the class to determine Brown's guilt or innocence. Evaluate the activity on the basis of group effort.

PAST TO PRESENT: The issue of slavery divided Americans in the 1850s. Assign students to collect newspaper and magazine articles that show issues that divide Americans today. Ask: *Are any of these issues sectional?*

CHAPTER 26: The Civil War Begins.

Opening It Up

MOTIVATING: Refer students to the map entitled "The Nation Divided, 1861." Ask: *What took place during the two years following John Brown's raid?* (The United States split apart.) Then discuss this 1861 statement by Jefferson Davis: "The time to compromise has passed and those who oppose us shall smell [gun]powder and taste Southern steel."

SETTING UP: Prepare copies of the quotation below and the Preamble to the U.S. Constitution. Teacher's manual resources include Chapter 26 answer key (p. 271), Chapter 26 Test (p. 120), and Chapter 26 Activity Sheet (p. 192).

TEACHING TIP

The Civil War was the first war to be documented by photographs. Ask students to study the photos in this chapter. Ask if these photos are primary or secondary sources of information. (primary) Have students list what each photo shows them about the war.

Teaching It Two Ways

LEARNING OBJECTIVES

- To trace events leading to the Civil War
- To weigh advantages of the North and the South at the start of war
- To describe how the war involved Americans from all backgrounds
- To name Union goals in the war

TO COMPARE PRIMARY SOURCES

Distribute copies of the preamble to the Confederate constitution. Have students compare this document to the Preamble to the U.S. Constitution. Have students list the differences between the two documents. (Tip: Have students look up the term *confederate.*)

We, the people of the Confederate States, each state acting in an . . . independent character, in order to form a . . . federal government . . . do establish this constitution. . . . [No] law denying . . . the right of property in Negro slaves shall be passed. . . . [Any slave] in any state . . . escaping into another shall be delivered . . . to the party to whom . . . such slave belongs.

TO COMPARE STRENGTHS AND WEAKNESSES

Have students make a chart. Column heads should include: Confederate States, Confederate Territories, Union States, Union Territories, Border States. Ask students to add up the states and territories for each side, excluding the border states. Ask: *Which side had the advantage?* Explore what might have happened if the border states had gone with the Confederacy. Have students imagine they were Abraham Lincoln. Ask them what policy they might adopt toward slavery in the border states and why. Tell students to write down their answers to check against Lincoln's actions in Chapter 27. Next, assign the Activity Sheet for this chapter.

Putting It All Together

SHARING: Write the terms *states rights'* and *slavery* on the chalkboard. Have students use these terms to explain the differences between the Confederate constitution and the U.S. Constitution. Next, use an opaque projector to show a completed Activity Sheet. Repeat a comment by Lincoln in 1861: "The hen is one of the wisest creatures of all the animal kingdom. She never cackles until after the egg is laid." Ask: *What did Lincoln mean?* (Don't brag until you win) *What reasons did he have to doubt a quick victory?*

ASSESSING: Based on the map on page 225, have students write a status report on the war from the Confederates' point of view. Ask: *Was it time for them to surrender? Why or why not?*

PAST TO PRESENT: Have students view photos of the Civil War. Ask: *Suppose TV had been available to broadcast the war. Would it have ended sooner? Why or why not?* Or have the students write reviews of the movie *Glory,* the story of the 54th Massachusetts Volunteer Infantry.

CHAPTER 27: The Union Is Saved.

Opening It Up

MOTIVATING: Read aloud this statement by Lincoln made early in the Civil War: "If I could save the Union without freeing *any* slave, I would do it; and if I could save it by freeing *all* the slaves, I would do it; and if I could do it by freeing some and leaving others alone, I would also do that." Ask students to identify Lincoln's main war goal. (saving the Union) Then tell them that they will learn which of these courses of action Lincoln chose.

SETTING UP: Make copies of the lines from the Gettysburg Address and the incomplete news story printed below. Teacher's manual resources include Chapter 27 answer key (p. 271), Chapter 27 Test (p. 121), and Chapter 27 Activity Sheet (p. 193).

TEACHING TIP

Many ESL/LEP students from foreign countries may not have the background to grasp abstract U.S. ideals such as liberty, equality, or government by the people. When possible, reinforce past learning. For example, link the Gettysburg Address to the Declaration of Independence.

Teaching It Two Ways

LEARNING OBJECTIVES

- To explain why Lincoln issued the Emancipation Proclamation
- To name victories or campaigns that turned the war in the North's favor
- To list economic and political effects of the war

TO IDENTIFY U.S. IDEALS

Distribute copies of the opening lines from the Gettysburg Address:

Four score and seven years ago our forefathers brought forth on this continent, a new nation, conceived in Liberty, and dedicated to the proposition [idea] that all men are created equal. Now we are engaged in a great civil war, testing whether that nation . . . can long endure.

Tell students to add the lines cited on page 231 of the text. Explain that *score* means 20. Ask: *What event happened 87 years earlier?* (American independence in 1776) Next, ask students to reread the discussion of the Preamble to the Declaration on pages 00–00 of the text. Direct them to list ideals that link the two documents.

TO INTERPRET A MAP

Have students review the guesses that they made in the Chapter 26 ESL/LEP activity about what action Lincoln might take regarding slavery in the border states. Call on volunteers to share their speculations. Next, assign the Activity Sheet for this chapter. When students have finished, have them write a news story on the Emancipation Proclamation from the point of view of a foreign nation such as Great Britain. To get students started, pass out copies of the following opening paragraph adapted from a story in the *London Gazette.*

London, January 26. The war in America has become a war between freedom and slavery. This change came when President Abraham Lincoln signed the Emancipation Proclamation. This document states that . . .

Putting It All Together

SHARING: Pass out the news stories. Ask: *What is Lincoln's position on slavery?* Have a student do a dramatic reading of the Gettysburg Address. Request a volunteer to role play Lincoln. Ask another student to explain how the Declaration of Independence inspired the address. Ask a third student to reread the address. Direct students to yell "Stop!" when they hear lines showing that Lincoln would have ended slavery everywhere if he could.

ASSESSING: Ask students to design a chart listing the social, economic, and political effects of the Civil War. Entries should reflect information in the text.

PAST TO PRESENT: Have students prepare a list of the Presidents studied thus far. Challenge them to rank order these individuals. Ask: *Where would you place Lincoln? Why?*

CHAPTER 28: The Nation Rebuilds.

Opening It Up

MOTIVATING: In 1871, African Americans from Kentucky told Congress: "Life, liberty, and property are not protected for Blacks. Bands of men roam the state. Most of them were soldiers in the Confederate army. They are taking away our rights. . . . We ask you to pass laws to protect us." Review conditions in the South after the Civil War. Explain that Chapter 28 explores efforts to change conditions.

SETTING UP: Make copies of the chart below, and have materials for drawing political cartoons. Teacher's manual resources include Chapter 28 answer key (p. 271), Chapter 28 Test (p. 122), Chapter 28 Activity Sheet (p. 194) and Unit 5 Test (p. 87).

TEACHING TIP

Political cartoons allow students to present opinions in a visual format. To familiarize ESL/LEP students with symbols commonly used by U.S. political cartoonists, create a bulletin board display with such items as Uncle Sam (the United States), a donkey (the Republicans), an elephant (the Democrats), and so on.

Teaching It Two Ways

LEARNING OBJECTIVES

- To describe advances and setbacks faced by African Americans in the South
- To list political rights won by African Americans during Reconstruction
- To identify shortcomings of Reconstruction

TO CLASSIFY INFORMATION

Have students work in groups and compile a list of advances made by African Americans during the years 1865-1877. In another list, have them name setbacks suffered by African Americans. Then distribute an expanded version of this chart:

Changes	Political	Economic	Social
Advances			families reunited
Setbacks	black codes passed		

Have students classify the various advances or setbacks in the appropriate columns. Sample answers have been provided to get students started.

TO INTERPRET A POLITICAL CARTOON

Distribute copies of the chapter Activity Sheet. Have students study the tips on reading a political cartoon. Focus on the use of symbols by cartoonists. The exercise mentions the eagle as a symbol of the United States. Ask: *What other symbols have you seen in political cartoons?* Students may be unfamiliar with common U.S. symbols so present some examples. (See Teaching Tip.) When students understand the idea of a symbol, have them name or draw some political symbols used in cartoons or posters in their home countries. (Political parties, for example, usually have symbols just like the United States.) Then have groups of students com-

Putting It All Together

SHARING: Draw an outline of the chart on the chalkboard. Have students share the items that they think should appear in each column. When the class chart is done, show the political cartoon on the activity sheet. Identify the subject of the cartoon. Ask: *In which column(s) would you place each of the conditions shown in the cartoon?*

ASSESSING: Instruct students to imagine it is 1877. Like Thomas Nast, who drew the cartoon on the Activity Sheet, they work for *Harper's Weekly.* Challenge them to create a political cartoon expressing their opinion of Reconstruction. Do students think it was a success or a failure? Cartoons should capture events that support their point of view.

PAST TO PRESENT: Have students read about the impeachment hearings into the activities of Richard Nixon in Volume 2, Chapter 19. Have them prepare an oral report comparing the impeachment hearings to the trial of Andrew Johnson.

CHAPTER 29: African Americans Face a Hostile World.

Opening It Up

MOTIVATING: Open by requesting volunteers read aloud the first two paragraphs of the chapter. Focus on remarks by T. Thomas Fortune. Using an opaque projector, reshow the political cartoon on the Chapter 28 Activity Sheet. Ask students how this cartoon validates, or proves, remarks by Fortune. Point out that Chapter 29 explains the reasons that Reconstruction failed.

SETTING UP: Prepare copies of the quotes below. Bring in index cards for a game of "Who Am I?" Teacher's manual resources include Chapter 29 answer key (p. 272), Chapter 29 Test (p. 123), and Chapter 29 Activity Sheet (p. 195).

TEACHING TIP

To help students focus on essential material in the lesson, have them develop and play content-oriented games such as "Who Am I?" or "20 Questions." These games give students a chance to try out their knowledge in a nontest situation. It also enables you to keep track of what they are learning.

Teaching It Two Ways

LEARNING OBJECTIVES

- To list laws that restricted the rights of African Americans
- To describe ways African Americans resisted Jim Crow
- To compare the ideas of Booker T. Washington and W.E.B. Du Bois
- To identify successful African Americans from the period

TO EVALUATE INFORMATION

Distribute copies of this quotation by Frederick Douglass. (Sentences have been numbered.)

[1] What advantage is the 13th Amendment? . . . [2] Slavery is not abolished until the black man can freely use the ballot. . . . [3] While the legislatures . . . retain the right to pass laws making any discrimination between black and white, slavery still lives.

Have students work in groups and list evidence that proves or refutes the claim made by Douglass in sentence 2. Have them repeat this exercise for sentence 3. Based on this information, challenge students to answer the question raised in sentence 1.

TO COMPARE LEADERS

Distribute copies of the activity sheet for this chapter. When students have completed the exercises, slowly read this quote to them.

Cast down your bucket [seize the opportunity] where you are. . . . Cast it down in agriculture, in mechanics, in commerce, in domestic service, and in the professions. . . . No race can prosper till it learns that there is as much dignity in tilling a field as in writing a poem. It is at the bottom of life we must begin and not at the top.

Ask: *Is the speaker Booker T. Washington or W.E.B. DuBois?* (Washington) *What clues in the quote tipped you off?*

Putting It All Together

SHARING: Ask a volunteer to role-play Frederick Douglass and deliver a speech entitled "Slavery Still Lives." In the speech, Douglass should name specific restrictions on the civil rights of African Americans. Then show one of the completed graphic organizers. Ask students to speculate what Booker T. Washington and W.E.B. DuBois might say to African Americans faced with these injustices.

ASSESSING: Distribute index cards. Have each student write an autobiographic description of one of the figures mentioned in the chapter. Each description should end with the words "Who Am I?" To play "Who Am I?" divide the cards and circulate them among groups in a round-robin fashion.

PAST TO PRESENT: Ask students to skim a copy of the Constitution to find the amendment (24th) ending poll taxes. Ask: *When was this amendment passed?* (1964) Challenge students to write a short statement explaining the connection of this amendment to the 15th Amendment.

CHAPTER 30: Americans Settle on the Great Plains.

Opening It Up

MOTIVATING: Tell students that at the end of Reconstruction tens of thousands of African Americans fled the South. Recalled Henry Adams of Louisiana: "We said that the whole South . . . had got into the hands of the very men that had held us slaves. . . . We felt there was no hope and we had better go." Ask: *If you had been in Adams's place, where would you go? Why?* Use students' comments to introduce the rush of people onto the Great Plains.

SETTING UP: Provide copies of the figures below, pieces of poster board, and felt-tipped pens. Teacher's manual resources include Chapter 30 answer key (p. 272), Chapter 30 Test (p. 124) and Chapter 30 Activity Sheet (p. 196).

TEACHING TIP

Whenever possible, relate events in U.S. history to experiences of ESL/LEP students. For example, after reading about new environments encountered by settlers on the Plains, ask ESL/LEP students what new environments they encountered when they came to the United States. Ask: *What aspects of the landscape were strangest?*

Teaching It Two Ways

LEARNING OBJECTIVES

- To name some of the challenges that faced settlers on the Plains
- To describe the link between ranching and the development of the West
- To trace the end of the horse-and-buffalo cultures of the Plains

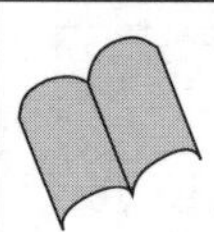

TO INTERPRET STATISTICS

Distribute copies of the figures below.

North American Buffalo Population, 1800–1900

Date	Size of Population	Date	Size of Population
1800	40,000,000	1880	395,000
1850	20,000,000	1890	1,091
1865	15,000,000	1895	800
1870	14,000,000	1900	1,024
1875	1,000,000		

Ask: *In which decade did the buffalo population decrease the most?* (1865–1875) *By how much?* (14 million) Tell students to imagine they are historians. Assign them oral reports explaining the reasons for this change.

TO INTERPRET A MAP

Assign the Activity Sheet for this chapter. After going over answers, review the different kinds of movement shown on the map. (the movement of cattle, the movement of railroads, etc.) Ask: *What groups of people were involved in these movements?* (cattleherders, railroad builders, etc.) Direct students to use the text to find other groups of people who moved onto the Plains. (Exodusters and settlers) Ask: *What peoples already lived there?* (Native Americans) Next, have students draw poster-size pictures that illustrate the life styles of each of the groups. Tell students to be sure to show how each group used the land or supported itself.

Putting It All Together

SHARING: Display students' posters on the wall. Conduct a class discussion on how the various ways of life differed. Ask: *What conflicts might erupt?* Next, have the "historians" deliver their reports on the destruction of the buffalo. Ask: *Which groups or lifestyles shown in the posters are linked to the destruction?*

ASSESSING: Have students write a short story in which a Native American grandparent tells a grandchild about changes that led the family to a reservation. Stories should reflect key events in the text.

PAST TO PRESENT: Some 755,000 Native Americans live on reservations today. Have interested students find the location of these reservations in a U.S. atlas. Ask: *In what regions are most found?*

CHAPTER 31: The United States Becomes an Industrial Nation.

Opening It Up

MOTIVATING: In 1893, Josiah Strong spoke on the growth of U.S. industry: "A few years ago, a skilled workman could make up three dozen pairs of sleeve buttons per day. Now, by the aid of the most improved machines, a boy can make up to 9,000 pairs or 250 times as many." Discuss the change produced by the "improved machines." Students will examine the positives and negatives of a new industrial age.

SETTING UP: Arrange for an opaque projector and materials for making posters. Teacher's manual resources include Chapter 31 answer key (p. 272), Chapter 31 Test (p. 125), and Chapter 31 Activity Sheet (p. 197).

TEACHING TIP

Line graphs show patterns of change over time. These patterns offer a chance to develop a grammar lesson on verb tenses. Ask students to write sentences about what the graph tells them. Have them make predictions. Ask them to underline the verbs. Have students note if the verbs reflect the past, present, or future.

Teaching It Two Ways

LEARNING OBJECTIVES

- To identify developments or inventions that spurred the growth of industry
- To describe new methods of production and business organization
- To cite reasons that workers organized labor unions

TO DRAW A LINE GRAPH

Read aloud the descriptions below:

MINER: We get old quickly. Powder, smoke, bad air—all combine to bring furrows to our faces and asthma to our lungs.

FACTORY GIRL: The shops were so crowded that we could hardly move from our benches. We had no ventilation and lacked even sanitary facilities and drinking water.

Have students identify the poor working conditions described in these quotes. Ask them to list other conditions cited in the text. Then distribute copies of the Activity Sheet. Challenge students to design posters that the miner or factory girl might have carried during a work stoppage.

TO ORGANIZE A TABLE

In a two-column table entitled: "An Age of Invention," have groups of students organize the inventions and inventors mentioned in the chapter. When they are done, tell each group to rank inventions in order of importance for the late 1800s. Have them repeat this process for the 1990s. Ask: *What differences can you find in the lists?* (For example, the automobile was of minor importance in the late 1800s.) Next, challenge each group to pick the invention that they think has had the most impact on the world. Tell them to design posters that celebrate this invention. (Students from other nations might show the effect of the invention on their homeland.)

Putting It All Together

SHARING: Use an opaque projector to show one of the line graphs. Then have students complete these sentences: "In the late 1800s, work stoppages _______." "In the 1900s, work stoppages _____." Use this activity to explore past and future verb tenses. Then display the two sets of posters. Use these posters to explore the positive and negative effects of industry and technology.

ASSESSING: People called the new business leaders by two names: "Captains of Industry" and "Robber Barons." Tell students to use a dictionary to figure out the meaning of these names. Then have them write a paragraph explaining which name best applied.

PAST TO PRESENT: Assign students to look up OPEC in an encyclopedia. Have them compare the goals of OPEC to those of Standard Oil.

CHAPTER 32: Immigrants Help Build the United States.

Opening It Up

MOTIVATING: Tell students that in 1882 a conference of Jews met in St. Petersburg, Russia. One delegate declared: "Either we get decent human rights or else let us go wherever our eyes may lead us." An outbreak of violence decided the issue. In the 1880s, tens of thousands of Jews followed their eyes to the United States. Their story forms part of this chapter. Have students skim section heads. Ask: *What other groups do you expect to learn about?*

SETTING UP: Copy quotes below and provide materials for a guidebook. Teacher's manual resources include Chapter 32 answer key (p. 272), Chapter 32 Test (p. 126) and Chapter 32 Activity Sheet (p. 198).

TEACHING TIP

The ESL/LEP strategy calls for students to make a guidebook for immigrants in the late 1880s. As an extension, you might ask students to prepare a guidebook for students new to your school. If one second-language group predominates, you might have the guidebook translated as a bilingual resource.

Teaching It Two Ways

LEARNING OBJECTIVES

- To distinguish the "new immigrants" of the late 1800s from earlier arrivals
- To cite examples of prejudice faced by Asian immigrants
- To list reasons that immigrants from Mexico, Puerto Rico, and Cuba came to the United States

TO WRITE A MOCK DIALOGUE

Distribute copies of this passage written by the son of a Jewish immigrant in 1900:

Our parents know English . . . but they speak only Yiddish, not just among themselves, but to us too, and even when our American friends come to visit us. . . . Imagine, even when we go with our father to buy something in a store on Fifth Avenue, New York, he insists on speaking Yiddish. . . . Is that nice? . . . They want keep only their old ways and don't want to take up our new ways.

Ask students to explain what this passage shows about the pains of assimilation. Then challenge them to create a mock dialogue in which the father and son explain their views on what it means to be a "real American."

TO DESIGN A GUIDEBOOK

Distribute copies from a guidebook for newcomers published by the city of Boston:

This little book . . . is a guide book and text book to help you over the rough places in this new land. It will show you something of our ways. It will tell you how . . . to feel less of a stranger here. . . . [It will help you] learn to understand America and to love it. It will be your country as much as ours.

Call on students to read this passage aloud. Discuss the purpose of the guidebook. Then have groups of students design a short guidebook of 5-10 tips to help immigrants in the late 1800s to "understand America." Encourage ESL/LEP students to draw on experiences that have helped them adjust to the United States.

Putting It All Together

SHARING: Make photocopies of the guidebooks and dialogues. Ask: *Which tips would help immigrants to become naturalized citizens? Which tips would Americanize them, or encourage them to assimilate?* Using the dialogues, explore how Americanization can cause conflict among generations.

ASSESSING: Have students use the outline map on page 253 to shade in nations that formed the *new immigration.* Tell them to label each nation and to write key phrases indicating the forces that "pushed" each group to the United States.

PAST TO PRESENT: Assign the Activity Sheet for this chapter. Then have students use an almanac to look up recent immigrants to the United States. Ask: *How many immigrants come from Asian nations? From Latin American nations?*

CHAPTER 33: The United States Becomes a Nation of Cities.

Opening It Up

MOTIVATING: Remind students that bar graphs make it possible to compare data at a glance. Ask: *What data does the bar graph on page 00 compare?* (the size of cities in 1880 with the size of cities in 1900.) *What does a comparison of the bars reveal?* (tremendous growth) *What caused this growth?* (immigration) Explain that Chapter 33 looks at city life—both the good and the bad—at the end of the century.

SETTING UP: Provide supplies for illustrations and postcards. Teacher's manual resources include Chapter 33 answer key (p. 272), Chapter 33 Test (p. 127), and Chapter 33 Activity Sheet (p. 199).

TEACHING TIP

Explain that a primary source is a written or visual record by a person who experienced the event. To find out if a primary source is valid, or accurate, it must be compared with other sources from the time. Have students compare the description of tenements by Jacob Riis in the Activity Sheet to photographs from the period. Ask: *Do the photos uphold Riis's description?*

Teaching It Two Ways

LEARNING OBJECTIVES

- To identify factors that led to the growth of cities
- To weigh the benefits and hardships of city living
- To describe how immigrants and reformers fought to improve city life

TO INTERPRET A PRIMARY SOURCE

Review primary and secondary sources of information. To practice distinguishing between these sources, have students examine the pictures in this chapter. Ask: *Which are primary sources? secondary sources?* Distribute the Activity Sheet for this chapter. Tell students to use Riis's description to review the description of tenements. Ask: *Is the text a primary or secondary source of information?* (secondary) *Does Riis's description uphold the authors' account? Why or why not? Which, if any, photos prove Riis's account?* Have students create a drawing of tenement life based on all of these sources. Ask: *What kind of source are these drawings?* (secondary) *Why?* (rely on other sources)

TO DESIGN A POSTCARD

Postcards are one of the most popular—and common items—found in the souvenir shops in most major cities. Tell students to imagine that it is the 1890s. They want to start a souvenir business for one of the cities mentioned in this chapter. Challenge them to design a postcard that captures some of the attractions of the city. As a tip, tell students that skyscrapers, elevators, elevateds, and subways were still new to most Americans. (In describing an elevator, one visitor said, "It's like being loaded into a basket and thrown upward like a feather in a hurricane.) When students have finished, display their postcards on the bulletin board.

Putting It All Together

SHARING: Compare illustrations of tenement life with the postcard display. Ask students to compare the two views of city life. Use students' comments to introduce the Study Hint activity.

ASSESSING: Ask students to imagine they have just read Jacob Riis's book. Have them write a letter to the mayor of New York City demanding change. The letters should reflect conditions described in the text.

PAST TO PRESENT: Have students conduct a straw poll (a nonscientific poll) to find out what their classmates think of city living. Have the pollsters ask: *Would you rather live in the city or the country? Are tenements a thing of the past? Do cities have attractions not found elsewhere?* Have students compile results and report their findings.

CHAPTER 34: Women Gain New Opportunities.

Opening It Up

MOTIVATING: Tell students that in 1900 author-feminist Charlotte Perkins Gilman declared: "Never before has so large a mass made so much progress in so short a time." When Gilman used the word "mass," she meant women. Have students skim the pictures and boldface heads in this chapter. Ask: *What evidence of "progress" can you spot?* Explain that this chapter takes a look at women at the turn of the century.

SETTING UP: Materials include copies of the quotation and poem below, outline map (p. 245), and supplies for commemorative postage stamps. Teacher's manual resources include Chapter 34 answer key (p. 272), Chapter 34 Test (p. 128) Chapter 34 Activity Sheet (p. 200).

TEACHING TIP

You might encourage pronunciation skills by developing rebuses. Explain that a rebus is a kind of puzzle consisting of pictures of objects, signs, letters, etc. whose combination suggests words or phrases. (A picture of a bee, a plus sign, and a picture of cows equals "because.")

Teaching It Two Ways

LEARNING OBJECTIVES

- To name some of the rights sought by women
- To list expanded work opportunities open to women in the late 1800s
- To describe how African American women tried to overcome prejudice

TO EVALUATE A QUOTATION

Distribute copies of this quotation from a 1897 speech by Susan B. Anthony.

The close of the nineteenth century finds every trade, vocation and profession open to women. . . . With but a few exceptions, the highest institutions of learning in the land are freely opened to girls as to boys. . . . There has been a radical revolution in the legal status of women too. . . . Only the department of politics has been slow to admit women. . . . If suffrage had been secured in the beginning, women would .

Have students find evidence in the chapter supporting or refuting each of Anthony's claims. Then challenge them to finish Anthony's speech by explaining how possession of the vote would have affected women's progress.

TO INTERPRET A MAP

Distribute copies of the Activity Sheet for this chapter. If students have difficulty with abbreviations for state names, display a wall map of the United States with full names of the states. When students have finished, go over their responses. Then distribute copies of this poem: "In Wyoming, our sisters fair / Can use the ballot well, / Why can't we do so everywhere, / Can't anybody tell?" Tell students that the word "fair" means "lovely." Ask if they need help defining any other words. Then have students relate the poem to the activity sheet. Ask: *What facts explain why this poem was written?* (Wyoming was the first state to give women equal voting rights. Most other states did not give women the vote.) To celebrate Wyoming's achievement, have students design a commemorative postage stamp for Women's History Month (celebrated each March).

Putting It All Together

SHARING: Display copies of the commemorative stamps. Then call on a volunteer to role play the completed Anthony speech. Ask: *Do you feel that Anthony accurately described the times? Why or why not? How did states such as Wyoming bring pressure on the "department of politics" to open its doors to women?*

ASSESSMENT: Assign students to design rebuses for some of the names mentioned in this chapter. (See Teaching Tip.) Challenge the rest of the class to solve the rebuses.

PAST TO PRESENT: List the jobs opened to women in the late 1800s. Then have students brainstorm or research jobs opened to women in the closing years of this century.

CHAPTER 35: The United States Becomes a World Power.

Opening It Up

MOTIVATING: Tell students that in 1898 a journalist wrote: "I am, heart and soul, an American. American ideals were the food of my youth. To see America converted into a senseless, Old World conqueror, embitters my old age." Refer students to the maps in the chapter. Ask: *What clues do these maps give you about events that saddened the journalist?* Explain that Chapter 35 traces U.S. empire building.

SETTING UP: Copy the selections below and the world outline map on page 248. Teacher's manual resources include Chapter 35 answer key (p. 272), Chapter 35 Test (p. 129), and Chapter 35 Activity Sheet (p. 201).

TEACHING TIP

Chapter 35 discusses four nations that have sent many immigrants to the United States: Cuba, Puerto Rico, the Philippines, and China. If you have students from these nations, ask them to prepare short profiles of their homelands. Ask them to recall how history books treated U.S. involvement in their homelands.

Teaching It Two Ways
LEARNING OBJECTIVES

- To describe how the United States acquired Hawaii and Alaska
- To discuss U.S. policy in China
- To list causes and effects of the Cuban-Spanish-American War

TO COMPARE POINTS OF VIEW

Assign the Activity Sheet. Distribute copies of the following quote by Manuel Luis Quezon, the first president of the Philippines.

As soon as [Dewey arrived], Aguinaldo . . . addressed the Filipino people telling them . . . that their freedom and independence were near at hand; that America, the mother of republics, had through Dewey assured him that if the Filipino people sided with the United States in the war against Spain, they would be granted independence at the [end] of the war.

Ask: *How did Aguinaldo view the U.S.? Based on the cartoon, did the U.S. honor its promise? How is the cartoon a biased, or slanted, view of events?*

TO ORGANIZE INFORMATION ON A MAP

Distribute copies of the outline map of the world. Have students shade in nations or territories acquired by the United States between 1865 and 1900. On or next to each area, have students write the date of acquisition and the method of acquisition (by purchase, by annexation, by treaty ending the war, etc.). Next, distribute copies of the following lyrics: "Take up the sword and rifle, / Send forth your ships with speed, / To join the nations' scramble, / And vie [compete] with them in greed." Ask a volunteer to read the lines aloud. Make sure students know the meaning of all the words. Then ask: According to *the poet, how did the United States acquire lands shown on the map?* (by force) Ask: *Do you agree? Why or why not?*

Putting It All Together

SHARING: Use an opaque projector to show a completed map. Have students reread the poem on U.S. acquisitions. Then show a completed Activity Sheet. Ask: *How might the political cartoonist respond to the poem? How would the people named in question 7 respond?*

ASSESSING: Have students compile a chart comparing U.S. actions in Alaska, Hawaii, Cuba, Puerto Rico, China, and the Philippines. Then review the definition of imperialism. Have students write an *I* next to policies that fit the definition. Discuss the reasons the United States flirted with imperialism in the late 1800s.

PAST TO PRESENT: Conduct the activity suggested in Teaching Tip. Allow time for students to share their profiles with the class.

CHAPTER 36: The American People Face the 20th Century.

Opening It Up

MOTIVATING: Review the meaning of *century* and *millennium* with students. Then write these dates on the chalkboard: 1900-2000. Ask: *What century will soon end?* (the 20th) *What millennium will end?* (the second) Have students imagine that they must prepare a time capsule to bury on December 31, 1999. Have them discuss the items they would include to celebrate U.S. accomplishments in the 20th century. Compare those items to items at the 1893 World's Fair introduced in Chapter 36.

SETTING UP: Copy the excerpt below. Teacher's manual resources include Chapter 36 answer key (p. 273), Chapter 36 Test (p. 130), Chapter 36 Activity Sheet (p. 202), and Unit 6 Test (p. 88).

TEACHING TIP

An essential skill for reading comprehension is the ability to predict what comes next. To practice this skill, read part of any passage to students. Discuss these sentences as well as any background knowledge that students may have. Then have students write material that logically concludes the passage.

Teaching It Two Ways

LEARNING OBJECTIVES

- To describe the products and achievements shown at the 1893 World's Fair
- To discuss what the World's Fair showed about prejudice at the turn of the century
- To list the values that held the diverse American people together

TO ANALYZE A QUOTATION

Explain that August 5, 1893, was Colored People's Day at the World's Fair. Ida Wells called for a boycott. But Frederick Douglass insisted upon giving a speech. Amid jeers, the aged abolitionist faced the crowd. Call on a student to do a dramatic reading of an excerpt from Douglass's speech.

People talk of the Negro problem. There is no Negro problem. The problem is whether the American people have loyalty enough, patriotism enough, to live up to their own Constitution. . . . We Negroes love our country. We fought for it. We only ask . . .

Have students state in their own words the problem raised by Douglass. Review obstacles faced by African Americans. Then have students write an ending for Douglass's speech.

TO WRITE A LETTER

Distribute copies of the Activity Sheet for this chapter. Read the introduction with students, going over any unfamiliar words. Then have a volunteer read aloud the opening sentences of Hamlin Garland's letter to his parents. Ask other students how Garland viewed the fair. Next, brainstorm a list of products or achievements that might have impressed Garland. (In addition to items in the text, you might tell students that the fair had the world's first ferris wheel, the latest phonograph by Thomas Edison, a peep-show device that showed the first moving picture, and the first grapefruits hauled in from Florida and California by refrigerated railroad cars.) Using this list, have students complete Garland's letter urging his parents to come to the fair.

Putting It All Together

SHARING: Ask volunteers to deliver Douglass's speech and others read Garland's letter. Encourage students to comment on the accuracy of the completed speeches and letters. Then analyze reasons for the two different responses to the fair.

ASSESSING: Write the title of this book on the chalkboard: *One Nation, Many People.* Challenge students to design a cover for a 1900 edition of the text. The cover should depict some of the people and values mentioned in Chapter 36.

PAST TO PRESENT: Review the time capsule suggestions in Motivating. Have students present their ideas in the form of a poster.

CHAPTER 1: The United States Faces the 1900s.

Opening It Up

MOTIVATING: Ask students to suggest inventions or ways of making things that have changed people's lives in recent years. Have students explain what changes those inventions caused. Then ask them to suggest ideas for inventions that they would like to see produced in years to come. Tell students as they read the chapter to make lists of inventions that changed the ways in which people in the United States lived about 100 years ago.

SETTING UP: Special materials include sheets of poster board and felt-tipped pens or tempera paints. Teacher's manual resources include: Chapter 1 answer key (p. 273), Chapter 1 Test (p. 131) and Chapter 2 Activity Sheet (p. 203).

TEACHING TIP

Remind students that a *cause* is a condition, person, or event that makes something happen. An *effect* is a result or outcome of a cause. One cause can have many effects. Some of those effects may be positive and some negative. Have students think of causes with both kinds of effects. Tell them to watch for such causes as they read.

Teaching It Two Ways

LEARNING OBJECTIVES

- To name factors that aided U.S. industrial growth in the early 1900s
- To describe problems that U.S. society faced at the turn of the century
- To recognize that progress and problems in a society often arise from the same causes

TO RECOGNIZE INTERELATIONSHIPS

Assign the work sheet for this chapter. After students have completed it, ask volunteers to explain how the two things shown on the graphs were related. (As railroad mileage increased, more iron was produced for tracks and engines).

Then have students skim through the chapter. As they skim, they should make lists of other things mentioned (e.g., automobiles, subways, electric trolleys, pipelines, new buildings) that would have helped to increase the demand for iron. Ask: *What other things mentioned would have increased business production?* (new inventions, assembly lines) Ask students if they think this increased production was good or bad for the United States.

TO RECOGNIZE PROBLEMS

Review the material on Mother Jones and her protests (page 10) with the students. Then have them form into small groups. The groups should skim through the chapter, and each should identify one condition that Americans of the early 1900s faced in their workplaces or their cities that needed correction.

Then let the groups use felt-tipped pens, paints, and poster board to make protest signs informing the public about their chosen problem. The protest signs may use words or pictures or a combination of the two. (ESL/LEP students can make their signs in their primary language, but should then prepare an English translation.)

Putting It All Together

SHARING: Show the graphs students developed. Ask volunteers to read their lists of things that caused increased iron production. Have the groups display their posters. Discuss whether factors leading to increased production contributed to any of the problems shown on the posters.

ASSESSING: Have students make lists or drawings of three improvements and three problems in U.S. life at the turn of the century.

PAST TO PRESENT: Review with students the problems that U.S. cities faced as the nation entered the 20th century. Ask if any of those problems still cause trouble for U.S. cities today. Ask: *What other problems do U.S. cities have to deal with today?* Write the suggestions on the chalkboard and develop a consensus list of the top five problems that cities face today.

CHAPTER 2: New Immigrants Contribute to the Nation.

Opening It Up

MOTIVATING: Divide the class into small groups. Give each group a penny, a nickel, a dime, and a quarter. Ask: *What words do all these coins have in common?* (*United States of America, Liberty, In God We Trust, E Pluribus Unum*) Tell them that *E Pluribus Unum* is Latin for "From many, one." Ask them why that phrase is on the coins. Tell them to keep those words in mind as they read the chapter on immigration at the turn of the century.

SETTING UP: Materials include pennies, nickels, dimes, quarters; colored pencils; an atlas. Copy the world outline map on page 248. Teacher's manual resources include Chapter 2 answer key (p. 273), outline map (p. 248), Chapter 2 Test (p. 132), and Chapter 2 Activity Sheet (p. 204).

TEACHING TIP

Tell students that they should think of themselves as detectives as they read the chapter. They should look for evidence. Evidence consists of facts that prove or disprove a statement or an idea. As they read, tell them to list facts that prove or disprove the motto on U.S. coins.

Teaching It Two Ways

LEARNING OBJECTIVES

- To describe the diverse origins of immigrants to the United States in the late 1800s and early 1900s
- To recognize the importance of immigration in U.S. history
- To identify factors that worked against immigrants to the United States

TO ANALYZE A STATEMENT

Read aloud to students the following statement by historian Oscar Handlin: "Once I thought to write a history of the immigrants in America; I discovered that the immigrants *were* American history." Ask students what they think Handlin means by this statement. Ask what evidence they can find in the chapter (examples of prejudice, riots, exclusion laws, etc.) that not all U.S. citizens of the late 1800s and early 1900s shared Handlin's view.

Then assign the Activity Sheet. After students have completed it, ask: *What continents are not represented by countries?* (Africa, Asia, South America) *What might account for this?* (prejudice, exclusion laws)

TO SHOW MOVEMENT ON A MAP

Divide the students into small groups. Give each group a copy of the outline map from p. 248 and several colored pencils. Be sure all groups have access to an atlas.

Tell the students first to look at the map on text page 16. Ask them to find on the outline map the countries mentioned in the text map. Tell them to color all those countries the same color.

Then tell students to skim through the chapter looking for other countries mentioned as sources of immigration. Ask students to color those countries another color.

Challenge each group to write one sentence describing immigration to the United States in the late 1800s and early 1900s.

Putting It All Together

SHARING: Display Activity Sheet graphs and the maps. Ask students to think again about the words on the U.S. coins: "From many, one." Ask: *How does the evidence of the maps and graphs support those words? Does anything you read in the chapter not support those words?* (exclusion laws, etc.)

ASSESSING: On the chalkboard write "IMMIGRANTS" and under it list two heads—"Reasons for Coming" and "Problems Faced Here." Direct students to copy this outline onto sheets of paper. Tell them to make as many entries as they can, either in words or in pictures, under each head.

PAST TO PRESENT: Ask students to suggest the major sources of immigration to the United States today. Write down a list of their top ten suggestions and put it aside until they read Unit 5. Then check to see how accurate they were.

CHAPTER 3: African Americans Move North.

Opening It Up

MOTIVATING: Open either by instructing students to turn to the map on text page 26 or by using an opaque projector to show the map. Make sure that students understand that the map shows changes in the African America population in key cities between 1910 and 1920. Ask them to compare population changes in New Orleans and Charleston with changes in New York and Chicago. Tell them that in this chapter they will learn why such a difference existed.

SETTING UP: Prepare a transparency for the quotation below. Teacher's manual resources include Chapter 3 answer key (p. 273), Chapter 3 Test (p. 133), and Chapter 3 Activity Sheet (p. 205).

TEACHING TIP

People migrate from one place to another for a variety of reasons. Factors such as drought or war may force them from their homes. These are called "push" factors. Other things such as jobs or climate can attract people to a certain place. These are "pull" factors. Tell students to look for "push-pull" factors as they read.

Teaching It Two Ways

LEARNING OBJECTIVES

- To identify "push-pull" factors behind the Great Migration
- To recognize efforts by African Americans to improve conditions for themselves
- To list leading African Americans of the late 1800s and early 1900s and their accomplishments

TO RECOGNIZE MOTIVATION

Display and discuss this 1917 quotation written by an African American from Alabama : "I am in the darkness of the South and I am trying my best to get out."

Tell the students to skim the chapter and write down all the reasons that an African American of that time would want to get out of the South.

Ask volunteers to read and compare their lists and make a master list of reasons for leaving the South on the chalkboard.

Point out to students that, bad as conditions were, the greatest number of African Americans chose to remain in the South. Challenge students to identify measures that African Americans took to improve conditions there.

TO INTERPRET A LETTER

Read aloud to students the following selection from a letter that an African American from Mississippi wrote to a friend back home after arriving in Philadelphia:

Well, . . . I am making [a] very good [life]. I make $75 dollars per month. I can ride in the electric street . . . car anywhere I get a seat . . . and if you are first in a place here shopping, you don't have to wait until the white folks get thro trading.

Ask students if they think the writer liked living in the North. Ask: *What reasons does the letter give for that?* Have them skim through the chapter. Ask them to suggest other things about Northern cities African Americans might have liked. Make a list of their suggestions. Then have groups complete the Activity Sheet.

Putting It All Together

SHARING: Display copies of activity sheet postcards and sheets with the quotation and lists on the bulletin board. Then ask students to identify "push-pull" factors behind the Great Migration.

ASSESSING: Tell students to make flash cards with the names of African Americans mentioned in the chapter on one side and their accomplishments on the other. Have students to hold up either side of a card and challenge classmates to identify either the person or the accomplishment.

PAST TO PRESENT: Have students review the part of Section 3 on African American artists of earlier years. Then ask them to name important African American artists, writers, musicians, and performers who are popular today.

CHAPTER 4: Latinos Build New Communities.

Opening It Up

MOTIVATING: Read aloud these lines from a speech made by a U.S. senator in 1898: "The ocean does not separate us from lands of our duty and desire—the oceans join us. . . . Cuba not contiguous [next to us]! Puerto Rico not contiguous! Our navy will make them contiguous." Ask students what the senator means by this speech. Tell them that in this chapter they will learn how the United States expanded its influence over lands where many Latinos lived.

SETTING UP: Materials include copies of prepared outline map of North and South America (p. 247). Teacher's manual resources include Chapter 4 answer key (p. 273), Chapter 4 Test (p. 134), and Chapter 4 Activity Sheet (p. 206).

TEACHING TIP

A good ESL/LEP strategy is to use students as resources for information on their native countries. Encourage Latino students to talk to relatives about how events in this chapter are taught in schools in their home countries. Have students share their findings with the class.

Teaching It Two Ways

LEARNING OBJECTIVES

- To chart changing relationships between the United States government and Cuba, Puerto Rico, and the Territory of New Mexico
- To recognize geographic areas in which historical events took place
- To illustrate key development in the histories of Cuba, Puerto Rico, and New Mexico

TO MAKE A CHART

Instruct students to copy this chart and fill it in as they complete the chapter.

	Relationship to U.S.	Major Legislation Passed
Cuba		
Puerto Rico		
New Mexico		

Ask students how the legislation on the charts showed expanded U.S. influence over Latinos in Cuba and Puerto Rico. Ask them to suggest how the U.S. might have expanded its influence over *nuevomexicanos* who already lived in U.S. territory during this period.

TO RECOGNIZE LOCATIONS ON A MAP

Prepare an outline map of North and South America by writing the following terms in random order in the ocean areas of the map: Platt Amendment, the *Maine* (Cuba); Foraker Act, Jones Act, *el Grito de Lares* (Puerto Rico); Ybor City (Florida, U.S.); *las Gorras Blancas* (New Mexico, U.S.). Make copies of the map and distribute them to students. Tell them, as they read the chapter, to draw lines connecting the terms to the places on the map to which the terms apply.

Then, assign the activity sheets. Tell students that they may write the captions for their illustrations in their native language.

Putting It All Together

SHARING: Display illustrations, maps, and charts. Point out that these deal with events in widely separate places. Have small groups study the displays. Challenge each group to come up with one sentence that links the events.

ASSESSING: Direct students to complete the following sentences: Under the terms of the 1902_____, the U.S. Army left _____. Further east, Latinos in _______ became U.S. citizens through the 1917 ______. Latinos in the territory of _______ had long been U.S. citizens when their homeland became a _____ in 1912.

PAST TO PRESENT: Ask students to suggest ways in which Latino cultures have become more visible in this country today. They might name foods, music, performers, etc.

CHAPTER 5: Workers Fight for Improved Conditions.

Opening It Up

MOTIVATING: Read aloud this description of pay for sales clerks around 1900: "Wages averaging from $2 to $4.50 a week were reduced by excessive fines. . . . A . . . girl who received $2 a week . . . for some trivial [tiny] mistake was fined 60 cents out of her $2. . . . One of the causes for fines . . . was sitting down." Explain that workers had no insurance or paid vacations. Ask: *What do you think of such conditions? What could workers do to improve conditions?*

SETTING UP: Copy the song below. Bring poster board, felt pens or paint. Teacher's manual resources include Chapter 5 answer key (p. 273), Chapter 5 Test (p. 135) and Chapter 5 Activity Sheet (p. 207).

TEACHING TIP

Making a chart is a form of sorting or categorizing information. Making a chart is a good way for ESL/LEP students to draw together and understand material spread out through a chapter. Distribute Activity Sheets to students before they begin this chapter and have them fill out the charts as they read.

Teaching It Two Ways

LEARNING OBJECTIVES

- To identify conditions that led U.S. workers to form labor unions
- To recognize the importance of songs as tools in the movement to organize labor
- To identify major labor organizations of the late 1800s and early 1900s

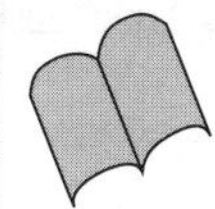

TO ANALYZE AND WRITE SONGS

Distribute copies of this song:

If the workers took a notion
They could stop all speeding trains;
Every ship upon the ocean
They can tie with mighty chains.
Every wheel in the creation
Every mine and every mill;
Fleets and armies of the nation,
Will at their command stand still.

Ask what weapon workers could use to achieve the results described in the song. (strike) Assign groups of students to write songs for a union or an event described in the chapter. They should not name the union or event.

TO DESIGN POSTERS AND HANDBILLS

Divide students into small groups. Have the groups complete the Chapter 5 Activity Sheet.

Then, the groups should select one of the unions or events described in the chapter. The groups should then create signs that could be carried on picket lines or handbills that could be passed out or hung up. Tell students that the signs or handbills should be designed to attract new members to a union, to support a strike, or to win sympathy from the general public. Groups may use pictures and words on their signs and handbills.

Putting It All Together

SHARING: Have volunteers read or sing their songs to the class. Challenge other class members to identify the union or event the song is about. Arrange a bulletin-board display of signs and handbills grouped together with any songs that might apply to them.

ASSESSING: Assign this cause-and-effect chart:

CAUSE	→	EFFECT
____________	→	Decline of Knights of Labor
Triangle Shirtwaist Fire	→	____________
____________	→	Laws to improve Illinois sweatshops

PAST TO PRESENT: Ask students to list what they think are the major problems facing U.S. workers today.

CHAPTER 6: Reformers Work to Improve American Life.

Opening It Up

Motivating: Write *Who? What? When? Where? Why? How?* on the chalkboard. Remind students that these are the questions that newspaper reporters try to answer in their stories. Tell them to skim through the chapter and see how many of those questions they can answer from chapter and section headings and illustration captions. Close by telling the class that newspapers and reporters played important roles in shaping events covered in this chapter.

Setting Up: Special materials include political cartoons from recent newspapers, magazines, and newsprint. Teacher's manual resources include Chapter 6 answer key (p. 274), Chapter 6 Test (p. 136), Chapter 6 Activity Sheet (p. 208), and Unit 1 Test (p. 89).

Teaching Tip

Use visual aids to help ESL/LEP students understand the many new vocabulary terms in the chapter. Direct them to make flash cards with bold-faced vocabulary words on one side and the definitions on the other. Tell students to quiz each other by using the cards.

Teaching It Two Ways

Learning Objectives

- To identify key reforms in U.S. society around the turn of the century
- To explain major reforms by writing newspaper articles
- To draw political cartoons expressing attitudes about the reform era

To Write Newspaper Stories

To help students understand the role of the muckrakers, assign the Chapter 6 Activity Sheet. When students have completed the sheets, ask: *How did the muckrakers help bring about reforms?*

Then, divide students into three groups. Tell the students to imagine that they are newspaper reporters and editors. Assign each group one of the sections in the chapter. Tell students to review their section carefully. Then each one should write a story or an editorial about a person, event, or idea discussed in the section. Tell the reporters to use the questions mentioned in the Motivating exercise. Have them write headlines for their articles and editorials.

To Draw Political Cartoons

Show and discuss copies of political cartoons from recent newspapers and magazines. You might also have students look at the historical cartoons in the text. Explain that cartoonists often exaggerate features to get ideas across. They also use symbols. Ask student to suggest symbols that cartoonists might use. Point out that cartoons have labels and captions.

Then divide students into three groups, assigning each group one chapter section. Tell students to draw political cartoons about some person, event, or idea in their section. If students cannot think of a cartoon idea, tell them to draw pictures that illustrate something in the section.

Putting It All Together

Sharing: Have the students who wrote articles for a chapter section and the students who made illustrations for that section lay out pages of a newspaper on newsprint. When layouts for the three sections are complete, have the class select a name for their paper and design a masthead (title) for it. Display the finished "Special Edition" on the bulletin board.

Assessing: Write the following words on the chalkboard: Politics, Business, Conservation, Women's Rights. Tell students to write down one reform in each area and explain why it was important.

Past to Present: Point out to students that Chapter 6 discussed early 20th-century reforms in politics, business, conservation, and women's rights. Ask students if they think additional reforms are needed in these areas today. If they do, list their ideas on the chalkboard and discuss them.

CHAPTER 7: The United States Is a Power in the Pacific.

Opening It Up

MOTIVATING: Use an opaque projector to display the map of the United States in the Pacific on text page 59. Identify U.S. possessions on the map. Ask: *Why might the United States have been interested in getting control of these lands.* (trade, defense) *What nations might have been concerned about U.S. acquisition of these lands?* (China, Japan, Russia) Tell them that in this chapter they will learn what happened as U.S. involvement in the Pacific grew.

SETTING UP: Special materials include an opaque projector. Teacher's manual resources include Chapter 7 answer key (p. 274), Chapter 7 Test (p. 137) and Chapter 7 Activity Sheet (p. 209).

TEACHING TIP

Point out to students that although this chapter covers events that occur in different places, some of those events took place at the same time. Making a chronology, or time table, is a good way to keep track of such events. Tell students to make notes of the dates of events as they read.

Teaching It Two Ways

LEARNING OBJECTIVES

- To gain an understanding of U.S. policy in the Pacific through reading maps
- To cite advantages and disadvantages arising from foreign policy decisions
- To recognize major events as the United States became more involved in the Pacific

TO MAKE A CHART

Tell students that in 1898, as the United States and Spain prepared to sign the treaty ending the war between them, the U.S. secretary of state called an aide over to a globe and said, "Let's see what we get by this."

Encourage students to think about what the United States got from its growing involvement in the Pacific. Remind them that foreign-policy decisions usually bring with them problems as well as benefits. Tell students to make charts tracking U.S. involvement in the Pacific. Charts should list major Asian areas of U.S. involvement discussed in the chapter. For each of these areas, students should list "Benefits" and "Problems" associated with involvement in the area.

TO READ A MAP

Divide the students into small groups. Have each group turn to the map of the United States in the Pacific Region on text page 59. Be sure that students understand how to use the scale on the map. Then tell them to compute approximate distances for the following: the 48 contiguous states to Alaska; California to Hawaii; Alaska to Japan; Philippines to China.

When the groups have completed the distance assignments, have them work from the map to make lists of U.S. possessions in the Pacific region. The lists should be arranged in the order in which the United States acquire d each possession.

Assign the Activity Sheet for Chapter 7.

Putting It All Together

SHARING: Display completed "Problem/Benefit" charts and map and Activity Sheet chronologies. Divide the students into groups. Have each group work up a brief description of U.S. policy in the Pacific during this era.

ASSESSING: Write *China, Japan,* and *Philippines* on the chalkboard. Under them, write *Emilio Aguinaldo, Gentlemen's Agreement, Open Door, Treaty of Portsmo uth, Boxer Rebellion, Battle of Manila Bay.* Tell students to copy the list of names and terms. After each item, they should write on the chalkboard the name of the nation that is most closely associated with that item. For extra credit, students can write a sentence giving the reason that each term is important.

PAST TO PRESENT: Ask students to describe ways the United States has been involved with Pacific Rim nations recently.

CHAPTER 8: The United States Controls Cuba and Puerto Rico.

Opening It Up

MOTIVATING: Read aloud this passage written by a Puerto Rican woman as she watched the first U.S. troops land on her homeland: "I thought . . . how sad and shameful it is to see [Puerto Rico] go from owner to owner without ever being her own master and to see her pass from sovereignty [power] to sovereignty without ruling herself." Ask volunteers to explain what they think the passage means. Tell them as they read the chapter to look for ways the United States limited the ability of Puerto Ricans and Cubans to rule themselves.

SETTING UP: Teacher's manual resources include Chapter 8 answer key (p. 274), Chapter 8 Test (p. 138) and Chapter 8 Activity Sheet (p. 210).

TEACHING TIP

In this chapter, students will be looking for evidence about issues. Evidence consists of the proof or facts that support the truth or falsity of something. *Evidence* comes from a Latin word for "visible," "clear." Tell students to ask themselves "What facts do I see here?" as they read this chapter.

Teaching It Two Ways

LEARNING OBJECTIVES

- To cite reasons for the expanded U.S. presence in the Caribbean
- To identify actions taken by the U.S. government in Cuba and Puerto Rico
- To recognize the effect that U.S. actions had on peoples of the Caribbean islands

TO GATHER EVIDENCE

Read aloud the follow ing statement made by a U.S. Senator during U.S. overseas expansion in the late 1800s:

Now, I claim that under the Declaration of Independence you cannot govern a foreign territory, a foreign people, another people than your own; that you cannot subjugate them and govern them against their will, because you think it is for their good, when they do not.

Divide the class into two groups. One group should review the chapter and list ways the United States thought it was acting for the good of Cuba, as well as any evidence that Cubans did not agree. The other group should do the same for Puerto Rico.

TO MAKE A CHART

Write this sentence on the chalkboard: "Members of the U.S. Congress had a major influence on the lives of the people of Puerto Rico and Cuba." Ask the students if they agree or disagree with this statement. What evidence can they find to support the statement?

Tell them that one way of assembling evidence for easy review is to turn it into a chart. Suggest that they make charts titled "The U.S. Congress Takes Action in the Caribbean." The chart should have these headings: "Acts Passed by Congress," "Date Passed," "Island Affected," "Details of the Acts."

Finally, have them complete the Activity Sheet for Chapter 8.

Putting It All Together

SHARING: Arrange to have the lists, charts, and Activity Sheets that the students have comple ted available for students to review. Then lead off a summary discussion with this question: Based on the evidence, who benefited most from U.S. involvement in the Caribbean? Look for them to support their respon ses with facts.

ASSESSING: Tell students to compose editorials that might have appeared in newspapers in the early 1900s. The editorials should support or oppose one of the following: Platt Amendment, Foraker Act, Jones Act.

PAST TO PRESENT: Ask: *In what way is the United States involved with Puerto Rico and Cuba today?* Tell students to bring in newspaper or magazine articles that show U.S. involvement. Have them look at the Table of Contents to see when they will be learning more about the islands.

CHAPTER 9: The United States Is Involved in Latin America.

Opening It Up

MOTIVATING: Read aloud this statement by José Martí, a Cuban hero who was killed in the struggle for independence from Spain. "It is my duty . . . to prevent, through the independence of Cuba, the U.S.A. from spreading over the West Indies and falling with added weight upon other lands of Our America." Ask students what they think Martí meant by this. Tell them to keep the statement in mind as they read the chapter.

SETTING UP: Copy the outline map of North and South America on p. 244. Teacher manual resources include Chapter 9 answer key (p. 274), Chapter 9 Test (p. 139), and Chapter 9 Activity Sheet (p. 211).

TEACHING TIP

To many, Theodore Roosevelt is both a great President and a hero. José Martí is one of the great heroes of Cuban history. If you have any students from other countries, ask them to tell the other students about some of their national heroes. Discuss what makes a hero.

Teaching It Two Ways

LEARNING OBJECTIVES

- To identify actions taken by the U.S. government in Mexico, Central America, and the Caribbean
- To explain the different policies of U.S. Presidents toward nations in these areas
- To identify on a map areas of U.S. involvement in Latin America

TO CATEGORIZE INFORMATION

Have students review actions taken by various U.S. Presidents in Latin America. Making a chart like the one below may help.

President	Nation Involved with	Action Taken

Then challenge students to create a brief phrase that describes the Latin America policy of each of the Presidents discussed.

Finally, assign students the Activity Sheet for Chapter 9.

TO INTERPRET A MAP

Divide the students into small groups. Give each group a copy of the outline map of North and South America.

Tell students the map can help explain why the United States wanted to build a canal at Panama. Be sure they understand how to use the scale on the map. Then ask: *How far would a ship have to sail to get from the southern tip of Florida to the U.S.-Mexican border on the Pacific coast if it went around the tip of South America?* (about 14,700 miles) *How far would it have to sail if it could go through Panama?* (about 4,800 miles)

Tell students to highlight and label those countries whose involvement with the United States they read about in Chapters 8 and 9.

Putting It All Together

SHARING: Have students display maps and charts that they have created while working on the chapter. Then reread the statement by José Martí from the Motivating exercise. Ask students to discuss whether Martí would be pleased with what happened in Latin America after Cuba won its independence. Students should point to maps and charts as evidence in their arguments.

ASSESSING: Tell students to draw a political cartoon about one of the events discussed in this chapter.

PAST TO PRESENT: Music is an important part of the culture of Latin America. Have volunteers go to a library and borrow samples of recordings from some of the countries mentioned in this chapter. Ask if any students in the class or any of their family members have examples of music from these countries that they might be willing to share. Play the music in class.

CHAPTER 10: The United States Fights World War I.

Opening It Up

MOTIVATING: Read aloud these words of President Woodrow Wilson: "There are, it may be, many months of fiery trial and sacrifice ahead of us. . . . We shall fight for the things which we have always carried nearest our hearts—for democracy, for the right of those who submit to lawful authority [obey the law] to have a voice in their own governments, for the rights and liberties of small nations, . . . [to] make the world itself at last free." Say that with these words the United States entered a huge war. Tell students to keep Wilson's speech in mind as they read the chapter.

SETTING UP: Copy the song below. Have paper, and colored pencils or crayons. Teacher manual resources include Chapter 10 answer key 9 (p. 274), Chapter 10 Test (p. 140), Chapter 10 Activity Sheet (p. 212), and Unit 2 Test (p. 90).

TEACHING TIP

Graphic organizers like the one in the Activity Sheet that help students organize data are part of prewriting. Students can move to the writing stage by drafting simple paragraphs. Tell students that paragraphs should have a topic sentence with a main idea and other sentences with supporting details.

Teaching It Two Ways

LEARNING OBJECTIVES

- To list combatants in World War I, reasons that the war broke out, and where it was fought
- To identify dates of major events connected with World War I
- To recognize reasons for U.S. entry into World War I

TO ANALYZE A SONG

Distribute copies of the verses below.

Let nations arbitrate their future troubles,
It's time to lay the sword and gun away,
There'd be no war today,
If mothers all would say,
"I didn't raise my boy to be a soldier.

Tell students that the lines are from a song popular in 1915-16. Ask: *Would the person singing the song favor U.S. neutrality? Which of President Wilson's 14 Points might have given the singer hope for the future?* (League of Nations). Challenge students to reply to the singer by writing (in verse if they wish) "Reasons Why Your Child Should Be a Soldier."

TO MAKE AN ILLUSTRATED TIMELINE

Write "1914," "1915," "1916," "1917," "1918" on separate sheets of paper. Post the sheets at equal intervals on the bulletin board. Divide students into groups, at least one for each section of the chapter. Give students sheets of drawing paper and colored pencils or crayons.

Tell students to illustrate some event described in their section. They should draw a picture on one side of the paper and a caption with the date of the event on the other. When students are finished, tell them to keep their pictures without showing them to other students. Then, assign the Chapter 10 Activity Sheet.

Putting It All Together

SHARING: When students have completed all activities, let volunteers who responded to the song give their reasons that U.S. citizens should have fought in the war. Students who drew pictures should hold them up for other students to identify. As the pictures are identified, they should be posted in the appropriate place on the bulletin board to create an illustrated time line. Ask students if they think that any reasons given for entering the war were still valid at its end.

ASSESSING: Have students write newspaper headlines for the events shown on the bulletin board time line.

PAST TO PRESENT: Bring copies of a recent atlas or almanac to the class. Have students compare the border of European nations before and after World War I (as shown on text p. 87) with current borders. Ask: *Are current borders like those of pre– or post–World War I Europe?*

CHAPTER 11: The 1920s Are a Time of Change.

Opening It Up

MOTIVATING: Write the following labels on the chalkboard: "Roaring 20s," "Golden 20s," "Jazz Age," "Aspirin Age," "Age of Wonderful Nonsense." Ask students what images the different labels call up in their minds. Tell students that people have used all those labels to describe the years they will read about in Chapter 11: the 1920s.

SETTING UP: Materials include sets of prepared index cards for ESL/LEP activity. Teacher's manual resources include Chapter 11 answer key (p. 274), Chapter 11 Test (p. 141), and Chapter 11 Activity Sheet (p. 213).

TEACHING TIP

The ESL/LEP exercise for this chapter is a variant on the graphic organizer called the idea cluster. By working together to group cards of names and terms, students get a chance to practice reading and speaking those names and terms as well as testing different associations among them.

Teaching It Two Ways

LEARNING OBJECTIVES

- To describe how conditions changed for groups of Americans during the 1920s
- To recognize interrelationships among ideas, people, and events of the 1920s
- To cite the effect of new laws on immigration to the United States

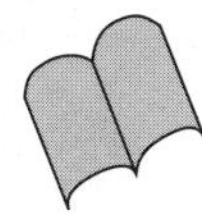

TO CREATE A CHART

Copy the chart below onto the chalkboard;

Group	Factors	Outcomes
Immigrants		
Women		
Workers		
African Americans		

Ask students to think about how conditions for various groups in the United States changed during the 1920s. As they read the chapter, they should look for factors that affected groups shown on the chart and should write in those factors. In the last column they should explain the effect of the factors. Students can add other groups if they wish.

Assign the Activity Sheet for Chapter 11.

TO CLUSTER IDEAS

Prepare several sets of index cards by writing one name or term from the chapter on each card. Some possible card entries are: *18th Amendment, speakeasies; 19th Amendment, League of Women Voters; Federal Highway Act, suburbs; Red Scare, Sacco and Vanzetti, quotas; Babe Ruth, Mary Pickford, Charles Lindbergh.*

Divide the students into small groups. Give each group a shuffled set of cards. Tell the students to arrange into clusters the cards that they think are related to each other. When they have completed the clusters, challenge them either to make a statement explaining why they have arranged each cluster or to write a card for each cluster that explains the group.

Putting It All Together

SHARING: Have students who made charts display and explain them to the class as a whole. Give students who have clustered index cards the opportunity to rearrange the cards based on the evidence of the charts. Then remind students of the labels for the decade you wrote on the chalkboard in the Motivating exercise. Challenge them to work in groups to create new labels for the 1920s.

ASSESSING: Write the following headings on the chalkboard: "Immigration," "Business," "Daily Life." Tell students to think of the person or event that had the greatest effect in each area during the 1920s. Students should write or deliver orally explanations for their choices.

PAST TO PRESENT: Ask students to think of the most prominent characteristics of the decade in which they are living. Tell them to suggest a label like the "Jazz Age" or the "Golden Twenties" that would apply to the current decade.

CHAPTER 12: African American Culture Thrives in the Jazz Age.

Opening It Up

MOTIVATING: Read aloud to students the following statement by Langston Hughes, one of the leading African American writers of the 20th century: "We younger Negro artists now intend to express our individual dark-skinned selves without fear or shame. If white people are pleased, we are glad. If they are not, it doesn't matter." Tell students that Hughes wrote these lines in the 1920s in Harlem. Tell them as they read the chapter to look for ways in which other African Americans besides artists shared these feelings.

SETTING UP: Teacher's manual resources include Chapter 12 answer key (page 274), Chapter 12 Test (p. 142), and Chapter 12 Activity Sheet (p. 214).

TEACHING TIP

Remind students of what propaganda is, material that tries to persuade people to think and act in a certain way. Advertisements are types of propaganda. Tell students to read all parts of ads carefully. For more clues about an ad's purpose, they should try to note when and where an ad appeared.

Teaching It Two Ways

LEARNING OBJECTIVES

- To understand problems that African Americans of the 1920s faced and how they fought against them
- To form generalizations about the African American experience in the 1920s
- To identify key figures of the Harlem Renaissance

TO MAKE GENERALIZATIONS

Read aloud these words about the Harlem Renaissance by African American writer James Weldon Johnson: "The picturesque Harlem was real, but it was the writers who . . . actually created the Harlem that caught the world's imagination." Explain that this is a generalization, a broad conclusion based on related facts. Challenge students to find facts to support this generalization.

Then, tell students to write their own generalizations about discrimination against African Americans in the 1920s, black nationalism, and the Harlem Renaissance. Students should be ready to defend each of their statements with at least two facts.

TO IDENTIFY HISTORIC FIGURES

Tell students to make identity flash cards as they read the chapter. The name of an individual in the chapter should be on one side of the card. On the other should be an identifying sentence in that person's voice: for example, "I organized . . ." or "I painted . . ." Challenge students to use visual identifiers: for example, a black star above a line for Garvey or a drawing of a cornet or trumpet for Armstrong. When students are finished, let them try to name the figures on each other's cards from the identifiers.

Before assigning the Activity Sheet, tell students to skim through Chapter 11 and review material relevant to this chapter.

Putting It All Together

SHARING: Have volunteers read their generalizations aloud. Tell students who have made flash cards to identify any of the figures on those cards whose actions supported the generalizations.

ASSESSING: Tell students to complete this postcard that an African American in New York City in the 1920s might have written to a friend: : Dear ______, Harlem is an exciting place to live right now because ________________."

Students who wish to may instead create a drawing for the other side of the postcard showing some aspect of the Harlem Renaissance.

PAST TO PRESENT: Marcus Garvey, the UNIA, and the *Negro World* are examples of important African American public figures, organizations, and publications from the 1920s. Ask students who and what are the leading public figures, organizations, and publications for African Americans today.

CHAPTER 13: A Great Depression Takes Hold.

Opening It Up

MOTIVATING: Remind students that in earlier chapters they learned how the United States had grown into the richest nation on earth. Then read this statement by humorist Will Rogers: "We've got . . . more of everything in the world than any nation that ever lived had, yet we are starving to death. We are the first nation in the history of the world to go to the poorhouse in an automobile." Say that in Chapter 13, they will find out what Rogers meant.

SETTING UP: Make copies of song lyrics. Have on hand graph paper and data for the exercises below. Teacher's manual resources include Chapter 13 answer key (p.275), Chapter 13 Test (p. 143), and Chapter 13 Activity Sheet (p. 215).

TEACHING TIP

Remind students of these basic economic terms and concepts: Most large U.S. companies are corporations in which people buy shares of ownership called stock. Businesses use the money from sales of stock to operate and grow. If many people sell stock rather than buy it, business activity slows.

Teaching It Two Ways

LEARNING OBJECTIVES

- To recognize contradictions between the industrial wealth of the United States and the hardships many of its citizens faced in the Great Depression
- To understand the meaning of the stock market crash
- To explain the effect of the Great Depression on different groups in U.S. society

TO INTERPRET AND WRITE SONGS

Tell students to read the song lyrics on page 13. Remind them that popular songs often capture the thinking and feeling of many people at a particular time. Distribute copies of these lines from a song by Woody Guthrie:

Lots of folks back east, they say,
Is leavin' home every day,
Beatin' a hot old dusty way to th' California line.
'Crost th' desert sands they roll
Gettin' outta that old dust bowl. . . .

Ask: *Who is the song about?* (Midwest farmers) *What problem did they face?* (loss of farms because of drought) Tell students to write songs about the problems of this or other groups in the chapter.

TO CREATE A GRAPH

Help students visualize what the term "stock market crash" means by drawing graphs. Divide students into small groups Distribute sheets of graph paper and copies of the following data:

Shares of Stock Sold (in millions)

1922—259	1923— 236	1924—282
1925—454	1926— 480	1927—577
1928—920	1929—1,125	1930—810
1931—577	1932— 425	

Review with them how to plot years on the horizontal axis and shares of stock sold on the vertical axis. Use intervals of 100 (million) from 0 to 1,200. Have students describe what the graphs show. Then assign the Activity Sheet for Chapter 13.

Putting It All Together

SHARING: Have volunteers read their song lyrics without identifying the subject. Let students who have done the Activity Sheets identify the group by projecting the appropriate sketches.

ASSESSING: Tell students to complete the following statement: "The three worst things about the Great Depression were ________." Remind students to give reasons for their choices.

PAST TO PRESENT: Remind students that the stock market remains a key part of U.S. economic life. Encourage students to bring financial pages of newspapers to class. Most sections run graphs that summarize stock activity over a period of several months; thus, students can get an idea of normal market changes compared to the 1929 plunge.

CHAPTER 14: The New Deal Brings New Hope.

Opening It Up

MOTIVATING: Write the words *relief*, *recovery*, and *reform* on the chalkboard. Ask the students for definitions of the words. (*Relief* means immediate help for a problem, *recovery* means getting back to normal, and *reform* means changing the way things are normally done.) Tell them to keep their definitions in mind as they read about FDR's efforts to solve the problems of the Depression.

SETTING UP: Special materials include index cards. Teacher's manual resources include Chapter 14 answer key (p. 275), Chapter 14 Test (p. 144), and Chapter 14 Activity Sheet (p. 216).

TEACHING TIP

Encourage the small groups of students who have received shuffled sets of cards in the ESL/LEP exercise to read the sentences on the cards aloud to each other. This will provide an opportunity to increase oral fluency and to practice organizing information received aurally.

Teaching It Two Ways

LEARNING OBJECTIVES

- To identify New Deal relief, recovery, and reform legislation.
- To understand how New Deal measures affected different groups in U.S. society
- To recognize how presidential elections reflected public attitudes toward the New Deal

TO ORGANIZE INFORMATION

Remind students of the three R's they defined in the Motivating exercise. Now tell them to make charts of the New Deal legislation.

Charts should list the name of each piece of legislation, what the legislation did, and whether the legislation fell into the category of relief, recovery, or reform. Measures from early in the New Deal are labeled in the text, but later measures are not labeled. Students will have to categorize these measures on their own. Tell them to be prepared to defend their labeling.

Assign Activity Sheet for Chapter 14. Ask volunteers to find similar maps and graphs for the elections of 1936 and 1940 in the school library and show them in class.

TO ORGANIZE IDEAS

Divide the students into four groups. Instruct each group to review material about one of the following: women, African Americans, Latinos, or Native Americans.

Tell each group to write a three-to-five sentence paragraph on how New Deal policies affected its group. When the groups have finished, distribute index cards. Tell the groups to write each sentence of their paragraphs on a separate card.

Students should then shuffle the cards and exchange them for those of another group. Groups should then try to arrange cards in the order that makes the most sense. When they tell how they ordered the cards, they should explain why they chose that order.

Putting It All Together

SHARING: Have volunteers display the charts of New Deal legislation. Encourage students who wrote paragraphs about groups to decide in which category legislation affecting their groups fell. Finally, ask students to determine what the American public thought of the New Deal based on the election maps and graphs of 1932, 1936, and 1940.

ASSESSING: Tell students to comment on some piece of New Deal legislation or on the New Deal as a whole by drawing political cartoons. Suggest that they review other cartoons in the textbook before drawing their own.

PAST TO PRESENT: Have students bring in copies of recent newspapers and newsmagazines. Tell them to skim through the periodicals for discussions of recent U.S. legislation. Ask if they can characterize as relief, recovery, or reform measures any of the bills discussed.

CHAPTER 15: The Nation Fights Another World War.

Opening It Up

MOTIVATING: From an almanac or encyclopedia, obtain a complete listing of nations involved in World War II. Without explaining the significance of the names, read them aloud to the class. Meanwhile, have volunteers locate those nations on a wall map or globe. Tell students that in Chapter 15 they will learn how those nations were swept into the world's largest conflict.

SETTING UP: Special materials include copies of the outline map of the world (p. 248). Teacher's manual resources include Chapter 15 answer key (p. 275), Chapter 15 Test (p. 145), and Chapter 15 Activity Sheet (p. 217).

TEACHING TIP

Remind students that World War II was a global conflict. You might reinforce this by requesting that ESL/LEP students ask parents or relatives to describe how World War II affected their homelands. ESL/LEP students can then present to the class oral reports of what they learned.

Teaching It Two Ways

LEARNING OBJECTIVES

- To recognize the global scope of World War II
- To cite and explain major events of the war
- To understand the chronology of events in the war

TO WRITE NEWS STORIES

Write these headlines on the chalkboard: GERMAN ARMY ATTACKS POLAND; CITIES BOMBED, PORT BLOCKADED and U.S. AT WAR! and V-J DAY!

Tell students that these are headlines from U.S. newspapers during World War II. Divide the class into three groups, one to cover events in Europe, one events in the United States, and one events in Asia. Challenge students in each group to write headlines and opening paragraphs about events in their area leading up to or during the war. Remind them of the *Who? What? When? Where? Why? How?* questions that reporters seek to answer.

TO PLOT EVENTS ON A MAP

Before students begin reading the chapter, distribute copies of the outline map of the world from the teacher's manual. Tell them whenever they read about an event in the chapter to write that event on the map in the country where it took place. If there is not room in the country, students can list events under the country's name on the edges of the map and draw an arrow from the country's name to its position on the map. Tell students to write all events that took place in one year in the same color and to use a different color for each year.

Distribute the Activity Sheet for Chapter 15 when students are almost at the end of the chapter.

Putting It All Together

SHARING: Post some of the student's maps on the bulletin board. Have students arrange news stories from the various groups around the maps with strings connecting the story to its map location. Then ask students to discuss whether the United States could or should have stayed out of World War II.

ASSESSING: Tell students to make lists of what they consider to be the three most significant events discussed in this chapter. They should write brief statements explaining why they made their selections.

PAST TO PRESENT: Challenge students to discover the effect that World War II had on people's lives. Tell students to interview adults about their memories of the war years or to ask adults who were too young to remember the war how they think the conflict influenced their or their parents' lives.

CHAPTER 16: Americans Support World War II on the Home Front.

Opening It Up

MOTIVATING: Tell students that after World War II, President Truman awarded a medal to a unit of U.S. troops for their gallant service and said to the soldiers: "You fought not only the enemy, you fought prejudice, and you have won." Soldiers in that unit were Japanese Americans. They and their relatives spent much of the war imprisoned in U.S. internment camps. In Chapter 16, students will learn what struggles Japanese Americans and other groups fought on the home front.

SETTING UP: Special materials include poster board and colored pencils or tempera paints. Teacher's manual resources include Chapter 16 answer key (p.275), Chapter 16 Test (p. 146), Chapter 16 Activity Sheet (p. 218), and Unit 3 Test (p. 91).

TEACHING TIP

Before assigning the Activity Sheet, give several ESL/LEP students the opportunity to read paragraphs from the selection aloud to the class as a whole. This will give them practice in developing oral fluency and in developing empathy for others.

Teaching It Two Ways

LEARNING OBJECTIVES

- To recognize the effect of World War II on the U.S. home front
- To explain how World War II provided new opportunities for some groups in U.S. society
- To understand that many groups still faced prejudice and discrimination despite their contributions to the war effort

TO FORMULATE HYPOTHESES

Tell students that one way to study an event or a period is to form a hypothesis to guide their research. A hypotheses is a temporary assumption or conclusion based on limited evidence created to explain a set of facts. As more evidence is obtained, the temporary conclusion can be changed.

Tell students to skim Chapter 16 before they read it, looking at illustrations and reading heads and captions and also to review Chapter 15. This is their limited starting information. Then they write a hypotheses about how World War II changed U.S. society as a whole and one of the groups in it. Collect and save their hypotheses until chapter study is complete.

TO DESIGN POSTERS

Tell students that during the war, the U.S. government used a great many posters to convince people to support the war effort by buying war bonds, saving scrap metal, growing their own vegetables, etc.

Divide the students into small groups. Let each pick one of the groups discussed in the text. Distribute poster board and colored pencils or paints. Tell students to design a poster intended to convince members of the group they selected to support the war effort. For example, one group might design a poster to convince women to take factory jobs. Another might try to convince interned Japanese Americans to join the armed forces.

Putting It All Together

SHARING: Display completed posters on the bulletin board. Then, without identifying the writers, read hypotheses about U.S. society and groups in it that students formulated before reading the chapter. Ask for suggestions about how those early hypotheses might be modified. In modifying the hypotheses, tell students to consider using evidence in the posters as well as in the chapter.

ASSESSING: Tell students to create charts in which they cite at least one positive and one negative effect that World War II had on women, African Americans, Latinos, and Japanese Americans.

PAST TO PRESENT: The United States has been involved in military conflicts since World War II. Ask students how involvement on the home front in recent conflicts like the Persian Gulf War was similar to or different from that involvement during World War II.

CHAPTER 17: The United States and the Soviet Union Fight a Cold War.

Opening It Up

MOTIVATING: Prepare two copies of outline maps from p. 248 in the Teacher's Resource Manual. On one, tint the maximum area controlled by Axis powers during World War II. On the other, tint areas held by Communist governments around 1949. Using an opaque projector, show the maps to the class. Ask why some people in the United States might have worried about the U.S.S.R. and its allies after the war.

SETTING UP: Special materials include prepared outline world maps and an opaque projector. Teacher's manual resources include Chapter 17 answer key (p.275), Chapter 17 Test (p. 147), and Chapter 17 Activity Sheet (p. 219).

TEACHING TIP

The Sharing exercise offers English-proficient students a chance to help out as "teachers" of ESL/LEP students. Suggest that, as ESL/LEP students fill in the charts, they offer suggestions of moves and countermoves for the English-proficient students to consider in their exercise.

Teaching It Two Ways
LEARNING OBJECTIVES

- To recognize reasons underlying the start of the Cold War
- To compare and contrast the United States and U.S.S.R. as Cold War superpowers
- To identify major Cold War confrontations

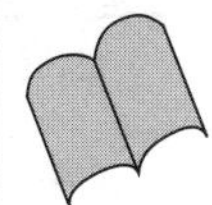

TO RECOGNIZE CAUSE AND EFFECT

Tell students to imagine a nation's relations with another as a cause-and-effect exercise. One nation makes a foreign policy move (cause). The other nation makes a countermove (effect) in response to the first one.

Tell the students to study the chapter and find three examples of such moves and countermoves in which the United States was involved. One example should be from Europe, one from Asia, and one from Cuba.

Finally, ask students which of these moves and countermoves they think posed the most serious threat to the United States. Tell them to write brief statements explaining their choice.

TO ORGANIZE INFORMATION

Copy the following chart onto the chalkboard as a model for students. Have them work in small groups to fill in their charts as they read the chapter. Tell them to leave the last row on the chart blank.

	U.S.	U.S.S.R.
Type of Government		
Economic System		
Leaders		
Basic Foreign Policy		
Alliances and Allies		

Finally, assign the Activity Sheet for Chapter 17.

Putting It All Together

SHARING: Have volunteers read aloud their choices for the most dangerous Cold War conflict. As they read, instruct other students to add a row labeled "Conflicts" to their charts and to make entries based on the conflicts that are described.

ASSESSING: Write these words on the chalkboard: "From this day we move forward . . . toward a new era of security at home . . . toward a new and better world of peace and international goodwill and cooperation." Tell students that President Truman spoke these words at the end of World War II. Tell them to write brief paragraphs explaining why they think his vision did or did not come true.

PAST TO PRESENT: Remind students that Korea remains a hot spot in world affairs. Ask volunteers to visit the library and prepare a report for the class on relations between North Korea and the United States today.

CHAPTER 18: The Years After World War II Bring Prosperity and Problems.

Opening It Up

MOTIVATING: Read aloud this statement by a European who had come to the United States in the 1950s: "No doubt, America is the land where people earn more, live better, and work under more agreeable conditions than anywhere else. . . ." Tell students to keep this quotation in mind as they read Chapter 18. Tell them to look for evidence that supports or refutes the statement.

SETTING UP: Special materials include sheets of poster board and tempera paints. Teacher's manual resources include Chapter 18 answer key (p.276), Chapter 18 Test (p. 148), and Chapter 18 Activity Sheet (p. 220).

TEACHING TIP

The lesson plan for this chapter is an extended cooperative learning activity. Circulate among the groups of correspondents and illustrators and encourage students in both categories to offer ideas to each other. The Activity Sheet for this chapter is appropriate for all students in the class.

Teaching It Two Ways

LEARNING OBJECTIVES

- To recognize that the wealth and opportunities of postwar United States were not open to all Americans because of fear, prejudice, and discrimination
- To understand the effects of the postWorld War II "Red scare" on U.S. society
- To explain the early stages of the African American Civil Rights Movement

TO PREPARE A NEWSCAST

Read aloud this statement by a historian about the 1950s: "The largest growth area was the exciting new medium of television. . . . TV boomed in the fifties. . . . By 1957, the three networks controlled the airwaves, reaching 40 million sets over nearly 500 stations." More and more Americans got their news from television.

Tell students to prepare a TV newscast from the 1950s. Divide the class into three groups, one for each section of the chapter. Students in each group should prepare brief reports about different aspects of the section that they will deliver orally as correspondents. When deciding on stories to cover, they should work closely with students doing the ESL/LEP exercise.

TO ILLUSTRATE IDEAS

Divide students into three groups that correspond to those in the adjacent exercise. Students in both exercises will work together to decide what stories from the section to cover.

Once stories have been chosen, students from the three groups in this part of the exercise will prepare visuals that will serve as illustrations for the correspondents' reports. Distribute poster board and tempera paints for students to work with. Tell them that illustrations may be pictures of individuals or events. Other visuals might include title cards—such as one saying "The Economy," with drawings of dollar signs and coins. Encourage students to be creative.

Putting It All Together

SHARING: Have the correspondents and illustrators for each section present their segment of the newscast. You might suggest that one person serve as anchor for each section. As correspondents present their reports, illustrators can display the appropriate visuals. Conclude by reminding students that newscasts often have a year-end wrap up of major stories. Have students choose the "Three Top Stories of the Chapter," picking one from each section.

ASSESSING: Tell students to write a complete paragraph supporting or refuting the statement in the Motivating exercise with evidence from the chapter.

PAST TO PRESENT: Have students monitor television newscasts for a week. Ask: *What are the top stories? Are any of the areas into which those stories fall similar to those from their 1950s newscast?*

CHAPTER 19: Three Presidents Shake Up the Nation.

Opening It Up

MOTIVATING: Write *1932, 1936, 1940, 1944,* and *1948* on the chalkboard. Write *Roosevelt* and *Truman* under the appropriate dates. Say that these were the nation's only leaders through five presidential terms. Write *1960, 1964, 1968, 1972,* and *1976* on the board. Explain that the nation had five Presidents during these terms. Ask what effect so many different leaders might have on the nation.

SETTING UP: Have poster board, paints, and index cards. Teacher's manual resources include Chapter 19 answer key (p. 276), Chapter 19 Test (p. 149), and Chapter 19 Activity Sheet (p. 221).

TEACHING TIP

When using cooperative learning activities, try to make sure that each student in the group has a special and specific responsibility in the overall project. This will help with control of the group, ensure that all students contribute, and prevent one or two from dominating.

Teaching It Two Ways

LEARNING OBJECTIVES

- To cite major accomplishments of the five Presidents discussed in the chapter
- To name the chief problems each President faced
- To identify major legislation of the period

TO WRITE CAMPAIGN SPEECHES

Divide students into five groups, one for each of the five President discussed in the chapter. Tell students to imagine that each of those Presidents had the chance to run for one more term.

Let some of the students in each group be campaign workers for that race. Tell them to write speeches their President might use in the race. Those speeches should stress the positive accomplishments, both foreign and domestic.

Tell the other students in the group that they represent the opposition. They should reread the sections dealing with their President and based on information in the section, should prepare arguments urging their President not to run again.

TO CREATE CAMPAIGN POSTERS

Assign the Activity Sheet for Chapter 19 to help students keep track of Presidents, ideas, and issues as they read the chapter. Then, divide the students into five main groups that correspond to those in the adjoining exercise. Distribute poster board and paints to each group.

Tell some in each group to create campaign posters calling for the reelection of their President. Students might think up campaign slogans for the posters or use illustrations that represent their President's major accomplishments in office. Others in the group should draw up posters opposing the President. Urge speech writers and poster makers for each President to work together.

Putting It All Together

SHARING: Have students hold campaign rallies for each of the five Presidents. Several students from each group should take turns delivering the campaign speech, while poster makers display their work. Opponents should present their speeches and visuals. Supporters should then have a chance to reply. You might conclude by holding elections in which students vote on whether each President should have another term.

ASSESSING: Distribute index cards to student groups. Tell them to write descriptions of some legislation or program mentioned in the chapter. Each card should end with the words "What Is It?" Collect cards and redistribute them to groups who will identify the law or program and write the answer on the other side of the card.

PAST TO PRESENT: Ask students which of the Presidents discussed in the chapter are still alive. Ask volunteers to do library research and report on what those Presidents are doing today.

CHAPTER 20: The United States Fights a War in Vietnam.

Opening It Up

MOTIVATING: Write the word *Vietnam* on the chalkboard. Ask a volunteer to locate Vietnam on a globe or map. Then brainstorm any information, images, or ideas the word calls up. Record in a cluster student responses on the chalkboard or overhead. Save the responses. Tell students that Chapter 20 deals with a complex period in U.S. history, one in which U.S. actions produced varied, and often opposing, responses in the American people.

SETTING UP: Special materials include index cards. Teacher's manual resources include Chapter 20 answer key (p. 276), Chapter 20 Test (p. 150), and Chapter 20 Activity Sheet (p. 222).

TEACHING TIP

Remember to use specifics whenever commenting on student group work. Rather than saying, "Great job, Group A," add "Group A, your cartoons dealt with all the major events in Section 1." This will provide students with an understanding of how to shape future performance.

Teaching It Two Ways

LEARNING OBJECTIVES

- To list major events in the course of the Vietnam War
- To recognize the chronological sequence of events in Vietnam
- To recognize differing attitudes the Vietnam War produced in U.S. society

TO DESIGN POLITICAL CARTOONS

Assign the Activity Sheet for Chapter 20 to get students thinking about political cartoons. After students have worked on the sheets, assign each student one section of the chapter. Review with them tools cartoonists use: caricature, symbolism, labels, captions. Tell students to draw a political cartoon about some event in their section.

After students have completed their cartoons, have them meet in groups according to section and decide what event or development discussed in their section was the most important. Each group should then select the carton that represents its choice and prepare a brief statement explaining the group's reasoning.

TO SEQUENCE EVENTS

Divide students into small groups. Distribute index cards to them. Tell each group to write a label or draw a picture of some important event in the history of U.S. involvement in Vietnam on one side of the card. On the other side, they should write the date of the events.

Collect each group's cards, shuffle them, and exchange them with the cards of another group. Tell the students in each group to arrange the cards in the order in which the events depicted or listed took place without looking on the back.

When all groups are done, have the authors check the sequences. Then have students select cards from each group to create the most complete story of the U.S. struggle in Vietnam.

Putting It All Together

SHARING: Have students who have worked with sequencing postcards show the most complete version of the war on the bulletin board. Cartoonists should post their works where they fall in the sequence. Then the groups should present their selections of the most significant events and give classmates a chance to critique their choices.

ASSESSING: Tell students to write statements about policy in Vietnam that might have been made by Presidents Eisenhower, Kennedy, Johnson, and Nixon. Have the students read the statements aloud. Ask class members to identify the Presidents from the statements.

PAST TO PRESENT: Tell students to ask adults about the Vietnam War period and what they think today. Show the cluster from the Motivating section. Add the findings to the cluster. Have volunteers summarize the ideas in the cluster.

CHAPTER 21: Changes in the American Way of Life Take Place.

Opening It Up

MOTIVATING: When Dwight Eisenhower took office in 1953, he said: "In the swift rush of great events, we find ourselves groping to know the . . . meaning of these changing times." When he took office in 1957, he said: "We do not fear this world of change. . . . Everywhere we see . . . seeds of growth." Ask students to identify the theme of both speeches. (change) Have them skim section heads. Ask: *What changes do you think were reshaping America?*

SETTING UP: Reproduce the survey findings below and have ready a clean overhead transparency. Teacher manual resources include Chapter 22 answer key (p. 276), Chapter 21 Test (p. 151), Chapter 21 Activity Sheet (p. 223), and Unit 4 Test (p. 92).

TEACHING TIP

The Chapter 21 Activity Sheet presents two stereotypes of teenagers. Tell students that a stereotype is a fixed idea about a group of people. Although a stereotype may have some factual basis, it does not take into account individual differences. Ask students to discuss the dangers of stereotyping.

Teaching It Two Ways

LEARNING OBJECTIVES

- To identify major population changes that took place in the United States between 1950 and 1980
- To describe how television and rock 'n' roll changed the nation
- To discuss some of the changes experienced by young people in the 1960s and 1970s

TO INTERPRET A SURVEY

Distribute copies of this 1950 survey of 400 Washington, D.C., households with TVs.

- Movie attendance has dropped by 72%.
- Adults spend 29.1% less time reading books.
- Children's reading has fallen by 15.7%.
- People attend wrestling and boxing 44.7% less; football, 40% less; baseball, 6.7% less.
- Nightly radio listening has dropped from an average of 3 hours 42 minutes to 24 minutes.
- Husbands now spend 42.% more of their leisure time at home; wives, 39.7% more; children, 41.3% more.

Have students write news stories announcing the survey's startling findings. Date lines should read: Washington, D.C., September 18, 1950.

ESL TO DESIGN AN ADVERTISEMENT

Copy the quote below on a transparency. Ask a volunteer to look up all unfamiliar words so that he or she can serve as a resource person.

Bill Levitt felt he had the right house. . . . The living room had a big picture window. . . . The kitchen shone with stainless steel cabinets and sink, a new refrigerator and automatic washer. He thought his price was right also: $7,900. Veterans could buy the house for $90 down and $58 a month (for 25 years). The payments covered taxes, fire insurance, mortgage payments and interest.

Show the transparency to the class, and encourage students to ask the "resource person" to define terms. Then have students design advertisements for a new Levitt home.

Putting It All Together

SHARING: Direct teams of students to combine the news stories, the extract on Levitt, and the ad for a Levitt home into a mock newspaper page. Use these pages to analyze the changes that TV and Bill Levitt brought to the U.S.

ASSESSING: Tell students to list the changes mentioned in this chapter. Then have students list these changes in order of importance. Challenge students to write speeches defending their choice for "Most Far-Reaching Change."

PAST TO PRESENT: Use the Activity Sheet to compare teenagers in the 1950s and 1960s with teenagers today. Have students identify stereotypes in the Activity Sheet or their own examples.

CHAPTER 22: African Americans Score Successes in Many Fields.

Opening It Up

MOTIVATING: In 1965, a 13-year-old African American named Cliff Morton explained why he marched for civil rights: "I have to do it. People should have done it before. When I grow up, . . . I don't want my children in a mess like we are now." Ask: *What were the limits on African American rights? What actions would you have taken in the 1960s to win equality?* Save student responses for comparison.

SETTING UP: Bring in copies of the U.S. outline map (p. 245), the quotes below, and a tape recorder. Teacher's manual resources include Chapter 22 answer key (p.276), Chapter 22 Test (p. 152) and Chapter 22 Activity Sheet (p. 224).

TEACHING TIP

To develop oral fluency in ESL/LEP students, you might have them script dialogues for tape recording. They should listen to the tape several times, editing as necessary. You might appoint an English-proficient resource person to help with pronunciation and grammatical construction.

Teaching It Two Ways

LEARNING OBJECTIVES

- To list gains and challenges of the Civil Rights Movement after 1960
- To describe how black nationalism changed the direction of the Civil Rights Movement
- To trace new directions in the struggle for equality after 1970

TO INTERPRET A MAP

Distribute copies of the quote below by SNCC civil rights worker Bruce Hartford.

Grenada is in the delta . . . in what you would call hard-core Mississippi. In the year I was there [1965], . . . we would start daily marches. . . . You could see Klan leaders trying to push into us. . . . The tension, the terror wears you down. . . . So we sang. The songs were our release—and our strength.

Ask: *What tactic did SNCC workers use to force change. What obstacles did they face? How did Hartford and others draw strength to resist?* Then hand out the Chapter 22 Activity Sheet and outline map. Have students locate Grenada. Ask: *Why do you think rioting might have broken out there.?*

TO CREATE A MOCK DIALOGUE

Ask students to tape record a mock dialogue in which Martin Luther King, Jr., Malcolm X, and Stokely Carmichael talk about the Civil Rights Movement. (See Teaching Tip) Tell students to avoid naming any of the speakers. Distribute copies of the following quotes as background.

King: "I have a dream that one day on the red hills of Georgia sons of former slaves and sons of former slaveowners will be able to sit down together at the table of brotherhood."

Malcolm X: "Well, if you and I don't use the ballot, we're going to be forced to use the bullet. . . . But let us try the ballot first."

Carmichael: "We've been saying freedom for six years and we ain't got nothin'. What we're going start saying now is black power."

Putting It All Together

SHARING: Play the dialogues and ask class members to identify the speakers. Compare and contrast the three views. Then go over the reports for the Kerner Commission. Ask: *Why was resolution of conflict so crucial in 1968?*

ASSESSING: Tell students that during the March on Washington thousands of placards announced the purpose of the demonstration. Ask each student to design a poster that he or she might have carried. Slogans and designs should reflect the goals mentioned in the text.

PAST TO PRESENT: In 1988, Jesse Jackson said: "Time . . . does not change things. It is courageous leaders who change things." Have students write a "Profile in Courage" about a leader in Chapter 22 who changed the United States.

CHAPTER 23: The Civil Rights Movement Advances.

Opening It Up

MOTIVATING: Open the lesson by referring students to the map on page 198. Ask: *What states have the largest African American populations? In what regions are these states located? Suppose a politician wanted to win the "African American vote," in what five states should she or he make speeches?* Tell students that Chapter 24 shows how African Americans exercised their power in politics and other areas of life.

SETTING UP: Prepare copies of the statistics and chart below. Teacher's manual resources include Chapter answer key (p. 276), Chapter 23 Test (p. 153), and Chapter 23 Activity Sheet (p. 225).

TEACHING TIP

The Chapter 23 Activity Sheet asks students to write a letter to their local newspaper. You might begin this activity by exploring how writing styles differ with audiences. Have students begin by writing this letter to a friend. Then have them rewrite it for the newspaper. Ask: *How do word choices differ?*

Teaching It Two Ways

LEARNING OBJECTIVES

- To name ways African Americans have shaped U.S. culture
- To assess the economic progress of African Americans
- To list examples of increasing African American political influence

TO DESIGN A SPECIAL PURPOSE MAP

Hand out copies of the outline map on page 250. Then have students use to data below to create a special-purpose map showing the geographic distribution of the nation's top 100 African American-owned businesses. Inform students that in the statistics () = number of businesses in a state. (Source: *Black Enterprise,* June 1993.) Based on the map, have students write short news stories that *Black Enterprise* might have run with the map.

Ala. (2); Ark. (1); Calif. (17); Conn. (2); Fla. (4); Ga. (8); Ill. (18); Ind. (5); Iowa (3); Ky. (3); La. (2); Md. (8); Mass. (4); Mich. (27); Minn. (1); Miss. (1); Mo. (2); Neb. (2); N.J. (5); N. Mex. (1); N.Y. (19); N.C. (5); Ohio (11); Okla. (2); Ore. (4); Pen. (4); S.C. (2); Tenn. (3); Texas (14); Va. (10); Wash. (5); W. Va. (2); Wis. (2)

ESL TO MAKE A CHART

Have students use the chart below to organize data on African American achievements.

Area	Person/Group	Achievement
Literature		
Music		
TV/Film		
Sports		
Business		
Politics/Law		

Putting It All Together

SHARING: Use an opaque projector to show copies of the completed map. Refer students to the population map on page 198. Ask: *What links can you identify between population distribution and the top 100 African American businesses?* Next, have volunteers read their news stories. Show a completed copy of the chart, focusing on business entries. Ask what new data students would add to the news stories.

ASSESSING: Based on the text and student charts, have the class design a series of biographical posters entitled "Famous Firsts."

PAST TO PRESENT: Hand out the Chapter 23 Activity Sheet. After going over directions, consider the use of the strategy in the Teaching Tip. Suggest that students save their letters to submit to their local newspaper in February.

CHAPTER 24: Women Fight for Their Rights.

Opening It Up

MOTIVATING: In 1968, African American Congresswoman Shirley Chisholm addressed Congress: "As a black person, I am no stranger to prejudice. But the truth is that in the political world I have been more often discriminated against because I am a woman than because I am black." Ask students what Chisholm's comments reveal about women's rights. Then tell them that Chapter 24 traces women's efforts to change this situation.

SETTING UP: Prepare copies of the quote below and materials for designing flash cards. Teacher's manual resources include Chapter 24 answer key (p. 277), Chapter 24 Test (p. 154), and Chapter 24 Activity Sheet (p. 226).

TEACHING TIP

The activity below asks students to set goals. Define short-term and long-term goals. Short-term goals often take less effort and bring quicker results. Long-term goals usually take more planning but can bring greater change. Short-term goals can be steps toward reaching long-term goals.

Teaching It Two Ways

LEARNING OBJECTIVES

- To list conditions that led to the women's movement
- To name laws that increased women's rights
- To describe the debate about the ERA
- To assess the role of women today

TO STATE GOALS

Distribute copies of the following statement of purpose adopted at NOW's first meeting in 1966.

To take action to bring women into full participation in the mainstream [most active part] of American society now, assuming all the privileges [rights] and responsibilities [duties] in truly equal partnership with men.

Ask a student to repeat the purpose of NOW in her or his own words. Then divide students into groups. Have each group list goals that NOW might have pursued in 1966 to fulfill its purpose. Ask them to distinguish short-term and long-term goals. (See Teaching Tip.) Then have each group pick one long-term goal. Have students identify the short-term goals (steps) that would help to achieve the long-term goal.

TO DESIGN BIOGRAPHICAL FLASH CARDS

With students, list the pioneering women mentioned in this chapter: Ruth Bader Ginsburg, Betty Friedan, Elizabeth Watson, Connie Chung, Geraldine Ferraro, Barbara Boxer, Dianne Feinstein, Carol Moseley Braun, Ella Grasso, Ann Richards, Sandra Day O'Conner, Jeane Kirpatrick, Madeleine Albright, Hillary Clinton. Then, challenge students to design flash cards that use pictures, symbols, and words to identify each person. (For example, Betty Friedan might hold her book or wear a T-shirt labeled NOW. State flags can serve as clues for the two women governors. A Supreme Court with eight male justices and one woman justice can be used for Sandra Day O'Conner. Dianne Feinstein might sit at a Senate seat labeled "California.")

Putting It All Together

SHARING: Show the flash cards and challenge the rest of the class to guess each person's identity. Then have the various groups present their long-term goals for NOW in 1966 and the steps they would have taken to achieve it. Ask: *Based on the achievements of the women in the flash cards, have any of these goals been met? Explain your thinking.*

ASSESSING: Assign the Chapter 24 Activity Sheet. Then divide the class into debate teams to conduct rounds of debate on the ERA. Make sure that ESL/LEP students are included on each team.

PAST TO PRESENT: Ask volunteers to look up in an almanac figures on men's and women's wages. Have them present their findings in the form of a table. Use these figures to raise the question of whether the ERA should be reintroduced in the 1990s.

CHAPTER 25: Mexican Americans Struggle for Equal Rights.

Opening It Up

MOTIVATING: Ask if students are familiar with Mohandas Gandhi. Recall Gandhi's nonviolent tactics for winning independence for India. Then read aloud this description of César Chávez by Art Torres, Mexican American state Senator from California. "He was our Gandhi," said Torres in 1993. "He showed us how to win human rights peacefully." Have students predict tactics that Chávez might have used to win equal rights for Mexican Americans.

SETTING UP: Prepare copies of the statistics below and materials for bar graphs and posters. Teacher's manual resources include Chapter 25 answer key (p. 277), Chapter 25 Test (p. 155), and Chapter 25 Activity Sheet (p. 227).

TEACHING TIP

The ESL/LEP activity calls for a skit. You might begin by introducing the idea of a dramatic *persona*—the personality that an actor wants to project to the audience. Before creating their skits, suggest that students develop a personality for each of the key characters.

Teaching It Two Ways

LEARNING OBJECTIVES

- To list conditions that led migrant farm workers to organize
- To name tactics that Mexican Americans used to gain equal rights
- To discuss issues that concerned Mexican Americans at the close of the 20th century

TO DESIGN A BAR GRAPH

Have students use the statistics below to create bar graphs on poster-size paper. Suggest that they plot percentages on the vertical axis in intervals of 5 percent, from 0 percent to 60 percent. The names of the groups should appear along the horizontal axis.

Migrant Workers, by Ethnic Group, 1992

Ethnic Group	Percent
Hispanic/other	2.0
Mexican	57.0
Non-Hispanic	29.0
Mexican American	9.0
Puerto Rican	3.0

(Source: U.S. Department of Labor)

TO DEVELOP A SKIT

Tell students that Mexican American protesters sometimes expressed their goals in the form of *actos,* or fast-moving plays. During the 1965 strike, migrant farm workers used *actos* to keep up their spirits. They devised on-the-spot skits that poked fun at vineyard owners and promised victory for *La Causa.* Challenge students to imagine they are part of the Delano strike. Working in small groups, have them develop short three-minute *actos.* Suggest that students begin by creating a dramatic *personae,* or personality for each key character. (See Teaching Tip.) Then have them devise a line of action. Encourage students to devise props, such as pro-strike posters.

Putting It All Together

SHARING: Allow time for students to present their *actos.* After each *acto,* call on class members to identify the message that the actors tried to get across. Then distribute copies of the Chapter 25 Activity Sheet. When students have completed the exercises, challenge them to create impromptu *actos* showing the role of Chávez in the 1965 strike.

ASSESSING: Using poster board, have students create murals illustrating the goals of *La Causa, El Movimiento,* or Mexican Americans today. The murals should reflect the goals mentioned in the text.

PAST TO PRESENT: Display copies of the bar graphs. Ask students which group makes up the largest percentage of migrant farm workers today. Ask: *What can you infer about Mexican immigration to the United States? What progress made in the 1960s and 1970s helps these new arrivals?*

CHAPTER 26: Cuban Exiles Become Americans.

Opening It Up

MOTIVATING: Open this chapter by referring students to the map on page 273. Ask them to use the scale to estimate the distance in miles between Cuba and Key West, Florida (about 90 miles). Then have students identify the boxed items that show some of the waves of Cuban immigration to the United States. Tell students that in Chapter 26 they will learn about how these and other waves of Cuban exiles have shaped U.S. culture.

SETTING UP: Prepare copies of the outline map (p. 245), the incomplete quote below, and materials for comic books. Teacher's manual resources include Chapter 26 answer key (p. 277), Chapter 26 Test (p. 156), and Chapter 26 Activity Sheet (p. 228).

TEACHING TIP

As with storyboards, students can create a short comic book that tells a story. You can arrange this activity as a traveling story in which groups of students build upon the account until the story is finished. Comics should include both pictures and dialogues.

Teaching It Two Ways

LEARNING OBJECTIVES

- To name reasons hundreds of thousands Cubans came to the United States after 1959
- To describe the geographic distribution of people of Cuban ancestry
- To list Cuban American contributions to the nation

TO INTERPRET A QUOTATION

Distribute copies of this incomplete quote by Cuban American politician Pedro Reboredo.

The face of Miami . . . has changed. . . . [W]hen Cuban refugees . . . realized that we wouldn't be going back to Cuba, we began to really buy into the American dream. Most are decent middle-class people who came from Havana. Like myself, almost all arrived penniless. [They have turned] the Eighth Street area [Calle Ocho] into a Little Havana. . . . They have (finish the speech).

Based on the text, challenge students to finish Reboredo's speech, citing other examples of Cuban contributions to Miami.

TO DESIGN A COMIC BOOK

Ask students to review the story of Little Havana in the text. Ask: *How did it start? What are some of its features?* Then have them retell this story in the form of a comic book. Students should begin by listing characters who will appear in the comic. (Characters can be a blend of real and fictional people.) Next, have students summarize the story that they plan to tell. Suggest that small groups of students be responsible for designing individual parts of the story. Arrange desks in a long row so that group members can walk back and forth to coordinate sequential frames and dialogues. You might bring some comics into class as models.

Putting It All Together

SHARING: Distribute photocopies of the comic book. When students have read it, challenge class members to design a cover. You might hold a vote to select the best cover. Place the finished book in the library. Next, request volunteers to read the completed speech by Reboredo. Ask students why Cuban Americans such as Reboredo take pride in Little Havana. Ask: *What other accomplishments are sources of pride to Cuban Americans?*

ASSESSING: Have students imagine that they work for the U.S. Bureau of the Census. Using facts and figures in the text, have them write a profile of Cuban Americans in the 1990s.

PAST TO PRESENT: Assign the Chapter 26 Activity Sheet. When students have finished, have them revise the profile written in Assessing. As a follow-up, have students design a travel poster entitled "Miami: Cuban Capital of America."

CHAPTER 27: Puerto Ricans and Dominicans Strive to Succeed.

Opening It Up

MOTIVATING: In 1993, a Puerto Rican in upstate New York exclaimed: "I am a United States citizen, *and* I am a Puerto Rican." Explore with students the special status of Puerto Ricans as members of two nations. Then refer students to the graph on page 00. Ask them why Puerto Ricans are not listed among the immigrants. (because they are U.S. citizens) Ask: *Of the people shown, which is the largest group coming to the U.S. today?* (Dominicans)

SETTING UP: Prepare copies of the lyrics and quote below and materials for posters. Teacher's manual resources include Chapter 27 answer key (p. 277), Chapter 27 Test (p. 157), and Chapter 27 Activity Sheet (p. 229).

TEACHING TIP

The activity below lists lyrics from Puerto Rico's national song. You might have ESL/LEP students bring in lyrics from the anthems of their nations of origin. Ask students to translate these lines into English. Then ask other students to identify sources of national pride.

Teaching It Two Ways

LEARNING OBJECTIVES

- To identify changes that took place in Puerto Rico after World War II
- To describe how Puerto Ricans adjusted to life on the mainland
- To discuss reasons large numbers of Dominicans have come to the United States

TO INTERPRET A NATION'S SONG

Distribute copies of the "La Borinquena," Puerto Rico's national song. (*Borinquen* is the Taino name for the island.) "The island of *Borinquen* / Where I was born / Is a tropical garden / Of magic splendor. / A sky that is always bright / It's like an enchanted [magic] canopy / And sing pleasant lullabies / The waves on your feet. / When Columbus arrived / Filled with admiration, he exclaimed: / Oh! Oh! Oh! / This beautiful land / I'm looking for / It's *Borinquen,* the daughter / The daughter of the sea and sun."

Have students copy the lyrics onto an illustrated poster. Then ask them to write letters in which mainland Puerto Ricans tell what they miss most about their island.

TO ANALYZE IMMIGRANT EXPERIENCES

Distribute copies of the quote below. In it, a young Dominican named Esmilda Maria Abreu describes her early life in the U.S.: "My grandmother worked in a sweatshop making purses. She earned the minimum wage and didn't speak any English. We lived in a one bedroom apartment. Yet, she was supporting my mom in medical school in the Dominican Republic as well as two uncles, an aunt, and myself."

Ask volunteers to read the quote aloud. Encourage students to help each other with pronunciations or word definitions. Then ask students what hardship Esmilda's family faced. Ask: *Why do think the family stayed in the United States?* To explore the experience of Dominican immigrants further, assign the Chapter 27 Activity Sheet.

Putting It All Together

SHARING: Display the illustrated lyrics from Puerto Rico's national song. Then have students read their letters. Discuss features of the island that immigrants might miss. Then use an opaque projector to show postcards. Encourage students to compare the experiences of Puerto Ricans and Dominicans in the United States. Ask: *Why has each group come to the mainland?*

ASSESSING: Challenge students to complete a balance sheet for Puerto Rican statehood. Column heads should include pro and con arguments. Ask: *If you lived on the island, how would you vote? Why?* Reasons should reflect factors named in the text.

PAST TO PRESENT: Arrange to hold a Caribbean festival in your class, complete with music, foods, and national costumes.

CHAPTER 28: Native Americans Fight for Their Rights.

Opening It Up

MOTIVATING: Read this Lakota saying to the class: "A people without history is like wind across the buffalo grass." Ask students what this saying means. (If a people forget their history, they might disappear.) Then tell students that Chapter 28 is about how Native Americans have attempted to reclaim their heritage. To evaluate Native American success, have students set up the chart described in Study Hint on page 235 of the text.

SETTING UP: Prepare copies of the quote below. Collect strips of computer paper for timelines. Teacher's manual resources include Chapter 28 answer key (p. 277), Chapter 28 Test (p. 158), and Chapter 28 Activity Sheet (p. 230).

TEACHING TIP

The Activity Sheet charts Native American populations in the Americas. You might use this activity to discuss the issue of indigenous cultures worldwide. Explore the threats of modernization and urbanization. Ask: *What responsibility does the global community have to preserve native cultures?*

Teaching It Two Ways

LEARNING OBJECTIVES

- To cite reasons for the start of a Native American rights movement
- To list tactics used by Native Americans to win equal rights
- To evaluate advances and setbacks experienced by Native Americans

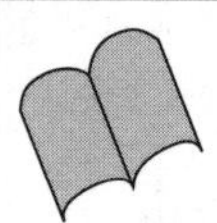

TO EVALUATE A QUOTATION

Hand out copies of this quote by a Hopi girl.

We are nothing to the white people; we are a few Hopis, but they are Americans, millions of them. My father told me that their leader . . . says to other nations: you had better pay attention, because we are big, and we will shoot to kill, if you don't watch out. My mother says all the big countries are like that, but I only know the Hopi nation. . . . [U.S. government] people come here . . . and give us their laws. . . . In case we have any objections, they have soldiers.

Ask students how the speaker saw the United States and her own people. Then have them list ways that Native Americans in the 1960s and 1970s tried to change this situation.

TO DRAW AN ILLUSTRATED TIME LINE

Refer students to the timeline on page 237 of the text. Ask students to identify the length of time covered by the timeline. (50 years) Ask: *What was the cause of many of the events on the timeline?* (policy of termination) *What entry shows that Native Americans still face an ongoing struggle for their rights?* (Reagan's cutbacks in aid to Native Americans) Next, have students design an illustrated version of this timeline for display on the classroom wall. Using connected sheets of computer paper, have students create the timeline and plot the events. Then have small groups of students devise pictures or symbols to depict each of the events shown.

Putting It All Together

SHARING: Display the completed timeline. Then have a volunteer read the quote by the Hopi girl. Discuss events that contributed to the plight of the Hopi. Have students read their lists of actions that Native Americans took to change such situations. Whenever a student cites an action on the timeline, have a volunteer point out the illustration.

ASSESSING: Go over the completed chart suggested in Motivating. Then challenge students to brainstorm goals Native Americans might pursue in the 2000s. Goals should reflect ways in which the setbacks listed on the chart can be corrected.

PAST TO PRESENT: Distribute copies of the Chapter 28 Activity Sheet. As an extension, follow the suggestion in Teaching Tip.

Opening It Up

MOTIVATING: Refer students to the chapter's map and graph. Ask students to identify the subject of each. Ask: *In what region are most of the top ten cities located?* (west) *How does this distribution reflect traditional immigration patterns?* (Eastward migrations out of Asia, as during the California Gold Rush.) Then, explain this chapter tells about Asian immigration and Asian Americans today.

SETTING UP: Bring in copies of the figures below and materials for a poster-size bar graph. Teacher's manual resources include Chapter 29 answer key (p. 277), Chapter 29 Test (p. 159), and Chapter 30 Activity Sheet (p. 231).

TEACHING TIP

The Chapter 29 Activity Sheet looks at the national origins of Asian American 8th graders. Have students poll social studies classes at their grade level to find out the main region their ancestors came from (Europe, Asia, Africa, Middle East, etc.) and if students are native born or foreign born.

Teaching It Two Ways

LEARNING OBJECTIVES

- To describe changes in U.S. policies toward immigration from Asia
- To name places where the most recent Chinese immigrants to the United States have settled
- To discuss how Japanese Americans challenged the injustice of the internment years
- To list reasons for Korean immigration

TO READ A TABLE

Assign the Chapter 29 Activity Sheet. Ask students to compare the statistics on Asian American 8th graders with immigration patterns in the text. (Point out the large number of Chinese and Korean immigrants.) Tell students that in Chapter 33 they will learn more about the recent immigration of other groups listed in the Activity Sheet. Next, work with students to develop a poll to determine the regional origins of students in their own grade. (See Teaching Tip.) Appoint a student to ask other social studies teachers for permission to distribute a questionnaire. Suggest the that questionnaire be anonymous (as in most polls). When students have finished, they should present the results in the form of a table.

TO DRAW A BAR GRAPH

Distribute copies of the following statistics on the percentage of Asian/Pacific Islanders by ethnic/national group who speak a language other than English at home. (The figures come from a 1989 poll conducted by the Asian American Health Forum, Inc.)

Hawaiian—0.5%; Japanese—40.5 %; Indian—55.3%; Filipino—59.9%; Samoan 63.2%; Korean—69.7%; Chinese—72.5%; Thai—72.5%; Laotian—77.4%; Vietnamese—80.7%; Cambodian—81.9%

Have students present these figures in a wall-size bar graph. Tell them to divide the vertical axis into 20-percent intervals, from 0 percent to 100 percent. Individual languages should be plotted along the horizontal axis.

Putting It All Together

SHARING: Ask students to summarize the profile of Asian American 8th graders. Then have them present the results of their poll. Ask: *From which region do most students trace their ancestry? Is there a large foreign-born population in your school? If so, from which region do they come?* Then post the bar graph. Based on this data, ask students to draw conclusions about language patterns among Asian American 8th graders.

ASSESSING: Ask two students to devise a Jeopardy-like game, setting up categories of answers. Then have two teams of "contestants" form questions for each answer. If a team member phrases an incorrect question, ask the "audience" to form it.

PAST TO PRESENT: Have students write a speech a Japanese American might have given upon passage of the Civil Liberties Act of 1988.

Opening It Up

MOTIVATING: In the 1980s, a Czech refugee in San Francisco told a reporter: "The people that I knew in eastern Europe still believed that America was the last place in the world where we could find freedom." Remind students that the lure of freedom had been a "pull" factor since the founding of the 13 Colonies. Then tell students that Chapter 30 looks at "push" factors that led European and Arab immigrants to this nation in the post-World War II era.

SETTING UP: Copy the quotations below. Teacher's manual resources include Chapter 30 answer key (p. 278), Chapter 30 Test (p. 160), Chapter 30 Activity Sheet (p. 232), and Unit 5 Test (p. 93).

TEACHING TIP

Have students start a diversity portfolio on post- World War II America. Tell them to include facts, graphs, photos, etc. that depict U.S. diversity. Ask students to think of people and culture. Begin by having them look up data on U.S. religions, including Islam (a topic in Chapter 30.)

Teaching It Two Ways
LEARNING OBJECTIVES

- To trace European immigration after World War II
- To name ways Middle Eastern immigrants have influenced U.S. life and culture

TO INTERPRET A QUOTE

Distribute copies of this quote by a Russian Jew who fled the Soviet Union in 1978.

The Communists wanted to eliminate [wipe out] religious faith. . . . They knew that the way to destroy the Jewish identity was to make it impossible for Jews to understand their religion. . . . The first step was to deny Jews a knowledge of their language. There was no Yiddish literature printed. The history of how the Jewish people came to Russia, . . . the traditions, the rituals, were all erased. What . . . made us decide to come to the West was when I came to accept that I am Jewish. I didn't belong to the Soviet society. I could no longer lie . . . to my child about her identity.

Have students write a summary of reasons Russian Jews came to the U.S. in the 1970s.

TO INTERPRET A QUOTATION

Distribute copies of the below quote.

In 1979, Islamic rebels overthrew the Shah [king] of Iran. My life was at risk because I worked for the government. My job was passport control. I rushed my daughter out of Iran. I stayed to help people escape the terror of the revolution. I was one of the last government people to get out. Now I work as a cab driver here in your nation's capital. But I am free. My daughter is free too. She is a science professor with her own apartment. Can you imagine that? We both love Islam. But the strict Islamic laws of Iran would make my daughter's life very different. Today we are Islamic U.S. citizens.

Have students underline the reasons that the former Iranian official came to the U.S.

Putting It All Together

SHARING: Ask pairs of volunteers to develop dialogues in which the Russian Jew and the Iranian explain why they came to the United States. Then distribute copies of the Chapter 30 Activity Sheet. Ask: *How does the dialogue explain the large number of immigrants from Iran? Given the dialogue and the figures on Israeli immigration, what can you infer about the nation's foreign-born Jewish population from the 1970s to 1990?*

ASSESSING: Assign or go over the chart suggested in the Study Hint on page 252.

PAST TO PRESENT: Ask volunteers to research and prepare an oral report on the Iranian Revolution. Ask: *Why did the United States. give asylum to so many Iranians?*

CHAPTER 31: The United States Shifts to Conservatism.

Opening It Up

MOTIVATING: Have a volunteer read aloud the definition of *budget deficit* on page 261. Then refer students to the line graph on page 262. Ask students why the budget deficit is a major issue for the nation. Challenge students to brainstorm solutions to this problem. Record these suggestions on the chalkboard. Then tell students to see which, if any, of the three Presidents tried these ideas.

SETTING UP: Materials include copies of the quotes below, poster board, and a black felt-tipped marker. Teacher's manual resources include Chapter 31 answer key (p. 278), Chapter 31 Test (p. 161), and Chapter 31 Activity Sheet (p. 233).

TEACHING TIP

Have students look up definitions of the terms *reactionary, conservative, moderate (middle-of-the-road), liberal, radical.* Then position the terms along a continuum. Ask: *Where would you place the three Presidents mentioned in the chapter? Where would you position yourselves?*

Teaching It Two Ways

LEARNING OBJECTIVES

- To identify key policies of Ronald Reagan
- To list George Bush's policy goals
- To describe Bill Clinton's approach to the deficit and health care

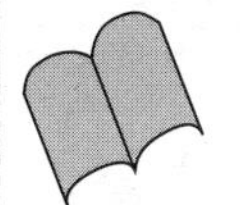

TO IDENTIFY ISSUES

Distribute copies of these Reagan quotes:

In the present crisis, government is not the solution to our problem; government is the problem. . . . It is time to check and reverse the growth of government.

Since 1960 our government has spent $5.1 trillion. Our debt has grown by $648 billion. Prices have exploded by 178 percent.

A second American Revolution . . . is gathering force . . . born of popular resentment against a tax system that is unwise, unwanted, and unfair.

Ask students to identify the issue in each quote and Reagan's opinion on this issue. Then have them compose a mock State of the Union Address that Reagan might have given in 1981.

TO ORGANIZE INFORMATION IN A TABLE

Divide students into three groups. Then distribute copies of the Activity Sheet for this chapter. Have each group fill in information on one of the three Presidents named in the table. When students have finished, have them reassemble. Direct them to construct a master table on a large piece of poster board. (Encourage students to edit each other's entries and to correct spelling or grammatical errors.) Challenge each group to compose a short autobiographical speech on the President that it researched. Tell students to avoid using the person's name. Each speech should end with the words "Who Am I?"

Putting It All Together

SHARING: Post the completed table at the front of the classroom. Then have students deliver their "Why Am I?" speeches. Challenge the rest of the class to identify each speaker. Next, call on volunteers to deliver the mock State of the Union Address. Ask: *Which of the table entries on Reagan are illustrated by the Address?*

ASSESSING: Develop the political continuum suggested in the Teaching Tip. After students have positioned each of the three Presidents on the continuum, challenge them to present oral arguments defending their placements.

PAST TO PRESENT: Have students conduct a school-wide poll on a single question: *Of all the Presidents, whom do you most admire?* Have students report the winner.

Opening It Up

MOTIVATING: Chapter 32 gives students a sweeping look at world events in the closing year of the 20th century. Ask volunteers to use an opaque projector to trace a large copy of the outline map of the world on page 248 onto pieces of poster board. Tape the completed map at the front of the room. At the end of each section, have a committee plot key sites on the map and add short descriptions and appropriate illustrations.

SETTING UP: Copy the excerpts below. Bring a video camera. Teacher's manual resources include Chapter 32 answer key (p. 278), Chapter 32 Test (p. 162), and Chapter 32 Activity Sheet (p. 234).

TEACHING TIP

A video camera is a useful tool for allowing students to review their own verbal performances. The Assessing activity calls for mock CNN reports from crisis scenes. You might videotape these reports. After viewing the videos, discuss how such on-the-scene reports help shape public opinion about war.

Teaching It Two Ways

LEARNING OBJECTIVES

- To identify effects of the breakup of the Soviet Union
- To describe how the United States became involved in conflicts in the Middle East and Africa
- To discuss U. S. interaction with nations in Latin America and the Caribbean

TO ANALYZE A NEWS STORY

Hand out copies of the following extract from the September 2, 1991, issue of *TIME*.

No Soviet Union? That huge blob . . . that dominated the maps of the Eurasian landmass for 70 years now broken up into a crazy quilt of [new nations]? . . . The concept is hard . . . to grasp. . . . [T]he Superpower that overshadowed the 20th century is no more.

Tell students that this piece is written in the colorful style of journalism. Ask them to reword the selection in the form of an encyclopedia entry (expository writing). Discuss: *How do the two styles differ? Why do they differ?* Have students compare the purpose of a magazine and an encyclopedia.

TO ANALYZE A NEWS STORY

Distribute copies of the following extract from the November 20, 1989, issue of *TIME*.

For 28 years it has stood as the symbol of the division of Europe and the world, of communist [power]. . . . It was a hideous [horrible] 28-mile-long scar through the heart of a once proud European capital. . . . And then—poof!—it was gone.

Tell students that reporters often use colorful words to catch the readers' attention. Point out the phrase "a hideous 28-mile-long scar." Note that the reporter does not tell readers what the scar is. Instead people must keep reading to find out. Ask students to guess the identity of the "scar." Have them copy facts from the text that support their answer.

Putting It All Together

SHARING: Have students read the two extracts aloud. Ask volunteers to share what they have learned about journalist writing. Then explore how these two stories are linked. Ask: *How did the collapse of the Berlin Wall signal the collapse of the Soviet Union? How did both events change history and geography?*

ASSESSING: Distribute copies of the Chapter 32 Activity Sheet. Assign groups of students one of the following crises: collapse of the Soviet Union, Persian Gulf War, UN intervention in Somalia, Haiti coup. Challenge students to use the Activity Sheets to develop an on-the-scene news report such as CNN might broadcast. (See the Teaching Tip for teaching variations.)

PAST TO PRESENT: Have students compare the Iran-Contra scandal to the Watergate scandal. Ask them what similarities or differences they find.

CHAPTER 33: New Immigrants Strengthen the American Multicultural Mix.

Opening It Up

MOTIVATING: In 1993, reporter Stanley Karnow said: "When I left Vietnam [in 1973], I never expected to see Saigon again. But I'm back there, at least in spirit. Vietnamese refugees have created a 'Little Saigon' right here in Orange Country, California." Ask: *What can you infer about Little Saigon from Karnow's comment?* (that it looks a lot like Vietnam) Have students find photos in Chapter 33 that show other ways immigrants have increased the diversity of our nation.

SETTING UP: Have on hand an opaque projector and copies of the figures and poem below. Teacher's manual resources include Chapter 33 answer key (p. 278), Chapter 33 Test (p. 163.), Chapter 33 Activity Sheet (p. 235.)

TEACHING TIP

One of the activities in this lesson asks students to write poetry. To help them with descriptive language, explain the idea of a simile, a comparison using "like" or "as." Tell students that poets use similes to create visual images. Then have them try to finish this simile: "History is like a __________."

Teaching It Two Ways

LEARNING OBJECTIVES

- To trace Vietnamese immigration to the United States
- To compare Indian society to U.S. society
- To name reasons South Americans fled their homelands for the United States

TO EVALUATE A GENERALIZATION

Write the following generalization by a leading population expert on the chalkboard. "Sometimes there is more divisity [divisions] within ethnic groups than between ethnic groups." Then distribute copies of these figures. Have students use the data to write a paragraph evaluating this generalization.

South Asians, 1990

Group	Numbers
Asian Indians	815,447
Pakistanis	27,876
Bangladeshi	11,838
Sri Lankan	10,970
Fijians of Indian Origin	7,000
Guyanese Indians	7,000–10,000

TO WRITE A POEM

Distribute copies of the following incomplete poem by a Vietnamese refugee.

With a pen our country was divided in two;
  in a blood bath, united. . . .
So we left on little wooden boats
  To search for . . .

Have students explain the meaning of the first two lines of the poem. (If they have trouble, refer them back to Chapter 20.) Then challenge students to add lines that describe a Vietnamese refugee's journey to the United States. ESL/LEP students can write the lines in their primary language and then translate them into English. Direct students to use at least one simile. (See Teaching Tip.)

Putting It All Together

SHARING: Use an opaque projector to show the table on South Asians. Then have students read their evaluations. Refer students to the remark by Amy Lan on page 281: "There is no such thing as an Asian American." Ask: *How would Amy respond to these evaluations?*

ASSESSING: Have students read their poems describing the experiences of a Vietnamese refugee. Then assign students to pick one of the groups of immigrants named in Sections 2 and 3. Have them write poems describing that group's experiences. Ask students to review each other's poems for accuracy.

PAST TO PRESENT: Assign the Chapter 33 Activity Sheet for this Chapter.

CHAPTER 34: The United States Faces Challenges.

Opening It Up

MOTIVATING: You might open this chapter by drawing a continuum on the chalkboard. Label entries on the continuum as follows: "Extremely Serious," "Serious," "Moderately Serious," "Not Very Serious." Then tell students to use the pictures and boldfaced heads to identify the challenges discussed in Chapter 34. List these on the chalkboard next to the continuum. With the class, reach a consensus on where each of these items should appear.

SETTING UP: Copy the table below. Have materials for making posters. Teacher's manual resources include Chapter 34 answer key (p. 278), Chapter 34 Test (p. 164), and Chapter 34 Activity Sheet (p. 236).

TEACHING TIP

To develop reading comprehension skills in ESL/LEP students, you might play a game of Sentence Scrambler. Take any paragraph in this chapter and mix up the sentences. As a closed-book exercise, have students try to unscramble the sentences and rebuild the paragraph so that it makes sense.

Teaching It Two Ways

LEARNING OBJECTIVES

- To list challenges facing Americans in the closing years of this century
- To cite reasons that these challenges are concerns for all Americans
- To name actions taken to meet each of these challenges

TO INTERPRET A TABLE

Distribute copies of these figures on school crime in 1993. Ask students to summarize the data in the form of a news story entitled: "Crime Goes to School—A National Tragedy."

Age	Total Number of Students	Victims at School	Violent Crime	Property Stolen
12	3,320,891	9%	2%	7%
13	3,318,714	10%	2%	8%
14	3,326,574	11%	2%	9%
15	3,214,109	9%	3%	7%
16	3,275,002	9%	2%	7%
17	3,273,628	8%	1%	7%
18	1,755,825	5%	1%	4%
19	231,348	2%	1%	2%

TO ORGANIZE INFORMATION ON A CHART

Refer students to the chart on page 288. Then go over the chart's basic organization. Ask: *What is the subject of the chart?* (the global environment) *What clue helped you with this answer?* (the title) *What three categories of information are included on the chart?* (issues, concerns, actions) To practice finding information on the chart, ask these questions: *(1) What four global issues threaten the environment? (2) Who or what is at risk from toxic waste? (3) What actions have been taken to save the rain forests?* When students understand the chart's structure, distribute copies of the Chapter 34 Activity Sheet. Working in groups, have students complete the activity.

Putting It All Together

SHARING: On the chalkboard, compile a master version of the chart with students. Then focus on the issue of crime. Distribute copies of the students' news stories. Have students underline statistics used in the story. Discuss: *What information in the chart explains reasons crime is so high among youth? In addition to actions named on the chart, what other suggestions can you make to curb crime?*

ASSESSING: Have students create posters to support one of the action projects mentioned in the chapter. Encourage them to use pictures and slogans to get their message across. Display these posters in the school.

PAST TO PRESENT: Request that students investigate rules regarding garbage and waste disposal in their community. Ask: *Which rules address environmental concerns named in the text?*

CHAPTER 35: Science and Technology Move Ahead.

Opening It Up

MOTIVATING: To illustrate the pace of change, have students name a "classic" rock song from the 1970s. Explain that in the 1970s, people usually bought this song in the form of a record. Ask: *In what form would young people buy it today?* (a tape or CD) Point out technology, not the song, has changed. As a lead into the chapter, have students brainstorm other technological changes.

SETTING UP: Have on hand copies of the events below, materials for a timeline, and an opaque projector. Teacher's manual resources include Chapter 35 answer key (p. 278), Chapter 35 Test (p. 165), and Chapter 35 Activity Sheet (p. 237).

TEACHING TIP

The ESL/LEP activity asks students to think about the future. You might use this exercise to practice past, present, and future verb tenses. For example, ask students to identify the verb in the chapter title. Ask: *What tense is it in?* Have students rewrite it in other tenses.

Teaching It Two Ways

LEARNING OBJECTIVES

- To name changes that computers have made in our lives
- To describe how medical advances have improved the quality of life
- To list United States achievements in space

TO DRAW A TIMELINE

Distribute copies of the list of events below. Have students design an illustrated timeline entitled "The U.S. Aims High."

1958: First U.S. rocket reaches the moon; Congress creates National Aeronautical and Space Administration (NASA). **1961:** First U.S. astronaut heads into space. **1962:** First U.S. astronaut orbits earth. **1967:** Three astronauts die in explosion on launch pad. **1969:** U.S. astronauts reach the moon. **1974:** U.S. launches first space station. **1977:** U.S. spaceship travels to end of solar system. **1981:** U.S. launches first space shuttle. **1986:** Space shuttle *Challenger* explodes, killing seven astronauts. **1988:** United States resumes space program. **1990:** United States launches Hubble space telescope. **1993.** NASA sends shuttle to repair Hubble.

TO MAKE PREDICTIONS

Distribute copies of the Chapter 35 Activity Sheet. Ask a volunteer to read the directions aloud. As a vocabulary exercise, focus on the definition of *futurology.* Ask students what other *-ology* words they know. To get them started, write the word *biology* on the chalkboard. When students have completed their list, remind them that *-ology* means "the study of." Ask: *What is the subject of study in each word?* To find out, have students use a dictionary to look up each root word. You might then use the suggestion in the Teaching Tip to develop grammatical skills. Ask students to write a sentence about each topic on the worksheet in the past, present, and future tense.

Putting It All Together

SHARING: Post the completed timeline. Ask students to name triumphs and setbacks in the space program. Then use an opaque projector to show the completed Activity Sheets. Ask: *What type of future do you predict for space exploration? What future do you predict for other topics on the Activity Sheet?*

ASSESSING: Ask students to draw posters illustrating the following concepts: network, information highway, automation, virtual reality. Hold up these posters, and ask other students guess the concept.

PAST TO PRESENT: Challenge students to create science fiction stories about the first space colony on the moon. One of the characters might be a handicapped scientist who does not need crutches to "walk" on the moon's surface.

CHAPTER 36: The American People Face the 21st Century.

Opening It Up

MOTIVATING: Prior to opening this chapter, ask volunteers to use an opaque projector to copy the outline map of the world on page 248 onto several large pieces of poster board. To introduce the concept of diversity, have students locate the nations or regions that they or their ancestors came from on the map. Shade in each area as it is named. When students are done, read aloud the definition of diversity on page 00. Ask: *How does the map illustrate this concept?*

SETTING UP: Have on hand copies of the figures below, materials for graphs, and an opaque projector. Teacher's manual resources include Chapter 36 answer key (p. 279), Chapter 36 Test (p. 166), Chapter 36 Activity Sheet (p. 238), and Unit 6 Test (p. 94).

TEACHING TIP

The Chapter 36 Activity Sheet compares census data from 1790 and 1990. As an enrichment activity, you might have students use a copy of an almanac to research additional tidbits about the American people. Have them present their findings in the form of a poster entitled: "Did You Know That. . . ."

Teaching It Two Ways

LEARNING OBJECTIVES

- To list ways that Americans have changed in the decades since 1900
- To name ways the elderly and disabled have worked to win equal rights
- To appreciate how diversity has enriched our American nation

TO INTERPRET A TABLE

Distribute copies of the table below. Have students use this table and the text to prepare a short oral report entitled: "The United States is Becoming More Diverse—Again." (Tip: Point to the first and last entries on the table.)

Immigration as a Percentage of
Total Population Growth, 1901–990

Period	Percent	Period	Percent
1900–10	39.6	1950–54	10.6
1910–20	17.7	1955–59	10.7
1920–30	15.0	1960–64	12.5
1930–34	0.1*	1965–69	19.7
1935–39	3.2	1971–80	19.4
1940–49	10.2	1981–90	32.8

*Immigration laws shut nation.
Source: U.S. Immigration and Natural Service

TO DRAW A LINE GRAPH

Distribute copies of the following data. Tell students to organize the data in the form of a line graph. Direct them to plot percentages on the horizontal axis in increments of five percent. Years should appear along the horizontal axis.

Growth of the Population
Age 65 and Over, 1910–030

Year	Percentage	Year	Percent
1910	4.3	1990	11.3
1930	4.7	2010	13.0
1950	8.1	2030	21.2
1970	9.8		

Source: Population Reference Bureau

Putting It All Together

SHARING: Have students present their tables and oral reports on increasing diversity in the United States. Ask: *What do you predict the percentage will be for the years 1990–2000?* Next, have students show their line graphs. Ask: *How has the age of the U.S. population changed since 1900? What do experts predict for the 2000s? How does this population change increase diversity?*

ASSESSING: Have students review the definition of a mosaic. Keeping this concept in mind, have students design a new cover for this book. The "mosaic" cover should include pieces that show the many peoples who make up the nation.

PAST TO PRESENT: Distribute copies of the Chapter 36 Activity Sheet. As an extension, use the Teaching Tip.

Name ______________________________ Date ____________________

UNIT 1 TEST: The Clash of Cultures in the Americas

I. MATCHING *Decide which definition in the right column best explains a term in the left column. Then write the letter of that definition in the space next to the term.*

_____	**1.** encomienda	**a.** beliefs and ways of life of a people
_____	**2.** diverse	**b.** Aztec's capital city
_____	**3.** Ghana	**c.** Spanish land grant
_____	**4.** Crusades	**d.** followers of the religion of Islam
_____	**5.** adobe	**e.** a series of wars fought over the Holy Land
_____	**6.** Tenochtitlan	**f.** six united Iroquois groups
_____	**7.** culture	**g.** an African empire
_____	**8.** Muslims	**h.** mud brick used by Pueblos to build houses
_____	**9.** nomads	**i.** different or varied
_____	**10.** League of Nations	**j.** people who moved from place to place in search of food

II. UNDERSTANDING THE UNIT *On a separate sheet of paper, answer each of the following questions in two or three sentences.*

11. How has immigration made the United States a diverse nation?
12. How did the discovery of farming affect the early Native Americans?
13. Why did the Europeans try to find new trade routes to Asia?
14. How did the encomienda system harm the Native Americans?
15. What led the Spanish to bring enslaved Africans to the islands of the Caribbean?

III. ESSAY *Choose two of the following topics. Then write your answers in paragraph form on a separate sheet of paper.*

A. The United States is described as a diverse nation. Explain why it is diverse and give three examples of its diversity.

B. Once the first Native Americans crossed the land bridge into North America, many changes in their way of life occurred. Describe these changes.

C. Imagine you are a Spanish official trying to get people to settle in Hispaniola. Design an advertisement that will encourage Spaniards to go to Hispaniola, using pictures and descriptions of the pictures.

Name ______________________________ Date ____________________

UNIT 2 TEST: New Cultures in the Americas

I. MATCHING *Decide which definition in the right column best explains a term in the left column. Then write the letter of that definition in the space provided next to the term.*

_____	**1.** mission	**a.** to persuade a person to join a religion
_____	**2.** famine	**b.** a resource or product sent from one country to another
_____	**3.** synagogues	**c.** the power to rule oneself
_____	**4.** nationalism	**d.** Jewish places of worship
_____	**5.** Jesuit	**e.** a plant that can be made into a blue dye
_____	**6.** export	**f.** a group that makes laws
_____	**7.** indigo	**g.** loyalty to or pride in one's country
_____	**8.** self-government	**h.** a member of a special Catholic order
_____	**9.** convert	**i.** a time when there is not enough food to eat
_____	**10.** assembly	**j.** a community run by the Catholic church

II. UNDERSTANDING THE UNIT *On a separate sheet of paper, answer the following questions in one or two sentences.*

11. Who was Father Kino?
12. What effect did tobacco have on the colonies?
13. Why was slavery more important in the South than in New England?
14. How did African slaves keep their culture alive?
15. How did the French king try to increase New France's population?

III. ESSAY *Choose two of the following topics. Then write your answers in paragraph form on a separate sheet of paper.*

A. How did missions protect and harm Native Americans?
B. What were the differences between North and South Carolina?
C. Why was there far less slavery in the North than in the South?

Name ______________________________________ Date ______________________

UNIT 3 TEST: From Revolution to Independence

I. MATCHING *Decide which definition in the right column best explains a term in the left column. Then write the letter of that definition in the space next to the term.*

______	**1.** boycott	**a.** a formal partnership between nations
______	**2.** Sons of Liberty	**b.** armed resistance to a government
______	**3.** Townshend Acts	**c.** to refuse to buy, sell, or use goods from another country
______	**4.** duty	**d.** a tax on imported goods
______	**5.** minutemen	**e.** a group of colonists who organized protests against the Stamp Act
______	**6.** Second Continental Congress	**f.** created a Continental Army with George Washington as its commander
______	**7.** rebellion	**g.** a goal someone tries to live up to
______	**8.** ideal	**h.** taxed imports from Britain such as cloth, paint, glass
______	**9.** alliance	**i.** members of the militia who were ready to fight with only one minute's notice
______	**10.** Proclamation of 1763	**j.** said colonists could not settle west of the Appalachians

II. UNDERSTANDING THE UNIT *On a separate sheet of paper, answer each of the following questions in two or three sentences.*

11. Why did Great Britain want the colonists to pay more taxes?

12. What were some of the ways that the colonists protested the British taxes?

13. Why were the battles of Lexington, Concord, and Bunker Hill important?

14. What important ideals are expressed in the second part of the Declaration of Independence?

15. What happened at Yorktown and why was it so important?

III. ESSAY *Choose two of the following topics. Then write your answers in paragraph form on a separate sheet of paper.*

A. Pretend that you are a member of the Sons of Liberty. Write a secret letter to a friend telling him what actions you plan to take against the British.

B. Write an eyewitness account of any one of the following important events: the Boston Massacre, the Boston Tea Party, the battles of Lexington and Concord, the Battle of Bunker Hill.

C. Draw a cartoon showing the colonists' point of view of one of the following: the Sugar Act, the Stamp Act, the Quartering Act. Be sure that you put a caption on your cartoon.

Name ______________________________ Date ____________________

UNIT 4 TEST: Growth of the New Nation

I. MATCHING *Decide which definition in the right column best explains a term in the left column. Then write the letter of that definition in the space provided next to the term.*

_____	**1.** canal	**a.** to change or revise
_____	**2.** amend	**b.** an act or decision that sets an example for later actions
_____	**3.** spiritual	**c.** a country where the people choose their own leaders
_____	**4.** embargo	**d.** a waterway built by people to connect two bodies of water
_____	**5.** tariff	**e.** to add territory to a nation
_____	**6.** executive	**f.** to refuse to sign a law
_____	**7.** annex	**g.** a religious song of enslaved African Americans
_____	**8.** republic	**h.** the branch of government headed by the President that carries out the laws
_____	**9.** veto	**i.** a tax on imported goods
_____	**10.** precedent	**j.** a government order forbidding trade with another nation

II. UNDERSTANDING THE UNIT *On a separate sheet of paper, answer each of the following questions in two or three sentences.*

11. Which compromises at the Constitutional Convention pleased the Southern states? Why?

12. What are the three branches of the U.S. government?

13. During the 1800s the United States grew much larger. How did the new nation double in size?

14. How did the North and South begin to grow apart in the first half of the 1800s?

15. Name two groups of people that the early Americans discriminated against?

III. ESSAY *Choose two of the following topics. Then write your answers in paragraph form on a separate sheet of paper.*

A. Design a poster that explains two of the first ten amendments to the Constitution.

B. Describe three ways that the Industrial Revolution changed life in the United States.

C. The U.S. government has a system of checks and balances to keep any one part of the government from becoming too powerful. Give two examples of this system of checks and balances.

Name ______________________________ Date ________________

UNIT 5 TEST: A Nation Divided; A Nation United

I. MATCHING *Decide which definition in the right column best explains a term in the left column. Then write the letter of that definition in the space next to the term.*

_____	**1.** immigrant	**a.**	Congress's plan to reunite the South with the Union
_____	**2.** women's rights movement	**b.**	African Americans released from slavery
_____	**3.** abolition movement	**c.**	laws passed by Southern states after the Civil War that took away many of the rights of the former slaves
_____	**4.** Fugitive Slave Act	**d.**	someone who leaves his or her country to settle in a new country
_____	**5.** Confederacy	**e.**	a movement in the 1800s to gain rights and fair treatment for women
_____	**6.** Civil War	**f.**	a movement that fought to end slavery
_____	**7.** Black Codes	**g.**	the new nation formed by seven Southern states
_____	**8.** Emancipation Proclamation	**h.**	conflict between the Confederate states and the Union
_____	**9.** freedmen	**i.**	law passed by Congress in 1850 that made it easier for slave owners to claim runaway slaves
_____	**10.** Reconstruction	**j.**	Presidential order freeing slaves in all areas held by the Confederacy

II. UNDERSTANDING THE UNIT *On a separate sheet of paper, answer each of the following questions in two or three sentences.*

11. Describe the greatest problem facing the United States from the Missouri Compromise in 1820 through the end of Reconstruction in 1877.

12. Why did thousands of German and Irish immigrants come to the United States between the 1840s and the 1860s?

13. Describe two of the main goals of the women's rights movement.

14. What roles did William Lloyd Garrison and Frederick Douglass play in the movement to abolish slavery?

15. Why did many freed African Americans in the South become sharecroppers after the Civil War?

III. ESSAY *Choose two of the following topics. Then write your answers in paragraph form on a separate sheet of paper.*

A. Explain the purpose of the Underground Railroad.

B. Draw a map of the United States that shows where at least four major battles of the Civil War took place.

C. Select the African American you think did the most to help bring freedom to enslaved people in the United States, and explain why you chose that person.

Name ________________________________ Date ____________________

UNIT 6 TEST: Challenges, Opportunities, and Achievements

I. MATCHING *Decide which definition in the right column best explains a term in the left column. Then write the letter of that definition in the space next to the term.*

_____	**1.** segregate	**a.** rights given to all citizens by the Constitution
_____	**2.** civil rights	**b.** science used in practical ways
_____	**3.** Homestead Act	**c.** a slum building with many apartments
_____	**4.** mass production	**d.** the building of colonial empires
_____	**5.** new immigrants	**e.** to separate people by races
_____	**6.** assimilate	**f.** jobs in which workers serve or help others
_____	**7.** tenement	**g.** ways of making large amounts of products quickly and cheaply
_____	**8.** service jobs	**h.** to adopt the customs of a culture or a country
_____	**9.** imperialism	**i.** an 1862 law that gave free land to anyone who would farm it for five years
_____	**10.** technology	**j.** people who came to the United States from Eastern and Southern Europe

II. UNDERSTANDING THE UNIT *On a separate sheet of paper, answer each of the following questions in two or three sentences.*

11. Who were the most important African American leaders of the nation in the late 1800s?

12. How were Jim Crow laws used to rob African Americans of their civil rights?

13. Why did farmers and ranchers in the West fight over the use of the land?

14. How did immigration to the United States change after 1885?

15. What were some new opportunities for women in the late 1800s?

III. ESSAY *Choose two of the following topics. Then write your answers in paragraph form on a separate sheet of paper.*

A. Draw a map showing the territories the United States controlled after the Cuban–Spanish-American War.

B. Explain how the Chicago World's Fair of 1893 showed many of the problems faced by Americans.

C. Explain why many of the new immigrant groups settled together in the same big city neighborhoods.

Name ______________________________ Date ____________________

UNIT 1 TEST: Into the Twentieth Century

I. MATCHING *Decide which definition in the right column best explains a term in the left column. Then write the letter of that definition in the space provided next to the term.*

_____	**1.** urban	**a.** the technique of production in which each worker makes only one part of a product
_____	**2.** Jim Crow laws	**b.** a run-down building divided into many small apartments
_____	**3.** *barrio*	**c.** having to do with cities
_____	**4.** American Federation of Labor	**d.** a civil rights group that sought to secure "equal rights and opportunities for all"
_____	**5.** assembly line	**e.** Southern laws that discriminated against African Americans
_____	**6.** muckrakers	**f.** section of a city where mostly Latinos live
_____	**7.** National Association for the Advancement of Colored People	**g.** a Spanish word meaning "a small grocery store"
_____	**8.** *bodega*	**h.** founded in 1886 by Samuel Gompers to organize skilled workers
_____	**9.** tenement	**i.** the right to vote
_____	**10.** suffrage	**j.** writers who exposed society's problems

II. UNDERSTANDING THE UNIT *On a separate sheet of paper, answer the following questions in one or two sentences.*

11. How did each of the following help workers gain rights: unions, strikes, and courts?

12. What was the role of the United States in bringing independence to Cuba?

13. How did the NAACP fight for African American rights?

14. Give two reasons why some Americans wanted to limit immigration.

15. What new ideas and inventions changed the way products were made in the late 1800s and early 1900s?

III. ESSAY *Choose two of the following topics. Then write your answers in paragraph form on a separate sheet of paper.*

A. If you were writing an article for a magazine on conditions in the early 1900s, what information would you include?

B. The Progressives worked for different ways to solve problems in society. If you were a Progressive, what problems would you have concentrated on solving, and why?

C. If you were an African American sharecropper living in the South in 1910, would you have moved north? Explain your answer.

Name ______________________________ Date ____________________

UNIT 2 TEST: Becoming a World Power

I. MATCHING *Decide which definition in the right column best explains a term in the left column. Then write the letter of that definition in the space next to the term.*

_____	**1.** colonialism	**a.** a group of countries that work together
_____	**2.** imperialism	**b.** a waterway dug by people to connect two bodies of water
_____	**3.** protectorate	**c.** a weak country that is under the control of a stronger country
_____	**4.** cultural imperialism	**d.** the taking over of foreign countries as colonies
_____	**5.** canal	**e.** the building of empires
_____	**6.** draftee	**f.** the desire to replace the culture of a colony with that of the ruling country
_____	**7.** migrant worker	**g.** the conducting of relations between countries
_____	**8.** alliance	**h.** a policy of not taking sides in a war
_____	**9.** neutrality	**i.** a farm worker who travels to find work
_____	**10.** diplomacy	**j.** a person taken into military service by the government

II. UNDERSTANDING THE UNIT *On a separate sheet of paper, answer each of the following questions in two or three sentences.*

11. What was the Open Door policy?

12. How did the United States gain control of the Cuban economy?

13. How did Theodore Roosevelt's and William H. Taft's policies differ on Latin America?

14. How were Mexican Americans discriminated against?

15. What caused the United States to declare war on Germany?

III. ESSAY *Choose two of the following topics. Then write your answers in paragraph form on a separate sheet of paper.*

A. Explain why the Platt Amendment was important to the United States and Cuba. Would you have been in favor of the amendment or opposed to it at the time it was passed?

B. Pretend you are one of the workers building the Panama Canal. In a letter home, discuss the conditions you face in Panama.

C. Describe the new opportunities open to women, Mexican Americans, and African Americans during World War I.

Name ______________________________ Date ____________________

UNIT 3 TEST: Times of Trial

I. MATCHING *Decide which definition in the right column best explains a term in the left column. Then write the letter of that definition in the space next to the term.*

_____	**1.** internment camp	**a.** to require a person to enter the military
_____	**2.** suburb	**b.** a policy of staying out of world affairs
_____	**3.** renaissance	**c.** a prison camp
_____	**4.** repatriation	**d.** a deep economic downturn
_____	**5.** tariff	**e.** period of rebirth
_____	**6.** depression	**f.** sending a person back to his or her own country
_____	**7.** dictator	**g.** an area people live in that surrounds a city
_____	**8.** draft	**h.** a ruler who has complete control and power
_____	**9.** fascism	**i.** a tax on imports
_____	**10.** isolationism	**j.** a system of government headed by a ruler who uses the military, nationalism, and racism to stay in power

II. UNDERSTANDING THE UNIT *On a separate sheet of paper, answer each of the following questions in two or three sentences.*

11. How did events after World War I lead to intolerance?

12. What were some of the contributions that African Americans made during the Harlem Renaissance of the 1920s?

13. Describe how life changed for many people during the Great Depression.

14. Describe three steps President Roosevelt took to end the Great Depression.

15. What role did women play in World War II, and how did they benefit from this role?

III. ESSAY *Choose two of the following topics. Then write your answers in paragraph form on a separate sheet of paper.*

A. Design a poster that shows some of the ways in which modern science helped during World War II.

B. Describe three ways in which World War II changed life in the United States.

C. What were some of the tragedies of World War II ?

Name ______________________________ Date ____________________

UNIT 4 TEST: A Challenging Period

I. MATCHING *Decide which definition in the right column best explains a term in the left column. Then write the letter of that definition in the space next to the term.*

_____	**1.** capitalism	**a.**	a list of people or organizations under suspicion or in disfavor
_____	**2.** communism	**b.**	an economic system in which most businesses and land are owned and controlled by the government
_____	**3.** blacklist	**c.**	an opponent of war
_____	**4.** boycott	**d.**	a way of living that clashed with traditional ways
_____	**5.** impeachment	**e.**	an economic system in which most businesses and land are privately owned
_____	**6.** pardon	**f.**	a war supporter
_____	**7.** hawk	**g.**	the bringing of charges against a government official
_____	**8.** dove	**h.**	to refuse to buy, sell, or use goods from certain companies, people, or countries
_____	**9.** counterculture	**i.**	an official act that releases someone from the penalty for a crime
_____	**10.** generation gap	**j.**	differences between parents and children

II. UNDERSTANDING THE UNIT *On a separate sheet of paper, answer each of the following questions in two or three sentences.*

11. What was the Cold War?
12. How did the U.S. economy change after World War II?
13. What did John Kennedy and Lyndon Johnson propose for America in their "New Frontier" and "Great Society" programs?
14. How did the war in Vietnam sharply divide Americans?
15. What major shifts in U.S. population took place between 1950 and 1980?

III. ESSAY *Choose two of the following topics. Then write your answers in paragraph form on a separate sheet of paper.*

A. Discuss at least three different ways in which America's fear of communism was expressed in the 1950s and 1960s.

B. Explain some of the great changes that occurred in the United States between 1950 and 1980. You should consider employment and wages, population shifts, housing, family life, and changes affecting racial minorities.

C. Describe the events leading up to the 1956 Supreme Court decision regarding segregation on Alabama's buses.

Name ______________________________ Date ____________________

UNIT 5 TEST: The Struggle for Equality

I. MATCHING *Decide which definition in the right column best explains a term in the left column. Then write the letter of that definition in the space next to the term.*

_____	**1.** sit-in	**a.** a Latino neighborhood of a city
_____	**2.** affirmative action	**b.** a proposed change in the Constitution calling for total equality for men and women under the law
_____	**3.** Black Caucus	**c.** a person who leaves a country for political reasons
_____	**4.** women's liberation	**d.** African American members of Congress who focus on issues that affect their people
_____	**5.** Equal Rights Amendment	**e.** to make persons from other countries citizens of the United States
_____	**6.** Chicana or Chicano	**f.** Native American organization formed in 1968
_____	**7.** political exile	**g.** a policy for correcting discrimination by increasing opportunities for certain groups
_____	**8.** *barrio*	**h.** an American of Mexican descent
_____	**9.** American Indian Movement	**i.** movement to free women of all discrimination
_____	**10.** naturalize	**j.** a protest in which people take a seat and refuse to leave

II. UNDERSTANDING THE UNIT *On a separate sheet of paper, answer each of the following questions in two or three sentences.*

11. How did Malcolm X and the Black Panthers inspire black nationalism in the 1960s?

12. How did César Chávez help Mexican Americans?

13. What was the Mariel boat lift from Cuba?

14. Why did the great migration from Puerto Rico begin after World War II?

15. How have conditions improved for Native Americans in recent years?

III. ESSAY *Choose two of the following topics. Then write your answers in paragraph form on a separate sheet of paper.*

A. Describe the actions the U.S. government has taken to remedy its treatment of Japanese Americans during World War II.

B. Make a chart with these headings: Government, Sports, Entertainment, Business. Under each heading, list African Americans who became leaders in these fields.

C. Explain why Betty Friedan and many other women founded the National Organization for Women (NOW) in 1966.

Name ______________________________ Date ____________________

UNIT 6 TEST: Facing a Changing World

I. MATCHING *Decide which definition in the right column best explains a term in the left column. Then write the letter of that definition in the space next to the term.*

_____	**1.** social programs	**a.** a UN attack in 1991 led by the United States to force Iraq to end its invasion of Kuwait
_____	**2.** free-market economy	**b.** a person who is forced to flee his or her home country
_____	**3.** Operation Desert Storm	**c.** waste that makes the air, water, or land unhealthy
_____	**4.** refugee	**d.** government programs that aid needy groups of people
_____	**5.** pollution	**e.** an economy in which there is little government control
_____	**6.** addict	**f.** a wide range of differences
_____	**7.** computer	**g.** a worldwide network of computers and satellites to send information
_____	**8.** automation	**h.** the use of machines to do jobs that were once done by humans
_____	**9.** diversity	**i.** a person who depends on drugs
_____	**10.** information highway	**j.** a machine for storing and processing information

II. UNDERSTANDING THE UNIT *On a separate sheet of paper, answer each of the following questions in two or three sentences.*

11. Why did the United States send soldiers to Somalia in 1992?

12. Why was President Reagan one of the most popular Presidents of modern times?

13. Who were the boat people who fled Vietnam for the United States?

14. What efforts did the United States make to try to end pollution?

15. What evidence is there to show that the United States is a land of great diversity?

III. ESSAY *Choose two of the following topics. Then write your answers in paragraph form on a separate sheet of paper.*

A. How have computers created a "revolution" in our lives today?

B. On a map of the world, color and label the nations of Asia, Africa, and Latin America that were trouble spots in the late 1980s and the 1990s that affected the United States.

C. In what ways had crime and drug abuse become such serious problems in the United States by the 1990s?

Name ______________________________ Date ____________________

CHAPTER 1 TEST: The United States Is a Diverse Nation.

I. MATCHING *Decide which definition in the right column best explains a term in the left column. Then write the letter of that definition in the space provided next to the term.*

_____ **1.** immigration

_____ **2.** Rocky Mountain Region

_____ **3.** Atlantic Coastal Plain

_____ **4.** democracy

_____ **5.** climate

a. the movement of people from their homeland to another country to live there

b. the average weather of a place over a period of years

c. the region of the United States that stretches from Alaska to Mexico

d. a form of government under which the people rule either directly or through their representatives

e. the region of the United States between the East Coast and the Appalachian Mountains that stretches from Florida to Maine

II. MULTIPLE CHOICE *Choose the answer that best completes the sentence or answers the question. Then write the letter of your choice in the space provided.*

_____ **6.** The United States is considered to be a diverse nation because all of the following are true EXCEPT: **a.** It has a variety of landforms. **b.** People of many cultures live there. **c.** It has a democratic form of government. **d.** It has many different climates.

_____ **7.** The population of the United States is: **a.** growing. **b.** shrinking. **c.** staying the same. **d.** the largest of any country in the world.

_____ **8.** For a nation like the United States to be considered multicultural, it must have: **a.** many different land forms. **b.** a very large population. **c.** many very wealthy people **d.** people of many different backgrounds and traditions.

_____ **9.** Climate affects all of the following EXCEPT: **a.** how people use the land **b.** the type of animals that live there **c.** the kind of government it has **d.** where people live

_____ **10.** Which of the following are natural resources? **a.** minerals and soil **b.** animals **c.** electricity **d.** airports and railway stations

III. ESSAY *Choose one of the following topics. Then write your answer in paragraph form on a separate sheet of paper.*

A. The natural environment has greatly influenced the history of the United States. Give two examples to support this statement.

B. If you could live in any region of the United States, which region would you choose? Describe its advantages and drawbacks.

Name ______________________________ Date ____________________

CHAPTER 2 TEST: The First Americans Develop Great Cultures.

I. MATCHING *Decide which definition in the right column best explains a term in the left column. Then write the letter of that definition in the space provided next to the term.*

_____	**1.** drought	**a.** Pueblo underground prayer room
_____	**2.** glacier	**b.** woodlands Native American group
_____	**3.** *kiva*	**c.** a giant sheet of ice
_____	**4.** tribute	**d.** a tax that a conquered nation must pay its conquerer
_____	**5.** Iroquois	**e.** a long period of dry weather

II. MULTIPLE CHOICE *Choose the answer that best completes the sentence or answers the question. Then write the letter of your choice in the space provided.*

_____ **6.** Nomads were: **a.** farming peoples. **b.** a Native American people later called the Iroquois. **c.** people who move from one place to another searching for food. **d.** people who built great cities.

_____ **7.** The important discovery one group of Native Americans made about 7,000 years ago that changed their way of life was the discovery of: **a.** fire. **b.** farming. **c.** fishing. **d.** gold.

_____ **8.** The buffalo was important to the Native Americans of the Great Plains because it was a source of all of the following EXCEPT: **a.** food. **b.** clothing and shelter. **c.** material tools and weapons. **d.** transportation.

_____ **9.** Which of the following is NOT true of Iroquois women? **a.** They could not vote **b.** They were in charge of planting and harvesting **c.** They owned all property **d.** They were village leaders

_____ **10.** The Maya are known for: **a.** their powerful army. **b.** their invention of an accurate 365-day calendar. **c.** the great pueblos they lived in. **d.** their beautiful gold jewelry.

III. ESSAY *Choose one of the following topics. Then write your answer in paragraph form on a separate sheet of paper.*

A. Imagine you are a Native American living in the Pacific Northwest. Give three examples of how you make use of the natural resources of your environment.

B. In the years after the first hunters migrated to North America, their way of life went through major changes. Describe these changes.

Name ______________________________ Date ____________________

CHAPTER 3 TEST: The Spanish Reach the Americas.

I. MATCHING *Decide which definition in the right column best explains a term in the left column. Then write the letter of that definition in the space provided next to the term.*

______	**1.** conquistador	**a.** an instrument used for showing direction
______	**2.** compass	**b.** opened a school for sea captains
______	**3.** Crusades	**c.** settlement Columbus founded on Hispaniola
______	**4.** Prince Henry	**d.** a Spanish soldier-explorer
______	**5.** Santo Domingo	**e.** a series of wars fought over the Holy Land

II. MULTIPLE CHOICE *Choose the answer that best completes the sentence or answers the question. Then write the letter of your choice in the space provided.*

______ **6.** Native Americans were used by Europeans for all of the following EXCEPT: **a.** finding a route to the Indies. **b.** working on farms. **c.** mining for gold and silver. **d.** building a cathedral in Santo Domingo.

______ **7.** Hatuey was: **a.** a Spanish conquistador. **b.** the governor of Hispaniola. **c.** an African conquistador. **d.** leader of the Taino Native Americans.

______ **8.** Conquistadors went to the Americas mainly to: **a.** find gold and glory. **b.** grow crops for trade. **c.** convert Native Americans to Christianity. **d.** find the "fountain of youth."

______ **9.** Which of the following is NOT true of the Muslims? **a.** They follow the religion of Islam. **b.** They controlled trade routes to Asia. **c.** They controlled the Holy Land. **d.** They invented the compass.

______ **10.** Which of the following does NOT show that Santo Domingo was an important center of Spain 's empire in the Americas? **a.** The government built the first American university and cathedral there. **b.** It produced much gold, silver, and cotton for Spain. **c.** It could not put down a rebellion by the Taino. **d.** The Spanish king and queen took control of Santo Domingo away from Columbus.

III. ESSAY *Choose one of the following topics. Then write your answer in paragraph form on a separate sheet of paper.*

A. Explain why Europeans tried to find a sea route to East Asia after the Crusades..

B. If you were a member of the Taino, how would you react to the arrival of Europeans on your land? What might you have done?

Name ______________________________ Date ______________

CHAPTER 4 TEST: Three Great Cultures Meet in the Americas.

I. MATCHING *Decide which definition in the right column best explains a term in the left column. Then write the letter of that definition in the space provided next to the term.*

______	**1.** Ghana	**a.** a system of owning people
______	**2.** Mecca	**b.** emperor of the Aztecs
______	**3.** slavery	**c.** a large grant of land offered to Spanish settlers
______	**4.** encomienda	**d.** African kingdom of gold
______	**5.** Montezuma	**e.** Muslim holy city

II. MULTIPLE CHOICE *Choose the answer that best completes the sentence or answers the question. Then write the letter of your choice in the space provided.*

______ **6.** Bartolomé de las Casas was: **a.** an Aztec emperor. **b.** opposed to the way landowners treated Native Americans. **c.** a wealthy plantation owner. **d.** a Spanish soldier.

______ **7.** All of the following were accomplishments of ancient Egypt EXCEPT: **a.** the development of a writing system. **b.** building huge pyramids. **c.** advances in math and medicine. **d.** the end of the encomienda system.

______ **8.** In the "silent trade" of ancient Ghana: **a.** slaves were bought and sold. **b.** gold was exchanged for silver. **c.** gold and salt were exchanged. **d.** salt from West Africa was exchanged for gold from North Africa.

______ **9.** Malinche was important to Cortés because she: **a.** helped him raise an army. **b.** taught him the Aztec language. **c.** persuaded Montezuma to surrender. **d.** told him about the Aztec god who was expected to return.

______ **10.** After conquering the Aztecs, Cortés did all of the following EXCEPT: **a.** tear down the Aztec capital. **b.** send Aztecs to work in the gold and silver mines. **c.** send many Aztecs to Spain to be educated. **d.** replace the old Aztec capital with a new city.

III. ESSAY *Choose one of the following topics. Then write your answer in paragraph form on a separate sheet of paper.*

A. Imagine that you are a visitor to the city of Timbuktu. Write a letter to a friend describing the city.

B. If you were an Aztec vassal, would you have helped Cortés conquer the Aztecs? Explain why you would or would not have.

Name ______________________ Date ______________

CHAPTER 5 TEST: Latino Culture Develops.

I. MATCHING *Decide which definition in the right column best explains a term in the left column. Then write the letter of that definition in the space provided next to the term.*

______	**1.** export	**a.** a colonist who was born in Spain
______	**2.** mission	**b.** a time when there is not enough food to eat
______	**3.** famine	**c.** to persuade a person to change his or her religion
______	**4.** peninsulare	**d.** to send a resource or product from one country to another
______	**5.** convert	**e.** a community run by the Catholic Church

II. MULTIPLE CHOICE *Choose the answer that best completes the sentence or answers the question. Then write the letter of your choice in the space provided.*

______ **6.** The poorest people in New Spain were: **a.** *criollos*. **b**. *mestizos*. **c.** African slaves and Native Americans. **d.** mulattos.

______ **7.** Which of the following is NOT true of the way people lived in New Spain? **a.** People had the right to build towns where they wanted. **b.** Farmers were told what to plant. **c.** There were distinct classes of people. **d.** People were expected to know their place.

______ **8.** Francisco Coronado is best remembered for: **a.** the way he encouraged farming in the Southwest. **b.** his search for the seven cities of gold. **c.** his friendly treatment of the Zuni. **d.** the many villages he founded.

______ **9.** The oldest town founded by the Spanish in the present-day United States is: **a.** Phoenix , Arizona. **b.** San Francisco, California. **c.** Santa Fe, New Mexico. **d.** St. Augustine, Florida.

______ **10.** Who was known as the "priest on horseback"? **a.** Ponce de León **b.** Popé **c.** Coronado **d.** Kino

III. ESSAY *Choose one of the following topics. Then write your answer in paragraph form on a separate sheet of paper.*

A. For a Native American in New Spain, what were some of the advantages and disadvantages of living in one of the missions run by the Catholic Church?

B. Give at least one example of the influence on the Latino culture of the Spanish, African, and Native American cultures.

Name ______________________________ Date ____________________

CHAPTER 6 TEST: The English Launch Colonies in North America.

I. MATCHING *Decide which definition in the right column best explains a term in the left column. Then write the letter of that definition in the space provided next to the term.*

_____ **1.** indentured servant

_____ **2.** Roanoke

_____ **3.** Mayflower Compact

_____ **4.** democracy

_____ **5.** Plymouth

a. an agreement signed by the Pilgrims to elect leaders and obey the law

b. a colony that was settled in 1620

c. a British colony that vanished

d. a system in which people govern themselves

e. a person who agrees to work for a set time without pay in exchange for transportation to a new land

II. MULTIPLE CHOICE *Choose the answer that best completes the sentence or answers the question. Then write the letter of your choice in the space provided.*

_____ **6.** The first British colony in the Americas was established at: **a.** Plymouth. **b.** Jamestown. **c.** Roanoke. **d.** Santa Fe.

_____ **7.** Which European group was the first to bring Africans to Virginia in 1619? **a.** the Dutch **b.** the French **c.** the English **d.** the Spanish

_____ **8.** Which of the following was NOT a strong belief of the Puritans? **a.** religious freedom for everyone **b.** the importance of good education **c.** democracy **d.** the need to purify the Church of England

_____ **9.** The first American town to guarantee religious freedom to all its people was: **a.** Plymouth, Massachusetts. **b.** Providence, Rhode Island. **c.** Williamsburg, Virginia. **d.** Newport, Rhode Island.

_____ **10.** Native Americans who fought to regain the land they had lost to the English settlers in 1675 were led by: **a.** Squanto. **b.** Samoset. **c.** Metacom. **d.** John Rolfe

III. ESSAY *Choose one of the following topics. Then write your answer in paragraph form on a separate sheet of paper.*

A. Describe the events that showed the growth of democracy in England's colonies.

B. If you had been a Pilgrim living in the 1600s, would you have tried to form a friendship with the Native Americans? Why or why not?

Name ______________________________ Date ____________________

CHAPTER 7 TEST: People from Many Lands Settle in the English Colonies.

I. MATCHING *Decide which definition in the right column best explains a term in the left column. Then write the letter of that definition in the space next to the term.*

______	**1.** debt	**a.** Jewish places of worship
______	**2.** synagogues	**b.** allowing other people to practice their own beliefs
______	**3.** toleration	**c.** people who can not pay their bills
______	**4.** cash crops	**d.** money that people owe
______	**5.** debtors	**e.** crops raised for sale rather than for a farmer's personal use

II. MULTIPLE CHOICE *Choose the answer that best completes the sentence or answers the question. Then write the letter of your choice in the space provided.*

______ **6.** The primary language spoken in 1744 in New York was: **a.** German. **b.** English. **c.** Dutch. **d.** French.

______ **7.** In which of these colonies were most African American slaves found? **a.** New England **b.** Southern **c.** Middle **d.** Swedish

______ **8.** The Act of Tolerance provided for: **a.** religious freedom. **b.** freedom of education. **c.** freedom of government. **d.** freedom of speech.

______ **9.** The largest farms were located in: **a.** the Southern colonies. **b.** the French colonies. **c.** the New England colonies. **d.** the Middle colonies.

______ **10.** In the 1700s, the greatest percentage of colonists lived: **a.** in small cities. **b.** on farms. **c.** on ships. **d.** in large cities.

III. ESSAY *Choose one of the following topics. Then write your answer in paragraph form on a separate sheet of paper.*

A. Explain why the colonists in the Middle Colonies were able to lead an easier way of life.

B. Create a mural that shows the different ways of life for the people living in the British colonies.

Name ______________________________ Date ____________________

CHAPTER 8 TEST: The People of the 13 Colonies Become Americans.

I. MATCHING *Decide which definition in the right column best explains a term in the left column. Then write the letter of that definition in the space provided next to the term.*

_____	**1.** assembly	**a.** someone who helps with childbirth
_____	**2.** nationalism	**b.** belief that one group is superior to others
_____	**3.** racism	**c.** horrifying trip for slaves across the Atlantic
_____	**4.** midwife	**d.** a group that makes laws
_____	**5.** middle passage	**e.** loyalty to or pride in one's country

II. MULTIPLE CHOICE *Choose the answer that best completes the sentence or answers the question. Them write the letter of your choice in the space provided.*

_____ **6.** Which of these was NOT true of most colonial women? **a.** There was equal education. **b.** Men controlled all family property. **c.** Women could read and write. **d.** Women could run the households.

_____ **7.** He was one of the first free African Americans to contribute to making laws in the colonies: **a.** John Smith **b.** Paul Cuffe **c.** Mathias De Sousa **d.** John Peter Zenger

_____ **8.** This colony was the first to pass laws stating that any child born to a slave mother was also a slave: **a.** Virginia **b.** Georgia **c.** Delaware **d.** Pennsylvania

_____ **9.** This enabled people to demand a greater voice in running their churches: **a.** the Great Awakening **b.** triangular trade **c.** nationalism **d.** self government

_____ **10.** The triangle trade involved: **a.** Africa, South America, and Europe. **b.** Africa, the Americas, and Europe. **c.** Africa and the British colonies. **d.** Europe and the British colonies.

III. ESSAY *Choose one of the following topics. Then write your answer in paragraph form on a seperate sheet of paper.*

A. Describe three things that led colonists to think of themselves as Americans.

B. Compare the treatment of women in Colonial times with the treatment of women today.

Name ______________________________ Date ____________________

CHAPTER 9 TEST: The French Set Up Colonies in North America.

I. MATCHING *Decide which definition in the right column best explains a term in the left column. Then write the letter of that definition in the space provided next to the term.*

______	**1.** *coureurs de bois*	**a.** founded a trading port at Port Royal in Nova Scotia
______	**2.** habitant	**b.** a member of a special Catholic order
______	**3.** ally	**c.** French fur traders
______	**4.** Jesuit	**d.** a small farmer in New France
______	**5.** Samuel Champlain	**e.** a person or group who joins with others for a common purpose

II. MULTIPLE CHOICE *Choose the answer that best completes the sentence or answers the question. Then write the letter of your choice in the spaces provided.*

______ **6.** Which was the first permanent French settlement in North America? **a.** Port Royal **b.** Quebec **c.** New Orleans **d.** Louisiana

______ **7.** Which river did Joliet and Marquette reach in 1673? **a.** the Hudson **b.** the Mississippi **c.** the St. Lawrence **d.** the Missouri

______ **8.** Farming in New France was difficult for all the following EXCEPT: **a.** thick forests. **b.** cold climate. **c.** trouble clearing the land. **d.** warm climate.

______ **9.** The Catholic Church played an important role in governing New France for all of the following EXCEPT: **a.** it was the only religion there. **b.** it owned land. **c.** it raised good crops. **d.** it ran schools.

______ **10.** In 1754, he surrendered at an important French fort in the Ohio valley: **a.** Edward Braddock **b.** George Washington **c.** La Salle **d.** William Pitt

III. ESSAY *Choose one of the following topics. Then write your answer in paragraph form on a seperate sheet of paper.*

A. Describe three French explorers and the territories they explored.

B. If you were a French woman in the 1600s, why might you have agreed to go to New France as one of the "king's daughters"?

Name ______________________________ Date ____________________

CHAPTER 10 TEST: The British Tighten Their Control.

I. MATCHING *Decide which definition in the right column best explains a term in the left column. Then write the letter of that definition in the space next to the term.*

______	**1.** Proclamation of 1763	**a.** to bring goods into a country illegally
______	**2.** Stamp Act	**b.** an announcement saying colonists could not move west of the Appalachians
______	**3.** Sons of Liberty	**c.** this put a tax on legal and other documents
______	**4.** smuggle	**d.** a group of colonists that organized protests against the Stamp Act
______	**5.** boycott	**e.** to refuse to buy, sell, or use goods from another country

II. MULTIPLE CHOICE *Choose the answer that best completes the sentence or answers the question. Then write the letter of your choice in the space to the left.*

______ **6.** The main reason for Pontiac's War was that the: **a.** Native Americans felt cheated and were afraid the British colonists wanted to take away their land. **b.** French did not want to trade with the Native Americans anymore. **c.** British soldiers attacked the Native Americans. **d.** British wanted to get back at the Native Americans for helping the French.

______ **7.** The Proclamation of 1763: **a.** made peace with the Native Americans. **b.** put a heavy tax on the colonists. **c.** was happily accepted by the colonists. **d.** made the colonists furious.

______ **8.** Which of the laws that the British passed in 1764 put taxes on imports such as sugar, molasses, coffee, and cloth? **a.** Navigation Acts. **b.** Sugar Act. **c.** Stamp Act. **d.** Quartering Act.

______ **9.** The colonists were angered by all of the new British laws, especially the Stamp Act, because: **a.** they had no representatives in the Parliament that passed the laws. **b.** the taxes made goods too expensive. **c.** they felt they should not be taxed since Americans purchases made many British companies rich. **d.** they thought the British king was trying to cheat them.

______ **10.** The meeting that the Colonies called to demand the repeal of the Sugar Act and the Stamp act was called the: **a.** Sons of Liberty. **b.** Protest Committee. **c.** Sugar Committee. **d.** Stamp Act Congress.

III. ESSAY *Choose one of the following topics. Then write your answer in paragraph form on a separate sheet of paper.*

A. Explain why Great Britain wanted the Colonists to pay more taxes.

B. Describe some of the main actions some Colonists took to protest the Stamp Act.

Name ______________________________ Date ____________________

CHAPTER 11 TEST: The Colonists Fight Back.

I. MATCHING *Decide which definition in the right column best explains a term in the left column. Then write the letter of that definition in the space next to the term.*

______	**1.** Townshend Acts	**a.** taxed goods imported from Great Britain such as cloth, paint, and glass
______	**2.** Boston Tea Party	**b.** citizens who act as soldiers in times of emergency
______	**3.** duty	**c.** a tax on imported goods
______	**4.** massacre	**d.** the cruel killing of a great number of people
______	**5.** militia	**e.** an incident in which chests of tea were smashed and thrown into the harbor

II. MULTIPLE CHOICE *Choose the answer that best completes the sentence or answers the question. Then write the letter of your choice in the space to the left.*

______ **6.** A successful form of protest that the colonists used was: **a.** hanging tax collectors from the Liberty Tree. **b.** boycotting British goods. **c.** burning customs offices. **d.** writing to King George III.

______ **7.** The group of Colonial women who organized protests against the Townshend Acts was called: **a.** the Daughters of Liberty. **b.** the Sons of Liberty. **c.** the Townshend Group. **d.** the Tea Party Dames.

______ **8.** One result of the Boston Massacre was: **a.** the British stopped collecting all taxes. **b.** most of the Townshend duties were repealed. **c.** the tax on tea was repealed. **d.** the port of Boston was closed.

______ **9.** The job of the Massachusetts Committee of Correspondence was to: **a.** write poems and plays that made fun of British officials. **b.** write letters to King George III. **c.** see that all newspapers in Boston printed anti-British news. **d.** make sure that news from Massachusetts reached the other colonies.

______ **10.** At the First Continental Congress, the colonies took all of the following actions EXCEPT: **a.** declaring the Colonies independent of Great Britain. **b.** deciding to boycott all British goods. **c.** declaring that the Colonies had the right to govern themselves. **d.** asking each Colony to set up a militia. .

III. ESSAY *Choose one of the following topics. Then write your answer in paragraph form on a separate sheet of paper.*

A. Describe what happened after the repeal of the Townshend Acts that drove the Colonies and Great Britain farther apart.

B. Describe the differences between how a Massachusetts Colonist and a member of the British Parliament would view the Boston Tea Party.

Name ______________________________ Date ____________________

CHAPTER 12 TEST The American Revolution Is Launched.

I. MATCHING *Decide which definition in the right column best explains a term in the left column. Then write the letter of that definition in the space next to the term.*

______	**1.** minutemen	**a.** a cruel ruler who takes away the rights of the people
______	**2.** Second Continental Congress	**b.** a person who represents others
______	**3.** rebellion	**c.** members of the militia who were able to fight with only a minute's warning
______	**4.** delegate	**d.** created a Continental Army with George Washington as its commander
______	**5.** tyrant	**e.** armed resistance to a government

II. MULTIPLE CHOICE *Choose the answer that best completes the sentence or answers the question. Then write the letter of your choice in the space provided.*

______ **6.** The reason that General Gage, the British governor of Massachusetts, sent troops to Concord was to: **a.** show the colonists how strong the British army was. **b.** see if the colonists would really fight. **c.** capture the weapons and supplies that the colonists had stored in Concord. **d.** capture George Washington's army.

______ **7.** After the battles at Lexington and Concord, as the British retreated to Boston: **a.** they captured many Colonial minutemen. **b.** they set fire to the entire countryside. **c.** they sang "Yankee Doodle." **d.** the minutemen shot at them from behind trees and fences.

______ **8.** The battles at Lexington and Concord were important because: **a.** most of the British army was killed or captured. **b.** thousands of colonists were killed, and the British thought this would end the rebellion. **c.** the British learned they could not defeat the colonists. **d.** they sent the message that the colonists were willing to die for their freedom.

______ **9.** The bloodiest battle of the Revolutionary War, which was won by the British, took place at: **a.** Breed's Hill. **b.** Lexington. **c.** Bunker Hill. **d.** Fort Ticonderoga.

______ **10.** The Second Continental Congress set up one committee to make a plan for a new government and the other to **a.** send another letter to King George III. **b.** write another pamphlet like *Common Sense* to encourage the Colonists to fight. **c.** decide where to send George Washington's army to fight. **d.** write a declaration of independence.

III. ESSAY *Choose one of the following topics. Then write your answer in paragraph form on a separate sheet of paper.*

A. Explain why you think the Colonists were able to win battles against the British, who had a much larger, better trained army.

B. Assume you are Thomas Paine writing the pamphlet Common Sense. Write a paragraph for the pamphlet that explains why the Colonies should declare their independence form Great Britain.

Name ______________________________ Date ____________________

CHAPTER 13 TEST: The Americans Declare Their Independence.

I. MATCHING *Decide which definition in the right column best explains a term in the left column. Then write the letter of that definition in the space next to the term.*

______	**1.** Patriots		**a.** an introduction
______	**2.** Loyalists		**b.** betraying one's country, including trying to overthrow the government
______	**3.** treason		**c.** supporters of the Declaration of Independence
______	**4.** preamble		**d.** a goal someone tries to live up to
______	**5.** ideal		**e.** people who remained loyal to Great Britain

II. MULTIPLE CHOICE *Choose the answer that best completes the sentence or answers the question. Then write the letter of your choice in the space provided.*

______ **6.** During the "great debate" at the Second Continental Congress, the delegates discussed whether to: **a.** write a letter to King George III. **b.** declare independence from Great Britain. **c.** ask the colonists to vote on the idea of independence. **d.** raise taxes on the colonists.

______ **7.** John Dickenson opposed declaring independence because he: **a.** feared the king. **b.** did not think most colonists favored independence. **c.** was afraid a war would cause great suffering and the colonies would not remain united. **d.** thought it would take too long to build a new country.

______ **8.** The delegates to the Continental Congress voted for independence: **a.** because they were sure of winning. **b.** even though they might be put to death for treason. **c.** because they expected help from other countries. **d.** because they expected to get rich after independence.

______ **9.** One part of the Declaration: **a.** blamed Parliament for what it had done to the colonies. **b.** declared that both Parliament and King George III were at fault. **c.** placed the blame on King George III. **d.** stated that the colonists should not have waited so long to declare their independence.

______ **10.** Which of the following statements is NOT true? **a.** Most African Americans supported the fight for independence. **b.** Some African Americans fought on the British side **c.** Most African Americans refused to support the war because the Declaration of Independence did not abolish slavery. **d.** Some African American minutemen fought at Lexington and Concord.

III. ESSAY *Choose one of the following topics. Then write your answer in paragraph form on a separate sheet of paper.*

A. Explain why most of the delegates to the Second Continental Congress wanted to declare independence from Great Britain.

B. Explain which ideas mentioned in the Declaration of Independence you think should still be followed today.

Name ________________________________ Date ____________________

CHAPTER 14 TEST: The Colonists Fight for Independence.

I. MATCHING *Decide which definition in the right column best explains a term in the left column. Then write the letter of that definition in the space provided next to the term.*

______	**1.** Hessians	**a.** to withdraw from or escape a battle
______	**2.** Battle of Saratoga	**b.** German soldiers hired by the British
______	**3.** Battle of Yorktown	**c.** a formal partnership between nations
______	**4.** retreat	**d.** a victory that was a turning point for the Americans
______	**5.** alliance	**e.** an American success that ended British hopes for victory

II. MULTIPLE CHOICE *Choose the answer that best completes the sentence or answers the question. Then write the letter of your choice in the space to the left.*

______ **6.** In the first British attack on Long Island in August 1776, George Washington: **a.** won the battle. **b.** had to retreat to New Jersey. **c.** was captured. **d.** held New York City.

______ **7.** On Christmas night in 1776, Washington's army surprised the Hessian troops and captured: **a.** New York City. **b.** Trenton. **c.** Boston. **d.** Saratoga.

______ **8.** The plan that British General John Burgoyne had for defeating the colonists was to: **a.** have the British navy surround all of the colonial port cities and cut off their trade. **b.** take a large army south from New York to capture George Washington. **c.** hire more Hessians and send them to fight at Princeton, New Jersey. **d.** cut off the New England Colonies from the rest of the colonies.

______ **9.** The American victory in the Battle of Saratoga was important to the Americans because: **a.** it convinced France to form an alliance with the Americans. **b.** the British had to retreat into Canada. **c.** it was the first battle that they had won. **d.** the Native Americans now joined the American side.

______ **10.** The American victory at Yorktown occurred when the French navy prevented British ships from coming to help Cornwallis and: **a.** French and American soldiers trapped the British. **b.** the Hessians revolted and helped the Americans. **c.** Loyalists fled to Canada so the British could no longer count on their help. **d.** the Americans found the secret battle plans of the British.

III. ESSAY *Choose one of the following topics. Then write your answer in paragraph form on a separate sheet of paper.*

A. Explain what advantages and problems each side had at the start of the American Revolution.

B. Explain why the American Revolution might be described as an international war.

Name ______________________________________ Date ______________________

CHAPTER 15 TEST: A New Government Is Formed.

I. MATCHING *Decide which definition in the right column best explains a term in the left column. Then write the letter of that definition in the space next to the term.*

_____	**1.** ratify	**a.** to change or revise
_____	**2.** amend	**b.** to approve
_____	**3.** republic	**c.** an agreement that gives each side part of what it wants
_____	**4.** compromise	**d.** a country where the people choose their own leaders
_____	**5.** constitution	**e.** the basic laws under which a country operates

II. MULTIPLE CHOICE *Choose the answer that best completes the sentence or answers the question. Then write the letter of your choice in the space provided.*

_____ **6.** In 1787, the United States was considered to have a weak government because: **a.** it had no Capitol building. **b.** it could not trade with foreign countries. **c.** it had no President or system of courts. **d.** it did not grant equal rights to enslaved African Americans.

_____ **7.** Under the Constitution, each state is represented in the Senate by: **a.** two senators. **b.** one senator for every 100,000 voters. **c.** four senators. **d.** the governor of the state.

_____ **8.** Supporters of the Constitution were called: **a.** Federalists. **b.** Anti-Federalists. **c.** delegates. **d.** citizens.

_____ **9.** The Bill of Rights was created to: **a.** elect a President. **b.** protect free trade. **c.** outlaw slavery. **d.** guarantee basic freedoms.

_____ **10.** The Constitution is considered to be a "living" document because: **a**. it can be changed. **b**. it is only a few hundred years old. **c**. it changes as the population grows. **d**. the descendants of the writers are still alive.

III. ESSAY *Choose one of the following topics. Then write your answer in paragraph form on a separate sheet of paper.*

A. Create an advertisement for a 1787 magazine that calls for a new, stronger government for the United States because the present government is weak.

B. You are a newspaper reporter attending the Constitutional Convention. Write an article for your paper explaining what the key compromises between the North and the South are.

Name ______________________________ Date ____________________

CHAPTER 16 TEST: The Constitution Is the Foundation of Our Government.

I. MATCHING *Decide which definition in the right column best explains a term in the left column. Then write the letter of that definition in the space provided next to the term.*

_____ **1.** legislature — **a.** the branch of government, headed by the President, that carries out the laws

_____ **2.** veto — **b.** the branch of government consisting of the Supreme Court and other federal courts

_____ **3.** executive — **c.** Congress; the branch of government that makes laws

_____ **4.** bill — **d.** the President's right to refuse to sign legislation passed by Congress

_____ **5.** judiciary — **e.** a proposed law

II. MULTIPLE CHOICE *Choose the answer that best completes the sentence or answers the question. Then write the letter of your choice in the space provided.*

_____ **6.** The job of Congress is to: **a.** build highways. **b.** make treaties with foreign governments. **c.** write laws. **d.** collect taxes.

_____ **7.** To become a law, all of the following are true EXCEPT: **a.** the President must sign it. **b.** it begins as a bill. **c.** it must be more than ten words in length. **d.** it must get a majority vote in both houses of Congress.

_____ **8.** An example of a check on the power of the President is that: **a.** the Senate must approve the people whom the President appoints to the Supreme Court. **b.** Congress must approve the President's speeches. **c.** the Supreme Court can block the President's choice of cabinet members. **d.** the House of Representatives must approve trips the President wishes to take.

_____ **9.** The first ten amendments to the Constitution are called the Bill of Rights because: **a.** they set forth how citizens are to be treated by Congress. **b.** they state what rights the people of the United States have. **c.** they state who has the right to be elected President. **d.** they explain what rights the President has.

_____ **10.** The term "due process of law" means: **a.** the government must follow the same rules for everyone. **b.** rich people can get better treatment by the courts. **c.** you can be arrested for no reason. **d.** everyone accused of a crime must have a lawyer.

III. ESSAY *Choose one of the following topics. Then write your answer in paragraph form on a separate sheet of paper.*

A. The federal judiciary is organized like a pyramid. Draw a picture showing the different layers and label each layer.

B. You are a lawyer for Oliver Brown. Write a statement you might make to the school board of Topeka arguing that their refusal to allow Brown's daughter to attend an all-white school is unconstitutional.

Name ______________________________ Date ____________________

CHAPTER 17 TEST: The New Government Begins to Work.

I. MATCHING *Decide which definition in the right column best explains a term in the left column. Then write the letter of that definition in the space provided next to the term.*

______	**1.** neutral	**a.** a tax on imported goods
______	**2.** cabinet	**b.** not taking sides in an argument
______	**3.** address	**c.** a speech
______	**4.** tariff	**d.** a group of advisers that help the President
______	**5.** precedent	**e.** an act or decision that sets an example for later actions

II. MULTIPLE CHOICE *Choose the answer that best completes the sentence or answers the question. Then write the letter of your choice in the space provided.*

______ **6.** Hamilton and Jefferson differed over: **a.** how much money to spend on the new capital. **b.** how much to tax whiskey. **c.** how much the post office should charge for letters. **d.** how much power the state and federal governments should have.

______ **7.** Thomas Jefferson and his supporters were known as: **a.** Democratic Republicans. **b.** Federalists. **c.** Republicans. **d.** Whigs.

______ **8.** When the government decided to tax whiskey, the farmers did all the following EXCEPT: **a.** refuse to pay the tax. **b.** join a huge march. **c.** attack the tax collectors. **d.** destroy the corn crops.

______ **9.** President John Adams avoided going to war with France over: **a.** the border with Canada. **b.** France's attacks on U.S. ships. **c.** France's interference in U.S. elections. **d.** France's demand for payment for its help during the American Revolution.

______ **10.** The election of 1800 was decided in the House of Representatives because: **a.** the Senate adjourned for the year. **b.** the Federalists had the majority there. **c.** Jefferson and Burr had the same number of votes. **d.** there were more than two candidates for President.

III. ESSAY *Choose one of the following topics. Then write your answer in paragraph form on a separate sheet of paper.*

A. George Washington is often called "the Father of Our Country." From what you have read about him in this chapter, explain why he deserves this name.

B. Why does the passage of the 12th Amendment support the idea that the Constitution is a "living" constitution?

Name ______________________________ Date ____________________

CHAPTER 18 TEST: Jefferson Strengthens the Nation.

I. MATCHING *Decide which definition in the right column best explains a term in the left column. Then write the letter of that definition in the space next to the term.*

	Term	Definition
______	**1.** embargo	**a.** a law
______	**2.** territory	**b.** a government order preventing trade
______	**3.** impressment	**c.** an area that was not yet a state
______	**4.** ordinance	**d.** forced service, especially in a navy or other armed force
______	**5.** diary	**e.** a daily record of notes and information

II. MULTIPLE CHOICE *Choose the answer that best completes the sentence or answers the question. Then write the letter of your choice in the space provided.*

______ **6.** One of the rules that the Northwest Ordinance set up: **a.** outlawed slavery. **b.** taxed whiskey. **c.** gave land to the Native Americans. **d.** allowed the navy to build ships.

______ **7.** Tecumseh had a plan to: **a.** build more towns for the Indians. **b.** visit New Orleans. **c.** push back the white settlers. **d.** cut down trees to build farms.

______ **8.** New Orleans was important to the United States because: **a.** it was a link to markets in the East and Europe. **b.** its people spoke French. **c.** it was part of the Northwest Territories. **d.** its large bay opened on the Pacific Ocean.

______ **9.** One purpose of Lewis and Clark's expedition was to: **a.** trade with the Native Americans. **b.** find a route through the Rockies to the Pacific Ocean. **c.** buy lumber to build naval ships. **d.** sign a treaty with the Shoshones.

______ **10.** All of the following are true of the War of 1812, EXCEPT: **a.** as a result of the war the United States received much new land. **b.** it proved that the United States could defend itself. **c.** it did not change relations between Britain and the United States. **d.** the United States made no new treaties with Britain.

III. ESSAY *Choose one of the following topics. Then write your answer in paragraph form on a separate sheet of paper.*

A. Explain what you think might have happened to the Louisiana Territory if President Jefferson had decided he did not have the constitutional right to buy it.

B. Describe the help that Lewis and Clark received on their expedition from people who were not white.

Name ______________________________ Date ____________________

CHAPTER 19 TEST: The North And South Take Different Paths.

I. MATCHING *Decide which definition in the right column best explains a term in the left column. Then write the letter of that definition in the space next to the term.*

	Term	Definition
______	**1.** spiritual	**a.** factory where cloth is made
______	**2.** boardinghouse	**b.** the person who watches over slaves' work
______	**3.** textile mill	**c.** a machine that removes seeds from cotton
______	**4.** overseer	**d.** a house where room and meals can be purchased
______	**5.** cotton gin	**e.** a religious song written and sung by enslaved African Americans

II. MULTIPLE CHOICE *Choose the answer that best completes the sentence or answers the question. Then write the letter of your choice in the space provided.*

______ **6.** Some of the changes that the Industrial Revolution brought about included: **a.** new machines to make goods faster. **b.** freedom for enslaved African Americans. **c.** high wages for workers. **d.** clean and pleasant factories for the workers.

______ **7.** This man was responsible for building the first U.S. cotton mill: **a.** Eli Whitney **b.** Samuel Slater **c.** Solomon Northup **d.** Francis Cabot Lowell

______ **8.** The South became a slave society because: **a.** more slaves were needed to grow much cotton. **b.** the North would not use slaves. **c.** slaves were needed to run the factories. **d.** slaves were needed to fight in the Industrial Revolution.

______ **9.** What did Eli Whitney invent that helped to make cotton "king " in the South? **a.** a machine that harvested cotton **b.** a machine that took cotton bales to market **c.** a machine that removed the seeds from the cotton **d.** a machine that planted cotton seeds.

______ **10.** Enslaved African Americans kept their culture alive by doing all of the following EXCEPT: **a.** developing spirituals. **b.** caring for one another's children. **c.** developing a feeling of closeness among themselves. **d.** buying farmland.

III. ESSAY *Choose one of the following topics. Then write your answer in paragraph form on a separate sheet of paper.*

A. Pretend that you own a boardinghouse in Lowell, Massachusetts. Make a poster advertising this place that gives the reasons women should come to your boardinghouse.

B. Imagine you are an African American slave on a cotton plantation in the South. One of your fellow slaves is planning an uprising against the owner of the plantation. Give reasons why you might want or not want to join in his plan.

Name ______________________________ Date ____________________

CHAPTER 20 TEST: Americans Move West.

I. MATCHING *Decide which definition in the right column best explains a term in the left column. Then write the letter of that definition in the space next to the term.*

	Term	Definition
_____	**1.** frontier	**a.** a waterway dug by people to connect two bodies of water
_____	**2.** wagon train	**b.** the edge of a country next to another country or region
_____	**3.** canal	**c.** land put aside for Native Americans west of the Mississippi River
_____	**4.** Indian Territory	**d.** a group of wagons that traveled to the Western frontier
_____	**5.** Oregon Country	**e.** land that became part of the United States in 1846

II. MULTIPLE CHOICE *Choose the answer that best completes the sentence or answers the question. Then write the letter of your choice in the space provided.*

_____ **6.** One of the most efficient ways of moving goods in the 1800s was: **a.** by stage-coach. **b.** by ship. **c.** by train. **d.** by canal.

_____ **7.** The benefits of the Erie Canal included all of the following EXCEPT: **a.** people and goods moved quickly over it. **b.** it was the cheapest way of transporting goods. **c.** large cities grew near the canals. **d.** it connected the Great Lakes with the Mississippi River.

_____ **8.** Before a frontier family could really live on the new land, they had to do all of the following EXCEPT: **a.** clear the land. **b.** build a shelter. **c.** raise crops. **d.** learn the Cherokee language.

_____ **9.** One reason the Cherokee were different from most other Native Americans is that they: **a.** could not ride horses. **b.** spoke English. **c.** built factories. **d.** set up a separate government.

_____ **10.** Many Cherokee hoped that the U.S. government would stop taking their land if they: **a.** learned to write a language. **b.** fought the British in the War of 1812. **c.** showed white settlers where gold could be found. **d.** learned the customs of the white man.

III. ESSAY *Choose one of the following topics. Then write your answer in paragraph form on a separate sheet of paper.*

A. You are a young Cherokee on the Trail of Tears. Write diary entries for several days that describe some of the things that happened to you and your family on the trail.

B. Explain why so many thousands of people left their homes in the East and traveled to the West in the years 1820 to 1860.

Name ______________________________ Date ______________________

CHAPTER 21 TEST: Cultures Clash in the Southwest.

I. MATCHING *Decide which definition in the right column best explains a term in the left column. Then write the letter of that definition in the space next to the term.*

	Term	Definition
_____	**1.** irrigation	**a.** to add onto a nation
_____	**2.** annex	**b.** treating people unfairly because they are of different cultural background, religion, or gender
_____	**3.** cadet	**c.** a system of bringing water to crops through ditches
_____	**4.** prejudice	**d.** a soldier in training
_____	**5.** discrimination	**e.** dislike of people who are different

II. MULTIPLE CHOICE *Choose the answer that best completes the sentence or answers the question. Then write the letter of your choice in the space provided.*

_____ **6.** Which of the following were NOT required of Americans if they wanted to stay in Texas? **a.** obey Mexican laws **b.** convert to Catholicism **c.** learn to speak Spanish **d.** become Mexican citizens

_____ **7.** Stephen Austin is important in U.S. history because he: **a.** fought against Santa Anna. **b.** signed the Treaty of Guadalupe Hidalgo. **c.** was the first American to start a sheep ranch in Texas. **d.** led the first group of U.S. settlers to Texas.

_____ **8.** Which of the following was NOT included in the Treaty of Guadalupe Hidalgo? **a.** All Mexicans who lived in the new U.S. territory had to move back to Mexico. **b.** The United States got almost half of Mexico's land. **c.** Mexico recognized that Texas was part of the United States. **d.** The Rio Grande became the southern border of Texas.

_____ **9.** One way in which gold seekers from the East prevented competition in the gold fields was through: **a.** the Foreign Miners' Tax of 1850. **b.** the Land Act of 1851. **c.** cutting off all immigration to California. **d.** organizing an army of Easterners.

_____ **10.** Which of the following had more rights in California than elsewhere in the United States? **a.** *tejanos* **b.** Chinese **c.** women **d.** African Americans

III. ESSAY *Choose one of the following topics. Then write your answer in paragraph form on a separate sheet of paper.*

A. Explain how the discovery of gold changed California.

B. Many people in the United States opposed the war with Mexico. If you had been living in the United States at that time, what reasons would you have given for opposing the war?

Name ______________________________ Date ____________________

CHAPTER 22 TEST: Immigrants Flock to the United States.

I. MATCHING *Decide which definition in the right column best explains a term in the left column. Then write the letter of that definition in the space next to the term.*

_____ **1.** immigrant — **a.** a poor area of a city

_____ **2.** famine — **b.** a traveling salesperson

_____ **3.** slum — **c.** someone who leaves his or her homeland to settle in a new country

_____ **4.** peddler — **d.** Chinese family and town groups who ran clubhouses for meetings and parties

_____ **5.** fong — **e.** a time when there is not enough food for people

II. MULTIPLE CHOICE *Choose the answer that best completes the sentence or answers the question. Then write the letter of your choice in the space provided.*

_____ **6.** The Great Famine in Ireland was caused by a disease that destroyed: **a.** cattle. **b.** corn. **c.** potatoes. **d.** wheat.

_____ **7.** From the 1840s to the 1860s, millions of immigrants arrived from all these countries EXCEPT: **a.** China. **b.** Germany. **c.** Ireland. **d.** Italy.

_____ **8.** Most Chinese immigrants to the United States in the 1840s and 1850s settled in California to: **a.** search for gold. **b.** found new cities. **c.** set up factories. **d.** seek religious freedom.

_____ **9.** The largest Chinese community in the United States was in: **a.** Los Angeles. **b.** New York. **c.** San Francisco. **d.** St. Louis.

_____ **10.** The new political party in the 1850s that opposed immigrant groups was the: **a.** Democratic party. **b.** Know-Nothing party. **c.** Whig party. **d.** Anti-Immigration party.

III. ESSAY *Choose one of the following topics. Then write your answer in paragraph form on a separate sheet of paper.*

A. Irish immigrant families who settled in the United States became important in the nation's fast-growing economy. Describe the kinds of jobs that many of them worked at and explain how they contributed to the growth of the United States.

B. Imagine that you are an immigrant who came to this country between 1840 and 1860. Write a letter to your family back in the old country describing the kinds of discrimination that you met in the course of a day.

Name ______________________________ Date ____________________

CHAPTER 23 TEST: Women Fight for Reform.

I. MATCHING *Decide which definition in the right column best explains a term in the left column. Then write the letter of that definition in the space next to the term.*

______	**1.** feminist	**a.** the right to vote
______	**2.** suffrage	**b.** a meeting held in 1848 that launched the movement for women's rights
______	**3.** reform	**c.** a supporter of the women's rights movement
______	**4.** women's rights movement	**d.** the attempt to improve society and people's lives
______	**5.** Seneca Falls Convention	**e.** the struggle to improve women's roles in society

II. MULTIPLE CHOICE *Choose the answer that best completes the sentence or answers the question. Then write the letter of your choice in the space provided.*

______ **6.** The Seneca Falls Declaration of Sentiments was modeled on: **a.** the abolitionist movement. **b.** the U.S. Constitution. **c.** the Iroquois League. **d.** the Declaration of Independence.

______ **7.** The former slave who worked to free slaves and gain rights for all women was: **a.** Elizabeth Cady Stanton. **b.** Sojourner Truth. **c.** Harriet Beecher Stowe. **d.** Maria Mitchell.

______ **8.** The leading reformer who helped improve conditions for the mentally ill and prisoners was: **a.** Sojourner Truth. **b.** Dorothea Dix. **c.** Horace Mann. **d.** Catherine Beecher.

______ **9.** Emma Hart Willard, Horace Mann, Lucy Stone, and Mary Lyon were some of the leading reformers in: **a.** education. **b.** women's suffrage. **c.** the temperance movement. **d.** medicine.

______ **10.** Louisa May Alcott and Harriet Beecher Stowe became famous as: **a.** reformers. **b.** doctors. **c.** temperance leaders. **d.** writers.

III. ESSAY *Choose one of the following topics. Then write your answer in paragraph form on a separate sheet of paper.*

A. Describe the most important gains made by the women's rights movement between 1820 and 1860.

B. If you were an educated woman living in 1860 and applying for entrance to a medical school, explain what your chances of being accepted might be. Explain your answer.

Name ______________________________ Date ____________________

CHAPTER 24 TEST: The Fight Against Slavery Gains Ground.

I. MATCHING *Decide which definition in the right column best explains a term in the left column. Then write the letter of that definition in the space next to the term.*

	Term	Definition
_____	**1.** *The Liberator*	**a.** the campaign to end slavery
_____	**2.** Underground Railroad	**b.** aggressive
_____	**3.** fugitive slave laws	**c.** an influential newspaper that called for the end of slavery
_____	**4.** abolitionist movement	**d.** laws that punished people who helped slaves run away
_____	**5.** militant	**e.** a network of people who helped slaves escape from the South

II. MULTIPLE CHOICE *Choose the answer that best completes the sentence or answers the question. Then write the letter of your choice in the space provided.*

_____ **6.** The Virginia slave who led a revolt against white slave owners was: **a.** William Lloyd Garrison. **b.** William Forten. **c.** Nat Turner. **d.** Frederick Douglass.

_____ **7.** The Compromise of 1850 did much to: **a.** make it easier for slaves to escape from the South. **b.** drive the North and the South farther apart. **c.** make Kansas a battleground over slavery. **d.** make John Brown a hero

_____ **8.** All of the following opposed the abolitionist movement EXCEPT: **a.** Northern business owners with ties to the South. **b.** slave owners. **c.** Northern workers, who feared slaves would take their jobs. **d.** African American churches.

_____ **9.** Frederick Douglass was: **a.** the best-known militant African American abolitionist. **b.** the head of the African Methodist Episcopal Church. **c.** a leader of Nat Turner's revolt. **d.** the leader of the moderate abolitionists.

_____ **10.** Among the most active supporters of the Underground Railroad were all of the following EXCEPT: **a.** African American churches. **b.** free African Americans in the North. **c.** white Southern owners of small farms. **d.** feminists.

III. ESSAY *Choose one of the following topics. Then write your answer in paragraph form on a separate sheet of paper.*

A. How do you think most Northerners regarded the abolitionists? Explain your answer.

B. If you were a fugitive slave escaping to the North on the Underground Railroad, what dangers would you face?

Name ______________________________ Date ____________________

CHAPTER 25 TEST: Slavery Divides the Nation.

I. MATCHING *Decide which definition in the right column best explains a term in the left column. Then write the letter of that definition in the space next to the term.*

	Term	Definition
______	**1.** Missouri Compromise	**a.** people who wanted to ban slavery in all new territories
______	**2.** Free Soilers	**b.** someone who runs away
______	**3.** Bleeding Kansas	**c.** the struggle between slave owners and those opposed to slavery who settled in Kansas
______	**4.** fugitive	**d.** a storage place for weapons
______	**5.** arsenal	**e.** agreement that provided that slavery was forbidden in the Louisiana Purchase north of Missouri's southern border

II. MULTIPLE CHOICE *Choose the answer that best completes the sentence or answers the question. Then write the letter of your choice in the space provided.*

______ **6.** The conflict over slavery grew because: **a.** free soilers settled all the territory west of the Mississippi. **b.** both Northern farmers and Southern planters moved into the western territory. **c.** the slave states began to outnumber the free states. **d.** the North and South refused to compromise.

______ **7.** What took place from 1846 to 1848 that caused the slavery issue to grow more serious? **a.** the Missouri Compromise **b.** the Dred Scott decision **c.** the Kansas-Nebraska Act **d.** the war with Mexico

______ **8.** Those who favored popular sovereignty believed: **a.** the people in the territories should decide the issue of slavery there. **b.** the territories should ban slavery. **c.** the territories should allow slavery. **d.** slaves in the territories should be freed within twenty years.

______ **9.** The Dred Scott decision was: **a.** a setback for the South. **b.** a victory for the abolitionists. **c.** a fair compromise by the Supreme Court. **d.** a defeat for the abolitionists.

______ **10.** The event that shocked the nation in 1859 and dramatized the growing struggle over slavery was: **a.** the trial of Anthony Burns. **b.** the fighting in Kansas. **c.** the arrest of Dred Scott. **d.** John Brown's raid.

III. ESSAY *Choose one of the following topics. Then write your answer in paragraph form on a separate sheet of paper.*

A. Explain how the war with Mexico, even though it did not directly affect slavery, increased the conflict over slavery.

B. In 1850, Senator Stephen Douglas of Illinois urged Americans to stop the debate over slavery. Do you think his advice was wise? Why did most people not accept it? Explain your answer.

Name ______________________________ Date ____________________

CHAPTER 26 TEST: The Civil War Begins.

I. MATCHING *Decide which definition in the right column best explains a term in the left column. Then write the letter of that definition in the space next to the term.*

_____	**1.** Civil War	**a.** the idea that states have the power to act without interference from the federal government
_____	**2.** states' rights	**b.** to withdraw from the Union
_____	**3.** Confederacy	**c.** the nation formed by the Southern states that left the Union
_____	**4.** secede	**d.** the armed conflict between the North and the South
_____	**5.** blockade	**e.** to shut off all trade to a nation's ports

II. MULTIPLE CHOICE *Choose the answer that best completes the sentence or answers the question. Then write the letter of your choice in the space provided.*

_____ **6.** The Confederacy named Jefferson Davis to be: **a.** head of its armed forces. **b.** ambassador to Great Britain. **c.** head of its supreme court. **d.** its president.

_____ **7.** Which one of the following was NOT true of the North? **a.** It had a larger population than the South. **b.** It had most of the nation's factories. **c.** It had most of the nation's railroads and ships. **d.** It had most of the best army officers.

_____ **8.** The Civil War began when: **a.** the Confederates fired on Washington, D.C. **b.** Union forces attacked Richmond, Virginia. **c.** the Confederates attacked Fort Sumter. **d.** President Lincoln ordered a blockade of the South.

_____ **9.** What do Clara Barton, Sara Edmonds, Harriet Tubman, Loreta Velázquez, and Phoebe Yates Pember have in common? **a.** They all aided the North during the Civil War. **b.** In various ways, they were all important to the war effort. **c.** They all took care of the wounded in hospitals. **d.** They all fought in the war, either on the side of the North or the South.

_____ **10.** To win the war by capturing the enemy's capital city, blockading its key ports, and taking control of the Mississippi was: **a.** the plan of the South. **b.** the advice the British gave to the Confederacy. **c.** the plan of the North. **d.** a war plan vetoed by Lincoln.

III. ESSAY *Choose one of the following topics. Then write your answer in paragraph form on a separate sheet of paper.*

A. Explain why Lincoln's election as President led to the Civil War.

B. If you were a New Yorker who was subject to the draft, how would you have felt about being forced to serve in the Union army? Explain your answer.

Name ______________________________________ Date ______________________

CHAPTER 27 TEST: The Union Is Saved.

I. MATCHING *Decide which definition in the right column best explains a term in the left column. Then write the letter of that definition in the space next to the term.*

	Term	Definition
______	**1.** border states	**a.** war in which an army destroys everything the enemy could use to fight with
______	**2.** Emancipation Proclamation	**b.** a speech made by President Lincoln in 1863
______	**3.** total war	**c.** four slave states that remained in the Union
______	**4.** assassination	**d.** presidential order freeing the slaves in areas held by the Confederacy
______	**5.** Gettysburg Address	**e.** the murder of a public person

II. MULTIPLE CHOICE *Choose the answer that best completes the sentence or answers the question. Then write the letter of your choice in the space provided.*

______ **6.** The Emancipation Proclamation: **a.** ended slavery in the border states. **b.** ended slavery in areas held by the Confederacy. **c.** caused the border states to join the Confederacy. **d.** ended slavery in the North.

______ **7.** The Union general who defeated Confederate forces in the West was: **a.** William Tecumseh Sherman. **b.** Robert E. Lee. **c.** George Meade. **d.** Ulysses S. Grant.

______ **8.** The war began to shift in favor of the Union in 1863 as a result of its victories at all of the following EXCEPT: **a.** Gettysburg. **b.**Vicksburg. **c.** Richmond. **d.** Chattanooga.

______ **9.** General Sherman's march through Georgia was an example of: **a.** a strategic retreat. **b.** total war. **c.** guerrilla war. **d.** unconditional surrender.

______ **10.** After the Civil War ended, the South: **a.** quickly began to rebuild. **b.** tried to restore slavery. **c.** was a land in ruins. **d.** tried to restore the Confederacy.

III. ESSAY *Choose one of the following topics. Then write your answer in paragraph form on a separate sheet of paper.*

A. Explain why the Civil War was such an important event in the history of the United States.

B. Assume you are a Union soldier who is still in the army. Write a letter to your parents back home in which you explain how you felt when you heard President Lincoln had been assassinated.

Name ______________________________ Date ____________________

CHAPTER 28 TEST: The Nation Rebuilds.

I. MATCHING *Decide which definition in the right column best explains a term in the left column. Then write the letter of that definition in the space next to the term.*

_____ **1.** Reconstruction — **a.** laws passed by Southern states that took away many of the newly freed African Americans

_____ **2.** freedmen — **b.** the period after the Civil War when the nation was to be restored

_____ **3.** Black Codes — **c.** farmer who pays part of his or her crop as rent to a landowner

_____ **4.** carpetbagger — **d.** enslaved African Americans who were set free as a result of the Civil War

_____ **5.** sharecropper — **e.** Northerner who went to the South after the Civil War

II. MULTIPLE CHOICE *Choose the answer that best completes the sentence or answers the question. Then write the letter of your choice in the space provided.*

_____ **6.** African American churches in the South helped freedmen rebuild their lives by: **a.** providing farming jobs. **b.** planning political campaigns. **c.** opening schools. **d.** setting up the Freedmen's Bureau.

_____ **7.** White Southerners tried to limit the freedom of African Americans by: **a.** passing Black Codes. **b.** passing laws that taxed carpetbaggers. **c.** imposing special taxes on former slaves. **d.** preventing them from attending school.

_____ **8.** Reconstruction ended when: **a.** the 13th Amendment was passed. **b.** when all Federal troops left the South. **c.** President Andrew Johnson was impeached. **d.** all the Southern states returned to the Union.

_____ **9.** Most African American families in the South were forced to make their living by: **a.** farming as sharecroppers. **b.** working on farms for wages. **c.** farming with poor whites. **d.** working at low-paying factory jobs.

_____ **10.** The 15th Amendment provided that African Americans: **a**. could not be enslaved. **b.** had the right to hold public office. **c.** born in the United States were citizens. **d.** could not be prevented from voting by any state.

III. ESSAY *Choose one of the following topics. Then write your answer in paragraph form on a separate sheet of paper.*

A. How did the U.S. government aid African Americans during and after the Civil War?

B. Keeping in mind what happened in the South during the years 1865 to 1876, would you say that Reconstruction was a success, a failure, or something in between? Explain your answer.

Name ______________________________ Date ____________________

CHAPTER 29 TEST: African Americans Face a Hostile World.

I. MATCHING *Decide which definition in the right column best explains a term in the left column. Then write the letter of that definition in the space next to the term.*

______	**1.** Jim Crow	**a.** to refuse to buy goods or services as part of a protest
______	**2.** segregate	**b.** the rights given to all U.S. citizens by the Constitution
______	**3.** *Plessy* v. *Ferguson*	**c.** laws in Southern states that kept African Americans and whites separate
______	**4.** civil rights	**d.** a Supreme Court decision that held the separation of African Americans and whites was legal
______	**5.** boycott	**e.** to separate by race

II. MULTIPLE CHOICE *Choose the answer that best completes the sentence or answers the question. Then write the letter of your choice in the space provided.*

______ **6.** Under the Jim Crow laws, African Americans were required to do all of the following EXCEPT: **a.** sit in separate sections of theaters. **b.** sit in separate railway cars. **c.** not attend school. **d.** drink from separate water fountains.

______ **7.** The Ku Klux Klan was an organization of white people that: **a.** ran schools for African Americans. **b.** kept African Americans from moving to the North. **c.** used terror, lynching, and violence against African Americans. **d.** tried to send African Americans to Africa.

______ **8.** In 1896, the body in the U.S. government that ruled that segregation was legal was the: **a.** Senate. **b.** House of Representatives. **c.** Department of State. **d.** Supreme Court.

______ **9.** One of the most courageous African American leaders in the fight against lynching was: **a.** Booker T. Washington. **b.** Sarah Breedlove. **c.** Madame C.J. Walker. **d.** Ida B. Wells.

______ **10.** By 1900, successful African American business owners were beginning to form: **a.** a black middle class. **b.** large national corporations. **c.** a new political party. **d.** new universities for African Americans only.

III. ESSAY *Choose one of the following topics. Then write your answer in paragraph form on a separate sheet of paper.*

A. Describe how African Americans fought against segregation and the denial of their civil rights in the years after the Civil War and Reconstruction?

B. Which leader, Booker T. Washington or W. E. B. DuBois, do you think did the most to help African Americans? Explain your answer.

Name ______________________________ Date ____________________

CHAPTER 30 TEST: Americans Settle on the Great Plains.

I. MATCHING *Decide which definition in the right column best explains a term in the left column. Then write the letter of that definition in the space next to the term.*

	Term	Definition
______	**1.** transcontinental	**a.** African Americans who settled on the Great Plains
______	**2.** Homestead Act	**b.** land set aside for Native Americans
______	**3.** Exodusters	**c.** something that crosses the continent
______	**4.** sod	**d.** law that gave 160 acres of land free to anyone who would farm it for five years
______	**5.** reservation	**e.** top layer of earth made tough by grass roots

II. MULTIPLE CHOICE *Choose the answer that best completes the sentence or answers the question. Then write the letter of your choice in the space provided.*

______ **6.** As a result of the Homestead Act of 1862: **a.** thousands of settlers flocked to the Great Plains. **b.** Native Americans were pushed from their homelands. **c.** the Great Plains became a land of farms and cattle ranches. **d.** All of the above are true.

______ **7.** All of these things about the Great Plains are true EXCEPT: **a.** rainfall was plentiful there. **b.** the soil was very rich. **c.** rain was scarce there. **d.** steel plows were used in farming.

______ **8.** The farmers and ranchers on the Great Plains became rivals because of the different way in which they used: **a.** the land. **b.** railroads. **c.** the reservations. **d.** sod houses.

______ **9.** In 1866, the Lakota people's fight to protect their land against the U.S. government was led by: **a.** Sitting Bull. **b.** Red Cloud. **c.** Crazy Horse. **d.** Osceola.

______ **10.** By the 1880s, most Native Americans on the Great Plains were: **a.** prosperous farmers. **b.** ranchers. **c.** living on reservations. **d.** aided by the Dawes Act.

III. ESSAY *Choose one of the following topics. Then write your answer in paragraph form on a separate sheet of paper.*

A. Explain why the settlers came into conflict with the Native Americans who were living on the Great Plains.

B. Imagine that you and your family are new farmers on the Great Plains in the 1880s. Write a letter to a friend back East that tells some interesting things about your new life.

Name ______________________________ Date ____________________

CHAPTER 31 TEST: The United States Becomes an Industrial Nation.

I. MATCHING *Decide which definition in the right column best explains a term in the left column. Then write the letter of that definition in the space next to the term.*

	Term	Definition
______	**1.** mass production	**a.** a company that raises money by selling shares in the business
______	**2.** corporation	**b.** refusal of workers to work until their demands are met
______	**3.** monopoly	**c.** a way of making large amounts of a product quickly and cheaply
______	**4.** national union	**d.** a company that has almost complete control over the production and market of a good or service
______	**5.** strike	**e.** a nationwide organization of workers

II. MULTIPLE CHOICE *Choose the answer that best completes the sentence or answers the question. Then write the letter of your choice in the space provided.*

______ **6.** Thomas Edison invented all of the following things EXCEPT: **a.** the electric light. **b.** the phonograph. **c.** the telephone. **d.** the storage battery.

______ **7.** The greatest change in the way workers now did their jobs was the result of: **a.** mass production. **b.** the AFL. **c.** new sources of power. **d.** monopolies.

______ **8.** The need for large amounts of money to buy costly machines and large factories and to hire many workers caused big business to form: **a.** unions. **b.** corporations. **c.** the Knights of Labor. **d.** non-profit companies.

______ **9.** The Haymarket Square incident was an example of: **a.** violence for which a union was blamed. **b.** a demonstration by farmers. **c.** a rally of voters in Chicago. **d.** a protest by Civil War veterans.

______ **10.** Which is true of most labor unions in the late 1800s? **a.** They did not accept women as members. **b.** They had only about ten percent of the workforce. **c.** They did not accept minorities as members. **d.** all of the above

III. ESSAY *Choose one of the following topics. Then write your answer in paragraph form on a separate sheet of paper.*

A. A government official in the late 1800s declared that "America has become known as the home of invention." Explain what that statement meant.

B. If you had been a worker in a factory in 1890, would you have joined a union? Explain why or why not.

Name ______________________________ Date ____________________

CHAPTER 32 TEST: Immigrants Help Build the United States.

I. MATCHING *Decide which definition in the right column best explains a term in the left column. Then write the letter of that definition in the space next to the term.*

	Term	Definition
_____	**1.** new immigrants	**a.** to adopt the customs of a culture or country
_____	**2.** tenement	**b.** people who came to the United States from Eastern and Southern Europe after 1885
_____	**3.** assimilate	**c.** a generalization or idea about a group that is not necessarily true
_____	**4.** Chinese exclusion acts	**d.** a slum apartment building with many small apartments
_____	**5.** stereotype	**e.** laws prohibiting Chinese people from coming to the United States

II. MULTIPLE CHOICE *Choose the answer that best completes the sentence or answers the question. Then write the letter of your choice in the space provided.*

_____ **6.** Most of the new immigrants to the United States after 1885 came from all these countries EXCEPT: **a.** Italy. **b.** Greece. **c.** Poland and Russia. **d.** England.

_____ **7.** Many Jews fled to the United States in the 1880s as a result of: **a.** famine. **b.** wars. **c.** pogroms. **d.** crop failures.

_____ **8.** Most of the immigrants on the West Coast came from: **a.** China and Russia. **b.** Italy and Japan. **c.** Japan and Korea. **d.** China and Japan.

_____ **9.** All of these facts about Chinese immigrants to the United States in the second half of the 1800s are true EXCEPT: **a.** most became wealthy mining gold. **b.** most were men. **c.** most worked as low-paid laborers and factory workers. **d.** they were not allowed to become citizens.

_____ **10.** Most Latino immigrants planned to: **a.** remain in the United States permanently. **b.** open shops in the big cities of the United States. **c.** return to their native countries. **d.** join labor unions.

III. ESSAY *Choose one of the following topics. Then write your answer in paragraph form on a separate sheet of paper.*

A. Describe how Eastern and Southern European immigrants were similar to those from Latino countries and how they were different.

B. Describe what life was like in a European immigrant neighborhood in a big U.S. city.

Name ______________________________ Date ____________________

CHAPTER 33 TEST: The United States Becomes a Nation of Cities.

I. **MATCHING** *Decide which definition in the right column best explains a term in the left column. Then write the letter of that definition in the space next to the term.*

	Term	Definition
______	**1.** heavy industry	**a.** a rapidly spreading outbreak of a disease
______	**2.** skyscraper	**b.** the manufacture of large items like trains and farm machines
______	**3.** settlement house	**c.** a new tall building made possible by the invention of safe elevators
______	**4.** epidemic	**d.** dishonest use of a government office for personal profit
______	**5.** graft	**e.** a center that served the needs of people of a poor neighborhood

II. **MULTIPLE CHOICE** *Choose the answer that best completes the sentence or answers the question. Then write the letter of your choice in the space provided.*

______ **6.** The main reason for the rapid growth of American cities was: **a.** the growth of farming. **b.** the growth of industry. **c.** the growth of railroads. **d.** the invention of skyscrapers.

______ **7.** Which one of these was NOT a cause of epidemics in big cities? **a.** impure drinking water **b.** uncollected garbage **c.** sewage disposal systems **d.** people living in overcrowded tenements

______ **8.** Even though dishonest politicians like "Boss" Tweed of New York stole public money, many of them also: **a.** helped city immigrant families. **a.** took graft. **b.** built skyscrapers. **c.** helped farmers. **d.** started new industries.

______ **9.** Hull House in Chicago was a settlement house that was started by: **a.** Jacob Riis. **b.** Malvina Maggia. **c.** Jane Addams. **d.** John Fitzgerald.

______ **10.** Immigrants improved their living conditions in the cities in all these ways EXCEPT by: **a.** moving into tenements. **b.** establishing social groups. **c.** opening church-run schools. **d.** starting special newspapers for their group.

III. **ESSAY** *Choose one of the following topics. Then write your answer in paragraph form on a separate sheet of paper.*

A. Explain what new kinds of transportation developed in U.S. cities during the late 1800s and how they affected people's lives?

B. The story of Alfredo and Malvina Maggia was typical of many immigrants in the late 1800s. Explain why this was true.

Name ______________________________ Date ____________________

CHAPTER 34 TEST: Women Gain New Opportunities.

I. MATCHING *Decide which definition in the right column best explains a term in the left column. Then write the letter of that definition in the space next to the term.*

_____	**1.** suffragette	**a.** women who fought for the right to vote
_____	**2.** service jobs	**b.** someone who works as a maid, a cook, or a laundry worker in someone's home
_____	**3.** domestic	**c.** jobs in which workers served or helped others
_____	**4.** suffrage	**d.** the right to vote
_____	**5.** office jobs	**e.** jobs in which women worked as typists and answered phones

II. MULTIPLE CHOICE *Choose the answer that best completes the sentence or answers the question. Then write the letter of your choice in the space provided.*

_____ **6.** Women first were given the right to vote by: **a.** Congress. **b.** Wyoming. **c.** New York. **d.** California.

_____ **7.** Elizabeth Blackwell was the first woman in the United States to become: **a.** a member of Congress. **b.** a lawyer. **c.** a labor leader. **d.** a doctor.

_____ **8.** Which one of the following was NOT true of women teachers in the late 1800s? **a.** They were not allowed to smoke. **b.** They seldom became principals or superintendents. **c.** They greatly outnumbered men teachers. **d.** They were paid the same wages as men teachers.

_____ **9.** Mary Seymour, who founded the first business school for women, was one of a group of women who: **a.** started their own businesses. **b.** hired only suffragettes. **c.** opened businesses in the new Western states. **d.** founded unions for women.

_____ **10.** The National Association of Colored Women was an organization of **a.** office workers. **b.** club members. **c.** teachers. **d.** domestics.

III. ESSAY *Choose one of the following topics. Then write your answer in paragraph form on a separate sheet of paper.*

A. In the late 1800s, men believed that a woman's place was in the home. Explain how they limited opportunities for women?

B. Describe the jobs held as office workers, and explain why women were hired for these jobs?

Name ______________________________ Date ____________________

CHAPTER 35 TEST: The United States Becomes a World Power.

I. MATCHING *Decide which definition in the right column best explains a term in the left column. Then write the letter of that definition in the space next to the term.*

	Term	Definition
______	**1.** imperialism	**a.** an area within a country that is controlled by another country
______	**2.** sphere of influence	**b.** attacks on foreigners by a Chinese secret society
______	**3.** Open Door policy	**c.** the policy of building an empire by acquiring colonies
______	**4.** Platt Amendment	**d.** U.S. plan to make sure that no country has an unfair advantage on trade in China
______	**5.** Boxer Rebellion	**e.** part of the Cuban constitution giving the U.S. the right to intervene in Cuba's affairs

II. MULTIPLE CHOICE *Choose the answer that best completes the sentence or answers the question. Then write the letter of your choice in the space provided.*

______ **6.** The United States gained control of the Philippines after: **a.** the Boxer Rebellion. **b.** the Open Door policy. **c.** the war with Spain in 1898. **d.** the overthrow of Queen Liliuokalani.

______ **7.** After Japan's victory over China in 1895 and 1896, several European nations: **a.** declared war on China. **b.** began to control parts of China. **c.** asked the United States to stay out of China. **d.** declared war on Japan.

______ **8.** The aim of the Chinese Boxers was to: **a.** force foreigners to leave China. **b.** protect China against Japan's invasion. **c.** invite the United States to protect China. **d.** overthrow China's weak ruler.

______ **9.** In 1895, an uprising against Spanish rule led by Jose Martí took place in: **a.** the Philippines. **b.** Puerto Rico. **c.** Central America. **d.** Cuba.

______ **10.** The event that led to the Cuban-Spanish-American War was: **a.** Dewey's victory in Manila Bay. **b.** the sinking of the battleship *Maine*. **c.** the U.S. occupation of Puerto Rico. **d.** Spain's refusal to agree to U.S. demands.

III. ESSAY *Choose one of the following topics. Then write your answer in paragraph form on a separate sheet of paper.*

A. Explain why the United States had such a great interest in ridding Cuba of Spanish control.

B. If you had been a Hawaiian in the 1890s, would you have supported Queen Liliuokalani? Explain your answer.

Name ______________________________ Date ____________________

CHAPTER 36 TEST: The American People Face the 20th Century.

I. MATCHING *Decide which definition in the right column best explains a term in the left column. Then write the letter of that definition in the space next to the term.*

	Term	Definition
_____	**1.** Chicago World's Fair	**a.** science used in practical ways
_____	**2.** technology	**b.** a system of roads that connect with one another
_____	**3.** calculator	**c.** a celebration to mark the 400th anniversary of Columbus's arrival in America
_____	**4.** network	**d.** a machine used to solve mathematical problems
_____	**5.** mural	**e.** a picture painted on a wall

II. MULTIPLE CHOICE *Choose the answer that best completes the sentence or answers the question. Then write the letter of your choice in the space provided.*

_____ **6.** The great changes that were rapidly transforming Chicago and other American cities were caused by: **a.** technology. **b.** government programs. **c.** labor unions. **d.** city officials.

_____ **7.** Ida B. Wells and Frederick Douglass strongly protested against the Chicago World's Fair because: **a.** it had Jim Crow rules against African Americans. **b.** it allowed only white visitors. **c.** it was celebrating Columbus's arrival in America. **d.** the African Americans who worked there were paid very low wages.

_____ **8.** The Midway amusement park at the Chicago World's Fair, with its models of an African village and German and Irish cities, was important because: **a.** it reflected America's multicultural population. **b.** it welcomed Native American visitors. **c.** it showed the contrast between rich and poor neighborhoods. **d.** it attracted visitors from Europe.

_____ **9.** The many different groups in the United States in 1900 shared a common belief in all these ideals EXCEPT: **a.** property rights. **b.** equal opportunity. **c.** equal protection by the laws. **d.** equality of wealth.

_____ **10.** In the late 1890s, the Constitution and the Declaration of Independence remained the great documents that: **a.** helped unite Americans by their ideals of equality and justice. **b.** granted women the right to vote. **c.** enforced the rights of African Americans. **d.** protected Native Americans.

III. ESSAY *Choose one of the following topics. Then write your answer in paragraph form on a separate sheet of paper.*

A. One visitor to the Chicago World's Fair remarked, "This American city, with all its problems and promise, is the future." Explain why you agree or disagree with this statement.

B. Explain why the Chicago World's Fair paid little attention to Native Americans.

Name ______________________________ Date ____________________

CHAPTER 1 TEST: The United States Faces the 1900s.

I. MATCHING *Decide which definition in the right column best explains a term in the left column. Then write the letter of that definition in the space provided next to the term.*

	Term	Definition
______	**1.** Elijah McCoy	**a.** African American inventor of the lubricating cup
______	**2.** Andrew Carnegie	**b.** a place for collecting freshwater
______	**3.** sweatshop	**c.** believed that wealthy people should help the poor
______	**4.** reservoir	**d.** run-down building divided into many small apartments
______	**5.** tenement	**e.** crowded room where workers made clothing or other products

II. MULTIPLE CHOICE *Choose the answer that best completes the sentence or answers the question. Then write the letter of your choice in the spaces provided.*

______ **6.** The electric light was invented by: **a.** Elijah McCoy. **b.** Thomas Edison. **c.** Henry Ford. **d.** John D. Rockefeller.

______ **7.** Which of the following was NOT an improvement in city life in the early 1900s? **a.** electricity **b.** building of reservoirs **c.** elimination of tenements **d.** formation of police departments

______ **8.** With the coming of mass production, which of the following took place? **a.** Many different items were made in one factory. **b.** Large quantities of goods were produced very quickly. **c.** Working conditions improved. **d.** Prices of goods rose.

______ **9.** Mary Harris Jones demanded laws that: **a.** protected child workers. **b.** protected men. **c.** allowed big business to operate without restriction. **d.** outlawed monopolies.

______ **10.** Between the late 1800s and the early 1900s the population of cities: **a.** stayed the same. **b.** shrank because of bad living conditions. **c.** grew. **d.** shrank because many people moved to farms.

III. ESSAY *Choose one of the following topics. Then write your answer in paragraph form on a separate sheet of paper.*

A. Many ideas and inventions helped big business grow in the early 1900s. Describe two of these advances.

B. What were working conditions in the factories like in the 1900s? Give four examples of these conditions.

Name ______________________________ Date ________________

CHAPTER 2 TEST: New Immigrants Contribute to the Nation.

I. MATCHING *Decide which definition in the right column best explains a term in the left column. Then write the letter of that definition in the space provided next to the term.*

	Term	Definition
______	**1.** self-help groups	**a.** having to do with a city
______	**2.** urban	**b.** an unfair opinion about a person made without knowing much about that person
______	**3.** prejudice	**c.** clubs that immigrants formed to adjust to life in the United States
______	**4.** ghetto	**d.** a section of a city where Jews were forced to live
______	**5.** persecution	**e.** harsh treatment of people because of their religion, ethnic group, or political ideals

II. MULTIPLE CHOICE *Choose the answer that best completes the sentence or answers the question. Then write the letter of your choice in the spaces provided.*

______ **6.** Most immigrants who came to the United States between 1880 and 1920: **a.** were skilled workers. **b.** had good jobs waiting for them. **c.** had to take jobs in the harshest, lowest-paying industries. **d.** came from big cities.

______ **7.** After arriving in the United States, immigrants generally moved into: **a.** sweatshops. **b.** ethnic neighborhoods with other people from their homeland. **c.** the suburbs. **d.** farming areas.

______ **8.** Many Chinese who immigrated to the United States: **a.** worked on fishing boats. **b.** left China because of a potato famine. **c.** were gold miners. **d.** took jobs no one else wanted and turned them into new opportunities.

______ **9.** One of the achievements of Japanese immigrants was that they: **a.** produced a large amount of California's food. **b.** opened many laundries. **c.** opened successful factories in the Midwest. **d.** were able to escape the prejudice other immigrants faced.

______ **10.** Among the changes in immigration that took place in the United States in the late 1800s were: **a.** growing prejudice against immigrants. **b.** efforts to cut down on the number of immigrants. **c.** state laws barring Asians from owning land. **d.** all of the above.

III. ESSAY *Choose one of the following topics. Then write your answer in paragraph form on a separate sheet of paper.*

A. Describe two reasons why immigrants left their homes for the United States.

B. Imagine you are an immigrant to the United States. Write a diary entry describing your first few days in the United States.

Name ______________________________ Date ____________________

CHAPTER 3 TEST: African Americans Move North.

I. MATCHING *Decide which definition in the right column best explains a term in the left column. Then write the letter of that definition in the space provided next to the term.*

_____ **1.** Jim Crow laws

_____ **2.** NAACP

_____ **3.** lynching

_____ **4.** W.E.B. Du Bois

_____ **5.** Booker T. Washington

a. organization founded to win "equal rights and opportunities for all"

b. a murder by a mob

c. Southern laws that discriminated against African Americans

d. the founder of Tuskegee University

e. the first African American to recieve a doctoral degree from Harvard University

II. MULTIPLE CHOICE *Choose the answer that best completes the sentence or answers the question. Then write the letter of your choice in the spaces provided.*

_____ **6.** During the Great Migration, thousands of African Americans moved: **a.** to the North. **b.** to the Caribbean. **c.** to Mexico. **d.** to Canada.

_____ **7.** In the South during the early 1900s, many African Americans: **a.** formed the NAACP. **b.** were allowed to vote. **c.** attended segregated schools. **d.** were active in local and state governments.

_____ **8.** Northern employers did all of the following to African Americans EXCEPT: **a.** hire them for the hardest labor. **b.** pay them less than whites. **c.** discriminate against them. **d.** provide decent housing.

_____ **9.** George Washington Carver was a famous: **a.** scientist. **b.** painter. **c.** writer. **d.** doctor.

_____ **10.** All of the following are African American colleges EXCEPT: **a.** Howard University. **b.** Spelman College. **c.** Tuskegee Institute. **d.** the University of Alabama.

III. ESSAY *Choose one of the following topics. Then write your answer in paragraph form on a separate sheet of paper.*

A. Imagine you are an African American sharecropper in the South during the early 1900s. Write a diary entry describing what your life might be like.

B. W.E.B. Du Bois and Booker T. Washington were both great African Americans who fought for their civil rights. However, they both had different ideas about what should be done to get those rights. Describe the differences between the two.

Name ______________________________ Date ____________________

CHAPTER 4 TEST: Latinos Build New Communities.

I. MATCHING *Decide which definition in the right column best explains a term in the left column. Then write the letter of that definition in the space provided next to the term.*

_____	**1.** *barrio*	**a.** a section of the city where large numbers of Latinos live
_____	**2.** Foraker Act	**b.** a Spanish word meaning "small grocery store"
_____	**3.** Platt Amendment	**c.** allowed the U.S. Army to return to Cuba if U.S. interests were threatened
_____	**4.** *bodega*	**d.** the act that gave U.S. citizenship to all Puerto Ricans that wanted it
_____	**5.** Jones Act	**e.** the act that gave the United States the right to appoint the Puerto Rican governor

II. MULTIPLE CHOICE *Choose the answer that best completes the sentence or answers the question. Then write the letter of your choice in the spaces provided.*

_____ **6.** After the United States gained control of Puerto Rico, what happened to many small farms there? **a.** They failed. **b.** The farmers moved to the southern United States and set up farms there. **c.** They were destroyed by the U.S. Army. **d.** Wealthy farmers bought them and turned them into large plantations.

_____ **7.** Many Cubans who moved to the United States worked in: **a.** the cigar industry. **b.** the clothing industry. **c.** mines. **d.** farming.

_____ **8.** *Nuevomexicanos* were Mexicans who: **a.** came from Spain. **b.** lived in New Mexico. **c.** lived in the Northeast. **d.** came to the United States and then returned to Mexico.

_____ **9.** Octaviano Larrayolo was: **a.** the owner of a cigar factory. **b.** New Mexican governor and senator. **c.** a shop owner in Los Angeles. **d.** author of the Platt Amendment.

_____ **10.** In the New Mexico constitution were articles that: **a.** protected *nuevomexicanos'* right to vote. **b.** made Spanish an official language. **c.** gave children of Spanish descent equality in the schools. **d.** provided all of the above.

III. ESSAY *Choose one of the following topics. Then write your answer in paragraph form on a separate sheet of paper.*

A. Pretend you are a Puerto Rican who has just arrived in New York. Write a diary entry explaining where you live and what your neighborhood is like.

B. Draw a poster aimed at recruiting *nuevomexicanos* to become members of *Las Gorras Blancos*.

Name ______________________________ Date ____________________

CHAPTER 5 TEST: Workers Fight for Improved Conditions.

I. MATCHING *Decide which definition in the right column best explains a term in the left column. Then write the letter of that definition in the space provided next to the term.*

	Term	Definition
_____	**1.** union	**a.** refusal to work until demands are met
_____	**2.** Triangle Shirtwaist Fire	**b.** first nationwide labor union
_____	**3.** Knights of Labor	**c.** union of skilled workers
_____	**4.** strike	**d.** a group of workers organized to protect their rights and improve working conditions
_____	**5.** American Federation of Labor	**e.** tragedy in which many workers died

II. MULTIPLE CHOICE *Choose the answer that best completes the sentence or answers the question. Then write the letter of your choice in the spaces provided.*

_____ **6.** Samuel Gompers founded which organization in 1886? **a.** American Federation of Labor **b.** Knights of Labor **c.** The Triangle Shirtwaist Company **d.** New York Consumers' League

_____ **7.** The Japanese-Mexican Labor Association fought for better conditions for: **a.** women. **b.** fishing boat workers. **c.** farm workers. **d.** clothing workers.

_____ **8.** What organization did Mary Kenney O'Sullivan found? **a.** the National Women's Trade Union League **b.** the Japanese-Mexican Labor Association **c.** the American Federation of Labor **d.** the Knights of Labor

_____ **9.** Florence Kelley and Josephine Goldmark won rights for workers by: **a.** strikes. **b.** taking labor cases to court. **c.** having laws changed. **d.** political campaigns.

_____ **10.** The Supreme Court decision in the case of *Muller* v. *Oregon* dealt with: **a.** working hours for women. **b.** child labor. **c.** wages for African Americans. **d.** wages for immigrants.

III. ESSAY *Choose one of the following topics. Then write your answer in paragraph form on a separate sheet of paper.*

A. Describe the Haymarket Riot and how it affected the Knights of Labor.

B. Women, Latinos, and some Asians faced discrimination at work and were also rejected by some existing unions. Describe the groups that these people formed.

Name ______________________________ Date ______________________

CHAPTER 6 TEST: Refomers Work to Improve American Life.

I. MATCHING *Decide which definition in the right column best explains a term in the left column. Then write the letter of that definition in the space provided next to the term.*

	Term	Definition
_____	**1.** initiative	**a.** making illegal payments to officials
_____	**2.** bribery	**b.** the first Progressive President
_____	**3.** Theodore Roosevelt	**c.** writers who exposed society's problems
_____	**4.** referendum	**d.** a method by which voters can propose and pass laws directly
_____	**5.** muckrakers	**e.** allows voters to strike down a law

II. MULTIPLE CHOICE *Choose the answer that best completes the sentence or answers the question. Then write the letter of your choice in the spaces provided.*

_____ **6.** Which of the following is not a reform introduced by Progressives? **a.** the initiative **b.** the income tax **c.** the recall **d.** the referendum

_____ **7.** The Sherman Anti-Trust Act of 1890 was a law that tried to: **a.** ban monopolies. **b.** preserve natural resources. **c.** outlaw lynchings. **d.** protect workers.

_____ **8.** Settlement houses provided services for: **a.** poor people in cities. **b.** immigrants. **c.** working women. **d.** all of the above.

_____ **9.** Which of the following is true of the way Progressives dealt with African American problems? **a.** They fought for reforms in the courts. **b.** They paid little attention to African Americans. **c.** They fought for laws outlawing discrimination. **d.** They forced the government to outlaw lynching.

_____ **10.** Which of the following inventions opened up new jobs for women in 1900? **a.** the automobile **b.** the telegraph **c.** the telephone **d.** the airplane

III. ESSAY *Choose one of the following topics. Then write your answer in paragraph form on a separate sheet of paper.*

A. Describe some of the methods suffragists used to win the right to vote for women.

B. Imagine you are a muckraker in the early 1900s. What problem would you choose to write about and why?

Name ______________________________ Date ____________________

CHAPTER 7 TEST: The United States Is a Power in the Pacific.

I. MATCHING *Decide which definition in the right column best explains a term in the left column. Then write the letter of that definition in the space provided next to the term.*

	Term	Definition
_____	**1.** colonialism	**a.** a secret Chinese military group
_____	**2.** "boxers"	**b.** a guarantee of equal trading rights to all foreign powers in China
_____	**3.** imperialism	**c.** the taking over of foreign countries as colonies
_____	**4.** Open Door policy	**d.** the building of empires
_____	**5.** compromise	**e.** an agreement that gives each side part of what it wants

II. MULTIPLE CHOICE *Choose the answer that best completes the sentence or answers the question. Then write the letter of your choice in the spaces provided.*

_____ **6.** In 1898, Manila was captured by: **a.** Ferdinand Magellan. **b.** George Dewey. **c.** Emilio Aguinaldo. **d.** William Howard Taft.

_____ **7.** What ended the most serious threat to the U.S. control of the Philippines? **a.** an attack by British warships **b.** the defeat of the Filipino army **c.** the arrest of Aguinaldo **d.** the shooting of Aguinaldo's lieutenants

_____ **8.** China was grateful to the United States because it: **a.** helped China remain an undivided country. **b.** helped educate many Chinese students. **c.** gave China money to maintain its army. **d.** helped improve the Shanghai harbor.

_____ **9.** In the early 1900s, the United States was suspicious of Japan because of: **a.** Japan's growing military and economic power. **b.** Japan's treatment of the Koreans. **c.** Japan's alliance with Russia. **d.** Japan's attack on the Philippines.

_____ **10.** Roosevelt reached a gentlemen's agreement with the Japanese government over: **a.** problems with fair schooling in San Francisco. **b.** the newspapers' unfair treatment of Japan. **c.** the Open Door policy in China. **d.** the treatment of Japanese workers in the United States.

III. ESSAY *Choose one of the following topics. Then write your answer in paragraph form on a separate sheet of paper.*

A. Pretend you are a Filipino in 1898. Would you have sided with Aguinaldo in his opposition to the United States, or with the Americans? Explain your answer.

B. Explain what led the United States to declare the Open Door policy in China.

Name ______________________________ Date ______________

CHAPTER 8 TEST: The United States Controls Cuba and Puerto Rico.

I. MATCHING *Decide which definition in the right column best explains a term in the left column. Then write the letter of that definition in the space provided next to the term.*

	Term	Definition
______	**1.** protectorate	**a.** a law that set up civil government in Puerto Rico
______	**2.** cultural imperialism	**b.** a law that gave U.S. citizenship to Puerto Ricans
______	**3.** Leonard Wood	**c.** a desire to replace the culture of a colony with that of the ruling country
______		
______	**4.** Foraker Act	**d.** the military governor of Cuba
______	**5.** Jones Act	**e.** a weak country that is under the control of a stronger country

II. MULTIPLE CHOICE *Choose the answer that best completes the sentence or answers the question. Then write the letter of your choice in the spaces provided.*

______ **6.** This allowed the United States to send its army into Cuba to keep order: **a.** the sugar economy **b.** the Foraker Act **c.** the Jones Act **d.** the Platt Amendment

______ **7.** In 1912, these people had almost no power in Cuba and were treated unfairly: **a.** Americans **b.** Asian Cubans **c.** African Cubans **d.** Puerto Ricans

______ **8.** During World War I, Cuban sugar mill owners became rich because: **a.** they switched to producing cigars. **b.** Cuba was the only country producing sugar. **c.** they sold their land to Americans. **d.** they produced the best sugar.

______ **9.** Unlike Cuba before 1898, Puerto Rico had been granted which of the following by Spain? **a.** limited self rule **b.** education **c.** Spanish citizenship **d.** the right to independence

______ **10.** Santiago Iglasias was a Puerto Rican who supported: **a.** complete independence from the United States. **b.** statehood for Puerto Rico. **c.** no change in Puerto Rico's relationship with the United States. **d.** alliance with Mexico.

III. ESSAY *Choose one of the following topics. Then write your answer in paragraph form on a separate sheet of paper.*

A. How was U.S. treatment of Cuba and Puerto Rico after the Cuban-Spanish American War the same for both islands? How was it different?

B. Who do you think did more for Cuba-Carlos Juan Finlay or Walter Reed? Explain your answer.

Name ______________________________ Date ____________________

CHAPTER 9 TEST: The United States Is Involved in Latin America.

I. MATCHING *Decide which definition in the right column best explains a term in the left column. Then write the letter of that definition in the space provided next to the term.*

	Term	Definition
______	**1.** migrant worker	**a.** popular Mexican revolutionary leader
______	**2.** Pancho Villa	**b.** a section of a city where there are a large number of Latinos
______	**3.** diplomacy	**c.** a worker who travels from farm to farm to find work
______	**4.** canal	**d.** the relations between countries
______	**5.** *barrio*	**e.** waterway dug by people to connect two bodies of water

II. MULTIPLE CHOICE *Choose the answer that best completes the sentence or answers the question. Then write the letter of your choice in the spaces provided.*

______ **6.** All of the following were related to the building of the Panama Canal EXCEPT: **a.** Panamanian desire for independance. **b.** quicker travel across North America. **c.** Colombian support. **d.** interests in business.

______ **7.** In 1904, Roosevelt used his "big stick" policy in Latin America in order to: **a.** prevent disease. **b.** guard the Panama Canal. **c.** be sure that the United States was the only one policing the Americas. **d.** pay off the U.S. debt.

______ **8.** President Taft's dollar diplomacy made relations with Latin American countries worse because: **a.** they wanted more land. **b.** U.S. businesses refused to invest in Latin America. **c.** dollars were scarce in Latin America. **d.** Latin American countries resented U.S. bankers collecting their taxes.

______ **9.** President Wilson's actions in Mexico took place while Mexico was involved in: **a.** a revolution. **b.** a war with Cuba. **c.** an economic boom. **d.** a series of earthquakes.

______ **10.** Most Mexican immigrants settled in this section of the United States: **a.** Northwest **b.** Southeast **c.** Southwest **d.** Northeast

III. ESSAY *Choose one of the following topics. Then write your answer in paragraph form on a separate sheet of paper.*

A. Do you think that the United States had the right to build the Panama Canal? Explain your answer.

B. Pretend you are a poor Mexican farmer who is undecided whether to fight in the Mexican revolution or to go to the United States to find work. Give reasons for making either decision.

Name ______________________________ Date ____________________

CHAPTER 10 TEST: The United States Fights World War I.

I. MATCHING *Decide which definition in the right column best explains a term in the left column. Then write the letter of that definition in the space next to the term.*

______	**1.** alliance	**a.** not taking sides in a war
______	**2.** neutrality	**b.** a close association of countries
______	**3.** ammunition	**c.** a person forced by the government to enter the armed forces
______	**4.** submarine warfare	**d.** military supplies such as bullets, bombs, and grenades
______	**5.** draftee	**e.** using submarines to sink ships bringing supplies to the enemy

II. MULTIPLE CHOICE *Choose the answer that best completes the sentence or answers the question. Then write the letter of your choice in the space provided.*

______ **6.** The immediate cause of the U.S. entry into World War I was the: **a.** sinking of the *Lusitania.* **b.** loss of U.S. ammunition shipments to France. **c.** air raids on London. **d.** German submarine warfare.

______ **7.** The Selective Service Act required men between the ages of 21 and 30 to: **a.** register for military service. **b.** go to military school. **c.** learn how to shoot a rifle. **d.** vote.

______ **8.** Thousands of African Americans served in the armed forces in World War I, but most of them: **a.** saw action in battle. **b.** served in labor units. **c.** were placed in the Marine Corps. **d.** were commanded by fellow African Americans.

______ **9.** World War I opened new job opportunities for: **a.** women. **b.** African Americans. **c.** Mexicans. **d.** all of the above.

______ **10.** Who was most responsible for the establishment of the League of Nations? **a.** U. S. senators **b.** President Wilson **c.** French and British leaders **d.** the Germans

III. ESSAY *Choose one of the following topics. Then write your answer in paragraph form on a separate sheet of paper.*

A. Describe the events that led to the outbreak of World War I in Europe.

B. If you had been a 21-year-old citizen of the United States in 1917, would you have volunteered to fight for your country? Why or why not?

Name ______________________________ Date ____________________

CHAPTER 11 TEST: The 1920s Are a Time of Change.

I. MATCHING *Decide which definition in the right column best explains a term in the left column. Then write the letter of that definition in the space next to the term.*

	Term	Definition
_____	**1.** prohibit	**a.** a tax on imports
_____	**2.** suburb	**b.** successful, especially in terms of wealth
_____	**3.** quota	**c.** to outlaw
_____	**4.** tariff	**d.** an area around a city that people live in
_____	**5.** prosperous	**e.** a limit

II. MULTIPLE CHOICE *Choose the answer that best completes the sentence or answers the question. Then write the letter of your choice in the space provided.*

_____ **6.** Workers formed unions for all of the following reasons EXCEPT: **a.** to demand better wages. **b.** to reduce working hours. **c.** to demand safer working conditions. **d.** to keep European goods off the market.

_____ **7.** The "Roaring Twenties" were known for all of the following EXCEPT: **a.** flappers. **b.** the start of many fads. **c.** Prohibition. **d.** the cause of World War II.

_____ **8.** Which of the following does not describe the Ku Klux Klan? **a.** They used violence. **b.** They were used to break strikes. **c.** They were a civil rights group. **d.** They murdered African Americans.

_____ **9.** After World War I the economy changed in all of the following ways EXCEPT: **a.** prices shot up. **b.** factories closed. **c.** jobs disappeared. **d.** wages increased.

_____ **10.** What was the Red Scare? **a.** a fear of new immigrants **b.** a drink invented during the 1920s **c.** a period in the 1920s when people were afraid of the communists **d.** an award given to union workers

III. ESSAY *Choose one of the following topics. Then write your answer in paragraph form on a separate sheet of paper.*

A. Design a poster that shows some of the changes that took place in U.S. life during the Roaring Twenties.

B. Describe the many new business opportunities that resulted when the automobile became popular during the 1920s.

Name ______________________________ Date ____________________

CHAPTER 12 TEST: African American Culture Thrives in the Jazz Age.

I. MATCHING *Decide which definition in the right column best explains a term in the left column. Then write the letter of that definition in the space next to the term.*

	Term	Definition
_____	**1.** casualty	**a.** someone who has been injured or killed
_____	**2.** black nationalism	**b.** period of rebirth
_____	**3.** autobiography	**c.** the story of one's own life written by oneself
_____	**4.** riot	**d.** African Americans' pride in themselves and in their African roots
_____	**5.** renaissance	**e.** a serious disturbance involving a large group of people

II. MULTIPLE CHOICE *Choose the answer that best completes the sentence or answers the question. Then write the letter of your choice in the space provided.*

_____ **6.** Marcus Garvey and W.E.B. Du Bois both: **a.** believed that African Americans should honor their African roots. **b.** founded a steamship company. **c.** appealed mostly to middle class African Americans. **d.** worked for the NAACP.

_____ **7.** The UNIA fell apart for all of the following reasons EXCEPT: **a.** bad investments. **b.** poor management. **c.** deportation of Marcus Garvey. **d.** members did not pay dues.

_____ **8.** The Harlem Renaissance refers to: **a.** an African American newspaper. **b.** a museum in Harlem. **c.** a rebirth of African American culture. **d.** a musicians' group in Harlem.

_____ **9.** Which of the following is NOT associated with African Americans? **a.** the NAACP **b.** the KKK **c.** the National Urban League **d.** the Great Migration

_____ **10.** The Harlem Renaissance came to an end when: **a.** the nation plunged into great poverty. **b.** many of its artists and writers died. **c.** discrimination against African Americans increased. **d.** living in Harlem became too expensive.

III. ESSAY *Choose one of the following topics. Then write your answer in paragraph form on a separate sheet of paper.*

A. Create an advertisement for an African American nightclub in Harlem during the twenties.

B. Describe the many ways in which Harlem operated as an African American cultural center during the 1920s.

Name ______________________________ Date ____________________

CHAPTER 13 TEST: A Great Depression Takes Hold.

I. MATCHING *Decide which definition in the right column best explains a term in the left column. Then write the letter of that definition in the space next to the term.*

	Term	Definition
______	**1.** depression	**a.** a line in which people stand to receive food
______	**2.** repatriation	**b.** help given to those in poverty or need
______	**3.** stock market	**c.** a deep economic downturn
______	**4.** relief	**d.** a place where stocks, or pieces, of companies are bought and sold
______	**5.** breadline	**e.** the shipment of a person back to his or her own country

II. MULTIPLE CHOICE *Choose the answer that best completes the sentence or answers the question. Then write the letter of your choice in the space provided.*

______ **6.** President Hoover refused to help the needy because: **a.** he thought they would rely on the government too much. **b.** he thought they were lazy. **c.** he believed the depression would not last long. **d.** he did not want to lose the next election.

______ **7.** Which of the following was NOT a result of the Great Depression? **a.** breadlines **b.** great unemployment **c.** homelessness **d.** a growth in business opportunities

______ **8.** The National Urban League helped African Americans during the Great Depression by: **a.** finding them jobs. **b.** providing food, clothing, and medical care. **c.** publishing a newspaper for sharecroppers. **d.** organizing a union of tenant farmers.

______ **9.** During the Great Depression many Mexican migrant workers were: **a.** sent back to Mexico from the United States. **b.** given jobs in cities of the Middle West. **c.** hired by the federal government. **d.** forced to send their children back to Mexico.

______ **10.** Which of the following is NOT associated with the Dust Bowl? **a.** strong winds carrying dry soil that blew across the land **b.** regions that were hit with droughts **c.** a famous football game **d.** farmers in the Southwest who abandoned their farms

III. ESSAY *Choose one of the following topics. Then write your answer in paragraph form on a separate sheet of paper.*

A. Pretend that you lived in Hooverville during the 1920s. Describe the problems you and your family experienced at that time.

B. Create a series of headlines for a newspaper describing the results of Black Thursday.

Name ______________________________ Date ____________________

CHAPTER 14 TEST: The New Deal Brings New Hope.

I. MATCHING *Decide which definition in the right column best explains a term in the left column. Then write the letter of that definition in the space next to the term.*

	Term	Definition
______	**1.** welfare	**a.** a ruler who has complete control and power
______	**2.** fireside chat	**b.** a government policy that provides pensions to retired people
______	**3.** social security	**c.** a radio talk President Roosevelt gave to the nation
______	**4.** dictator	**d.** a system in which the government makes payments to people who are needy
______	**5.** unemployment insurance	**e.** regular government payments to people who lose their jobs

II. MULTIPLE CHOICE *Choose the answer that best completes the sentence or answers the question. Then write the letter of your choice in the space provided.*

______ **6.** The New Deal was President Franklin D. Roosevelt's plan to: **a.** stop the Great Depression. **b.** declare a bank holiday. **c.** raise farm prices. **d.** organize labor unions.

______ **7.** The Tennessee Valley Authority was a success for all the following reasons EXCEPT: **a.** it provided many jobs. **b.** it brought cheap electricity to thousands of people. **c.** it controlled flooding in the Tennessee Valley. **d.** it set up Tennessee as a state.

______ **8.** The New Deal was not popular with many Americans because: **a.** they thought it made people too dependent on the government. **b.** they feared it would make the government too powerful. **c.** they believed it wasted money. **d.** of all of the above reasons.

______ **9.** The appointment of Mary McLeod Bethune helped: **a.** African American young people get an education. **b.** Mexican Americans get work on government projects. **c.** end discrimination against African Americans. **d.** Native Americans preserve their cultures.

______ **10.** The New Deal helped Native Americans in all of these ways EXCEPT: **a.** it fought hard for their rights. **b.** it helped them preserve their cultures. **c.** it ended Indian reservations. **d.** it worked to prevent their lands from being sold.

III. ESSAY *Choose one of the following topics. Then write your answer in paragraph form on a separate sheet of paper.*

A. Pretend that you are President Roosevelt giving a fireside chat. Tell the people how you plan to help the economy during the next hundred days.

B. Create a poster advertising the TVA and its benefits. Show how it will improve life for many people in the area.

Name ______________________________ Date ____________________

CHAPTER 15 TEST: The Nation Fights Another War.

I. MATCHING *Decide which definition in the right column best explains a term in the left column. Then write the letter of that definition in the space next to the term.*

	Term	Definition
_____	**1.** draft	**a.** hatred of the Jewish people
_____	**2.** isolationism	**b.** person or nation that does not take sides in a dispute
_____	**3.** neutral	**c.** a policy of staying out of world affairs
_____	**4.** fascism	**d.** a system of government ruled by a dictator who uses the military, nationalism, and racism to stay in power
_____	**5.** anti-Semitism	**e.** to require a person to enter the military

II. MULTIPLE CHOICE *Choose the answer that best completes the sentence or answers the question. Then write the letter of your choice in the space provided.*

_____ **6.** This country was NOT one of the Allied Powers in World War II: **a**. Soviet Union **b.** Britain **c.** France **d.** Italy

_____ **7.** Which of the following was NOT one of Hitler's goals? **a.** to make Germany the most powerful nation in the world **b.** to rid Germany of Jews **c.** to bomb Hiroshima **d.** conquer more land in Europe.

_____ **8.** Even though the United States was not on any side at the start of World War II, it: **a.** supplied the Allies with war materials. **b.** supplied the Axis powers with war materials. **c.** refused to send war materials to either side in the war. **d.** sent U.S. soldiers to France and Britain.

_____ **9.** Dorie Miller was: **a.** an African American who fought at Pearl Harbor. **b.** the first woman in the WACS. **c.** an American naval officer. **d.** an African American pilot who flew fighter planes over Europe.

_____ **10.** The contribution of the Navajos in World War II was important because they: **a.** used a secret code the enemy could not break. **b.** volunteered for the armed forces more than any other minority. **c.** invented a special telescope. **d.** flew so many bombers over Europe.

III. ESSAY *Choose one of the following topics. Then write your answer in paragraph form on a separate sheet of paper.*

A. Pretend that you are a reporter at Pearl Harbor on December 7, 1941. Write a news article describing what you saw there.

B. Create a poster that pictures the important events of World War II.

Name ______________________________ Date ____________________

CHAPTER 16 TEST: Americans Support World War II on the Home Front.

I. MATCHING *Decide which definition in the right column best explains a term in the left column. Then write the letter of that definition in the space next to the term.*

	Term	Definition
_____	**1.** *bracero*	**a.** a contract laborer from Mexico
_____	**2.** internment camp	**b.** a person who is not in the military
_____	**3.** ration	**c.** a prison camp
_____	**4.** civilian	**d.** to portion or limit such resources as food, clothing, or fuel
_____	**5.** price control	**e.** the setting of prices on certain goods and services by the government

II. MULTIPLE CHOICE *Choose the answer that best completes the sentence or answers the question. Then write the letter of your choice in the space provided.*

_____ **6.** Which of the following was NOT a way in which Americans on the home front contributed to the war effort? **a.** They held civil defense drills. **b.** They built victory gardens. **c.** They took part in blackouts. **d.** They bought more meat than their ration coupons allowed.

_____ **7.** The economy was boosted during the war because: **a.** many things were produced by the war industries, thus providing jobs. **b.** the soldiers came home and spent money. **c.** women saved money on day care. **d.** civilians spent money on big items like cars, trucks and refrigerators.

_____ **8.** Women who worked during the war faced all of these problems EXCEPT: **a.** lack of day-care centers for their children. **b.** having to do the housework after a day on the job. **c.** support of the family if their husbands were in the armed forces. **d.** the threat of unemployment.

_____ **9.** A. Philip Randolph was: **a.** an African American who demanded an end to job discrimination during World War II. **b.** an African American who urged young blacks to volunteer for the armed services. **c.** a *bracero* who worked in California. **d.** commander of Japanese internment camps.

_____ **10.** Even though their people underwent the most severe discrimination during World War II, many young Japanese Americans: **a.** volunteered for the U.S. armed services. **b.** offered to work in defense factories without pay. **c.** refused to learn how to speak Japanese. **d.** were smuggled into Japan to spy for the United States.

III. ESSAY *Choose one of the following topics. Then write your answer in paragraph form on a separate sheet of paper.*

A. Pretend that you are a Japanese American student who has been put into an internment camp. Write three entries into your journal describing what life was like and what you may have missed when you were in the camp.

B. Create a political cartoon that pictures one of the following: "Rosie the Riveter," Double V, zoot suits, Japanese internment, or blackouts.

Name ______________________________ Date ____________________

CHAPTER 17 TEST: The United States and the Soviet Union Fight a Cold War.

I. MATCHING *Decide which definition in the right column best explains a term in the left column. Then write the letter of that definition in the space provided next to the term.*

	Term	Definition
______	**1.** United Nations	**a.** symbolic dividing line between Eastern and Western Europe after World War II
______	**2.** capitalism	**b.** an economic system in which most businesses and land are privately owned
______	**3.** communism	**c.** group formed to defend against Soviet attack
______	**4.** Iron Curtain	**d.** organization formed just after World War II to maintain peace around the world
______	**5.** North Atlantic Treaty Organization	**e.** an economic system in which most businesses and land are owned and controlled by the government

II. MULTIPLE CHOICE *Choose the answer that best completes the sentence or answers the question. Then write the letter of your choice in the space to the left.*

______ **6.** The conflict between the United States and the Soviet Union in which they competed to gain control of other countries was called: **a.** the Great War. **b.** World War II. **c.** the Cold War. **d.** the Korean War.

______ **7.** Between 1945 and 1948 the Soviet Union set up Communist dictatorship in Poland, Romania, Bulgaria, Hungary, and Czechoslovakia. These countries were called: **a.** Soviet satellites. **b.** Western Europe. **c.** puppet governments. **d.** NATO countries.

______ **8.** One reason that the Soviet Union wanted to control the Eastern European countries was to: **a.** profit from trade with those countries. **b.** be able to maintain a very large military force. **c.** create a protection for themselves so no European power could invade their country again. **d.** be able to make those countries more modern.

______ **9.** Germany was split into two countries because: **a.** it was easier to govern. **b.** the Soviet Union would not end the Berlin Blockade. **c.** world leaders feared the power of a single Germany. **d.** during the Cold War the allies could not agree on reforms to rebuild Germany's economy.

______ **10.** Which of the following was NOT a result of the Korean War? **a.** U.S. troops saved South Korea from becoming Communist. **b.** The war ended in a draw that cost the United States 50,000 killed and 100,000 wounded. **c.** The United States armed forces became integrated with African Americans and white soldiers fighting in the same units. **d.** Communist China took over North Korea.

III. ESSAY *Choose two of the following topics. Answer the following questions in two or three sentences.*

A. How did the Truman Doctrine and the Marshall Plan aid Western Europe?

B. Why did people in the United States feel especially threatened by a Communist government in Cuba?

Name ______________________________ Date ______________

CHAPTER 18 TEST: The Years After World War II Bring Prosperity and Problems.

I. MATCHING *Decide which definition in the right column best explains a term in the left column. Then write the letter of that definition in the space next to the term.*

	Term	Definition
______	**1.** inflation	**a.** a period of great prosperity
______	**2.** boom	**b.** a list of people or organizations under suspicion or in disfavor
______	**3.** suburb	**c.** a rapid rise in prices that reduces the value of money
______	**4.** blacklist	**d.** a community near a city
______	**5.** boycott	**e.** to refuse to buy, sell, or use goods from certain companies, people, or countries

II. MULTIPLE CHOICE *Choose the answer that best completes the sentence or answers the question. Then write the letter of your choice in the space provided.*

______ **6.** Which of the following was true of the economy after World War II? **a.** Consumer spending replaced government spending. **b.** Factories switched from military to consumer goods and stayed busy. **c.** During the 1950s, the income of the average American doubled. **d.** All of the above.

______ **7.** Which of the following was provided by the GI Bill of Rights? **a.** money for veterans to go to school **b.** equal rights for all returning soldiers **c.** a job for all returning soldiers **d.** equal pay for equal work

______ **8.** In Montgomery, Alabama, Rosa Parks was arrested because she: **a.** refused to pay her taxes. **b.** would not move to the part of the bus where African Americans were required to sit. **c.** burned the American flag. **d.** led a boycott of the city's buses.

______ **9.** In 1954 the U.S. Supreme Court decided in the case of *Brown* v. *Board of Education* that: **a.** public schools could remain segregated. **b.** school districts in all states had to desegregate right away. **c.** separate schools for whites and blacks were legal as long as they were equal. **d.** each state could make its own rules for its schools.

______ **10.** Dr. Martin Luther King, Jr. believed that the best way to fight segregation was to: **a.** use nonviolent, peaceful methods. **b.** organize into military units and fight the police. **c.** do nothing until it slowly went away. **d.** bomb businesses and other organizations that practiced segregation.

III. ESSAY *Choose one of the following topics. Then write your answer in paragraph form on a separate sheet of paper.*

A. What benefits and problems did peace after World War II bring to the United States?

B. How did the Cold War affect feelings about communism in the United States?

Name ______________________________ Date ____________________

CHAPTER 19 TEST: Five Presidents Shake Up the Nation.

I. MATCHING *Decide which definition in the right column best explains a term in the left column. Then write the letter of that definition in the space next to the term.*

______	**1.** New Frontier	**a.** the bringing of charges against a government official
______	**2.** Civil Rights Act of 1964	**b.** President Kennedy's plan to to fight poverty, improve education, health care, and social justice
______	**3.** assassination	**c.** an official act that releases someone from the penalty for a crime
______	**4.** impeachment	**d.** a law forbidding discrimination based on race, religion, sex, or national origin
______	**5.** pardon	**e.** a planned murder of an official

II. MULTIPLE CHOICE *Choose the answer that best completes the sentence or answers the question. Then write the letter of your choice in the space provided.*

______ **6.** Most of Kennedy's proposals did not become law because: **a.** Republicans and some Democrats in Congress teamed up to block them. **b.** they were too old-fashioned. **c.** no one else thought they were important. **d.** Kennedy was too busy with foreign affairs to push them through Congress.

______ **7.** On November 22, 1963, President John Kennedy: **a.** signed a civil rights act into law. **b.** was killed in Dallas, Texas. **c.** married. **d.** watched men land on the moon.

______ **8.** Most of President Johnson's programs were passed by Congress, but he became an unpopular president because: **a.** of his handling of the war in Vietnam. **b.** his programs cost too much money. **c.** many people thought he was too powerful. **d.** he did not get along with people very well.

______ **9.** Richard Nixon is the only President ever to have: **a.** gone to jail. **b.** been defeated for a second term. **c.** resigned from the office of President. **d.** been impeached by the House of Representatives.

______ **10.** Both Presidents Ford and Carter had to: **a.** deal with serious economic problems such as unemployment and inflation. **b.** face impeachment charges because of Watergate. **c.** turn down the heat in the White House because of the energy crisis. **d.** increase taxes.

III. ESSAY *Choose one of the following topics. Then write your answer in paragraph form on a separate sheet of paper.*

A. After President Nixon left office, many people looked to him for his advice on foreign affairs. Do you think they are right in asking his advice? Why or why not?

B. Explain how U.S policy in Vietnam was influenced by the Cold War.

Name ______________________________ Date ______________

CHAPTER 20 TEST: The United States Fights a War in Vietnam.

I. MATCHING *Decide which definition in the right column best explains a term in the left column. Then write the letter of that definition in the space provided next to the term.*

	Term	Definition
______	**1.** amnesty	**a.** a war supporter
______	**2.** Viet Cong	**b.** a slow but steady increase in the level of warfare
______	**3.** escalation	**c.** South Vietnamese guerrillas, also known as Vietnamese Communists
______	**4.** hawk	**d.** an opponent of war
______	**5.** dove	**e.** a pardon for political offenses

II. MULTIPLE CHOICE *Choose the answer that best completes the sentence or answers the question. Then write the letter of your choice in the space to the left.*

______ **6.** The idea that if Vietnam fell to the Communists, the other nations of Southeast Asia would also fall was called: **a.** the Gulf of Tonkin Resolution. **b.** the domino theory. **c.** Vietnamization. **d.** the Tet Offensive.

______ **7.** The President who sent the first U.S. soldiers to fight on the ground in South Vietnam and who ordered bombing raids on North Vietnam was: **a.** Eisenhower. **b.** Kennedy. **c.** Johnson. **d.** Nixon.

______ **8.** The U.S. policy of turning the fighting over to the South Vietnamese army and bringing American troops home was called: **a.** escalation. **b.** the domino theory. **c.** Vietnamization. **d.** amnesty.

______ **9.** The U.S. signed agreements with the North Vietnamese guerrillas and the last U.S. ground troops came home in 1972. However, the war continued until 1975, when: **a.** the United States reentered the war and bombed North Vietnam. **b.** North Vietnam attacked the capital of South Vietnam. **c.** the North Vietnamese surrendered. **d.** North Vietnam and the guerrillas won the war and made the North and South on Communist nation.

______ **10.** American protest against the war ended in bloodshed in May of 1970 when four college students were killed by National Guardsmen at: **a.** Saigon. **b.** Kent State University. **c.** the Vietnam Veterans Memorial in Washington, D.C. **d.** the White House.

III. ESSAY *Choose one of the following topics. Answer the following questions in two or three sentences.*

A. What was President Nixon's plan for ending the war?

B. What were the feelings of Americans about the Vietnam War?

Name ______________________________ Date ____________________

CHAPTER 21 TEST: Changes in the American Way of Life Take Place.

I. MATCHING *Decide which definition in the right column best explains a term in the left column. Then write the letter of that definition in the space next to the term.*

	Term	Definition
_____	**1.** baby boom	**a.** young people of the 1960s who rebelled against society
_____	**2.** rock 'n' roll	**b.** differences between parents and children
_____	**3.** hippies	**c.** large increase in population that took place in the 20 years after World War II
_____	**4.** Sunbelt	**d.** blend of African American R & B with white country-and-western musical traditions
_____	**5.** generation gap	**e.** states in the southern and southwestern United States

II. MULTIPLE CHOICE *Choose the answer that best completes the sentence or answers the question. Then write the letter of your choice in the space provided.*

_____ **6.** To meet the great demand for homes after World War II, a builder named Arthur Levitt did all of the following EXCEPT: **a.** use fewer workers. **b.** use mass-production methods. **c.** build many houses at the same time. **d.** sold his houses at low prices.

_____ **7.** Many African Americans from the South headed for Northern cities in the 1950s because: **a.** they wanted to live in their own communities. **b.** mechanical cotton pickers were taking their jobs on the farms. **c.** they were afraid to continue to live in the South. **d.** the Northern communities were integrated.

_____ **8.** In the North many aging factories were closing and moving to: **a.** Canada. **b.** Europe. **c.** the South and Southwest. **d.** other Northeastern cities.

_____ **9.** Which of the following is NOT true about the power of television? **a.** So few people had sets that TV had no power. **b.** It could unite Americans especially in a time of crisis. **c.** It gave Americans a front-row view of history, such as civil rights demonstrations and the Vietnam War. **d.** It had a great influence on the lives of teenagers.

_____ **10.** Many young people of the 1960s and 1970s: **a.** focused their energies on political and social action. **b.** did not rebel against society but fought in the Vietnam War and supported President Nixon's conservative policies. **c.** showed a deep interest in religion. **d.** did all of the above.

III. ESSAY *Choose one of the following topics. Then write your answer in paragraph form on a separate sheet of paper.*

A. Describe the changes that made life in the years after World War II different from life before the war.

B. Imagine you were opening a business in 1950, explain what products you would sell and why.

Name ______________________________ Date ____________________

CHAPTER 22 TEST: African Americans Struggle for Rights and Equality.

I. **MATCHING** *Decide which definition in the right column best explains a term in the left column. Then write the letter of that definition in the space next to the term.*

	Term	Definition
_____	**1.** sit-in	**a.** a strong, negative response to a group or an idea
_____	**2.** freedom ride	**b.** a way of achieving a goal
_____	**3.** backlash	**c.** a policy for correcting discrimination by increasing opportunities for certain groups
_____	**4.** affirmative action	**d.** a bus trip to test African Americans' rights
_____	**5.** tactic	**e.** a protest in which people take a seat and refuse to leave

II. **MULTIPLE CHOICE** *Choose the answer that best completes the sentence or answers the question. Then write the letter of your choice in the space provided.*

_____ **6.** The tactics of the civil rights groups in the 1960s were based on the philosophy of: **a.** violent protest. **b.** affirmative action. **c.** nonviolence. **d.** party politics.

_____ **7.** One result of the freedom rides was that federal courts ordered that: **a.** commuter trains be desegregated. **b.** city buses be desegregated. **c.** interstate buses be open equally to all races. **d.** African Americans be hired as bus drivers.

_____ **8.** The African American protest marches against bombings and violence by officials in Birmingham, Alabama, stirred national sympathy for civil rights because of: **a.** appeals by church leaders. **b.** television coverage of the events. **c.** the actions of President Kennedy. **d.** the presence of federal marshals.

_____ **9.** All of the following were actions against civil rights workers in Southern states in the 1960s EXCEPT: **a.** attacks on freedom riders. **b.** the murder of three civil rights workers. **c.** the bombing of a church in Birmingham. **d.** the March on Washington.

_____ **10.** Which one of the following was NOT a cause of the split in the civil rights movement in the late 1960s? **a.** the appearance of fiery new leaders **b.** continuing high unemployment and segregated, rundown housing for African Americans **c.** the slow progress in gaining racial equality **d.** the Vietnam War

III. **ESSAY** *Choose one of the following topics. Then write your answer in paragraph form on a separate sheet of paper.*

A. Explain the tactics of civil rights groups in the 1960s.

B. What victories did the Civil Rights Movement have? What problems remained unsolved?

Name ______________________________ Date ____________________

CHAPTER 23 TEST: African Americans Score Successes in Many Fields.

I. MATCHING *Decide which definition in the right column best explains a term in the left column. Then write the letter of that definition in the space next to the term.*

______	**1.** Black Caucus	**a.** government body that passes a state's laws
______	**2.** entrepreneur	**b.** the state of being widely known to people
______	**3.** state assembly	**c.** someone who owns a business
______	**4.** prominence	**d.** a group that works together to achieve shared political goals
______	**5.** caucus	**e.** African American members of Congress who focus on issues that affect their people

II. MULTIPLE CHOICE *Choose the answer that best completes the sentence or answers the question. Then write the letter of your choice in the space provided.*

______ **6.** The first African American to receive the Nobel Prize for literature was: **a.** Lorraine Hansberry. **b.** James Baldwin. **c.** Toni Morrison. **d.** Ralph Ellison.

______ **7.** All of the following were true of African American businesses in the 1990s EXCEPT: **a.** their sales grew at twice the rate of other businesses. **b.** their sales climbed to almost $8 billion. **c.** most were small businesses. **d.** most were large businesses.

______ **8.** One result of the spread of voting rights was that more African Americans were: **a.** elected to Congress. **b.** given cabinet posts. **c.** named to the Supreme Court. **d.** named ambassadors.

______ **9.** After Thurgood Marshall, the first African American to serve on the Supreme Court, resigned, he was replaced by: **a.** Robert C. Weaver. **b.** Adam Clayton Powell. **c.** David Dinkins. **d.** Clarence Thomas.

______ **10.** The increase in the number of African American voters since the 1960s has meant all of the following EXCEPT: **a.** the number of African Americans who were elected as government officials increased from 300 in 1964 to about 8,000 today. **b.** more laws favorable to African Americans were passed. **c.** both political parties try to attract African American votes. **d.** African Americans always vote for candidates of their own race.

III. ESSAY *Choose two of the following topics. Then write your answer in paragraph form on a separate sheet of paper.*

A. Select a field in which African Americans have became famous and describe some of their achievements.

B. What progress have African Americans made in the economy?

Name ______________________________ Date ______________

CHAPTER 24 TEST: Women Fight for Their Rights.

I. MATCHING *Decide which definition in the right column best explains a term in the left column. Then write the letter of that definition in the space next to the term.*

	Term	Definition
______	**1.** feminism	**a.** prejudice based on gender
______	**2.** liberation	**b.** the fight for women's political, economic, and social rights
______	**3.** sexism	**c.** freeing a person or group from discrimination
______	**4.** women's liberation	**d.** a proposed change in the Constitution calling for total equality for men and women under the law
______	**5.** Equal Rights Amendment	**e.** the movement to free women from all discrimination

II. MULTIPLE CHOICE *Choose the answer that best completes the sentence or answers the question. Then write the letter of your choice in the space provided.*

______ **6.** All of the following were problems women faced during the 1950s EXCEPT: **a.** fewer women now went to college. **b.** women workers earned less money than men for the same work. **c.** they had trouble borrowing money. **d.** they often could not get credit cards.

______ **7.** Leaders of the women's liberation movement used many of the methods of: **a.** the "pro-life" movement. **b.** the union movement. **c.** the abolition movement. **d.** the Civil Rights Movement.

______ **8.** Feminists worked for all of the following goals EXCEPT:**a.** equal job opportunities. **b.** the success of NOW. **c.** new roles for women. **d.** the defeat of ERA.

______ **9.** The Equal Rights Amendment, passed by Congress in 1972, was : **a.** adopted as the 29th amendment to the Constitution. **b.** defeated when only 12 states ratified it. **c.** ratified by 34 states but rejected by the voters. **d.** ratified by 35 states by 1982, when the deadline for approval passed.

______ **10.** Which one of the following had ceased to be a major problem faced by women in the second half of the 1990s? **a.** juggling careers and children. **b.** equal pay with men. **c.** career advancement **d.** legal restrictions.

III. ESSAY *Choose one of the following topics. Then write your answer in paragraph form on a separate sheet of paper.*

A. Explain what gains women have made in politics in recent years and explain why they are important.

B. Which woman in the chapter has made the most important contribution? Why do you think so?

Name ______________________________ Date ____________________

CHAPTER 25 TEST: Mexican Americans Struggle for Equal Rights.

I. MATCHING *Decide which definition in the right column best explains a term in the left column. Then write the letter of that definition in the space next to the term.*

	Term	Definition
______	**1.** migrant worker	**a.** admit that a union represents workers
______	**2.** Chicana or Chicano	**b.** in two languages
______	**3.** recognize	**c.** an American of Mexican descent
______	**4.** bilingual	**d.** a person who harvests crops in different places
______	**5.** United Farm Workers	**e.** a union of migrant farm workers

II. MULTIPLE CHOICE *Choose the answer that best completes the sentence or answers the question. Then write the letter of your choice in the space provided.*

______ **6.** The struggle for full Latino rights in the 1960s was called: **a.** La Causa. **b.** *El Movimiento.* **c.** Chicano self-help. **d.** *La Raza Unida.*

______ **7.** César Chávez's efforts to help Latino migrant workers was based on: **a.** nonviolent action. **b.** forming a political party. **c.** new trade policies with Mexico. **d.** direct, violent action.

______ **8.** Congress passed the Bilingual Education Act in 1968 to: **a.** help elect Latinos to federal offices. **b.** support efforts by Latinos to win civil rights in court. **c.** aid students who did not read or speak English. **d.** curb illegal immigration.

______ **9.** NAFTA was sponsored by Mexico and the United States to: **a.** raise tariffs. **b.** end illegal immigration. **c.** promote trade between the two countries. **d.** form a military alliance.

______ **10.** The Immigration Reform and Control Act of 1986 was passed to help solve the problem of: **a.** legal immigrants from Mexico. **b.** poverty among Mexican Americans. **c.** lack of jobs for Latinos. **d.** illegal immigration from Mexico.

III. ESSAY *Choose one of the following topics. Then write your answer in paragraph form on a separate sheet of paper.*

A. Select the Mexican American leader you think was the most important in helping Latinos improve their lives in the United States and give reasons for your choice.

B. Draw a map of the United States or use an outline map, to show the states where most Mexican Americans live today.

Name ______________________________ Date ____________________

CHAPTER 26 TEST: A Cuban Presence Grows in the United States.

I. MATCHING *Decide which definition in the right column best explains a term in the left column. Then write the letter of that definition in the space next to the term.*

	Term	Definition
_____	**1.** multinational	**a.** operation to bring refugees to safety by sea
_____	**2.** political exile	**b.** an order preventing trade with another nation
_____	**3.** boat lift	**c.** a company doing business in several countries
_____	**4.** embargo	**d.** a person who leaves a country for political reasons
_____	**5.** Little Havana	**e.** the Miami neighborhood in which many Cubans settled

II. MULTIPLE CHOICE *Choose the answer that best completes the sentence or answers the question. Then write the letter of your choice in the space provided.*

_____ **6.** When Fidel Castro came to power in Cuba, he ruled the nation as a: **a.** democracy. **b.** communist state. **c.** free enterprise economy. **d.** multinational corporation.

_____ **7.** One reason Castro stopped people from leaving for the United States in 1973 was that: **a.** Cuba was sending people to Spain. **b.** Cuba was losing too many people. **c.** Castro needed more people for the army. **d.** Castro was preparing to go to war with the United States.

_____ **8.** Which one of the following is NOT true of "Little Havana"? **a.** It is called "the capital of Latin America." **b.** Ninety percent of all Cubans live there. **c.** It is 200 miles from Cuba. **d.** It is the center of Cuban life in the United States.

_____ **9.** Which of the following is NOT true of Cuban Americans? **a.** They have the highest income of Latino groups. **b.** Most have graduated from high school. **c.** Many of them live in San Francisco. **d.** Many Cuban Americans own businesses.

_____ **10.** The U.S. embargo and the collapse of the Soviet Union in 1991 caused Castro's rule in Cuba to: **a.** grow stronger. **b.** come to an end. **c.** face a revolution. **d.** grow weaker.

III. ESSAY *Choose one of the following topics. Then write your answer in paragraph form on a separate sheet of paper.*

A. If you were a Cuban American, would you return to Cuba if Castro's dictatorship is replaced by a free government? Explain your answer.

B. In what ways have Cuban exiles changed life in Miami?

Name ______________________________ Date ____________________

CHAPTER 27 TEST: Puerto Ricans and Dominicans Strive to Succeed.

I. MATCHING *Decide which definition in the right column best explains a term in the left column. Then write the letter of that definition in the space next to the term.*

	Term	Definition
______	**1.** Operation Bootstrap	**a.** a self-governing nation with strong political and economic ties to another nation
______	**2.** *autonomismo*	**b.** a Dominican neighborhood in New York
______	**3.** Young Lords	**c.** Spanish for self-rule
______	**4.** commonwealth	**d.** Muñoz Marín's program for Puerto Rico
______	**5.** Washington Heights	**e.** mainland Puerto Ricans who pushed for full civil rights

II. MULTIPLE CHOICE *Choose the answer that best completes the sentence or answers the question. Then write the letter of your choice in the space provided.*

______ **6.** During the "great migration" of people from Puerto Rico to mainland United States, most Puerto Ricans settled in: **a.** Los Angeles. **b.** New York City. **c.** Miami, Florida. **d.** Philadelphia.

______ **7.** Puerto Ricans came to mainland United States for all these reasons EXCEPT: **a.** to find jobs. **b.** to earn higher wages. **c.** to build better lives. **d.** to leave their relatives.

______ **8.** In 1993, the people of Puerto Rico voted to: **a.** make Puerto Rico a state. **b.** keep Puerto Rico a commonwealth. **c.** make Puerto an independent nation. **d.** separate from the United States.

______ **9.** Which one of these facts about the Dominican Republic in the 1980s was NOT true? **a.** One fourth of the people had no jobs. **b.** A recent hurricane had caused $1 billion in damage. **c.** It owed a debt of $4 billion. **d.** Few of its people migrated to New York City.

______ **10.** In the 1990s, all of these things were true of the Dominicans living in mainland United States EXCEPT: **a.** They sent $800 million back to family members in the Dominican Republic. **b.** Few become U.S. citizens. **c.** More than 700,000 lived in New York City. **d.** They were the fastest-growing immigrant group.

III. ESSAY *Choose one of the following topics. Then write your answer in paragraph form on a separate sheet of paper.*

A. By 1970, the Puerto Rican population in New York City was twice as large as the population of San Juan, Puerto Rico. Why do you think this happened?

B. You are a reporter for a newsmagazine assigned to write an article on the Dominican community in New York City. What features of this community would you highlight in your article?

Name ______________________________ Date ______________________

CHAPTER 28 TEST: Native Americans Fight for Their Rights.

I. MATCHING *Decide which definition in the right column best explains a term in the left column. Then write the letter of that definition in the space next to the term.*

	Term	Definition
______	**1.** termination	**a.** Native American organization that seized Wounded Knee
______	**2.** American Indian Movement	**b.** the belief that Native Americans should take charge of their lives.
______	**3.** National Congress of American Indians	**c.** an organization whose members called for "Red Power"
______	**4.** National Indian Youth Council	**d.** group formed in 1944 by representatives from many Native American peoples
______	**5.** Red Power	**e.** U.S. policy to end of self-government by Native Americans

II. MULTIPLE CHOICE *Choose the answer that best completes the sentence or answers the question. Then write the letter of your choice in the space provided.*

______ **6.** During the 1960s, Native Americans renewed their struggle for: **a.** reservation lands. **b.** full civil rights. **c.** the right to vote. **d.** citizenship.

______ **7.** The goal of many Native American peoples in the 1940s and 1950s was to: **a.** end termination. **b.** restore the Indian Bureau. **c.** appoint the U.S. Commissioner of Indian Affairs. **d.** sell reservation land.

______ **8.** Which of the following was NOT true of Native American life on reservations by the 1960s? **a.** Many people lived in rundown housing. **b.** The jobless rate was high. **c.** Native Americans gained full civil rights. **d.** The death rate was higher than in the rest of the nation.

______ **9.** During the 1970s, Native Americans won back some of their land and gained other benefits by all of the following EXCEPT: **a.** court decisions. **b.** armed conflicts. **c.** new Presidential programs. **d.** agreeing to leave the reservations.

______ **10.** One subject on which Native Americans disagree is whether they should mix more completely into U.S. society or: **a.** try to set up their own government. **b.** make strong efforts to keep the old ways alive. **c.** move back to the reservations. **d.** prevent Native American women from attending college.

III. ESSAY *Choose one of the following topics. Then write your answer in paragraph form on a separate sheet of paper.*

A. Why did the U.S. government begin the termination policy? What were the effects? How did Native Americans respond?

B. What conditions led Native Americans to take direct action? What were some results of their actions?

Name ______________________________ Date ____________________

CHAPTER 29 TEST: Americans From Asia Are a Fast-Growing Part of the U.S. Population.

I. MATCHING *Decide which definition in the right column best explains a term in the left column. Then write the letter of that definition in the space next to the term.*

	Term	Definition
______	**1.** The McCarran-Walter Act	**a.** to return to the country where a person was born
______	**2.** The Immigration Act of 1965	**b.** a law that allowed immigration from most Asia countries
______	**3.** naturalize	**c.** to make persons from other countries citizens of the United States
______	**4.** The Civil Liberties Act of 1988	**d.** a law that allowed 20,000 immigrants from each Asian country to enter the United States each year
______	**5.** repatriate	**e.** a law that paid $20,000 to Japanese who had been interned during World War II

II. MULTIPLE CHOICE *Choose the answer that best completes the sentence or answers the question. Then write the letter of your choice in the space provided.*

______ **6.** Large numbers of Asian Americans have come to the United States from all of these Asian nations EXCEPT: **a.** Vietnam. **b.** China. **c.** Korea. **d.** Japan.

______ **7.** Immigration from China did not increase greatly until the tensions of which period began to ease? **a.** the Cold War **b.** the Korean War **c.** the Vietnam War **d.** World War II

______ **8.** Over 60 percent of the immigrants from China live in: **a.** Florida. **b.** California. **c.** California and New York. **d.** New York.

______ **9.** During World War II, the U.S. government decided that Japanese Americans threatened the security of the country and: **a.** kept them in internment camps. **b.** shipped them to Japan. **c.** put them in prisons. **d.** ordered them to work in munitions factories.

______ **10.** During the 1960s, the government of South Korea: **a.** encouraged its citizens to emigrate. **b.** tried to prevent emigration. **c.** forced its citizens to become communists. **d.** ended all emigration.

III. ESSAY *Choose one of the following topics. Then write your answer in paragraph form on a separate sheet of paper.*

A. Why did Congress in 1983 declare that the treatment of Japanese Americans during World War II had been "a grave injustice"?

B. Today Asians are one of the fastest-growing immigrant groups in the United States. What prediction can you make about the U.S. population in the future?

Name ______________________________ Date ____________________

CHAPTER 30 TEST: Immigrants from Europe and the Middle East Make New Lives in the United States.

I. MATCHING *Decide which definition in the right column best explains a term in the left column. Then write the letter of that definition in the space next to the term.*

	Term	Definition
______	**1.** displaced persons	**a.** Jewish state established in 1948
______	**2.** mosque	**b.** people who have been forced out of their homeland by war
______	**3.** Displaced Persons Act of 1948	**c.** people who live in Israel and in the nearby Arab nations
______	**4.** Israel	**d.** law that let 100,000 people per year from Eastern and Southern Europe beyond the quota limit enter the United States
______	**5.** Middle Easterners	**e.** Islamic house of worship

II. MULTIPLE CHOICE *Choose the answer that best completes the sentence or answers the question. Then write the letter of your choice in the space provided.*

______ **6.** During the Cold War, many people came to the United States to escape from: **a.** Communist governments in Western Europe. **b.** Communist governments in Eastern Europe. **c.** Islamic governments in the Middle East. **d.** Islamic governments in Africa.

______ **7.** As a result of the Immigration Act of 1965, many new immigrants came to the United States from: **a.** Europe. **b.** Africa. **c.** Europe and Africa. **d.** Asia and Latin America.

______ **8.** Most of the new immigrants to the United States from the Middle East are: **a.** Jews. **b.** Christian Arabs. **c.** Muslim Arabs. **d.** Israelis.

______ **9.** Donna Shalala, Secretary of Health and Human Services in President Clinton's cabinet, is: **a.** an Arab American. **b.** a displaced person. **c.** the founder of a huge clothing business. **d.** a Jewish American.

______ **10.** Many Arab Americans fear that prejudice against their people will rise because of: **a.** the collapse of the Soviet Union. **b.** terrorism in the Middle East. **c.** the treatment of Arabs in Israel. **d.** the dependence of the United States on oil in the Middle East.

III. ESSAY *Choose one of the following topics. Then write your answer in paragraph form on a separate sheet of paper.*

A. Explain why immigration from Europe declined after World War II.

B. Describe some of the achievements of Arab Americans in the United States, as well as some of the problems they face.

Name ______________________________ Date ____________________

CHAPTER 31 TEST: New Leaders Search for New Solutions.

I. MATCHING *Decide which definition in the right column best explains a term in the left column. Then write the letter of that definition in the space next to the term.*

	Term	Definition
____	**1.** sunbelt	**a.** a sharp downturn in business
____	**2.** recession	**b.** a debt created when government spends more than it takes in
____		
____	**3.** social programs	**c.** southern and western United States
____	**4.** conservative	**d.** government programs that aid groups of needy people
____	**5.** budget deficit	**e.** a person who believes in reducing the size of government and giving business more freedom

II. MULTIPLE CHOICE *Choose the answer that best completes the sentence or answers the question. Then write the letter of your choice in the space provided.*

____ **6.** All of the following are true of President Reagan EXCEPT: **a.** he was the oldest person ever elected President. **b.** he was one of the most popular of modern Presidents. **c.** he favored more spending on social programs. **d.** he had been governor of California.

____ **7.** Reagan's policies about taxes and defense spending resulted in a: **a.** lower budget deficit. **b.** increase in the deficit. **c.** balanced budget. **d.** a long recession.

____ **8.** Reagan appointed Sandra Day O'Connor as the first woman to serve as a member of the: **a.** Senate. **b.** Supreme Court. **c.** Joint Chiefs of Staff. **d.** cabinet. **e.** Federal Reserve Board.

____ **9.** All of the following are true of George Bush EXCEPT: **a.** he served as Vice-President under Reagan. **b.** he was a World War II hero. **c.** he was director of the CIA. **d.** he was a Democrat.

____ **10.** President Bush's action in trying to lower the deficit without raising taxes led to: **a.** a recession. **b.** a depression. **c.** business boom. **d.** his reelection in 1992.

III. ESSAY *Choose one of the following topics. Then write your answer in paragraph form on a separate sheet of paper.*

A. Explain why President Reagan's policies fit the mood of so many Americans in the 1980s.

B. Why do you think President Bush wanted to become known as the "Education President"?

Name ______________________________ Date ______________________

CHAPTER 32 TEST: The United States Is Challenged by World Problems.

I. MATCHING *Decide which definition in the right column best explains a term in the left column. Then write the letter of that definition in the space next to the term.*

_____	**1.** trade deficit	**a.** a nation in which the government has little control of the economy
_____	**2.** free-market economy	**b.** a situation that arises when a country buys more goods and services from other countries than it sells to them
_____	**3.** Operation Desert Storm	**c.** a place where there are no taxes on trade between countries
_____	**4.** free-trade zone	**d.** The UN offensive, led by the United States, against Iraq's invasion of Kuwait
_____	**5.** Palestine Liberation Organization	**e.** The group that led the fight to recover the land of the Palestinians from Israel

II. MULTIPLE CHOICE *Choose the answer that best completes the sentence or answers the question. Then write the letter of your choice in the space provided.*

_____ **6.** In the late 1980s, communism collapsed in all of these nations EXCEPT: **a.** the Soviet Union. **b.** East Germany. **c.** Poland. **d.** Iraq.

_____ **7.** Iraq's invasion of oil-rich Kuwait threatened a takeover of one of the world's main supplies of oil in: **a.** Iran. **b.** Somalia. **c.** Saudi Arabia. **d.** Israel.

_____ **8.** In August 1993, the world was surprised when: **a.** the PLO and Israel signed a peace agreement. **b.** Israel and the PLO refused to accept President Clinton's offer of peace. **c.** Israel and Saudi Arabia signed a peace agreement. **d.** the PLO and Saudi Arabia broke off relations.

_____ **9.** The armed conflict between the Contras and the Sandinistas took place in: **a.** Panama. **b.** Guatemala. **c.** Haiti. **d.** Nicaragua

_____ **10.** The overthrow of President Aristide by the army caused a crisis in: **a.** Panama. **b.** Nicaragua. **c.** Haiti. **d.** the Dominican Republic.

III. ESSAY *Choose one of the following topics. Then write your answer in paragraph form on a separate sheet of paper.*

A. Explain why the collapse of the Soviet Union challenged the U.S position as world leader.

B. Which of these two statements do you think best describes the U.S. actions in the war with Iraq: "Operation Desert Storm was a war by the United States to protect its main source of oil." "Operation Desert Storm was a key test of the U.S. policy of opposing powerful nations that invade their weaker neighbors." Explain your answer.

Name ______________________________ Date ____________________

CHAPTER 33 TEST: New Immigrants Make the United States a More Diversified Nation.

I. MATCHING *Decide which definition in the right column best explains a term in the left column. Then write the letter of that definition in the space next to the term.*

	Term	Definition
_____	**1.** refugee	**a.** Vietnamese who escaped their land by leaving in open boats
_____	**2.** Shining Path	**b.** a person who is forced to flee his or her home country
_____	**3.** boat people	**c.** the way many immigrants think of the United States
_____	**4.** the Land of Promise	**d.** a campaign to arrest people who were opposed to Argentina's military government
_____	**5.** the "dirty war"	**e.** a terrorist group in Peru

II. MULTIPLE CHOICE *Choose the answer that best completes the sentence or answers the question. Then write the letter of your choice in the space provided.*

_____ **6.** Almost half of the immigrants to the United States in the 1980s came from: **a.** Central America. **b.** Latin America. **c.** Europe. **d.** Asia.

_____ **7.** The Vietnamese who fled their land to escape the Communist government became: **a.** repatriates. **b.** refugees. **c.** pirates. **d.** plane people.

_____ **8.** Most of the Vietnamese people who came to the United States: **a.** met prejudice everywhere they settled. **b.** found work and became productive Americans. **c.** settled in cities in the Northeast. **d.** became shrimp fishers.

_____ **9.** All of the following is true of Indian immigrants to the United States EXCEPT: **a.** most are well educated. **b.** they all plan to return to their homeland someday. **c.** many have opened their own businesses. **d.** they own 15,000 motels in the U.S.

_____ **10.** South Americans continue to immigrate to the United States even though: **a.** democracy has spread in South America. **b.** many prefer to go to Spain to live. **c.** U.S. laws discriminate against them. **d.** most newcomers are unemployed.

III. ESSAY *Choose one of the following topics. Then write your answer in paragraph form on a separate sheet of paper.*

A. Select one of the groups of recent immigrants to the United States and describe some of the opportunities and problems they faced.

B. Jaime Escalante has become a role model for many young South American immigrants. Explain why.

Name ______________________________ Date ____________________

CHAPTER 34 TEST: The United States Faces Challenges.

I. MATCHING *Decide which definition in the right column best explains a term in the left column. Then write the letter of that definition in the space next to the term.*

	Term	Definition
______	**1.** pollution	**a.** the income below which people are considered poor by the U.S. government
______	**2.** acid rain	**b.** a person who depends on drugs
______	**3.** recycle	**c.** waste that makes the air, water, or land unhealthy
______	**4.** poverty line	**d.** to use again
______	**5.** addict	**e.** harmful rain caused by factory wastes in the air

II. MULTIPLE CHOICE *Choose the answer that best completes the sentence or answers the question. Then write the letter of your choice in the space provided.*

______ **6.** What action did the U.S. government take in 1993 to cut down on pollution from automobiles? **a.** It raised the speed limit to 60 miles per hour. **b.** It required factories to use nuclear fuel. **c.** It set a limit on how many miles a person may drive in a year. **d.** It set a goal of making cars get 80 miles on a gallon of gasoline.

______ **7.** In 1970, President Nixon created what government agency to enforce laws against pollution? **a.** Earth Day **b.** the Clean Air Act **c.** the Clean Water Act **d.** the Environmental Protection Agency

______ **8.** All of the following are causes of homelessness EXCEPT: **a.** mental illness. **b.** drug abuse. **c.** lack of low-cost housing. **d.** government loans.

______ **9.** Food stamps, welfare, job training, and special education classes are among the government programs designed to fight: **a.** pollution. **b.** poverty. **c.** mental illness. **d.** crime.

______ **10.** The Brady Bill was a law passed by Congress in 1993 to: **a.** fight drug use. **b.** make it more difficult for people to buy a handguns. **c.** seek a cure for AIDS. **d.** pay for repair and fix up homes for the poor.

III. ESSAY *Choose one of the following topics. Then write your answer in paragraph form on a separate sheet of paper.*

A. What government programs have been set up to aid poor Americans? Explain why you think they have succeeded or failed.

B. Draw a poster warning against the use of drugs, showing the dangers of selling and using drugs.

Name ______________________________________ Date ________________________

CHAPTER 35 TEST: Science Changes the Way Americans Live.

I. MATCHING *Decide which definition in the right column best explains a term in the left column. Then write the letter of that definition in the space next to the term.*

	Term	Definition
______	**1.** computer	**a.** the use of machines to do jobs that were once done by humans
______	**2.** program	**b.** a powerful beam of light that can be used to perform surgery
______	**3.** automation	**c.** something that circles the earth or another body in space
______	**4.** laser	**d.** a machine for storing and processing information
______	**5.** satellite	**e.** a series of instructions for a computer

II. MULTIPLE CHOICE *Choose the answer that best completes the sentence or answers the question. Then write the letter of your choice in the space provided.*

______ **6.** The "brains" of a modern computer is the: **a.** modem. **b.** program. **c.** chip. **d.** instructions.

______ **7.** Automation allows companies to make more goods and provide more services by using: **a.** more workers. **b.** less machinery. **c.** giant robot machines. **d.** more hand labor.

______ **8.** Scientists are linking computers with satellites in a plan to create: **a.** a network. **b.** an information highway. **c.** laser technology. **d.** a model of the human brain.

______ **9.** Which of the following is NOT an important tool in modern medicine? **a.** CAT scans **b.** brain transplants **c.** optical fibers **d.** lasers

______ **10.** Critics of the U.S. space program attack it by saying that: **a.** the money should be spent on more important things. **b.** the results have not been worth the money spent on it. **c.** other countries have done a better job with less money. **d.** it is prejudiced against minorities.

III. ESSAY *Choose one of the following topics. Then write your answer in paragraph form on a separate sheet of paper.*

A. What do you think has been the most important breakthrough in science in recent years? How has it changed Americans' lives?

B. Draw a picture of a space launch or a space shuttle in orbit, with a caption in which you identify what is happening.

Name ______________________________ Date ____________________

CHAPTER 36 TEST: The American People Face the 21st Century.

I. MATCHING *Decide which definition in the right column best explains a term in the left column. Then write the letter of that definition in the space next to the term.*

_____	**1.** diversity	**a.** a work of art or anything made up of smaller pieces
_____	**2.** melting pot	**b.** giving up working because of age
_____	**3.** mosaic	**c.** a wide range of differences
_____	**4.** mainstreaming	**d.** putting disabled students into classes with other children
_____	**5.** retirement	**e.** the idea that people from other lands and cultures would lose their "foreign ways" and become "American"

II. MULTIPLE CHOICE *Choose the answer that best completes the sentence or answers the question. Then write the letter of your choice in the space provided.*

_____ **6.** Immigrants to the United States today are like past immigrants in all of the following ways EXCEPT: **a.** they come to find better lives. **b.** they come to escape political unrest. **c.** they come to escape poverty. **d.** they come mainly from Southern and Eastern Europe.

_____ **7.** The elderly are an important voice in society for all of the following reasons EXCEPT: **a.** they organized to protect their rights. **b.** there are so many of them today. **c.** all of them can afford to contribute to politicians' campaigns. **d.** they have clear ideas about what they want done.

_____ **8.** The main goal that elderly Americans began to work for about 30 years ago was: **a.** retirement benefits. **b.** the right to retire. **c.** forced retirement. **d.** retirement at age 70.

_____ **9.** All of the following are true of the U.S. population today EXCEPT: **a.** many elderly Americans can now work at private jobs until age 70. **b.** the number of elderly Americans is increasing. **c.** African Americans now make up about 12 percent of the population. **d.** fewer disabled Americans are mainstreamed.

_____ **10.** In what way has the United States been changing in recent years? **a.** The population is growing, but more slowly than in the past. **b.** Americans are marrying later in life. **c.** Americans are having fewer children. **d.** all of the above.

III. ESSAY *Choose one of the following topics. Then write your answer in paragraph form on a separate sheet of paper.*

A. The official motto of the U.S., "*E Pluribus Unum*," means "from out of many, there is one." Do you think this supports the idea of the melting pot or of a cultural mosaic of people? Explain your answer.

B. Make a chart listing ways in which Americans with disabilities have the right to be helped to enter and use all public places, like restaurants, libraries, schools, sports arenas, and movie theaters.

Name ______________________ Date ______________

CHAPTER 1 Activity Sheet
Interpreting Statistics

The United States has been called "a nation of immigrants." For more than 300 years, immigrants have been writing the story of the United States. Immigrants have made the United States the diverse, multicultural nation that it is is today. The line graph and table on this page show how immigration is still adding to the variety of our nation. Study this information and answer the questions that follow.

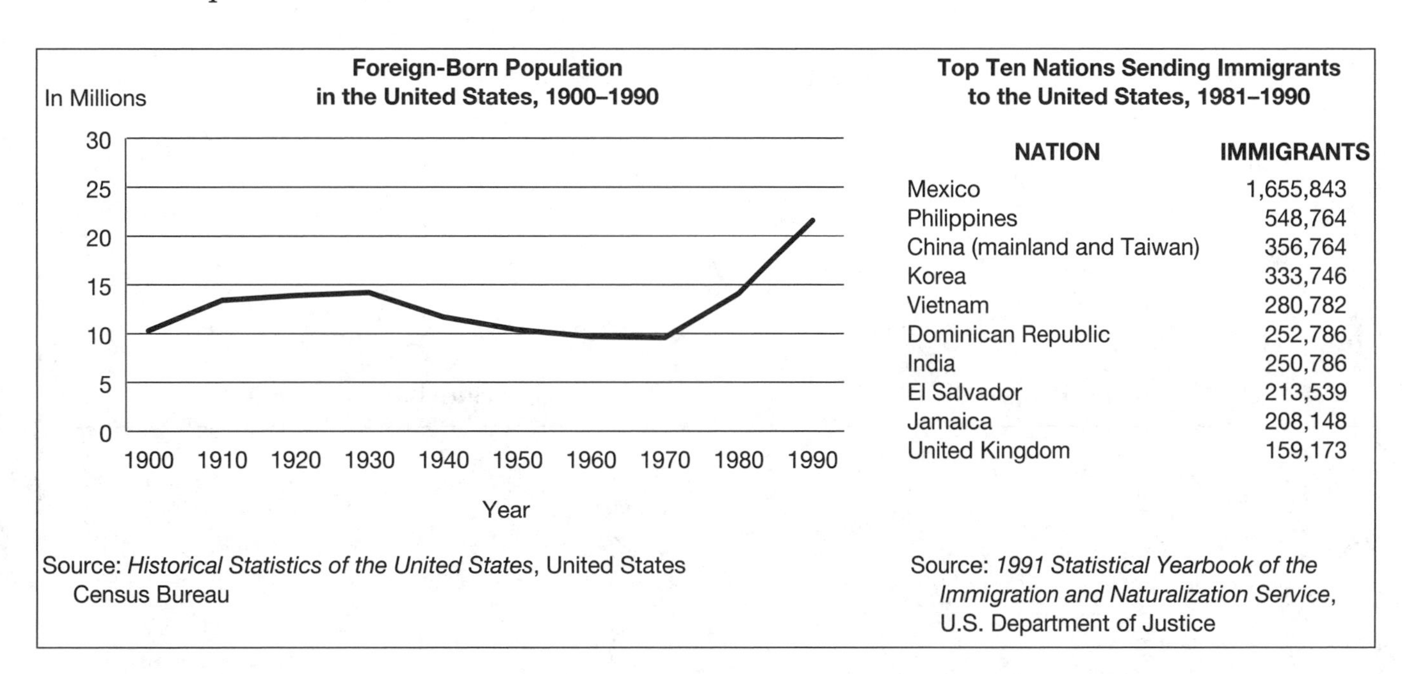

Top Ten Nations Sending Immigrants to the United States, 1981–1990

NATION	IMMIGRANTS
Mexico	1,655,843
Philippines	548,764
China (mainland and Taiwan)	356,764
Korea	333,746
Vietnam	280,782
Dominican Republic	252,786
India	250,786
El Salvador	213,539
Jamaica	208,148
United Kingdom	159,173

Source: *1991 Statistical Yearbook of the Immigration and Naturalization Service*, U.S. Department of Justice

1. What information is shown in the line graph? ______________________

2. What information is shown in the table? ______________________

3. In what ten-year period did the nation's foreign-born population begin to drop? __________

4. Suppose you were a population expert in 1970. Based on the figures on this line graph, would you predict that the foreign-born population would go up or down? Why? __________

5. Which nation sent the most immigrants during the 1980s? ______________________

6. Based on the table, from which two regions did most immigrants come: Europe, Africa, Asia, the Middle East, or Latin America? ______________________

7. Does the graph and table support the idea of the United States as a nation of many cultures? Explain. ______________________

Name ______________________________ Date ____________________

CHAPTER 2 Activity Sheet
Comparing the First American Cultures

Draw a sketch in each square that shows the way of life for each culture named.

Plains People	Southwest People
Eastern Woodlands People	Northwest People
The Maya	The Aztec

Name ______________________________ Date ____________________

CHAPTER 3 Activity Sheet
Interpreting Primary Sources

Like most sea captains, Christopher Columbus kept a log, or diary, of his ship's travels. This log is known as a **primary source.** Primary means first, or original. Columbus's log is a primary source because it is an original, firsthand look at his journey across the Atlantic. To step back into the past, read the following entries. Then answer the questions that follow.

Sunday, September 9, 1492
This day we completely lost sight of land, and many men sighed and wept for fear they would not see it again for a long time. I comforted them with great promises of lands and riches.

Monday, September 24, 1492
I am having serious trouble with the crew. . . . I am told by a few trusted men (and they are few in number!) that if I persist in going onward, the best course of action will be to throw me into the sea some night.

Monday, October 1, 1492
The pilot of the *Santa Maria* calculated that we had traveled 1,734 miles. . . . My personal calculation shows that we had come 2,121 miles. I did not reveal this figure to the men because they would become too frightened.

Thursday, October 11, 1492
About 10 o'clock at night, while standing on the sterncastle [rear deck], I thought I saw a light to west. It looked like a little wax candle bobbing up and down. . . . I am the first to admit that I was so eager to find land that I did not trust my senses. . . . Then at two hours after midnight, the *Pinta* fired a cannon, the signal for the sighting of land.

Friday, October 12, 1492
No sooner had we . . . taken possession of the island than people began to come to the beach. . . . They are friendly and bear [carry] no arms except for small spears, and they have no iron. I showed one my sword, and . . . he grabbed it by the blade and cut himself. . . . They ought to make good and skilled servants. . . . I think they can easily be made Christians for they seem to have no religion.

1. Why was Columbus's crew fearful? ____________________

2. What tricks did Columbus use to keep his crew going onward? ____________________

3. What worries did Columbus have? ____________________

4. How many days did his ships sail without any sight of land? ____________________

5. On what date did Columbus arrive in the Americas? ____________________

6. What was one of Columbus's first actions when he landed? ____________________

7. How did Columbus view the culture of the people that he met? ____________________

8. What conflicts do you think might erupt if Columbus stayed on this island? Explain. ______

____

____

Name ________________________ Date ________________

CHAPTER 4 Activity Sheet
Reading a Historical Map

Historical maps present information about the past. The historical map on this page shows the connection between the growth of trade and the growth of West African empires. Read this map, and answer the questions that follow. The key will help you unlock the map's meaning.

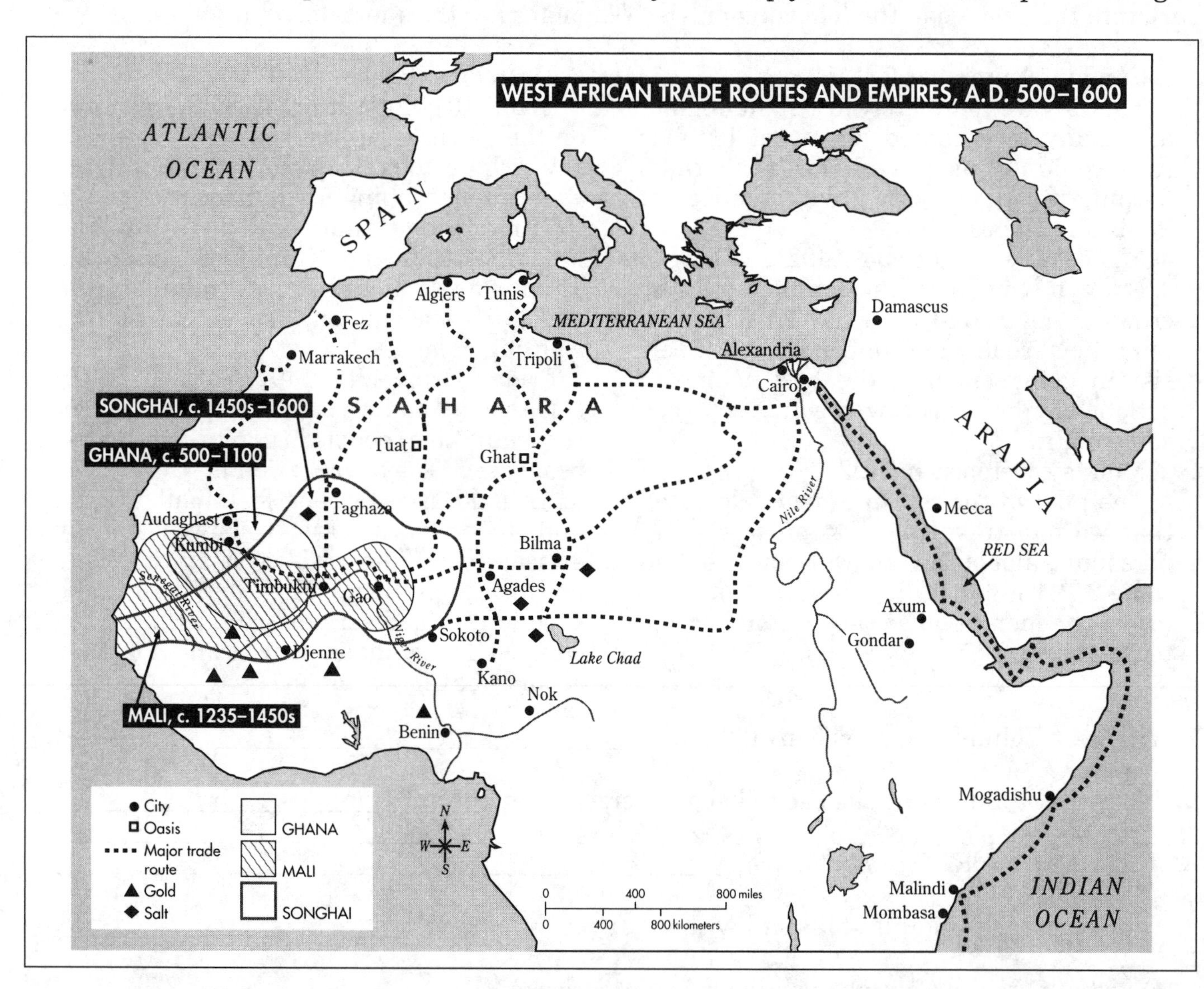

1. What three empires are shown on the map? ________________________

2. What two trade items enriched these empires? ________________________

3. Suppose you were a Muslim scholar at the University of Timbuktu. Which route(s) would you travel to get to the Muslim holy city of Mecca? ________________________

____

Name ______________________ Date ______________

CHAPTER 5 Activity Sheet
Reading a Bar Graph

Graphs are important tools for organizing statistical information in an easy-to-read diagram. The graph on this page is called a **bar graph** because it uses bars to show amounts. Other graphs use different symbols to show amounts. **Line graphs** use indicator lines. **Circle graphs** use parts of circles. **Pictographs** use pictures or symbols. You begin reading any graph by identifying the information on it. Next, you compare this information. What differences in size or amount can you spot? Can you see any patterns or changes over time? To practice these skills, study the graph below. Then answer the questions that follow.

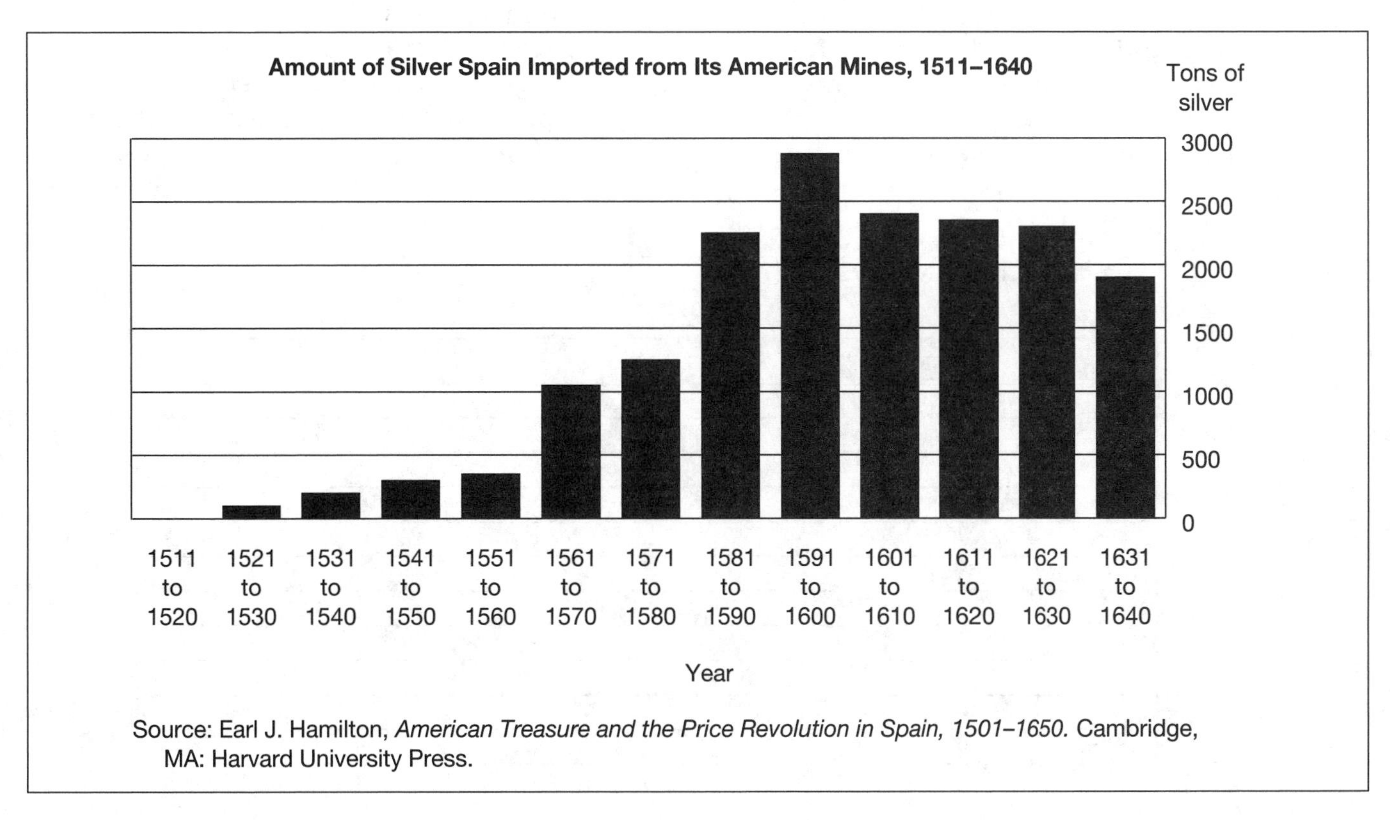

Source: Earl J. Hamilton, *American Treasure and the Price Revolution in Spain, 1501–1650.* Cambridge, MA: Harvard University Press.

1. What is the subject of this graph? ______________________

2. What information is shown on the **horizontal axis**, or line that runs sideways across the bottom of the graph? ______________________

3. What information is shown on the **vertical axis**, or line that runs up and down? ____________

4. In what ten-year period did silver exports top 500 tons? ______________________

5. In what ten-year period did silver exports reach their highest point? ______________________

6. Based on this graph, would you expect silver exports to go up or down for the period 1641–1650? Why? ______________________

Name ______________________________ Date ______________

CHAPTER 6 Activity Sheet
Understanding Chronology

A **chronology** is a list or table of events organized in the order in which they occurred. It shows the event that happened first, the event that happened second, and so on. Find the correct date in Chapter 6 for each of the events below. Use these dates to complete the chronology that follows. When you are done, write a title for your chronology. Then pick the event that most interests you and illustrate it in the box at the bottom of the page.

______ First Africans arrive in Virginia.
______ Pilgrims write the Mayflower Compact.
______ England smashes the Spanish navy.
______ Roger Williams seeks religious freedom at Providence.
______ Puritans found Salem.
_____ King Philip's War begins.
_____ John White founds Roanoke.
_____ English settlers build Jamestown.
_____ Virginia forms the House of Burgesses.
_____ The "starving time" nearly destroys Jamestown.
_____ Puritans pass the first public-school law.

Title

Date	Event

Name ______________________________ Date ______________

CHAPTER 7 Activity Sheet
Interpreting a Table

The table below shows the growth of the colonial population between 1660 and 1760. Study the information in this table. Then answer the questions that follow.

Population of the Thirteen Colonies

Colony	1660	1700	1760
New Hampshire	1,555	4,958	39,093
Massachusetts*	20,082	55,941	202,600
Rhode Island	1,539	5,894	45,471
Connecticut	7,980	25,970	142,470
New York	4,936	19,107	117,138
New Jersey	——	14,010	93,813
Pennsylvania	——	17,950	183,703
Delaware	540	2,470	33,250
Maryland	8,426	29,604	162,267
Virginia	27,020	58,560	339,726
North Carolina	1,000	10,720	110,442
South Carolina	——	5,704	94,074
Georgia	——	——	9,578

* The figure includes Maine, which was part of Massachusetts. Source: U.S. Department of Commerce, Bureau of the Census, *Historical Statistics of the United States, Colonial Times to 1970*, Part 2, (Series Z 1–19), p. 1168.

1. Which two colonies had the largest populations in 1660? ______________________

2. Which two colonies had the largest populations in 1760? ______________________

3. Which region had the largest population by 1760? ______________________

4. In 1760, which colony was the least densely populated? ______________________

5. What information in the text explains this fact? ______________________

6. Review the line graph on page 55. What does this graph tell you about one of the causes of population growth in the Southern colonies? ______________________

7. Another cause of population growth in the colonies was the birth of children. What other causes can you discover in the text? ______________________

Name ______________________________ Date ____________________

CHAPTER 8 Activity Sheet
Interpreting a Diagram

A diagram is a drawing or plan that explains how something works. The diagrams on this page show how a slave ship worked. These drawings were done in 1788 by a group of people who studied a slave ship named *Brookes*. The drawings labeled View A, View B, and View C show what a slave ship looked like if you sliced it open from front to back or from top to bottom. The drawing labeled View D shows what it looked like if you sliced off the upper deck and looked at one of the inside platforms. Study these diagrams and answer the questions below.

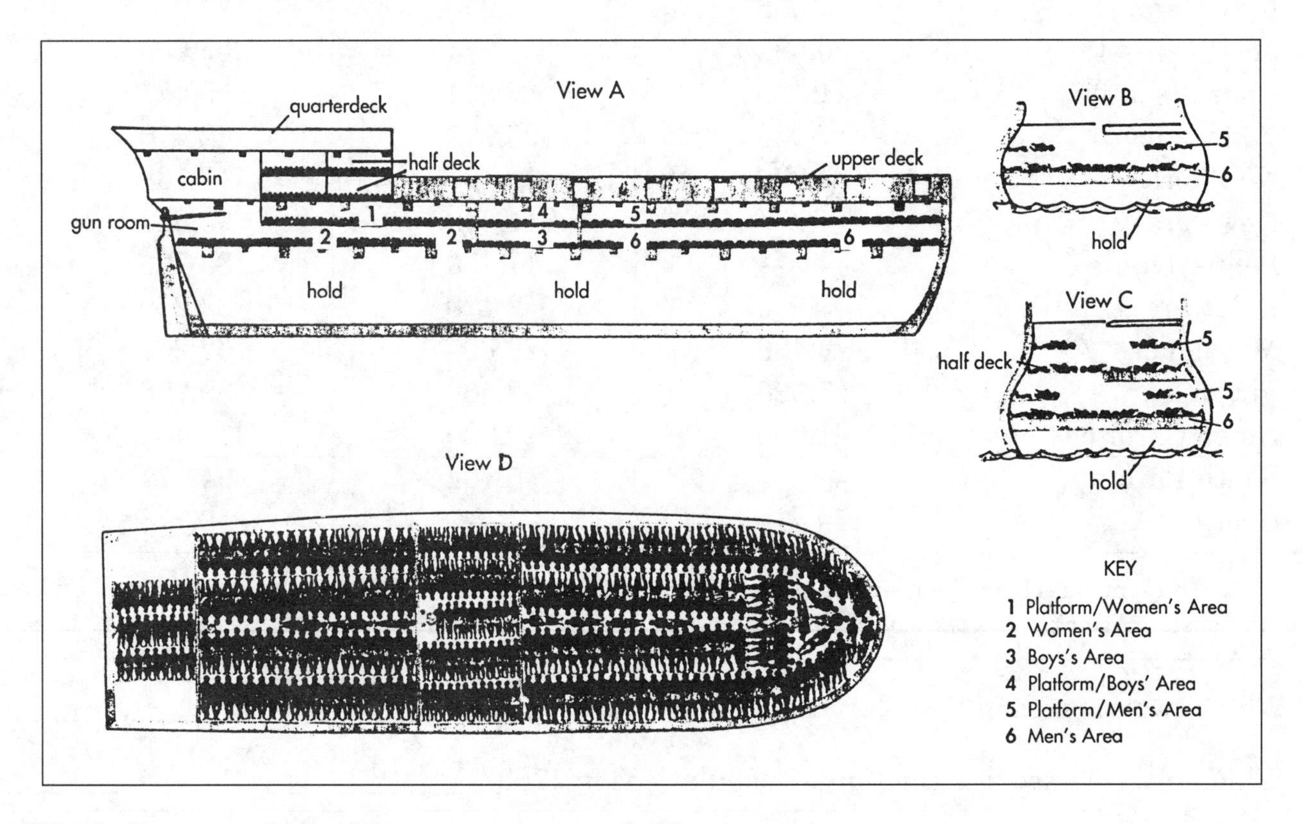

1. Which diagram shows where women traveled? ______________________________

____

2. What view explains why so many enslaved Africans died on the voyage? ______________

____

3. Imagine you are reporting on the slave trade in 1788. Complete the following description. "I found the conditions aboard the *Brookes* to be __________. Trapped below deck, the enslaved Africans receive little __________. They are forced to ______________."

Name ______________________________ Date ____________________

CHAPTER 9 Activity Sheet
Understanding Cause and Effect

Understanding cause and effect is an important part of understanding history. To identify cause and effect, keep these tips in mind. A **cause** produces a result, or effect. An **effect** is the result of a cause. To discover the cause of an event, ask yourself: "Why did this event happen?" To discover the effects of an event, ask yourself: "What happened as a result of this event?" The diagram below will help you organize the causes and effects of the French and Indian War. If you need more boxes, add them. Also, if you can't fill up all the boxes, don't worry. This chart is a tool for taking notes.

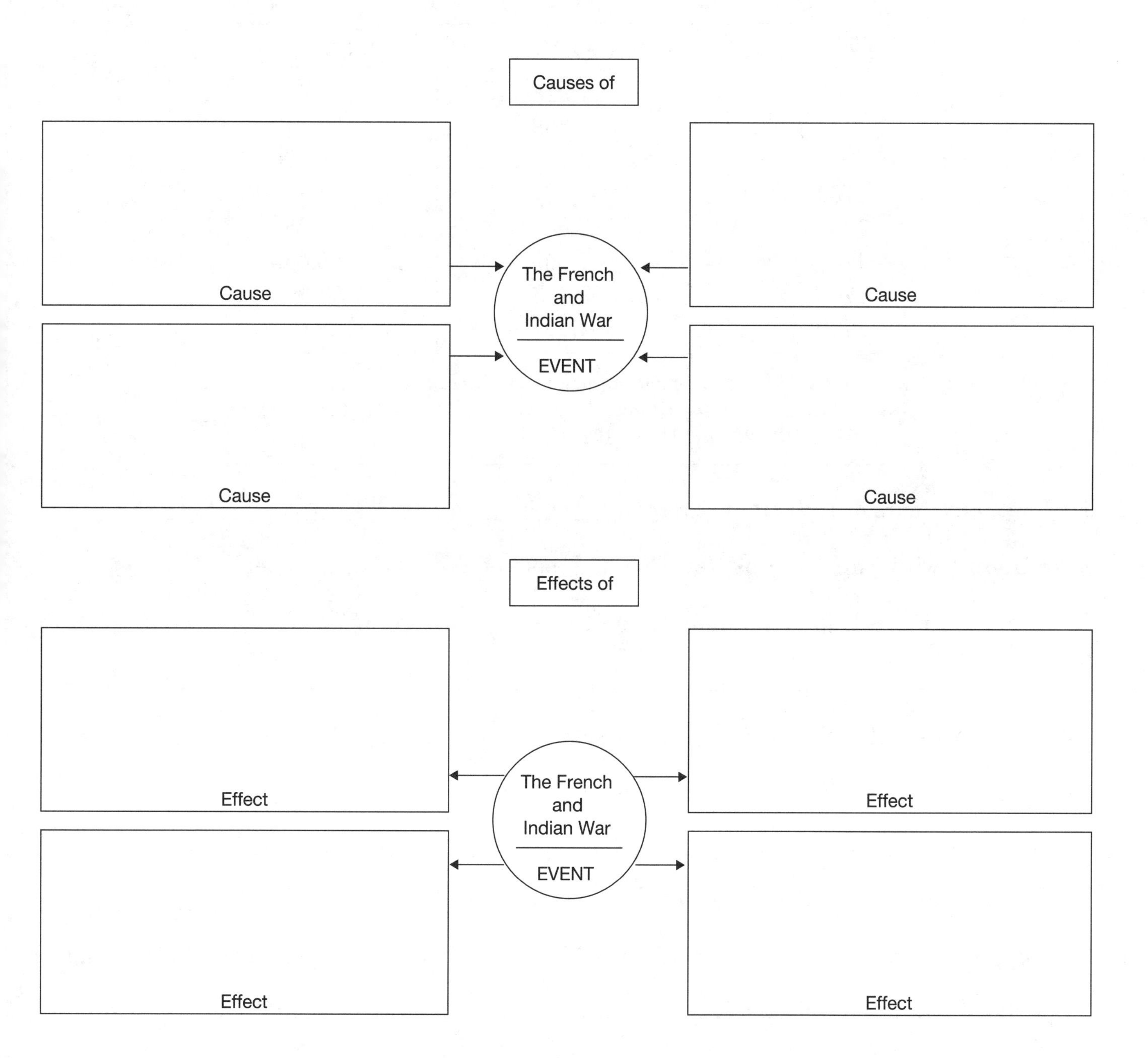

Name ______________________________ Date ______________________

CHAPTER 10 Activity Sheet
Interpreting a Table

The table on this page compares the growth of New England imports and exports. (Imports are the goods brought into a country. Exports are the goods sent out of a country.) The figures represent the value of these goods in pounds sterling, the unit of money used by England. (Dollars had not yet been invented! They came after the American Revolution and independence.) Study this table. Then answer the questions that follow.

New England Trade with England, 1700-1770

Year	Imports	Exports
1700	91,918	41,486
1710	106,338	31,112
1720	128,767	49,206
1730	208,196	54,701
1740	171,081	72,389
1750	343,659	48,455
1760	599,647	37,802
1770	394,451	148,011

Source: U.S. Department of Commerce, Bureau of the Census, *Historical Statistics of the United States, Colonial Times to 1970,* Part 2 (Series Z 213-226), pp. 1176–1177

1. How many years does the table cover? ______________________

2. In trading with England, was New England more of a "buyer" or a "seller"?______________

3. Do you think this trading relationship helped or hurt England? Explain. ______________

____

4. In what decade did imports from England drop the most?______________________

5. What event(s) cited in the textbook explain this drop? ______________________

6. Suppose you were the British prime minister in 1770. How would you respond to the changes that took place in trade between 1760 and 1770?______________________

7. Suppose you were a member of the Sons of Liberty? How might you respond to these same changes? ______________________________

Name ______________________________ Date ____________________

CHAPTER 11 Activity Sheet
Describing Place and Time

Bad roads and slow travel kept most colonists close to home. Many of the people who attended the First Continental Congress had never been outside of their colonies. So they saw the trip to Philadelphia as a great adventure. Imagine you are from a colony north or south of Pennsylvania. Design a postcard that shows something about your journey or the city of Philadelphia.

Use the space below to design the front of your postcard.

Greetings from ____________

Now that you have designed your postcard, write a message about your trip. Include the date.

Date:

To: ____________
____
____
____

Name ______________________ Date ______________

CHAPTER 12 Activity Sheet
Summarizing Chronological Information

Chapter 12 focuses on a short period of time. It runs from March 1775 to May 1776. But a lot happened in those months. To see why this period is so important, fill in the missing items in the chart below. Then write a sentence summarizing what has happened in the colonies in just 14 months.

Event	Date	Description
Patrick Henry addresses the Virginia assembly.		
	April 1775	The first shots of the American Revolution are fired.
Battle of Concord	April 1775	
	May 1775	Colonists capture badly needed cannon.
		Delegates from 13 colonies meet in Philadelphia. They send a list of complaints to the king.
Battle of Bunker Hill		
Common Sense is published.		
	May 1776	A delegate asks the Second Continental Congress to declare independence.

Summary: *By May of 1776,* ______________________

____

____

____

____

______________________.

Name ______________________________ Date ______________________

CHAPTER 13 Activity Sheet
Debating an Issue

The best debaters always try to guess the arguments used by the other side. This helps them to put together their own arguments more effectively. To practice preparing arguments for a debate, complete the exercises below.

Issue: ______________________________

Should colonists support the Declaration of Independence? ______________________________

Possible Pro Arguments ______________________________

Possible Con Arguments ______________________________

Position: ______________________________

Argument: ______________________________

Evidence: ______________________________

Argument: ______________________________

Evidence: ______________________________

Argument: ______________________________

Evidence: ______________________________

Summary Argument:

We support/oppose the Declaration because ______________________________

____

____

____

____

____

Name ______________________ Date ______________

CHAPTER 14 Activity Sheet
Comparing Accomplishments

1. Identify how each of the following people helped to win the Revolution.

   George Washington ______________________

   Mary Ludwig Hays ______________________

   Marquis de Lafayette ______________________

   James Armistead ______________________

   Baron von Steuben ______________________

   Bernardo de Gálvez ______________________

   Thaddeus Kosciusko ______________________

   Count Casimir Pulaski ______________________

2. If you had to pick one of these people to honor on the next July 4 holiday, which person would you pick? Why? "I would pick ____________ because ______________________ ______________________."

3. Design a special stamp that the government might issue to honor this person.

Name ______________________________ Date ____________________

CHAPTER 15 Activity Sheet
Interpreting a Table

The Revolution had barely ended when a new battle erupted. This time Americans fought over a new plan of government known today as the Constitution. To see where the toughest fights took place, study the following table. (States are listed alphabetically.) Then answer the questions below.

Ratification of the Constitution

State	Rank in Population	Date of Vote	Votes For	Votes Against
Connecticut	8	January 9, 1788	128	40
Delaware	12	December 7, 1787	30	0
Georgia	11	January 2, 1788	26	0
Maryland	6	April 28, 1788	63	11
Massachusetts	2	February 6, 1788	187	168
New Hampshire	10	June 21, 1788	57	47
New Jersey	9	December 18, 1787	38	0
New York	5	June 26, 1788	30	27
North Carolina*	4	November 21, 1789	194	77
Pennsylvania	3	December 12, 1787	46	23
Rhode Island*	13	May 29, 1790	34	32
South Carolina	7	May 23, 1788	149	73
Virginia	1	June 25, 1788	89	79

* After the Constitution went into effect and the Bill of Rights was added, North Carolina and Rhode Island held new votes.

1. What was the first state to ratify the Constitution? ______________________

2. What was the last state to ratify it? ______________________

3. Nine states were needed to ratify the Constitution. What state claimed the honor of making the Constitution "the law of the land"? ______________________

4. In which four states was the vote the closest? ______________________

5. Which two states did not ratify the Constitution until after it became law? ______________________

6. Review the debate between large and small states. What reason might Rhode Island have had for fighting ratification? ______________________

Name ______________________________ Date ______________

CHAPTER 16 Activity Sheet
Interpreting a Chart

The authors of the Constitution feared the misuse of power. So they divided power in two important ways. First, they divided power among three branches of government—the legislative, executive, and judicial. Second, they divided power among federal and state governments. The definitions and chart on this page help you to understand how this second division of power works. Study this information, and then complete the exercise that follows.

Federal System: a system in which power is divided between a national government and state governments

Reserved Powers: powers that the Constitution reserves, or sets aside, for state governments

Delegated Powers: powers that the Constitution delegates, or gives, to the national government

Concurrent Powers: powers that national and state governments share (Concurrent means to "hold together.")

Read the list of government services below. Decide which level of government has the power to

Federal Government Powers
(Delegated Powers)

- Regulate foreign trade
- Regulate trade between the states
- Coin and print money
- Create and support armed forces
- Declare war and make peace
- Conduct relations with other nations
- Establish post offices and roads
- Govern U.S. territories
- Admit new states
- Create federal courts
- Set up a system of weights and measures
- Make copyright laws
- Control immigration
- Establish citizenship laws

Shared Federal and State Powers
(Concurrent Powers)

- Collect taxes
- Borrow money
- Establish courts
- Provide for the well-being of the people
- Enforce the laws
- Charter banks

State Government Powers
(Reserved Powers)

- Regulate trade with the state
- Estbablish local governments
- Conduct elections
- Determine voting qualifications
- Establish and support public schools
- License professional workers
- Make laws about marriage and divorce
- Create laws for business firms
- Provide for public safety
- Carry out all powers not given to the federal government nor denied to the states

provide this service. In the space provided, write *F* if the power belongs to the federal government, *S* if the power belongs to the state governments, and *B* if it belongs to both governments.

1. ____ Signing a peace treaty with Russia

2. ____ Increasing income taxes

3. ____ Deciding when election polls open

4. ____ Coining a new silver dollar

5. ____ Changing to the metric system

6. ____ Increasing the school year

7. ____ Enlisting soldiers in the army

8. ____ Creating a new county government

9. ____ Reducing the length of time to become a citizen

10. ____ Taking a loan to provide low-income housing

Name ______________________________________ Date ______________________

CHAPTER 17 Activity Sheet
Writing a News Story

Below is an eyewitness description of George Washington's arrival in New York City. Within hours, he would be sworn in as the first President of the United States. Pretend you are a reporter watching this scene. Write down details that you would include in a story for your local newspaper. (Remember that reporters answer the questions *Who? What? Where? When? Why?* and *How?*) Use these details to write a news story in the space below. In the box, design a picture to accompany your article.

> The barge [in which he crossed the Hudson River] was built . . . by the citizens of New York. . . . [It] was rowed by thirteen pilots, all dressed in white. . . . His Excellency [Washington] was also accompanied by some well-equipped ships . . . with citizens of New Jersey and New York on board. . . . When the presidential barge passed, a Spanish ship fired thirteen guns. Again thirteen guns were fired when the President landed. . . . The rush of people to see their beloved General Washington was amazing. . . . At night the whole city was lighted.

"____"(Headline)

April 30, 1789, New York City

Story by ______________________________________

Name ______________________________ Date ________________

CHAPTER 18 Activity Sheet
Analyzing History through Literature

Americans gained strong feelings of patriotism, or pride in their nation, as a result of the War of 1812. One American expressed these patriotic feelings in a poem called "The Star-Spangled Banner." Read how Francis Scott Key came to write this poem.

In August 1814, a British army of 4,000 soldiers landed at Chesapeake Bay. Its goal was to capture Baltimore, Maryland, and Washington, D.C. On August 24, they entered Washington and set fire to the White House, the Capitol, and other government buildings.

The British Army then headed north to complete its victory by capturing Baltimore. At Baltimore, however, the U.S. forces had several strong forts. For several days, British ships fired on these forts with heavy shells and rockets.

Francis Scott Key, an American lawyer, was a prisoner on one of the British ships. He was very worried as he watched the British bombing Fort McHenry. Key feared that the British might conquer the fort. Baltimore then would have to surrender. All that night, he watched anxiously as the heavy shelling continued. Finally, at about 1:00 A.M. on September 14, the firing stopped. Then Key saw something wonderful. The large U.S. flag at Fort McHenry was still waving in the breeze! Key knew that the Americans had defeated the British.

Early that morning, Francis Scott Key began to write down his feelings of joy and relief. On the back of a letter that he was carrying, he wrote:

> O say! can you see, by the dawn's early light,
> What so proudly we hail'd at the twilight's last gleaming,
> Whose broad stripes and bright stars, thro' the perilous fight,
> O'er the ramparts we watch'd were so gallantly streaming?
> And the rockets' red glare, the bombs bursting in air,
> Gave proof thro' the night that our flag was still there.
> O, say, does that Star-Spangled Banner yet wave
> O'er the land of the free and the home of the brave?

Key's poem was published by several Baltimore newspapers. Within a few months, the poem was being used as the words to a popular tune. That song became the national anthem of the United States, "The Star-Spangled Banner."

1. Why do you think Francis Scott Key wrote "The Star-Spangled Banner"? ________________

____

2. How did the song show the growing patriotic feeling among Americans? ________________

____

3. Why do you think "The Star-Spangled Banner" is still important to Americans today? _____

____

____

Name ________________________________ Date ____________________

CHAPTER 19 Activity Sheet
Interpreting Poetry

In 1828, teachers at the New York African Free School asked their students to write poems on the subject of slavery. The school's African American students were free. But they still felt the pain of enslaved African Americans in the South. The poem on this page was written by a 12-year-old student named George R. Allen.

If you read the poem out loud, you'll discover that each line ends with words that *rhyme,* or sound alike. You also may stumble across some strange terms. George wrote in a formal style of English that we no longer use. Study the vocabulary list below. Then try reading the lines to a classmate. Together answer the questions that follow.

bands: restrains, ties
dost: do
impart: give
seize: take by force
stain: dark spot
thou: you
smart: stinging pain
woes: sorrows

On Slavery,
by George R. Allen

Slavery, oh, thou cruel stain,
Thou dost fill my heart with pain.
See my brother, there he stands
Chained by slavery's cruel bands.

Could we not feel a brother's woes,
Ease all the wants he undergoes!
Seize him from slavery's cruel smart,
And to him freedom joys impart?

1. Who is the "brother" that George mentions? ____________________

2. Why do you think George used an exclamation point at the end of the sixth line?__________

3. What emotions does George ask the readers to feel? ____________________

4. What action does he want them to take?____________________

5. Suppose you were a former enslaved African American. Complete the letter below.

Dear George,

I just read your poem. ____________________

____

____

____

Name ______________________ Date ______________

CHAPTER 20 Activity Sheet
Interpreting a Primary Source

From 1843 to 1863, some 350,000—550,000 people traveled the Oregon Trail. They made up the largest voluntary **migration**, or movement, of people in history. One of the travelers who rode the trail wrote: "It seems as if the whole human family has set its face westward." To find out what the journey was like, read the following diary entries by Lydia Allen Rudd.

May 6, 1852 Left the Missouri River for our long journey across the . . . plains. In front of us as far as vision could see extended the green hills covered with fine grass.

May 9 We passed a new made grave today . . . a man from Ohio. We also met a man that was going back. He had buried his Wife this morning. She died from measles.

May 14 Just after we started this morning we passed four men digging a grave. . . . The man that had died was taken sick [with] . . . cholera.

July 4 This is the day of our nation's . . . liberty. . . . Encamped for the day to celebrate our independence. We had some gooseberry sauce for dinner gathered from the bluff. Harry killed an antelope.

July 15 Some . . . Indians came to our camp this morning. I swapped some hard bread for some good berries.

October 2 A Frenchman came to us this morning from the mountains. Says we cannot cross the mountains for the snow. . . . Nothing for us to do but to . . . go down [the Columbia River].

October 14 I am so anxious to get some place to stop and settle that my patience is not worth much.

October 27 We reached Burlington [a town in Oregon Territory]. . . . There is one store, one blacksmith shop, and three or four . . . houses. . . . There is no house we can get to winter in.

October 27 We are to live in the back part of the store for this winter. . . . This is the journey's end.

1. For how long did Lydia travel the Oregon Trail? ______________________

2. What were some of the landscapes over which Lydia traveled? ______________________

3. What hardships did she meet along the way? ______________________

4. (a) What American beliefs did Lydia carried west? (b) What diary entry supports your answer? ______________________

5. What difficulties faced Lydia after she arrived in Oregon? ______________________

6. Why do you think so many people risked their lives to travel into the Oregon Territory? ___

____

____

Name ______________________ Date ______________

CHAPTER 21 Activity Sheet
Organizing Historical Information

The diagrams below use some of the reporter's questions to help you to collect key facts about the Texas Rebellion and the Mexican War. Fill in these diagrams with information from the text.

The Texas Rebellion

WHEN
was it fought?

WHERE
was it fought?

WHAT
was it?

WHO
fought in it?

WHY
was it fought?

The Mexican War

WHEN
was it fought?

WHERE
was it fought?

WHAT
was it?

WHO
fought in it?

WHY
was it fought?

Name ______________________ Date ______________

CHAPTER 22 Activity Sheet
Interpreting a Primary Source

Below is a letter written by a young Irish immigrant named Patrick Murphy to his mother in Ireland. Read this letter carefully. Then answer the questions that follow.

> My dear Mother,
>
> I hope that you are very well, as I am. This letter is written for me by Tom Rooney, for I am no scholar. You remember how much more time I spent in the hills than in the schoolroom. I told you in my last [letter], I am stopping [staying] with Tom and his wife, Sally, who are fine people. So you should not worry about me. I am very comfortable and eat well. Now that I am here [in the United States] awhile, I like it better than ever. New York is a grand, handsome city. But you would hardly know you had left Ireland, there are so many Irish people here. Some of them have become rich. Some of them are big men in government. For most of us it is hard work. But there is plenty of it. And the pay is all right. They are always building things here. Tom . . . has got me a job working with him on the new streets they are making in this city. . . . Soon I will be sending you some money I have saved. I know that will help you and you will not feel so bad about how I had to leave you. Well, Mother, I must end now. . . . There are plenty of good Catholic people here, and no fear of losing our way. . . . I will write you again soon.
>
> Your son,
> Pat

1. Why does Pat have a friend write his letter? ______________________

____

2. What is Pat's opinion of New York City? ______________________

3. Why has it been easy for him to adjust to living in the United States? ______________

____

4. What accomplishments by Irish immigrants does he mention? ______________

5. How does Pat view opportunity in the United States? ______________________

6. What does Pat mean when he says there is "no fear of losing our way"? ______________

____

7. Suppose you were Pat's mother. On a separate sheet of paper write a reply to his letter. Mention some of the conditions that Tom has left behind in Ireland. ______________

____

Name ______________________ Date ______________

CHAPTER 23 Activity Sheet
Interpreting a Primary Source

In 1847, Emily Dickinson attended Mount Holyoke. Dickinson later went on to become one of America's best-known women poets. In the selection below, the future poet describes her school day. As you read this selection, keep in mind your own school day. Then answer the questions that follow.

> I will tell you my order of time for the day. At 6 o'clock we all rise. We [eat] breakfast at 7. Our study hours [are] at 8. At 9 we all meet in the Seminary Hall for prayers. At 10:30 I recite a review of ancient history from our reading. At 11 I recite a lesson . . . [in poetry]. At 12 I practice calisthenics [exercises]. At 12:15 I read until dinner, which is at 12:30.
>
> After dinner, from 1:30 until 2 I sing in Seminary Hall. From 2:45 until 3:45 I go to Section. [Here] we give in all our accounts of the day. This includes absence, tardiness, breaking silent study, and ten thousand other things. At 4:30 we go into Seminary Hall and receive advice from Miss Lyon.
>
> We have supper at 6 and silent study hours from then until the retiring bell. This rings at 8:15. One thing is certain. Miss Lyon and all the teachers [think] . . . of our happiness in everything they do. You know that is pleasant.

1. How long is the school day at Mount Holyoke? ______________________

2. What are some of the subjects studied at the school? ______________________

3. What happens during "Section"? ______________________

4. What do these activities tell you about discipline at the school? ______________________

____

5. How does Dickinson view her school life? ______________________

6. In the space below, list some of the similarities and differences between Dickinson's schooling and your own schooling.

Similarities	Differences
______________	______________
______________	______________
______________	______________
______________	______________

Name ______________________________ Date ____________________

CHAPTER 24 Activity Sheet
Interpreting a Political Advertisement

William Lloyd Garrison tried to convince women to join the abolitionist movement. The advertisement on this page ran in Garrison's newspaper *The Liberator.* Study this advertisement, and then answer the questions that follow. A vocabulary list will help you with difficult words in the advertisement's poem.

LADIES' DEPARTMENT.

"Am I not a Woman and a Sister?"

White Lady, happy, proud and free,
Lend awhile thine ear to me ;
Let the Negro Mother's wail
Turn thy pale cheek still more pale.
Can the Negro Mother joy
Over this her captive boy,
Which in bondage and in tears,
For a life of wo she rears ?
Though she bears a Mother's name,
A Mother's rights she may not claim ;
For the white man's will can part,
Her darling from her bursting heart.

From the Genius of Universal Emancipation.
LETTERS ON SLAVERY.—No. III.

bears: carries
bondage: held in slavery
bursting: breaking
captive: prisoner
emancipation: freedom from bondage
genius: wisdom, very smart
lend: give
pale: colorless
rears: raises
thine: your
universal: present everywhere
wail: loud cries
will: wish
wo: woe, sadness

1. How does Garrison show that he is appealing to women readers? ______________________________
____

2. What kind of life does the poem say an enslaved African American woman can expect for her children? ______________________________

3. Why can't she claim "a Mother's rights"? ______________________________

4. What does the phrase "Genius of Universal Emancipation" mean? ______________________________
____

5. If Garrison did not print the poem, could you still figure out the ad's message? Explain. ___
____
____

Name ______________________________ Date ____________________

CHAPTER 25 Activity Sheet
Interpreting an Interview

A short time after John Brown's arrest at Harpers Ferry, several people interviewed him. They included Senator James M. Mason of Virginia and Representative Clement L. Vallandigham of Ohio. (Vallandigham sided with the South.) A reporter for the *New York Herald* recorded the interview. Read the passage below from that interview. Then answer the questions that follow.

Vallandigham: Mr. Brown, who sent you here?

Brown: No man sent me here; it was my own prompting and that of my Maker, or that of the Devil—whichever you please to [think].

Mason: What is your object in coming?

Brown: We came to free the slaves, and only that.

Mason: How do you justify your acts?

Brown: I think, my friend, you [slave owners] are guilty of a great wrong against God and humanity. . . . It would be perfectly right for anyone to interfere with you so far as to free those you willfully and wickedly hold in bondage. I do not say this insultingly.

Mason: I understand that.

Brown: I think I did right, and that others will do right who interfere with you. . . . I hold with the Golden Rule. [It says] "Do unto others as you would have others do onto you." [This rule] applies to all who would help others to gain their liberty. . . . I pity the poor in bondage that have none to help them. . . . I don't think the people of the slave states will ever consider the subject of slavery in its true light.

Reporter: I do not wish to annoy you. But if you have anything further you would like to say, I will report it.

Brown: I wish to say . . . that . . . all you people of the South had better prepare yourselves for a settlement of the question [of slavery]. . . . You may dispose [get rid] of me very easily. I am nearly disposed of now; but this question is still to be settled. . . . I mean, the end of it is not yet [come].

1. What was Brown's goal at Harpers' Ferry? ______________________________

2. What sentence shows that Brown knew he would be seen as either a hero or a villain? ____

____

3. What rule did Brown use to defend his actions? ______________________________

____

4. Why did Brown feel that such forceful actions were needed? ______________________________

____

5. What prediction does Brown make? ______________________________

6. Based on information in the text, what effect did Brown's raid have on the United States?

____

Name ______________________________ Date ____________________

CHAPTER 26 Activity Sheet
Comparing Strengths and Weaknesses

The graphs below compare the North and South at the start of the Civil War. They are based on the 1860 census. Study this data. Then complete the exercises that follow.

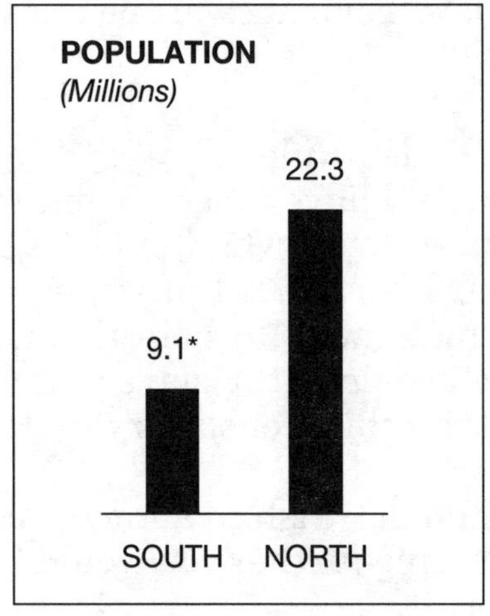

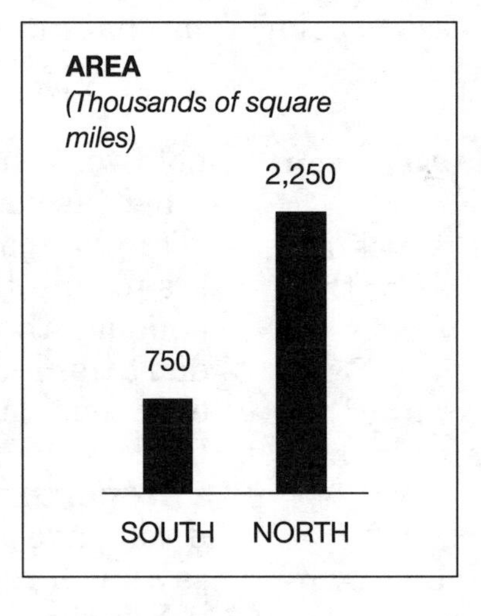

*Including 4 million enslaved African Americans

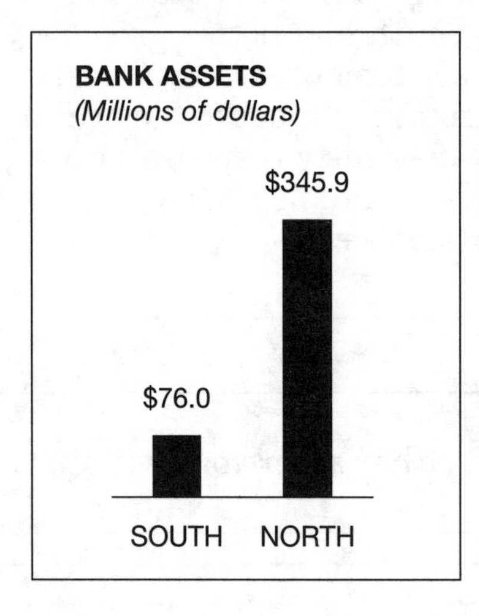

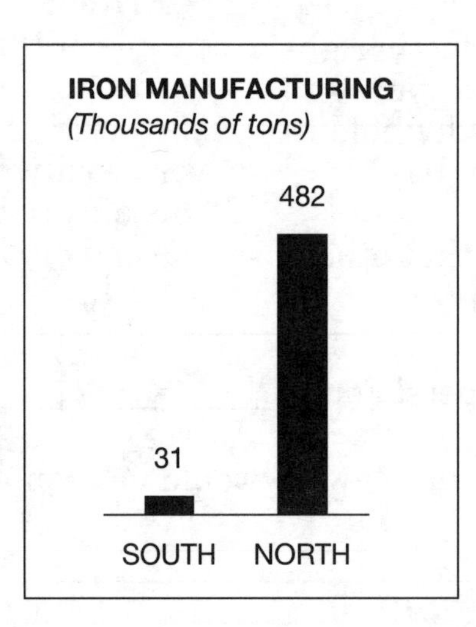

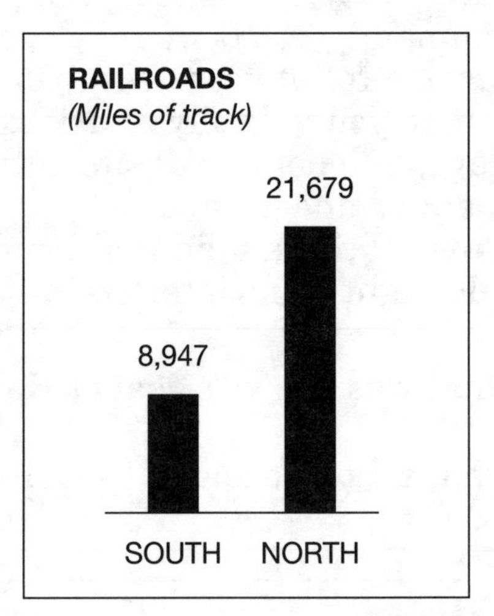

1. How many more people lived in the North than in the South? ____________________

2. How much bigger was the North than the South in terms of land area? ____________

3. What industrial advantages did the North have over the South? ____________________

4. How much more **capital,** or money, did the North have to invest in the war? __________

5. Based on this information, which prediction would you make about the outcome of the war?

____

Name ______________________________ Date ____________________

CHAPTER 27 Activity Sheet
Interpreting a Chart

Emancipation means freedom from bondage. *Proclamation* means official announcement. So the Emancipation Proclamation was an official announcement of freedom from bondage. Suppose you were an enslaved African American. You might think the United States had just declared an end to slavery. But it hadn't. What exactly did the Emancipation Proclamation do? Study the chart and answer the questions below.

EFFECT OF THE EMANCIPATION PROCLAMATION, 1863			
Free States of the Union	Border States Loyal to the Union	Confederate Areas Held by the Union	The Confederate States of America*
Maine, Vermont New Hampshire Massachusetts Rhode Island Connecticut Pennsylvania Michigan, New Jersey New York, Ohio Indiana, Illinois Wisconsin Minnesota Kansas Nebraska Territory Dakota Territory Indian Territory Colorado Territory Utah Territory Nevada Territory New Mexico Territory California Washington Territory Oregon	Delaware Maryland West Virginia Kentucky Missouri	Parts of the following states: Virginia North Carolina South Carolina Georgia Florida Louisiana Tennessee Arkansas Alabama	Virginia North Carolina South Carolina Georgia Florida Louisiana Tennessee Arkansas Alabama Texas *Where the Emancipation Proclamation applied

1. Where did the Emancipation Proclamation apply? ______________________________

2. Where did it not apply? ______________________________

3. If the federal government took no other action, would slavery still exist in the United States at the end of the war? Why or why not? ______________________________

____

4. Read page 229 in the text. If the Emancipation Proclamation did not end slavery, why did Lincoln issue it? ______________________________

Name ______________________________ Date ______________

CHAPTER 28 Activity Sheet
Interpreting Political Cartoons

A political cartoon is like a letter to the editor. It expresses a point of view, or opinion, about a person, issue, or event. You begin reading a political cartoon by looking at its details. Keep in mind that a cartoonist often uses **symbols**, or drawings with special meaning. The eagle in the cartoon on this page, for example, is a symbol of the United States. (Look at a quarter, and you will find the same eagle.) Cartoonists also use **caricatures**. These are sketches that exaggerate, or distort, a person's features. Caricatures can be positive or negative, depending upon a person's point of view. Finally, a cartoonist uses labels and words to help you figure out the cartoon's message. To practice your skill at reading a political cartoon, study the cartoon below. Then answer the questions that follow.

1. Who do the two standing figures represent? ______________________________

2. Who do the kneeling figures represent? ______________________________

3. What do the words "The Union as it was" mean? ______________________________

4. Which set of figures want the Union that way? ______________________________

5. How can you tell? ______________________________

6. What does the burning schoolhouse and the words "Worse than slavery" tell you about what is happening in the South? ______________________________

7. What is the cartoonist's opinion of these events? ______________________________

8. What evidence supports your answer? ______________________________

____

Name ______________________________ Date ____________________

CHAPTER 29 Activity Sheet
Comparing Leaders

The diagram below will help you compare the lives and ideas of Booker T. Washington and W. E. B. DuBois. Some areas for comparison have been suggested. Think of others. If you want to add even more areas, create new diagrams on the back of this sheet.

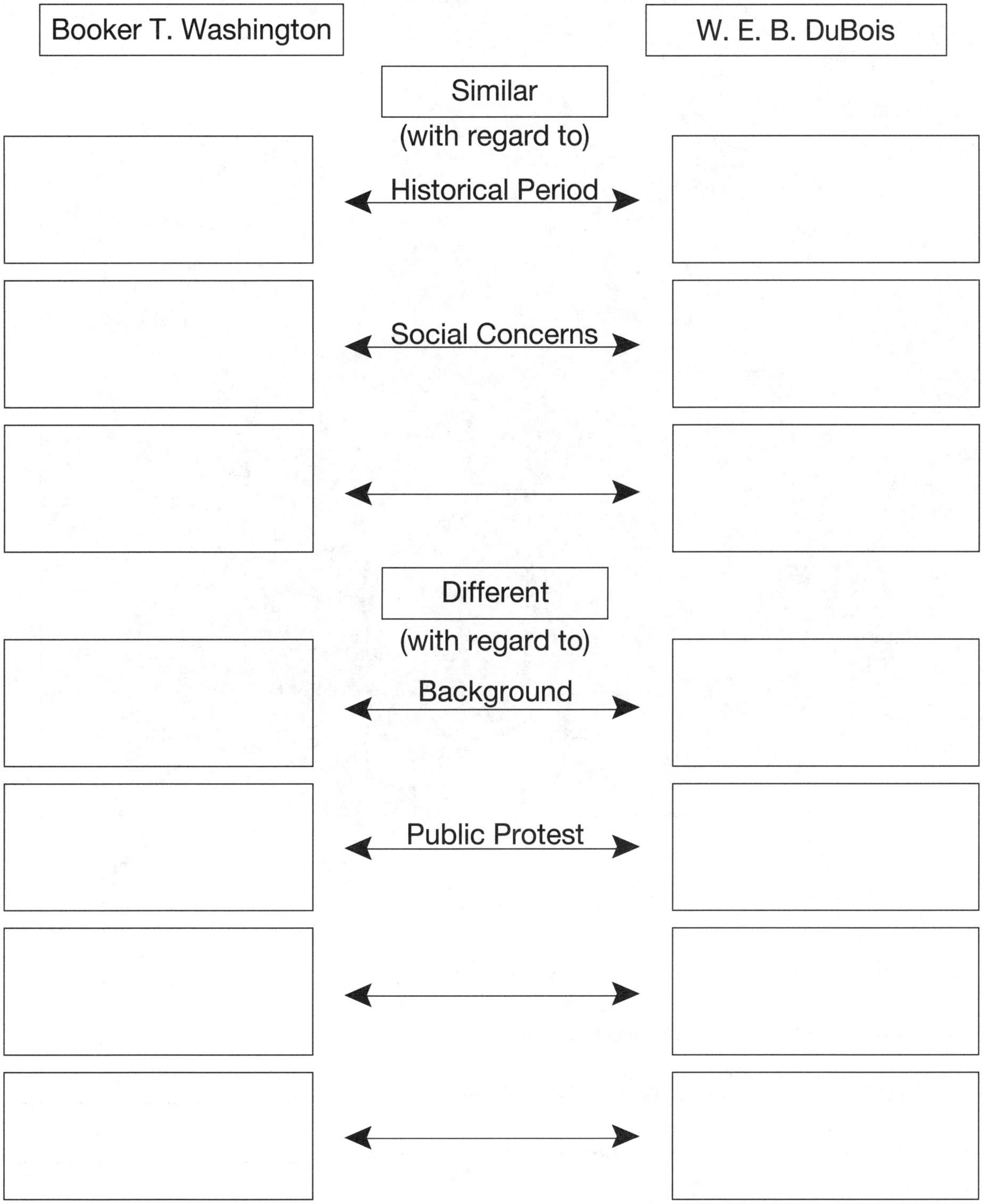

Booker T. Washington		W. E. B. DuBois
	Similar (with regard to)	
	← Historical Period →	
	← Social Concerns →	
	←→	
	Different (with regard to)	
	← Background →	
	← Public Protest →	
	←→	
	←→	

Name ______________________ Date ______________

CHAPTER 30 Activity Sheet
Interpreting a Map

Study this map carefully. Then answer the questions that follow.

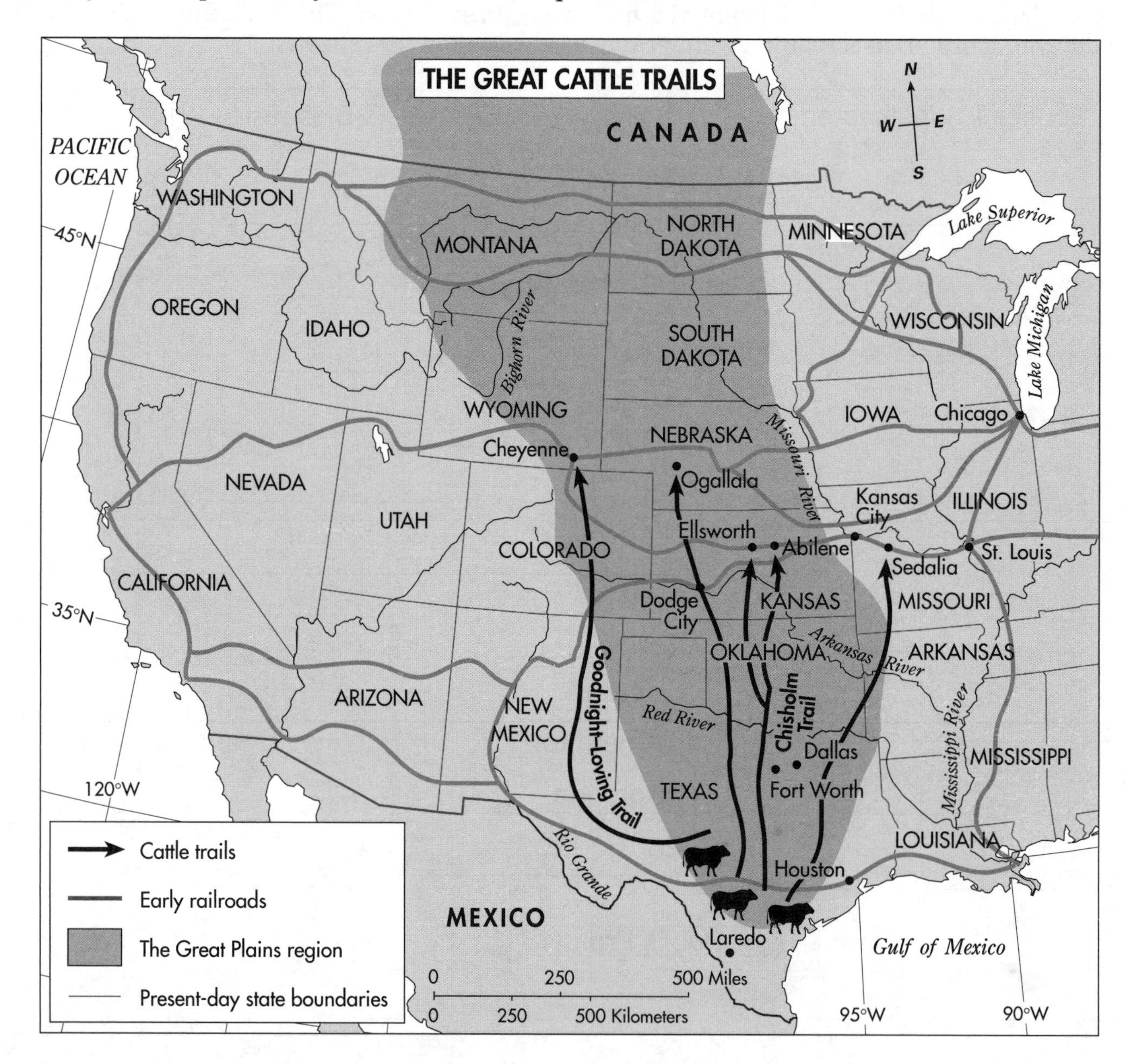

1. How would you describe the location of the Great Plains? ______________________

2. In what direction did most of the cattle trails head? ______________________

3. In what two directions did most of the railroads head? ______________________

4. In what present-day state did most of the cattle drives start? ______________________

5. What railroad town was the end of the Goodnight-Loving Trail? ______________________

Name ______________________ Date ______________

CHAPTER 31 Activity Sheet
Drawing a Line Graph

The figures below show the number of work stoppages for the years 1881–1900. As you might guess, a **work stoppage** is a form of protest in which workers stop working until their demands are met. A strike is one example of a work stoppage. Use the figures below to draw a line graph showing the number of worker protests during the last years of the 1800s. Then answer the questions that follow.

YEAR	WORK STOPPAGES
1881	477
1882	476
1883	506
1884	485
1885	695
1886	1,572
1887	1,503
1888	946
1889	1,111
1890	1,897

YEAR	WORK STOPPAGES
1891	1,786
1892	1,359
1893	1,375
1894	1,404
1895	1,255
1896	1,066
1897	1,110
1898	1,098
1899	1,838
1900	1,839

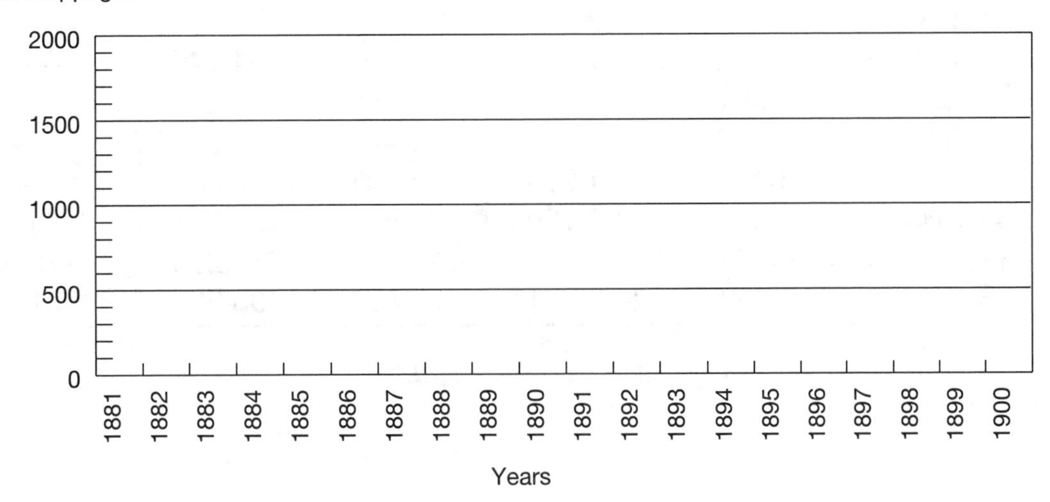

1. What title would you give your line graph? ______________________

2. In what year did the most work stoppages occur? ______________________

3. Would you expect the number of work stoppages to go up or down in the 1900s? How did you come up with your answer? ______________________

4. Based on the text, why do you think work stoppages dramatically increased after 1885?

____

Name ______________________ Date ______________

CHAPTER 32 Activity Sheet
Linking Past and Present

In the 1800s, immigrants from Asia began arriving in the United States in large numbers. Then prejudice against Asians slammed the nation's doors shut. When the doors reopened, Asian immigrants entered the United States in record numbers. Today, nearly 40 percent of all immigrants to the United States come from nations in Asia. The only region to send more immigrants is Latin America. The table below shows you how Asian immigration has changed over time. Study this table. Then answer the questions that follow.

Asian Immigration by Nation of Origin, 1850–1990

Decade	Chinese	Japanese	Asian Indian	Korean	Filipino	Vietnamese
1850–1860	41,397	——	43	——	——	——
1861–1870	64,301	186	69	——	——	——
1871–1880	123,201	149	163	——	——	——
1881–1890	61,711	2,270	269	——	——	——
1891–1900	14,799	25,942	68	——	——	——
1901–1910	20,605	129,797	4,713	7,697	——	——
1911–1920	21,278	83,837	2,082	1,049	869	——
1921–1930	29,907	33,462	1,886	598	54,747	——
1931–1940	4,928	1,948	496	60	6,159	——
1941–1950	16,709	1,555	1,761	——	4,691	——
1951–1960	9,657	46,250	1,973	6,231	19,307	——
1961–1970	34,764	3,998	27,189	34,526	98,376	3,788
1971–1980	12,326	49,775	164,134	271,956	360,216	179,681
1981–1990	366,622	43,248	261,841	338,824	495,271	401,419

Source: *Statistical Record of Asian Americans*, Gale Research, Inc., 1993.

1. By how much did Chinese immigration drop in the 1880s: (a) 10 percent, (b) 25 percent, (c) 50 percent, (d) 90 percent? ______________________

2. Which event in the text explains this drop? ______________________

3. What Asian nations began sending immigrants in the 1900s? ______________________

4. In which ten year period did Asian immigration reach its peak? ______________________

5. Write a sentence summarizing the changes in Asian immigration since the late 1880s. ____

____

Name ______________________ Date ______________

CHAPTER 33 Activity Sheet
Interpreting a Primary Source

In 1890, a Danish reporter named Jacob Riis took a look at the dark side of American life. With notebook and camera in hand, he visited the tenements of Cherry Street, on Manhattan's Lower East Side. Riis's pictures and words take us inside the tenements. Read the selection below from his book *How the Other Half Lives.* Then answer the questions that follow.

Be a little careful, please! The hall is dark and you might stumble over the children pitching pennies back there. Not that it would hurt them; kicks and cuffs are their daily diet. They have little else. Here where the hall turns and dives into utter [complete] darkness is a step, and another, another. A flight of stairs. You can feel your way, if you cannot see it. Close [stuffy]? Yes! . . . All the fresh air that ever enters these stairs comes from the hall-door that is forever slamming, and from the windows of dark bedrooms that in turn receive from the stairs their sole supply of [air and sunlight].

Here is a door. Listen! That short hacking cough, that tiny, helpless wail [cry]—what do they mean? . . . Oh! a sadly familiar story. . . . The child is dying of measles. With half a chance it might have lived; but it had none. That dark bedroom killed it.

Come over here. . . . This gap [between tenements] is the yard. . . . This tenement is much like one in front that we just left, only fouler and darker. A hundred thousand people lived in back tenements in New York last year.

What sort of answer, do you think, would these tenement-dwellers give to the question, "Is life worth living?"

1. What dangerous or unhealthy conditions does Riis describe? ______________________

____

2. What effect does Riis say these conditions have on children? ______________________

____

3. How are back tenements different from front tenements? ______________________

____

4. Reread the last sentence of the selection. How do you think the tenement-dwellers on Cherry Street might answer this question? ______________________

____

5. Based on the text, how did reformers and immigrant organizations try to relieve the misery of the tenements? ______________________

Name ______________________________ Date ______________

CHAPTER 34 Activity Sheet
Interpreting a Map

In 1869, an amendment to give women the right to vote was brought up in Congress. But few members paid any attention to it. More than 50 years would pass before Congress would approve such an amendment. Some states refused to wait on the issue of equal voting rights for women. These states are listed in the table below. Using a colored pencil, shade in these states on your copy of the outline map. Then create a title and a key for your map. Based on the table and map, answer the questions that follow.

Arizona	1912	South Dakota	1918	New York	1917
Michigan	1918	Colorado	1893	Washington	1910
Oregon	1912	Nevada	1914	Kansas	1912
California	1911	Utah	1896	Oklahoma	1918
Montana	1914	Idaho	1896	Wyoming	1896

1. What were the first states to grant women equal voting rights? ______________

____

____

____

2. How many states had granted women equal voting rights by the time that Congress passed the 19th Amendment in 1919? ______________

____

____

3. What region led the way in giving women the right to vote? ______________

____

____

4. What information in the text helps to explain why states in this region gave women the right to vote? ______________

____

____

Name ______________________________ Date ____________________

CHAPTER 35 Activity Sheet
Interpreting a Political Cartoon

In 1776, the 13 British colonies fought a war of independence. The colonists gave their lives to defend an important ideal—the ideal of self-government. But what happened when the United States won colonies of its own? How did Americans view other people's efforts to win independence in these colonies? The cartoon on this page shows how one political cartoonist saw the Filipino struggle for freedom. Study this cartoon. Then answer the questions that follow.

1. (a) Who is the tall figure in the center of the cartoon? ____________________

   (b) What does the figure symbolize? ____________________

2. Who are the other figures in the cartoon? ____________________

3. (a) What is the tall figure holding? ____________________

   (b) What does he intend to do? ____________________

4. The figure behind the tree is Emilio Aguinaldo, the leader of the Filipinio independence movement. What is the cartoonist's opinion of this movement? ____________________

5. What details in the cartoon support your answer? ____________________

6. How does the cartoonist see other U.S. possessions? ____________________

Name ______________________________ Date ______________________

CHAPTER 36 Activity Sheet
Using Historical Imagination

On May 1, 1893, a great world's fair opened in Chicago. It was named the World's Columbian Exposition. It honored the 400th anniversary of Columbus's first voyage to the Americas. On opening day, more than 200,000 people came to the fair. By the time the fair closed, some 27 million had visited it.

Among the fair's visitors was a 33-year-old writer from the Great Plains named Hamlin Garland. He sent a letter describing the fair to his parents on their North Dakota farm. Imagine that you are Garland. Tell your parents all about the fair's many wonders. Below are the opening two sentences from Garland's letter.

May 26, 1893

Dear Ma and Pa,

Sell the cook stove if necessary and come. You must see this fair!

____

____

____

____

____

____

____

____

____

____

____

____

____

Your son,

Hamlin

Name ______________________________ Date ____________________

CHAPTER 1 Activity Sheet
Making a Graph

Graphs are a good way of presenting data about numbers in visual form. One type of graph uses a symbol to represent amounts of something. Follow the instructions to create graphs giving information about U.S. industrial growth around 1900. First, study the two tables below:

IRON PRODUCTION		RAILROADS	
Year	Tons of U.S. Iron Produced	Year	Total Miles of U.S. Railroad Track
1870	1,500,000	1870	53,000
1880	3,400,000	1880	93,000
1890	8,100,000	1890	167,000
1900	12,300,000	1900	193,000

1. Choose two symbols—one for iron produced and the other for miles of railroad track. Let each symbol for iron produced stand for 1 million tons of iron. Let each symbol for miles of track stand for 25,000 miles of track. Now, find the number of symbols you will need on each graph. For iron production, divide the total amount of iron produced in each year by 1 million. For miles of railroad track, divide the total miles of track for each year by 25,000. If you get numbers like 2.5, then you would use two and a half symbols.

a) How many symbols for iron produced will you need for 1880? ____________________

b) How many symbols for railroad track will you need for 1890? ____________________

2. Now complete the graphs below. Give each graph a title. Draw the symbols you have chosen for iron produced and miles of railroad track in the graph keys. Then, on the line next to the year, draw the correct number of symbols for iron produced and total miles of railroad track.

Title: ____________________	Title: ____________________
1870 ____________________ 1880 ____________________ 1890 ____________________ 1900 ____________________	1870 ____________________ 1880 ____________________ 1890 ____________________ 1900 ____________________
Key ________ = 1 million tons of iron	Key: ________ = 25,000 miles of track

3. Write a statement that describes what your graphs show. ____________________

____

____

____

Name ______________________ Date ______________

CHAPTER 2 Activity Sheet
Reading a Circle Graph

One common form of graph is the circle graph. Circle graphs are a good way of giving information about the relations of the parts of something to the whole. Circle graphs are often called pie graphs. You can think of the complete circle in a circle graph as a whole pie. If you gave a number value to the whole pie, it would be 100 percent. The parts of information that make up the whole circle can be thought of as pieces of the pie. If you divided up a whole pie into four equal pieces, each piece would make up a quarter, or 25 percent, of the whole pie.

When you work with circle graphs, be sure to carefully read the graph title and any labels on the graphs. They contain important information that will help you understand the graph. Now study the graph below and answer the questions that follow it.

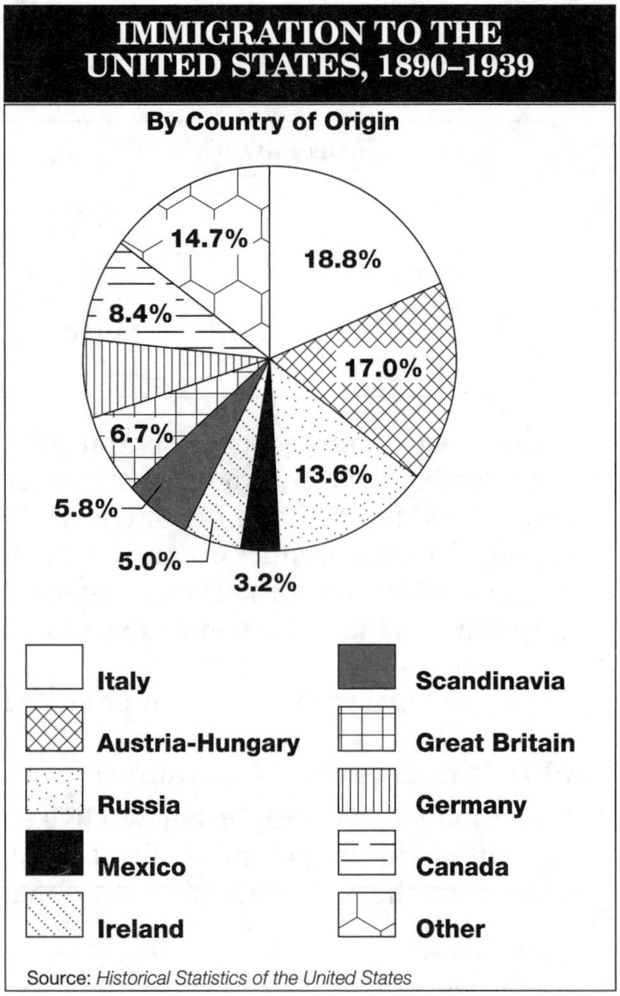

IMMIGRATION TO THE UNITED STATES, 1890–1939

By Country of Origin

14.7%
18.8%
8.4%
17.0%
6.7%
13.6%
5.8%
5.0%
3.2%

Italy
Austria-Hungary
Russia
Mexico
Ireland
Scandinavia
Great Britain
Germany
Canada
Other

Source: *Historical Statistics of the United States*

1. What is the subject of this graph? ______________________

2. For what period does the graph give information? ______________________

3. From what nation did the largest number of immigrants come? ______________________

4. What percentage of immigrants came from Ireland? ______________________

5. What nation sent the smallest number of immigrants? ______________________

6. **a**) What percentage of immigrants do you think came from Germany during this period: 50.7 percent, 33.2 percent, 25.4 percent, or 6.8 percent? ______________________

   b) Why? ______________________

7. Where would immigrants from Japan be represented on this graph? ______________________

Name ______________________________ Date ____________________

CHAPTER 3 Activity Sheet
Describing Place and Time

Over a million African Americans left the South in the 20 years after 1910. Most of them moved to cities of the North. There, they found conditions very different from the farms that most of them left in the South.

Imagine that you are an African American from the South who has moved to a Northern city in 1915. You are going to send a postcard to a friend back home. In it, you will say something about your new life.

First, use the space below to show some part of life in the city. Review pictures of cities in this unit of your textbook to get a sense of what cities looked like then.

Greetings from ____________________

Next, write a message to a friend. You might say why you like or do not like the city. You might tell your friend reasons to move North or stay in the South.

Date:

To: ____________________
____
____

Name ______________________ Date ______________

CHAPTER 4 Activity Sheet
Illustrating Events

Review Chapter 4. Then, for each of the sections in the chapter choose one event. Draw a picture illustrating that event in one of the boxes below. For each picture, write a one-sentence caption that tells why that event was important.

CUBA

Caption:

____

____

PUERTO RICO

Caption:

____

____

NEW MEXICO

Caption:

____

____

Name ______________________ Date ______________

CHAPTER 5 Activity Sheet
Making a Chart

Making a chart is a good way to sum up information about different groups. In this chapter, you read about labor groups that formed in the late 1800s and early 1900s. Skim through the chapter again to complete the chart below. Some of the entries have been made already.

Labor Group	Date of Founding	Type of Workers Group Appealed To	Persons or Events Associated with Group
Knights of Labor			
American Federation of Labor		skilled laborers	
Women's Alliance			Elizabeth Morgan
Japanese-Mexican Labor Association			
National Women's Trade Union League			
International Ladies Garment Workers Union	1900		

Name ______________________ Date ______________

Chapter 6 Activity Sheet
Analyzing a Primary Source

Early in the 1900s, articles in U.S. newspapers brought many problems in U.S. society to the attention of large numbers of readers for the first time. The people who wrote those articles were called **muckrakers,** because they stirred up unpleasant facts and brought them to light. One of those muckrakers was Ida Tarbell. Her "History of the Standard Oil Company" was one of the most famous muckraking reports. Read the selection below, and then answer the questions that follow. (Remember: A **trust** is a group of companies run by a single board of directors.)

The profits of the present Standard Oil Company are enormous. For five years [they] have been averaging $45 million a year. . . . Consider what must be done with the greater part of this $45 million. It must be invested. The oil business does not need it. . . . The money must go into other industries. Naturally, these other industries will be connected to oil. One such interest will be gas, and we have the Standard Oil people steadily taking over the gas interests of the country. Another will be railroads, for all industries depend on transportation. Besides, railroads are one of the great consumers of oil products and must be kept in line as buyers. So we have the directors of the Standard Oil Company acting as directors on nearly all of the great railways of the country. They will go into steel. . . . They will go into banking. . . . The crucial question is still that of transportation. . . . As long as it is possible for a company to own the carrier on which a great natural product depends for transportation, and to use this carrier to limit a competitor's supply or to cut it off entirely, it is foolish to talk about constitutional amendments limiting trusts. As long as the Standard Oil Company can control transportation, as it does today, it will remain master of the oil industry. The people of the United States will pay a high price for oil because of their indifference in regard to transportation.

1. How much profit does the Standard Oil Company make a year? ______________

2. According to Tarbell, what must the company do with the profits? ______________

3. What kinds of businesses is Standard Oil involved with? ______________

____

4. Which of those businesses is Standard Oil most interested in? ______________

5. How could Standard Oil harm competitors through investments in railroads? ______________

____

____

6. Explain what you think Tarbell means by her last sentence. ______________

____

____

Name ________________________________ Date ____________________

CHAPTER 7 Activity Sheet
Making a Chronology

A **chronology** is a list or table of events organized in the order in which they took place. Complete the chronology below to gain a better understanding of U.S. involvement in the Pacific area. First, read the sentences above the table that describe events in the Pacific. Skim through the chapter to find the correct date for each event. Then, write the date and the event in the chronology with the earliest event at the top and the most recent event at the bottom. When you are done, pick one of the events and draw a picture illustrating it in the box at the bottom of the page. Write a caption for the picture in the space provided.

U.S. troops capture Emilio Aguinaldo.
Japan defeats China in a war.
San Francisco segregates Japanese schoolchildren.
Emilio Aguinaldo becomes leader of Philippine independence movement.
U.S. calls for Open Door Policy.
Japan defeats Russia in a war.
U.S. troops capture Manila.
Boxer Rebellion breaks out.

Date	Event

Caption: ____

____

Name ______________________ Date ______________

CHAPTER 8 Activity Sheet
Working with Main Ideas and Supporting Details

After the Cuban-Spanish-American War, the United States took charge of Spain's colonies in the Caribbean. Cuba became a U.S. protectorate, a weaker nation under the control of a stronger one. Puerto Rico became a U.S. possession.

The paragraph above is organized like most of those in your textbook and in other forms of written matter as well. The first sentence of the paragraph is the **topic sentence.** It contains the main idea of the paragraph. The other sentences give facts that back up or explain the main idea. Such facts are called **supporting details.**

For practice using main ideas and supporting details, complete the paragraphs below. A topic sentence or sentences with supporting details are provided. Your job is to complete the paragraph by writing sentences that contain either supporting details or a main idea. Skim through the chapter to find ideas and details.

1. Yellow fever was a serious problem in Cuba in the late 1800s. (Write two sentences that give supporting details.) ______________________

____

2. (Read the following sentences. Then, write a main idea for the paragraph.) ______________________

____

____

Under its terms, the United States built a naval base at Guantánamo Bay. It also sent troops to Cuba in 1906 and 1912.

3. During World War I, Cuba profited as sugar production in many other countries was shut down. ______________________

____

4. The Foraker Act limited the political freedom of people in Puerto Rico. ______________________

____

5. ______________________

____

Puerto Ricans raised about $10 million in U.S. war bonds. Also, nearly 20,000 islanders served in the U.S. armed forces during the struggle.

Name ______________________________ Date ____________________

CHAPTER 9 Activity Sheet
Interpreting a Political Cartoon

Political cartoons are drawings that express opinions about people, issues, and events. Cartoonists use **symbols,** drawings that stand for something else. Review Chapter 9. Then study the cartoon and answer the questions that follow. (Hints: The Dominican Republic was once known as Santo Domingo.)

1. Who is the main figure in the cartoon? ____________________

2. How do you know the identity of the figure? ____________________

3. Where does the action in the cartoon take place? ____________________

4. What countries are identified by labels in the cartoon? ____________________

5. What point do you think the cartoonist is trying to make? ____________________

____

6. Name an event that you have read about in Chapter 9 for each of the countries identified in the cartoon that might support the cartoonist's point. ____________________

____

____

Name ______________________________ Date ____________________

CHAPTER 10 Activity Sheet
Organizing Historical Information

Filling in the diagram below can help you organize what you have learned about World War I in Chapter 10. Skim through the chapter and fill in the boxes with facts that answer the questions.

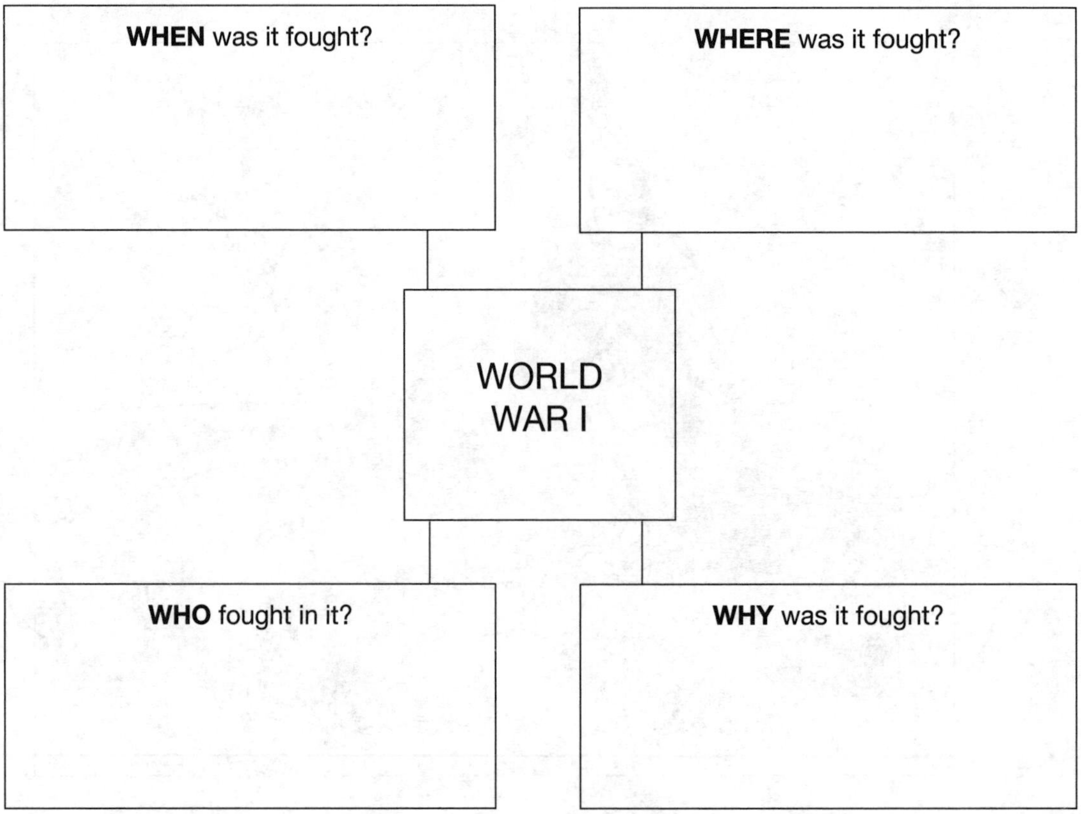

WHEN was it fought?

WHERE was it fought?

WORLD WAR I

WHO fought in it?

WHY was it fought?

Review the information in the diagram. Then, on the lines below, write a brief paragraph about World War I that uses information from at least two of the boxes.

Name ______________________________ Date ____________________

CHAPTER 11 Activity Sheet
Comparing Graphs

Graphs present data about numbers in visual form. Comparing two graphs helps you to see how numbers of things have changed over time. The graphs below give information about immigration to the United States. Study them and answer the questions that follow.

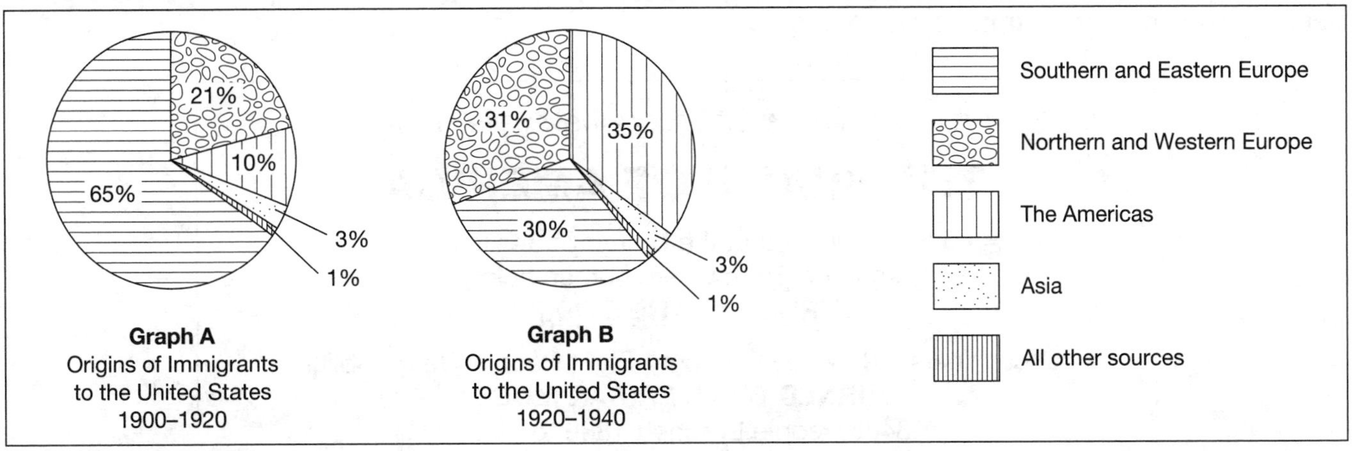

21%
10%
65%
3%
1%

Graph A
Origins of Immigrants
to the United States
1900–1920

31%
35%
30%
3%
1%

Graph B
Origins of Immigrants
to the United States
1920–1940

Southern and Eastern Europe
Northern and Western Europe
The Americas
Asia
All other sources

1. The graphs above give information about what two periods? ____________________

2. What information do the graphs provide? ____________________

3. What percentage of all immigrants came from Asia in the years shown on Graph A? ________

____

4. From where did most immigrants come in the years shown on Graph B? ____________________

5. From what area did immigration fall by the greatest amount in the years shown on the two graphs? ____________________

____

6. Based on Chapter 11, what caused the changes in immigration shown on the two graphs?

____

____

7. Write a sentence that summarizes these graphs. ____________________

____

____

Name ______________________ Date ______________

CHAPTER 12 Activity Sheet
Analyzing an Advertisement

Advertisements that appear in newspapers and magazines can provide valuable information about the time in which they first appeared. Study carefully the copy of the advertisement that appears below. Review Chapter 12 of your textbook. Then answer the questions that follow. When you have answered the questions, design on a separate sheet of paper another advertisement on the same topic as the one below.

THE NEW YORK TIMES, THURSDAY, NOVEMBER 13, 1922

THE SHAME OF AMERICA

Do you know that the United States is the
Only Land on Earth where human beings are
BURNED AT THE STAKE?

In Four Years, 1918–1921, Twenty-Eight People Were Publicly
BURNED BY AMERICAN MOBS
3436 People Lynched 1889 to 1922

AND THE LYNCHERS GO UNPUNISHED

THE REMEDY
THE DYER ANTI-LYNCHING BILL IS NOW
BEFORE THE UNITED STATES SENATE
TELEGRAPH YOUR SENATORS TODAY YOU WANT IT ENACTED

NATIONAL ASSOCAITION FOR THE ADVANCEMENT OF COLORED PEOPLE
36 Fifth Avenue, New York City

This Advertisement is Paid for in Part by the Anti-lynching Crusaders

1. When did the advertisement appear? ______________________

2. Where did it appear? ______________________

3. According to the advertisement, what is "the shame of America"? ______________________

____

4. How many people died of mob violence between 1889 and 1922? ______________________

5. According to your textbook, what were some of the causes of this problem? ______________________

____

6. Why did the advertisement appear at this time? ______________________

7. What did the advertisement want readers to do? ______________________

Name ______________________________ Date ____________________

CHAPTER 13 Activity Sheet
Recognizing Problems

Review Chapter 13. Then in each square below, draw a picture that represents a problem that each of the groups named there faced during the Great Depression.

Bank Depositors	Mexican Americans
African Americans	Stock Market Investors
Workers in U.S. Businesses	Farmers of the Great Plains

Name ______________________ Date ______________

CHAPTER 14 Activity Sheet
Interpreting a Graph

The line graph below shows the number of unemployed people in the United States between 1915 and 1945. Study it carefully, then answer the questions that follow.

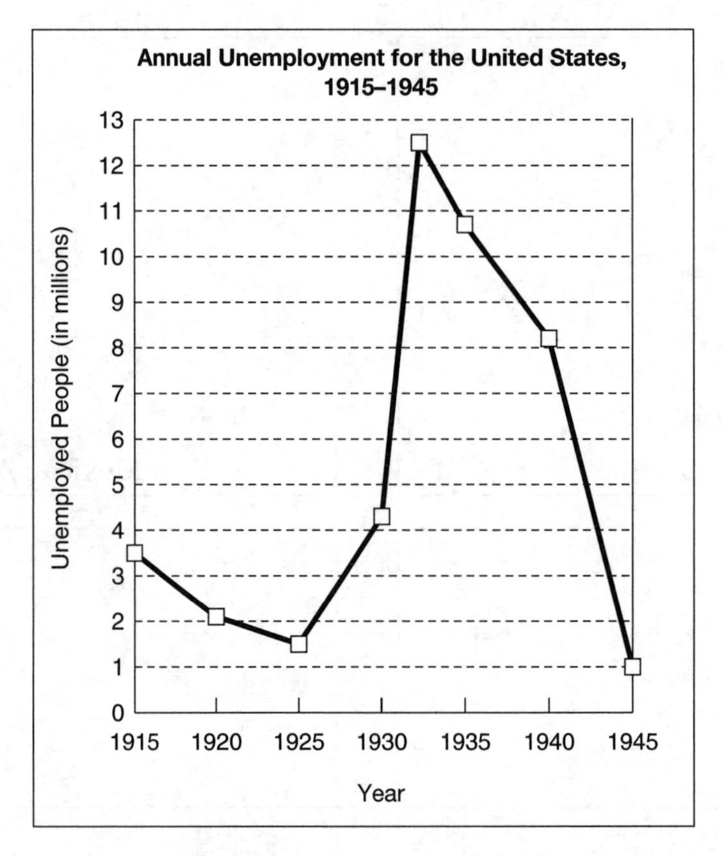

1. What important period in U.S. history does this graph show? ______________________

____

2. About how many people were unemployed in 1933? ______________________

3. What happened to the number of unemployed people after Franklin Roosevelt became President in 1933?______________________

4. By how much did unemployment drop between 1940 and 1945? ______________________

5. Write a statement that summarizes the information shown on this graph.______________

____

____

____

Name ______________________ Date ______________

CHAPTER 15 Activity Sheet
Organizing Ideas and Chronology

History is made up of people, places, and things interacting with each other. This exercise will help you think about how some things came together in the years leading up to and during World War II.

Below you will see clusters of terms. Use the terms in a cluster to write a sentence about an event before or during the war. When you have written five sentences, number them in the order in which the events took place.

Order

____ **A.** United States Japan Hawaii Pearl Harbor

____ **B.** France English Channel Allies D-Day

____ **C.** Adolf Hitler Germany depression Nazi party

____ **D.** Nagasaki United States Hiroshima Japan

____ **E.** Germany western Czechoslovakia England France

Name ______________________ Date ______________

CHAPTER 16 Activity Sheet
Interpreting a Primary Source

What was it like to be confined in an internment camp during World War II? A primary source document can help you understand the feelings of the Japanese Americans held behind barbed wire. The passage below is taken from an account written by Monica Sone, who was a college student when the war began. Read it, then answer the questions below.

Camp Minidoka was located in the south-central part of Idaho, north of the Snake river. It was a semidesert region. When we arrived I could see nothing but flat prairies, clumps of greasewood shrubs, and jack rabbits. And of course the hundreds and hundreds of barracks to house 10,000 of us.

Our home was one room in a large army-type barracks, measuring about 20 by 25 feet. The only furnishings were an iron pot-belly stove and cots. . . .

Idaho summer sizzled on the average of 110 degrees. For the first few weeks I lay on my cot from morning till night, not daring to do more than go to the mess hall three times a day. . . .

By fall, Camp Minidoka had bloomed into a full-grown town. Children went to school in the barracks, taught by professional teachers among the evacuees and people hired from the outside. Except for members of the administration staff, the evacuees themselves supplied the entire labor force in the camp. . . .

During our spare hours, we confiscated [took] scrap lumber, piece by piece from a lumber pile. Tables and chairs gradually made their appearance in our tiny apartment. Rows of shelves lined the bare walls. . . . It had everything except the kitchen sink and privacy.

We had lived in camps through the four seasons, and each season had served as a challenge to us. In the meantime, we had drifted farther and farther away from the American scene. We had been set apart, and we had become adjusted to our existence. The great struggle in which the world was engaged seemed far away.

Then one day a group of army personnel marched into our camp on a special mission. They made a startling announcement. . . . "We have come to recruit volunteers [for the army]."

1. Where was the camp Monica Sone was writing about located? ______________

2. What was land around the camp like? ______________

3. Who did most of the necessary work around the camp? ______________

4. What do you think the writer felt was the major hardship in the camp? ______________

____

5. Why was the announcement by army personnel "startling"? ______________

____

Name ______________________ Date ______________

Chapter 17 Activity Sheet
Reading a Diagram

Diagrams can provide useful information about how an organization is set up and how it operates. Study the diagram of the organization below. Then answer the questions that follow.

THE UNITED NATIONS

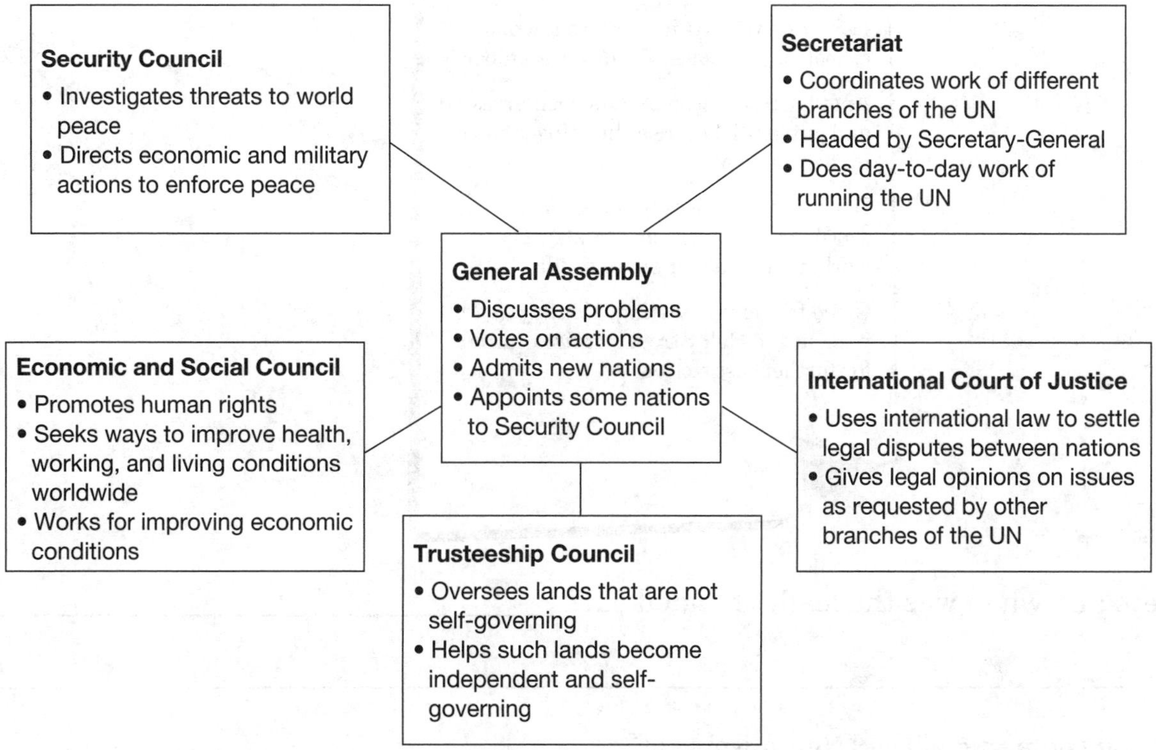

Security Council
- Investigates threats to world peace
- Directs economic and military actions to enforce peace

Secretariat
- Coordinates work of different branches of the UN
- Headed by Secretary-General
- Does day-to-day work of running the UN

General Assembly
- Discusses problems
- Votes on actions
- Admits new nations
- Appoints some nations to Security Council

Economic and Social Council
- Promotes human rights
- Seeks ways to improve health, working, and living conditions worldwide
- Works for improving economic conditions

International Court of Justice
- Uses international law to settle legal disputes between nations
- Gives legal opinions on issues as requested by other branches of the UN

Trusteeship Council
- Oversees lands that are not self-governing
- Helps such lands become independent and self-governing

1. What does this diagram show? ______________________

2. How many major branches does the organization have? ______________________

3. What branch seems to be the most important? Why? ______________________

4. To what branch would two nations turn in order to settle an argument about the right to mine minerals from the sea floor off their coasts? ______________________

5. What branch would draw up a Declaration of Human Rights? ______________________

6. What branch would be in charge of distributing reports to other branches? ______________________

7. What branch oversaw actions in Korea in the 1950s? ______________________

____

Name ______________________ Date ______________

CHAPTER 18 Activity Sheet
Interpreting a Leaflet

The leaflet below was handed out during the 1950s. Read it, then skim through Chapter 18 to answer the questions that follow.

> Don't ride the bus to work, to town, to school, or any place Monday, December 5.
>
> Another Negro woman has been arrested and put in jail because she refused to give up her bus seat.
>
> Don't ride the buses to work, to school, or anywhere on Monday. If you work, take a cab, or share a ride.
>
> Come to a mass meeting, Monday at 7:00 p.m., at the Holt Street Baptist Church for further instruction.

1. Where and when was the leaflet handed out? ______________________

____

2. What is the name of the "Negro woman"? ______________________

3. Whom do you think the leaflet is addressed to? ______________________

4. What does the leaflet ask them to do? ______________________

____

5. Why do you think such action might be effective? ______________________

____

6. What was the final result of actions called for in the leaflet? ______________________

____

On a separate sheet of paper, design a poster that you think would convince people to take the action that the leaflet calls for.

Name ______________________________ Date ____________________

CHAPTER 19 Activity Sheet
Organizing Information

Chapter 19 covers 20 years and deals with the activities of five Presidents. One of the best ways to keep track of this much information is to arrange it in a chart. As you read the chapter, write information you discover into the proper columns. The completed chart will be a handy tool for reviewing the chapter.

President	Party	Years in Office	Foreign Policy Issues	Domestic Issues	Reason for Leaving Office

Name ____________________ Date ____________

CHAPTER 20 Activity Sheet
Interpreting a Political Cartoon

Cartoonists use their artwork to express points of view about issues. The cartoon below comments on one aspect of the Vietnam War. As always when studying a political cartoon, read all labels and captions to understand the message the artist is trying to get across. Study this cartoon carefully, then answer the questions that follow. Reviewing Chapter 19 before you begin may help you.

'DEAR SON — I'M PROUD THAT YOU'RE DEFENDING THE FREEDOM WE'RE TRYING TO GET...'

1. Who is the main figure in the cartoon? ____________________

2. Where is the cartoon set? How do you know? ____________________

____

3. What is the soldier doing? ____________________

4. What does the cartoon caption refer to? ____________________

____

5. Express in your own words what you think the cartoonist is saying here. ____________________

____

____

____

____

Name ____________________ Date ____________________

CHAPTER 21 Activity Sheet
Making Comparisons

Below are two descriptions of teenagers in the 1950s and 1960s. Read these decriptions carefully. Then answer the questions that follow.

1950s

"They [teenagers] are well-dressed. . . . They are well mannered. . . . They are noisy. They love to have a listener. They are addicted to radio ("top-tune" programs) and the 30-minute telephone call. They are not taken with television. . . . Their slang is dreary [dull] to most adults. 'Cool'—'hep'—'flip'—'crazy'—this is the jargon [special language] of teens."

Look, May 24, 1956

1960s

"The young people use rock 'n' roll to say to the world, 'We can be independent. This is our way of life. We're revolutionaries. . . . . We shall overcome our parents' misunderstanding of us. We shall overcome poverty and sickness and the fact that there's a war. We will dress and act differently [from our parents].'"

Bill Graham, Rock Club Owner, *An Oral History of the Sixties*

1. What made teenagers different from adults in the 1950s? ____________________

____

2. According to Bill Graham, how did teenagers in the 1960s see themselves? ____________________

____

3. To what war do you think Graham was referring? ____________________

4. Which comments by Graham show evidence of a "generation gap"? ____________________

____

5. What, if any, similarities did teenagers in the 1950s and 1960s share? ____________________

____

6. Do teenagers in your generation fit any of these descriptions? Explain. ____________________

____

____

____

Name ______________________________ Date ____________________

CHAPTER 22 Activity Sheet
Interpreting a Chart

As the 1960s opened, the struggle over civil rights became more intense. For a time, national attention focused on the sit-ins and freedom rides in the South. But Senator Robert Kennedy predicted that trouble was brewing elsewhere. Warned Kennedy in 1964: "Cities where blacks are trapped in pockets of poverty—Harlem, Watts, South Side [Chicago]—are riots just waiting to happen." From 1965 to 1968, cities across the nation exploded. The chart on this page shows where the largest riots took place. With this chart and an outline map of the United States, answer the questions that follow.

Civil Rights Riots, 1965–1968

Cities with riots	Outcome
Americus, Georgia	fatalities
Atlanta, Georgia	fatalities
Boston, Massachusetts	
Chicago, Illinois	fatalities
Cincinnati, Ohio	
Cleveland, Ohio	fatalities
Dayton, Ohio	
Detroit, Michigan	fatalities
Grenada, Mississippi	
Kansas City, Missouri	
Los Angeles (Watts), California	fatalities
Louisville, Kentucky	

Cities with riots	Outcome
Milwaukee, Wisconsin	fatalities
Nashville, Tennessee	
New York, New York	fatalities
Newark, New Jersey	fatalities
Philadelphia, Pennsylvania	
Pontiac, Michigan	fatalities
Portland, Oregon	
Rochester, New York	fatalities
San Francisco, California	fatalities
Tampa, Florida	fatalities
Tucson, Arizona	
Washington, D.C.	

1. In what major western cities did riots occur? ______________________________

2. In what major cities of the South did riots occur? ______________________________

3. In what cities along the Great Lakes did people die during the rioting? ______________

4. What region saw the most civil-rights riots during the years 1965–1968? ______________

5. Suppose you were a member of the Kerner Commission. (See text pages 190–191.) Write a brief paragraph summarizing the riots. Your report should include the following information: (a) the number of cities in which riots occurred, (b) the numbers of riots with fatalities, and (c) geographic patterns of the riots. ______________________________

____

____

Name ______________________________ Date ____________________

CHAPTER 23 Activity Sheet
Comparing Past and Present

February is Black History Month. At this time, people focus on the progress made by African Americans. In February 1988, the *Washington Post* asked African American students to write letters about how the Civil Rights Movement had changed their lives. Below is one of the letters printed by the newspaper. Read this letter carefully. Using a blue pen, underline sentences that show what things were like at the start of the Civil Rights Movement. Using a red pen, underline sentences that show how things have changed. Then, write a letter that you might send to your local newspaper during Black History Month.

My dad has told me of not being able to get into a restaurant because he is an Afro-American. I have seen stories on television of how blacks used to be banned [kept] from doing everyday activities. Today, you can easily find a restaurant owned by a black person.

At the beginning of the Civil Rights Movement, there weren't any black Supreme Court Justices. There weren't any black people running for President. A black man could be beaten up in his own home and the [attacker] could get away unpunished.

The accomplishments in the last 25 years are remarkable [amazing]. What is equally important is the determination [strong desire] for black people to maintain [hang onto] their equal status [position in society]. Although we have not reached the totally integrated [racially mixed] society that Martin Luther King Jr. and others dreamed of, we are well on our way.

Dear Editor:

____

____

____

____

____

____

____

____

____

____

____

Sincerely,

Name ______________________________ Date ____________________

CHAPTER 24 Activity Sheet
Debating an Issue

People all across the United States debated passage of the Equal Rights Amendment (ERA). Think about what position you might have taken on this issue. Read the statement below. Then prepare to attack or defend this amendment by filling out the chart on this page.

The Equal Rights Amendment, Proposed 3/22/72

Equality of rights under the law shall not be denied or abridged [limited] by the United States or by any State on account of Sex [gender].

Issue: *Should the ERA be passed?*	
Possible Pro Arguments	Possible Con Arguments

Position: ______________________________

Argument:
Evidence:

Argument:
Evidence:

Argument:
Evidence:

Summary Argument: *We support/oppose the ERA because* ______________________________

____

____

____

____

____

____

Name ______________________________ Date ____________________

CHAPTER 25 Activity Sheet
Writing an Obituary

On April 23, 1993, César Chávez died at age 66. He had spent more than 30 years of his life working to win greater rights for migrant farm workers. Pretend that you are a reporter. Your newspaper has just assigned you to write an obituary on Chávez. An **obituary** is a notice of death. It usually includes a short biography.

Below are some notes on Chávez's early life. Like notes taken in research, they are written in incomplete sentences. Study these notes. Then add some other interesting facts about Chávez from the text. Use these notes to write an obituary in the space provided.

Background Notes	Additional Notes
• Born on March 31, 1927, near Yuma, Arizona.	
• Second of five children of Juana and Librado Chávez.	
• Parents lost family farm in Great Depression.	
• Worked alongside his parents as a migrant farm worker.	
• Served in the navy during World War II.	
• Married Helen Fabela after the war and worked as a migrant in Delano, California.	

"____" (Headline)

April 24, 1993. Keene, California.

Story by ____________________

____

____

____

____

____

____

____

____

____

____

Name ______________________ Date ______________

CHAPTER 26 Activity Sheet
Creating a Special Purpose Map

Today people of Cuban ancestry live in every state of the Union. The chart below shows the distribution of the Cuban population by region and state. Use this chart to fill in your outline map of the United States. Then answer the questions that follow.

Cuban Population by Geographic Region and State (in thousands)

West		Midwest		East		South	
Washington	2	North Dakota	(0)	Maine	(0)	Texas	18
Oregon	1	South Dakota	(0)	Vermont	(0)	Oklahoma	1
California	72	Minnesota	2	New Hampshire	1	Arkansas	(0)
Nevada	6	Iowa	(0)	Massachusetts	8	Louisiana	9
Idaho	(0)	Nebraska	1	Rhode Island	1	Mississippi	(0)
Montana	(0)	Kansas	1	Connecticut	6	Kentucky	1
Wyoming	(0)	Missouri	2	New York	74	Tennessee	2
Utah	(0)	Illinois	18	Pennsylvania	7	Alabama	1
Colorado	(0)	Wisconsin	2	New Jersey	85	Georgia	8
Arizona	2	Michigan	5			Florida	674
New Mexico	(1)	Indiana	2			South Carolina	2
Hawaii	1	Ohio	4			North Carolina	4
Alaska	(0)					West Virginia	(0)
						Virginia	6
						Maryland	6
						Delaware	1

Source: *Statistical Abstract of the United States, 1992,* U.S. Bureau of the Census, CB91-215

1. What information is shown in the chart? ______________________

2. What two states have the largest Cuban populations? ______________________

3. How many people of Cuban ancestry live in each of these states? (Remember to multiply the numbers by 1,000.) ______________________

4. What region has the largest number of people of Cuban ancestry? ______________________

5. Write a generalization about the geographic distribution of people of Cuban ancestry in the United States. ______________________

____

____

Name ______________________ Date ______________

CHAPTER 27 Activity Sheet
Writing a Postcard

Below is the front of a postcard. You have recently moved from the Dominican Republic to Washington Heights (see text on page 232). Draw a picture of your neighborhood.

Here is the back of that postcard. Write a letter to a friend in Santo Domingo, the capital of the Dominican Republic, describing your new home.

Address:

____

____

____

Name ______________________ Date ______________

CHAPTER 28 Activity Sheet
Making Global Connections

Chapter 28 talks about Native Americans in our country. But Native Americans once claimed *all* the land in the Americas as their home. How many Native Americans live in the Americas today? To find the answer to this question, study the table below. Then answer the questions that follow.

Native American Populations in the Americas by Country, 1991

Country	Estimated Population	Percent of Total Population
Mexico	10,537,000	12.4
Peru	8,097,000	38.6
Guatemala	5,423,000	60.3
Bolivia	4,985,000	71.2
Ecuador	3,753,000	37.5
United States	1,959,000	0.8
Canada	892,000	3.4
Chile	767,000	5.9
Colombia	708,000	2.2
El Salvador	500,000	10.0
Argentina	477,000	1.5
Brazil	325,000	0.2
Venezuela	290,000	1.5
Panama	194,000	8.0
Honduras	168,000	3.4
Paraguay	101,000	2.5
Nicaragua	66,000	1.7
Guyana	29,000	3.9
Costa Rica	19,000	0.6
Belize	15,000	9.1
Surinam	11,000	2.9
French Guyana	1,000	1.2
Uruguay	0	0.0
TOTAL	39,317,000	5.8

Source: *Report on the Americas,* Volume XXV, No. 3, December 1991

1. Which country has the largest Native American population? ______________

____

2. In which country do Native Americans make up the largest percentage of the population? ______________

____

3. How many Native Americans live in the United States? ______________

____

4. Canada, Mexico, and the United States make up North America. How many Native Americans live in this region? ______

____

____

____

5. Write a generalization about the distribution of Native Americans in the Americas. ______

____

____

____

Name ______________________________ Date ____________________

CHAPTER 29 Activity Sheet
Reading a Table

Changing patterns of immigration affect everyone in our nation. Perhaps you can see the effect of these patterns in your own school district. Do you have any students from foreign lands in your school? If so, from what nations do they come?

The table below presents facts about eighth graders who trace their ancestry to Asia. This table helps you to read and compare these facts by organizing them into columns. Read the column heads, and identify the different categories of information shown on this chart. Then answer the questions that follow. (Remember to multiply numbers by 1,000.)

Asian American Eighth Graders, 1988

Ethnic or National Group (in thousands)	Number	Percent	Native-born	Foreign-born
Asian, total	1,505	100.0	52.4%	47.6%
Chinese	309	17.4	54.3%	45.9%
Filipino	288	20.2	52.0%	48.2%
Japanese	92	6.0	59.1%	31.0%
Korean	188	11.0	69.1%	31.0%
Southeast Asian	240	12.7	15.3%	84.9%
Pacific Islander	99	8.8	85.6%	14.6%
South Asian	126	8.7	45.0%	54.6%
Other Asian*	163	15.3	67.0%	33.1%

* Listed as "Other Asians" because of small numbers and location on or near the Asian continent.

Source: *Statistical Record of Asian Americans,* Gale Research Inc., 1993.

1. What was the total number of Asian American eighth graders in 1988? ______________

2. Were more Asian American eighth graders born inside or outside the U.S.? ______________

3. Which two groups of eighth graders had the highest percentage born in Asia? __________

____

4. Which four groups accounted for the largest number of eighth graders? ______________

____

5. On the basis of this table, what conclusions can you draw about Asian immigration? _____

____

____

____

Name ______________________ Date ______________

CHAPTER 30 Activity Sheet
Identifying Trends

The Middle East is a global region. The nations in the region share a similar location in between the continents of Europe and Asia. Most of the nations also share a common Arab culture. The majority of people speak Arabic languages and practice Islam. The one non-Arab nation in the region is Israel. Here people speak Hebrew and practice the Jewish religion.

Until recently, immigration from the Middle East lagged behind other world regions. However, since 1960, revolutions and religious wars have forced many people to flee. Some of the wars have been between Arab nations and Israel. Other battles have been caused by different ideas about the way in which Islam should be practiced. Struggles over government and land have also caused trouble. To see how immigration from the Middle East has changed, study the table on this page. Then answer the questions that follow.

Immigration from the Middle East, 1961–1990
(in thousands)

Country	1961–1970	1971–1980	1981–1990
Afghanistan	0.04	2.0	26.6
Iran	10.4	46.2	154.2
Israel	12.2	26.6	36.3
Jordan	14.0	29.6	32.6
Lebanon	7.5	33.8	41.6
Syria	4.6	13.9	20.6
Turkey	6.8	18.6	20.9

Source: U.S. Immigration and Naturalization Service, *Statistical Yearbook.*

1. Add up the number of immigrants in each column. How many immigrants arrived from the Middle East for each period shown? ______________________

2. Which nation has sent the least immigrants to the United States since 1961? ____________

3. Which nation has sent the most immigrants to the United States since 1961? ____________

4. A **trend** is a consistent pattern of change over time. What trend can you identify on this table? ______________________

5. Based on this trend, what prediction can you make for the future? ______________________

____

6. What is the connection between your prediction and the growth of Islam in the United States? ______________________

Name ______________________ Date ______________

CHAPTER 31 Activity Sheet
Making Comparisons

As you have seen, a table organizes information into categories. Once a table is completed, you can easily make comparisons by looking for similarities and differences between information recorded in each column or row. The table on this page will help you to compare the three Presidents covered in this chapter. Use information in the text to fill in each box in the table. One item requires your own original answer. How do you think the public viewed Bill Clinton? Is he more or less popular than Ronald Reagan and George Bush?

Comparing Presidents

Background and Policies	Ronald Reagan	George Bush	Bill Clinton
Personal Background			
Character Traits			
Political Party			
Economic Policies			
Social Policies			
Area(s) of Greatest Personal Concern			
Public Opinion			

Name ______________________________ Date ________________

CHAPTER 32 Activity Sheet
Organizing Historical Information

The diagram below uses a reporter's questions to help you collect key facts about one of the foreign-policy crises covered in this chapter. Select which crisis you would like to study. Then fill in the diagram with information from the text.

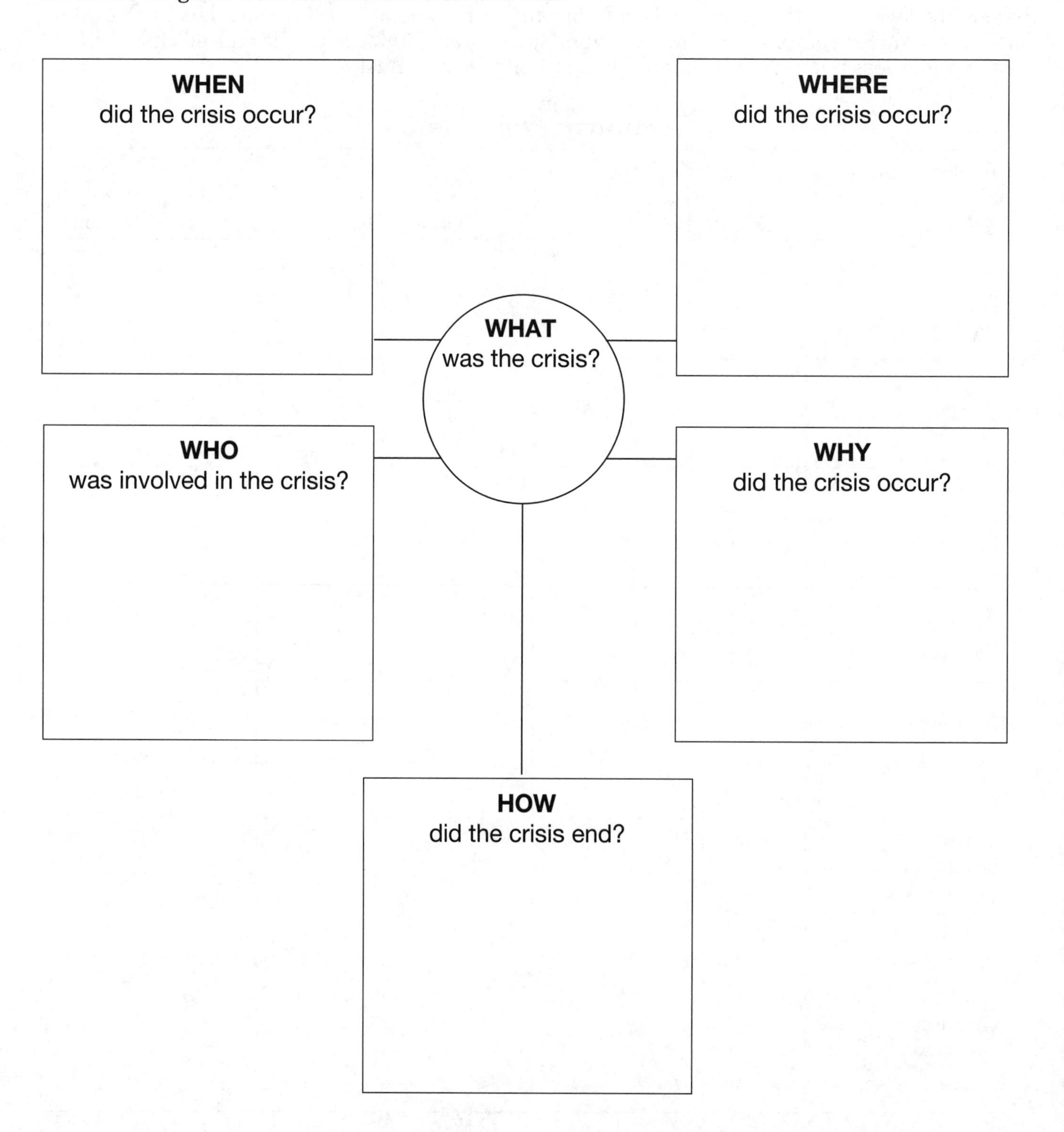

Name ______________________ Date ______________

CHAPTER 33 Activity Sheet
Understanding Demographics

Demography is the study of statistics about population. Statistics about population are known as demographics. People who study demographics are called demographers. Pretend that you are a demographer studying the demographics on this page. Begin by identifying the subject of each set of figures. Then answer the questions that follow.

1 ______

Top Ten Ancestry Groups of All Americans, 1990

	millions
1. German	58
2. Irish	39
3. English	33
4. African	24
5. Italian	15
6. Mexican	12
7. French	10
8. Polish	9
9. Native American	9
10. Dutch	6

2 ______

Top Ten Nations of Origin for Immigrants, 1992

	percent
1. Mexico	22
2. Vietnam	8.0
3. Philippines	6.3
4. Former Soviet Union	4.5
5. Dominican Republic	4.3
6. China	4.0
7. India	3.8
8. El Salvador	2.7
9. Poland	2.6
10. United Kingdom	2.1

3 ______

Top Ten Languages Spoken in the United States, 1990

	millions
1. English only	198.6
2. Spanish	17.3
3. French	1.7
4. German	1.5
5. Italian	1.3
6. Chinese	1.2
7. Tagalog *	0.8
8. Polish	0.7
9. Korean	0.6
10. Vietnamese	0.5

* A Filipino language

1. To what four ethnic groups do most Americans trace their ancestry? ______________________

____

2. The groups named in Table 1 come from Europe, Africa, and the Americas. What other region sent large numbers of immigrants in 1992? ______________________

3. How do Tables 1 and 2 help explain why so many people speak Spanish in the United States?

____

4. Based on these tables, write a generalization about the population of the United States.

____

____

____

____

Name ______________________ Date ______________

CHAPTER 34 Activity Sheet
Organizing Information on a Chart

To analyze the challenges discussed in this chapter, fill in the chart below.

Meeting the Nation's Challenges

Issue	Concern	Action
Pollution Wastes that make the air, water, or land unhealthy	 **At Risk:**	
Poverty Lack of resources to live a healthy and comfortable life	 **At Risk:**	
Drug Addiction Dependence upon a harmful substance	 **At Risk:**	
Crime Violation of the law	 **At Risk:**	

Name ______________________________ Date ____________________

CHAPTER 35 Activity Sheet
Predicting the Future

The word **future** means "the time to come." It is the days, months, and years that lay ahead of us. **Futurology** is the study of the future. (The suffix *-ology* means "the study of.") A futurologist is the person who does the studying. To study the future, futurologists gather the facts about the past and present. They then look for patterns of change. Based upon these changes, they make a prediction about the time that lies ahead (the future). Pretend that you are a futurologist. Draw a picture of at least one change that you see happening in the following areas.

Use of Computers

Medical Advances

Space Exploration

Name ______________________________ Date ____________________

CHAPTER 36 Activity Sheet
Comparing Past and Present

One of the best pictures of the American people comes from the data collected by the U.S. Bureau of the Census. The Constitution requires that a **census,** or official population count, be taken every ten years. The Census Bureau took its first census in 1790. It took its most recent census in 1990. Below are two statistical "snapshots" from each of these surveys. Study these figures. Then answer the questions that follow.

The Way We Were

- A total of 3,929,214 people lived in the United States, including enslaved Africans. (Untaxed Native Americans were not counted.)
- Four-fifths of the population came from northern Europe.
- One-fifth of the population came from Africa.
- People of English ancestry made up 60.9% of the population.
- Germans, Scots, and Scots-Irish made up 23% of the population.
- Only about .05% of Americans lived in cities.
- The nation had more men than women.
- Nearly 50% of all households had six or more people.
- The nation was young. The average American was a teenager.

Source: *Historical Statistics of the United States, Colonial Times to 1970.*

The Way We Are

- A total of 248,709,873 million people live in the United States.
- More Americans report German ancestry than any other group.
- African Americans total 12.3% of the population.
- Latinos total 9% of the population. By 2000, Latinos are expected to be the nation's largest minority.
- Asian and Pacific Islanders total 2.9% of the population. But in the 1980s, their numbers grew by 107.8%.
- More than 75% of Americans lived in cities.
- Women outnumber men by 6.2 million.
- Average household has 2.63 people.
- Average age of Americans is 33 years.

Sources: *The Universal Almanac,* 1994; *The New York Times,* July 26, 1992, p. E 5.

1. By how much has the nation's population grown since 1790? ____________________

____

2. Write a description of the "average" American in 1790. ____________________

____

3. Write a description of the "average" American in 1990. ____________________

____

4. Would you expect the nation to become more or less diverse by 2000? Explain. __________

____

____

____

▶INTEGRATING THE LANGUAGE ARTS INTO ▶THE TEACHING OF HISTORY

In recent years educators have become increasingly aware of the need to integrate the language arts into other subject areas. Usually when people think of the language arts, they think of reading and writing, but listening and speaking are equally important. Listening and speaking, like reading and writing, are essential elements in the communication of knowledge.

THE READING PROCESS

Every kind of reading material, no matter what the content area, has peculiarities that must be identified and mastered by the reader. History, for instance, has a specialized vocabulary, its own logic of organization, and its own kind of sentence structure.

An added complication is that students also bring a wide variety of skills to the task of reading history materials. Every teacher has faced the problem of having students who read quickly and with excellent comprehension in the same class with students who struggle to decode text.

As you know, prior experience is a significant factor in the comprehension of text; it is often more important than the student's ability to decode individual words. Since experience varies so much from student to student, it is important to have students share their understandings with one another—and correct their misunderstandings—before approaching the text. This sharing of information and perceptions is easily accomplished by using graphic organizers.

GRAPHIC ORGANIZERS

Graphic organizers are diagrams that illustrate the connections among ideas. Such organizers may take many forms, such as semantic maps, webs, timelines, and idea clusters. The point is to create a visual display of the associations or properties of topics. For instance, suppose that students are about to read a chapter from *One Nation, Many People* that discusses why U.S. settlers in Texas broke away from Mexico. Most students will have a limited knowledge of this subject. In order to prepare students to understand the chapter, you can help them share what knowledge they have in an idea cluster.

A typical idea cluster might look like this:

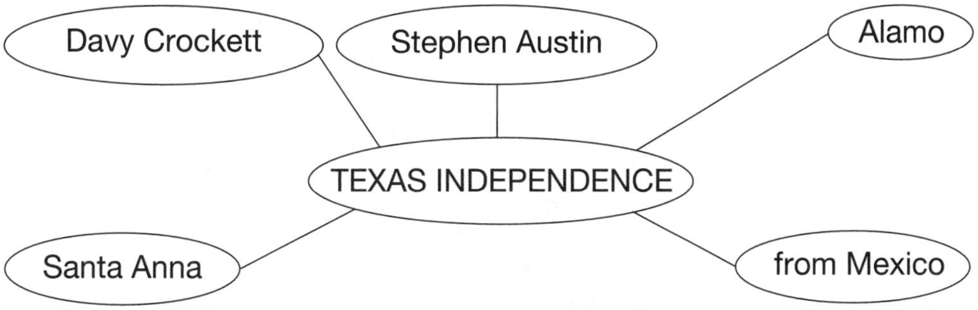

Davy Crockett
Stephen Austin
Alamo
TEXAS INDEPENDENCE
Santa Anna
from Mexico

The students create an idea cluster by listing all the words and images that come to their minds when they hear the name of a topic, in this case, Texas independence. You write these ideas on the chalkboard as students share them. One advantage of this technique is that all students are able to participate in, and learn from, this activity. As the students dictate their ideas, you will have an opportunity to introduce and use in context any unfamiliar vocabulary that students encounter in the text. Through discussion, you are also able to correct any information students may have that is incorrect or inaccurate.

Such diagrams are pictures of the collective knowledge of the group about the topics. In order to develop the diagrams, the students have to draw upon their experience and generate meaning. As they read the chapters and learn additional relevant details, they can add to their graphic organizers, which then become a visual representation of their new learning.

PREDICTION GUIDES

Another way of directing student attention and building needed background information is through the use of prediction guides. A prediction guide is merely a series of statements that students write concerning the material that they are about to read. The statements are written so that thinking is stimulated at the literal, interpretive, and applied levels.

Example:

Literal — Christopher Columbus first sailed from Palos, Spain.
I agree__________ I disagree __________

Inferential — Iron weapons and gunpowder gave Europeans an advantage over Native Americans of the Caribbean.
I agree__________ I disagree __________

Applied — The weapons of the Spaniards aided them in conquering the native people of the Caribbean.
I agree__________ I disagree __________

As the students respond to these statements, they are predicting what they will read. (The prediction guides should not be graded for accuracy.) This prereading focus gives students the chance to read with a purpose as they judge their preconceptions and change their ideas.

Vocabulary is another factor in understanding content-area material. All the research that has been done in the area of language acquisition reveals that unfamiliar words should always be taught in context if students are to retain their meaning. One way to teach new vocabulary is to give the students sentences in which the words are used in context and then require the students to infer the meaning. After students complete their inferences, they check their dictionaries for the correct meanings.

Example:

The Spanish used horses, dogs, and guns to subjugate the Taino of Hispaniola.

I think the word subjugate means ______________________________

Dictionary definition: ______________________________

DIRECTED READING

It is often necessary to focus the students' attention as they read. In *One Nation, Many People,* the text itself provides purpose-setting questions to direct the reading experience. These questions appear at the beginning of each section of the chapter. Students should consider the questions before reading begins. Discussion should always follow silent reading. It is important that students be asked to provide information and opinions and that they be required to substantiate their opinions by reading pertinent text aloud. In whole-class lessons, it is important that students be encouraged to discuss their answers with one another as well as with you.

Another method of guiding silent reading encourages students to pose their own questions about events and ideas in the text. With this method, you preview the chapter with the students. Together, you examine the visuals that appear in the chapter. In discussing these images, you give the students a chance to predict what they are going to read. You may also wish to mention some key ideas or events covered in the test.

In another method, you divide the class into small discussion groups of five or six students and ask them to list questions about the text. Turning section heads into questions is a good study technique. Next, have students read to find the answers to their own questions.

META-COGNITIVE SKILLS

Students who have difficulty reading text need to be taught comprehension-monitoring skills. Reading teachers refer to these skills as *metacognitive*. This terms means that students must develop awareness of themselves as readers. They must learn to think about how they process the text. Such students read aloud portions of the text that are difficult for them to decode and interpret during independent reading. They explain why portions of the text were hard to understand and demonstrate how they worked with the text to create meaning. Working with these students to recognize problems of text interpretation, you can lead them to identify their own strategies for getting meaning from print. As they deal with their reading difficulties, students benefit from using alternative sources of knowledge, particularly information learned from listening and speaking.

LISTENING

In this "information age," much of what students learn comes from listening. They listen constantly to radio and television. However, this is usually passive listening in which they are being entertained. Students are not listening for information, and often what they actually retain is incomplete or inaccurate. Ask any student about a current controversial public issue and you will frequently discover that the issue is poorly understood, at best.

To a great extent, this lack of listening comprehension can be attributed to the fact that few students are taught *how* to listen. Most people in the United States come from cultures that have rich oral traditions. Yet this emphasis on oral learning has been eclipsed by the availability of print materials. In our eagerness to teach students how to read, we have neglected to teach them how to listen.

One method of teaching listening skills to your students is to read a section of connected text to your class daily. After reading to them, ask your students to summarize what they have heard. If the students are typical, the information in their summaries will be disappointing at first. Once they begin to listen for who, what, when, where, why, and how—with a purpose, that is—the students will be able to report the content of what you have read more and more accurately.

SPEAKING

Just as the development of listening skills has been neglected, the development of speaking skills has also been given little attention. Of course, most social studies classrooms are filled with discussion. However, the same students often seem to do most of the talking. Often the less articulate students sit silently. In addition, a student may talk freely and comfortably with his or her peers. However, when he or she stands up in front of a classroom filled with those very same peers, gasps, stammers, and many "uh's" and "uhm's" can be heard.

Speaking in front of a group does not seem safe to many people. That is why creating an environment in which students feel safe to speak is so important in the development of speaking skills. The first step in creating such an environment is to limit the number of people in the audience. Extremely inarticulate students may need to be paired with a single partner at first. Gradually, as the student becomes more confident, the number of participants may be increased.

The most nonthreatening situation for listening and speaking is the cooperative learning group. In this situation, all the students are equal. Properly monitored, a cooperative learning group can be effective in turning a fearful speaker into a confident one. The key to teaching the reluctant speaker is structure. Whereas being called upon to speak extemporaneously on an issue to the whole class might cause reactions of terror in some students, the task of reporting a piece of discrete and limited information to a small group does not seem so threatening. You can arrange the group assignments with this in mind. After a time, the students with stage fright will grow more confident and can be given more challenging assignments.

WRITING

Writing should be an important part of every social studies lesson. Students learn to write the same way they learn to play the piano—by practicing. Just as practicing makes better pianists, it also makes better writers.

Writing also makes better readers. One way to increase your students' comprehension of written text is to make them write about a passage before they read it. This is a particularly effective way to prepare your students to read difficult primary source material. Students often struggle to read material written in previous centuries. Quite often the vocabulary is beyond them and the content does not seem relevant to their own lives. Writing is the way to make the connections for them.

Suppose, for example, that your students are about to read an excerpt from an autobiography of Frederick Douglass. This is challenging text, so it is advisable to work with students to create an idea cluster. Since the text concerns Douglass's experiences as an enslaved African American in 19th century Baltimore, students should think of what their feelings and experiences might be if they were in the same situation.

The resulting idea cluster might look like this:

As soon as the students finish listing ideas, have them take out a piece of

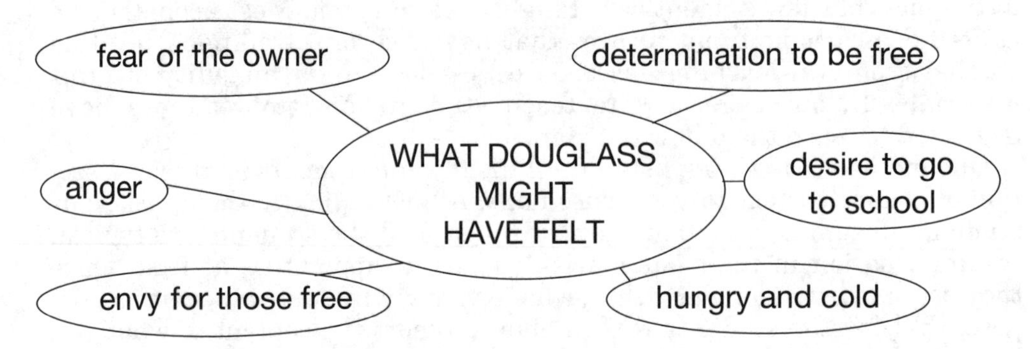

paper and write very quickly what sort of experiences they think they will read about in the life of Frederick Douglass. Tell students that they will not receive a mark for their brief essay and that they should not worry about spelling or punctuation, since this is not for publication.

Be certain that everyone writes something down on paper. The important thing about this assignment is that it be strictly stream of consciousness; it is designed to rid students of writer's block that is often caused by fear of writing something inaccurate or "dumb."

After students have been writing for two or three minutes, tell them to put down their pens. Ask if anyone in the groups wants to share what he or she has written. You will find many students eager to share their efforts. Write their predictions about the Douglass autobiography on the chalkboard. Tell the students that they should now read the text to verify the accuracy of their predictions. After students finish reading the text (this may be done silently or aloud), refer to the list of predictions on the chalkboard and discuss with the class which of their predictions were accurate.

This entire activity will take only 10 or 15 minutes of class time. Yet it will yield obvious dividends in reading comprehension, student interest, and student participation in learning.

Using Maps with *One Nation, Many People*

This chart lists mapping activities to give students practice with geographic elements in the study of United States history. Each activity is correlated to one or more of the themes of geography and can be done by completing one of the five outline maps on pp. 244–248. Most activities cam be completed using the text. Activities requiring research appear in italics.

	Map	Mapping Activity	Geographic Theme
Unit 1 Vol. 1	The United States	Regions of the United States	region
	The Americas	Native American nations	location, movement
	World	European trade routes	movement, place
		Routes of explorers	movement, interaction
		African empires	location, movement
	The Americas	The Spanish colonial empire	place, movement, interaction, region
Unit 2 Vol. 1	The Americas	European colonies	place, movement, interaction, region
	Eastern United States	English colonies	place, movement, interaction, region
	World	Triangle trades	movement, place, region
Unit 3 Vol. 1	Eastern United States	*Battles of the Revolutionary War*	Location, movement, interaction
Unit 4 Vol. 1	The United States	Louisiana Purchase/Louis and Clarke route	region, movement
		Slave and free states	interaction, region
		U.S. expansion into the Southwest	movement, region, interaction
	Eastern United States	*Slave rebellions*	location
Unit 5 Vol. 1	World	Migration	movement, interaction
	The United States	Underground Railroad	movement
		The compromises	interaction, region
		The Union and the Confederacy	region
	Eastern United States	Effects of the Emancipation Proclamation	region, movement
Unit 6 Vol. 1	The United States	Settlement on the Great Plains	movement, region, place
		Native American removal	movement, region
		Cattle drives	movement
		Roads, railroads, canals, trails	movement, region
	The World	New immigration patterns	movement, region
		Expansion in the Pacific	region, location, place
		Cuban-Spanish-American War	region, place, region
Unit 1 Vol. 2	The United States	U.S. cities in the 1900s	location, place, interaction
		The Great Migration	movement, region
	The Americas	*Latino migration in the 1900s*	movement, region
	World	Immigration patterns	movement, region
Unit 2 Vol. 2	North and South America	United States in Latin America	location, place, movement
		Panama Canal	movement, interaction
	World	U.S. global expansion	region, location
		Allies and Central powers	region, location
		Battles of World War I	location
Unit 3 Vol. 2	World	Allies and Axis nations	region, location
		Battles of World War II	location
	The United States	Internment camps	region, location
Unit 4 Vol. 2	World	Cold War enemies	region, location
		Korean and Vietnam Wars	region, location
	The United States	Migration to the Sun Belt	movement, region
		Civil-rights encounters	place, movement
Unit 5 Vol. 2	The Americas	Latino immigration	movement, region
	The United States	Reservations today	location, region
	World	Asian immigration	movement, region
Unit 6 Vol. 2	World	New Asian immigrants	movement, region
		Trouble spots	location, interaction
	The United States	Diverse populations in the United States	movement, place, region

Name ______________________ Date ______________

OUTLINE MAP 1: NORTH AMERICA

Name ________________________________ Date ____________________

OUTLINE MAP 2: THE UNITED STATES

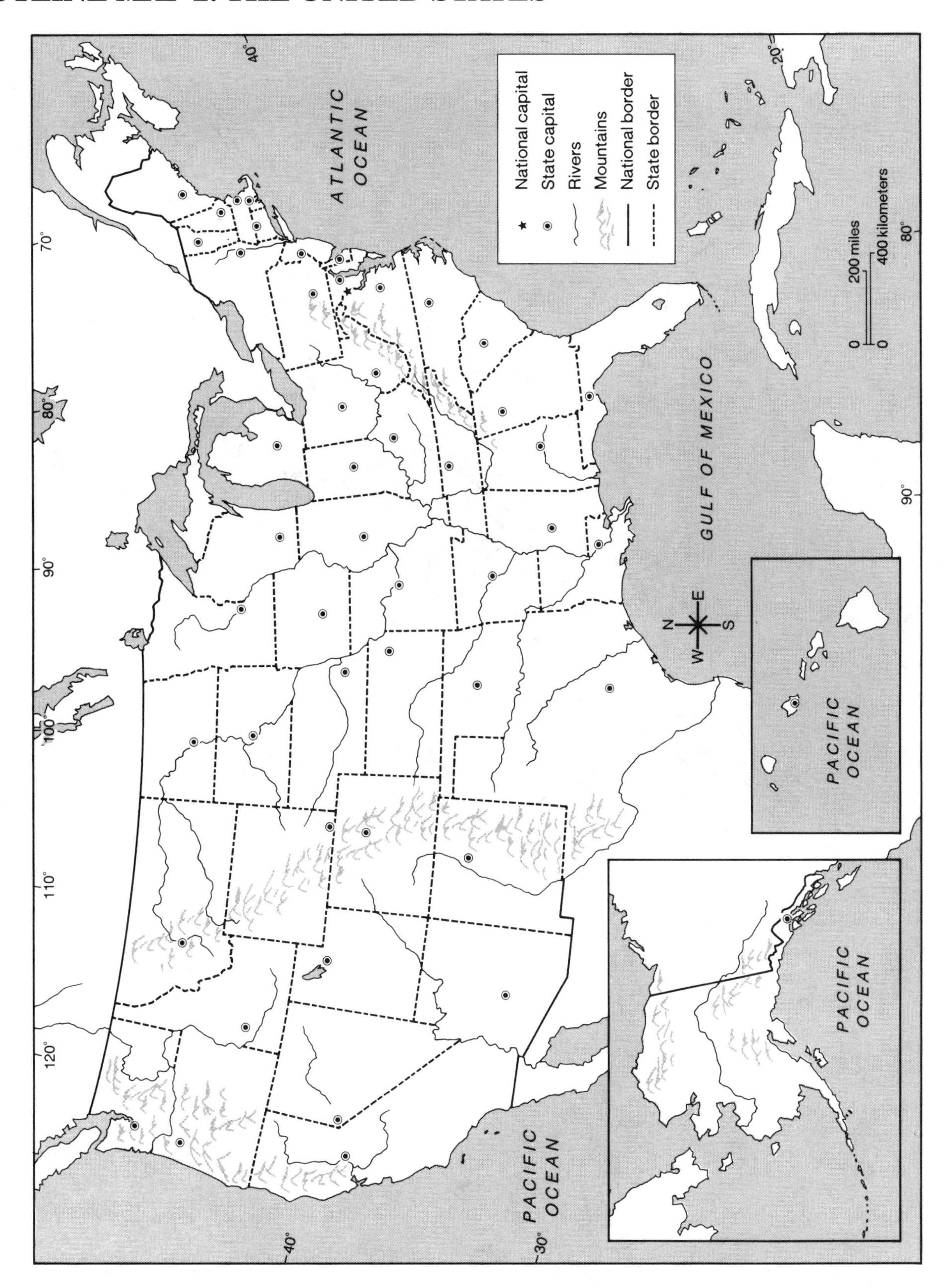

Name ______________________ Date ______________

OUTLINE MAP 3: THE THIRTEEN COLONIES

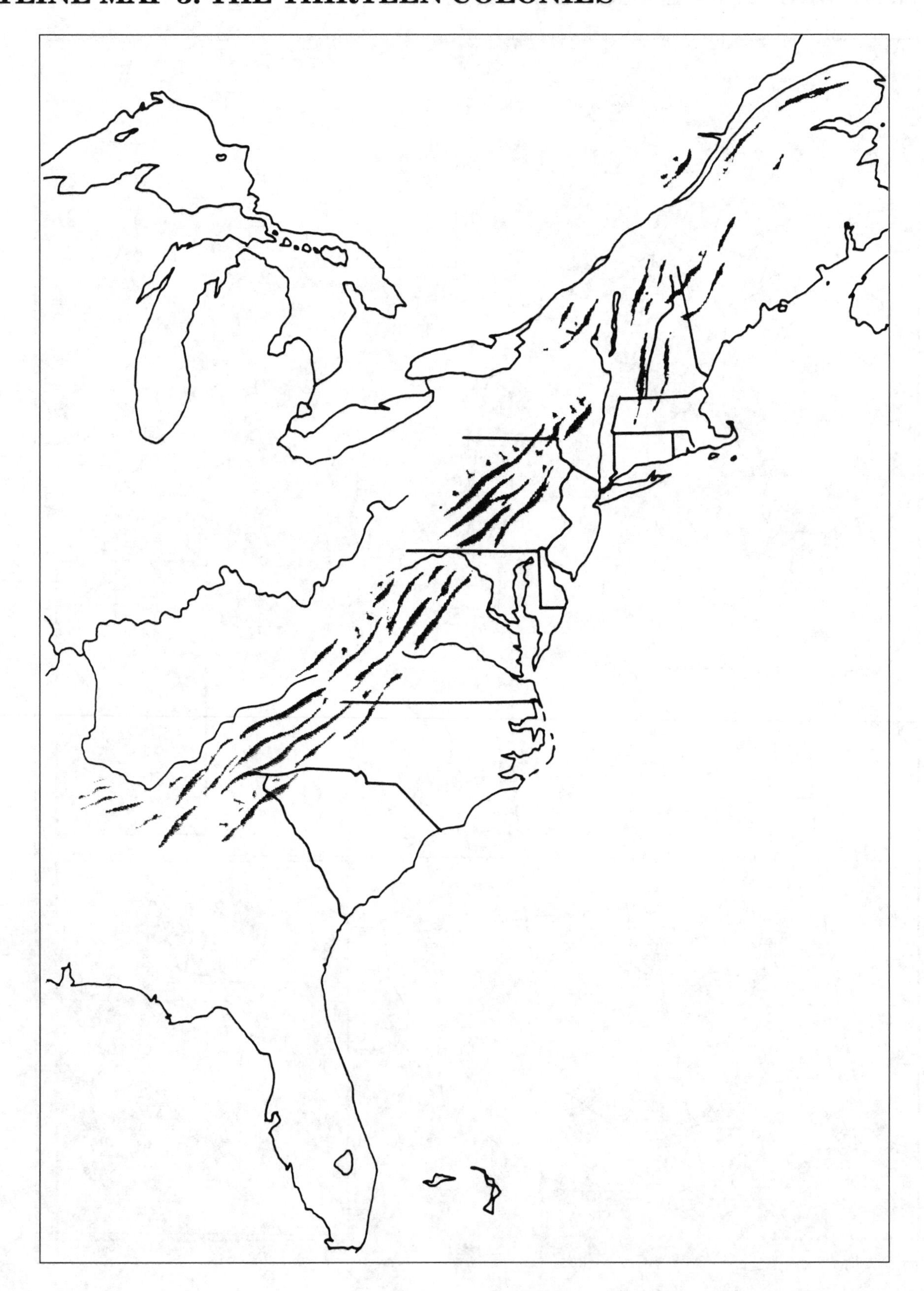

Name ______________________ Date ______________

OUTLINE MAP 4: THE AMERICAS

Name ______________________________ Date ____________________

OUTLINE MAP 5: THE WORLD

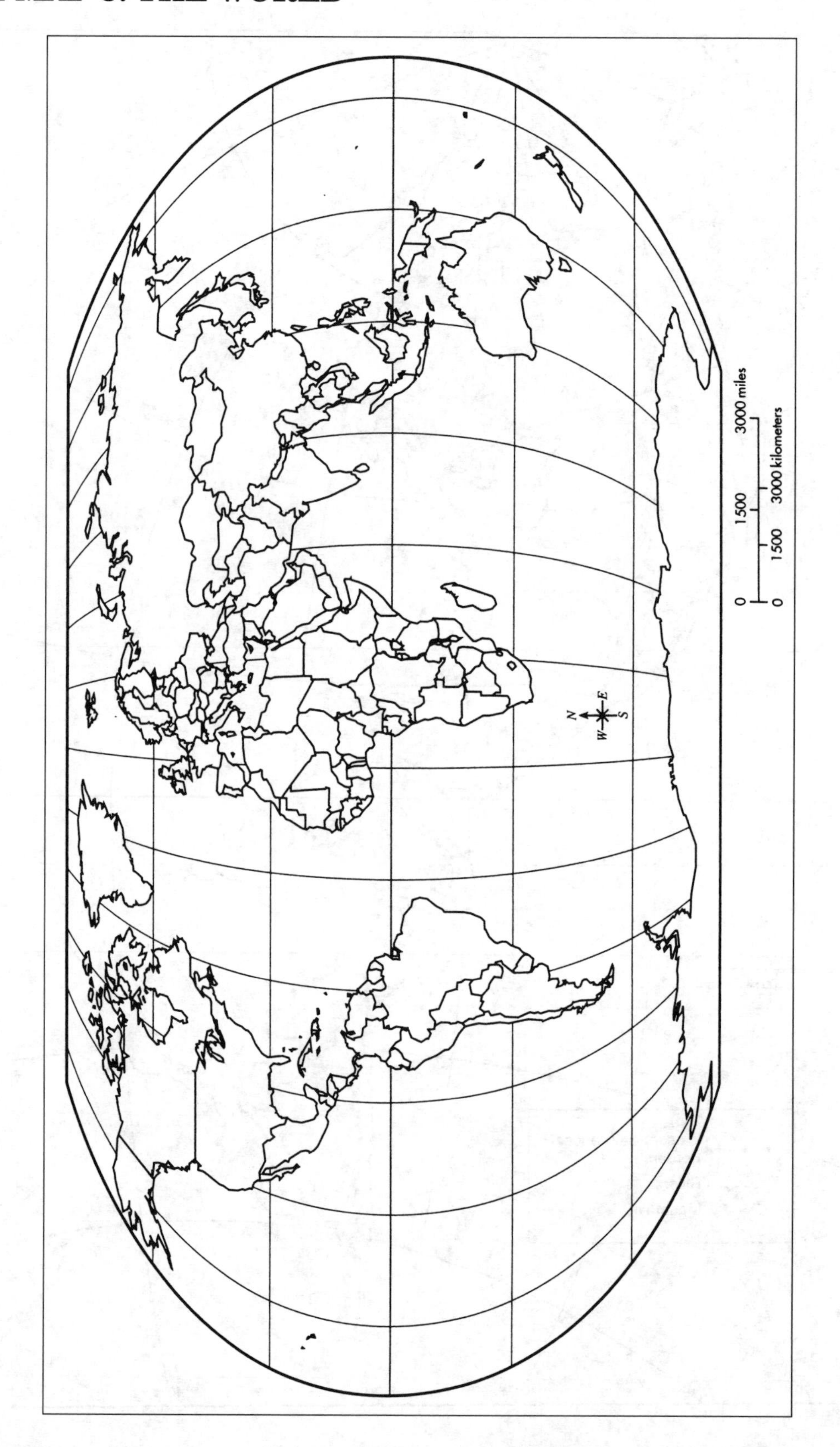

☆ WRITING WORKSHOP EVALUATION

Writer ______________________________ Title ______________________________________

Write comments about the content, organization, style, and spelling, usage, and mechanics in the space below.

Content

Well-done: ____

____

____

Needs Improvement: ____

____

____

Organization

Well-done: ____

____

____

Needs Improvement: ____

____

____

Style

Well-done: ____

____

____

Needs Improvement: ____

____

____

Spelling, Usage, Mechanics

Well-done: ____

____

____

Needs Improvement: ____

____

____

☆ WRITING WORKSHOP EVALUATION

Writer ______________________________ Title ______________________________

To evaluate a paper holistically, first read the paper. Then, with your first impression in mind, use this scoring guide as a basis for your assessment.

SCORE	CRITERIA
4	clear, concise sentences varied sentence structure specific or descriptive details special flair; uses imagination or makes thoughtful comments effective word choice good use of transitions writes to the topic well-organized excellent spelling, usage, mechanics other: ______________________________
3	clear, concise sentences some detail, imagination, or thoughtful ideas writes to the topic some use of transitions mechanical or usage problems do not interfere adequate organization appropriate paragraphing other: ______________________________
2	some incomplete sentences lacks organization partial development of the topic errors interfere with understanding faulty paragraphing other: ______________________________
1	little or no organization short and underdeveloped wanders from the topic many mechanical problems other: ______________________________
0	inappropriate illegible off the topic blank page

Name ______________________________ Date ____________________

✩ WRITING WORKSHOP

Reporting Facts

A biography is an account told of a person's life. Biographies give facts about the person.

Facts tell *who, what, where, when, how*, or *why*. Suppose that you were asked to write a brief biography of Malinché, an important member of Cortés's group. You would first introduce your subject in a topic sentence. Then you would add details, usually in time order. Those details would tell who Malinché was, what Malinché did, where that took place, when she lived, and so on.

Discover
- **What is the topic sentence of each paragraph?**
- **What facts are used to support this main idea?**

Without the help of Malinché, Hernando Cortés would probably have failed to conquer the Aztec. The daughter of a powerful Native American chief, Malinché had been sold into slavery upon her father's death. She was given to Cortés by Gulf Coast Native Americans and quickly became a valuable member of Cortés's group. Malinché spoke the Aztec language and understood Aztec life. She quickly learned Spanish and became Cortés's teacher and interpreter. She also was Cortés's special delegate to Native American chiefs. During the two-year Spanish expedition in Mexico, Malinché kept the Spanish from getting into trouble many times.

Look at the Model

Understand
- **How the writer uses facts to answer questions**
- **How the writer organizes facts in time order**

1. What is the topic sentence of the paragraph? ______________________________

____

____

2. List these facts in time order: Malinché was sold as a slave, Malinché was the daughter of a powerful chief, Malinché learned Spanish. ______________________________

____

____

____

____

____

Name ______________________ Date ______________

1 Prewriting

Choose Your Topic

Think of an important or interesting person from the time period you are studying. That person will be the topic of your paper. You will write a two-paragraph biography about that person's life. No matter which person you choose, your biography must (1) report facts about the person and (2) organize those facts in sequence, or time order.

Think about your *purpose*. Will your biography inform, persuade, or entertain? Think about your *audience*. Who will read this biography? How much does your audience already know about the topic? Now choose the topic about which you will write. Write your choice below.

____

Tell what your purpose is: ______________________

Tell who your audience is: ______________________

Make a Time Line

Organize facts about your topic by making a time line. First write a topic sentence for your first paragraph. Then jot down events in the order in which they occurred. Include dates where possible. Look at the example.

Without the help of Malinché, Cortés would probably have failed to conquer the Aztec.	Born the daughter of a powerful chief	Sold into slavery	Given to Cortés	Became Cortés's teacher and interpreter

Topic Sentence ← **Event 1** — **Event 2** — **Event 3** — **Event 4** →

Now make similar lines for the two paragraphs of your biography.

____

____

____

Topic Sentence 1 ← **Event 1** — **Event 2** — **Event 3** — **Event 4** →

____

____

Topic Sentence 1 ← **Event 1** — **Event 2** — **Event 3** — **Event 4** →

Name ____________________ Date ____________________

2 Writing

First Draft

Use this space to write a first draft of your biography. Do not worry about errors in spelling or punctuation. You will have time later to correct these errors. Use information from your time line to write facts in sequence. Use the guidelines on the left as you organize your draft.

Write a topic sentence that introduces your topic. (Remember your purpose. Does your topic sentence explain why you are writing?)

Use your time line to write complete sentences that tell facts in time order.

Use dates and transition words such as *then, next,* and *finally* to make the order of events clear. (Think about your audience. How much do they already know about when things took place?)

Follow the same process to write your second paragraph.

Name ______________________________ Date ________________

Talk It Over

Choose a partner. Listen as your partner reads his or her work aloud two times. The first time, listen to be sure that the facts are organized in an order that makes sense. The second time, try to answer these questions:

1. Are all the facts about the topic here? Could any facts be left out, or should additional facts be added?
2. Are the transitions from one event to the next clear? Could transition words or dates be added to make the sequence clearer?

After the second reading, you should answer the questions for the writer. Then change places. Follow the same steps with your partner.

Check for Sequence

Whenever you use dates, you must check to make sure they are in order. Read the sentences below. Rearrange them so that they are in the proper sequence.

Cabral claimed Brazil for Portugal in 1500. The French set up a settlement in 1555, but were forced out by the Portugese in 1567. The first permanent Portuguese colony was established there in 1532.

Make the Changes

Reread your first draft. Are your events in the proper sequence? Think about your partner's comments and suggestions. Make only those changes that improve your biography. Then copy the revised biography on a clean sheet of paper.

Capitalize any proper nouns or adjectives.
Henry the Navigator Portuguese Lisbon

Find and correct five capitalization errors in this paragraph. Use these proofreading marks:

[≡] capitalize [/] change to lower case

Pedro Alvarez cabral was on an Expedition to India when he veered off course and landed on the Coast of brazil. He was apparently not the first european explorer to land there.

Proofread your biography. Be sure you have capitalized proper nouns and adjectives correctly. Look for other mistakes in spelling and punctuation. Then make a final neat copy of your work.

Name ______________________________ Date ____________________

☆ WRITING WORKSHOP

Persuasive Writing

Suppose you are convinced that you have the right opinion about an issue. How can you persuade other people to agree with you? Read some editorials. They are good examples of persuasive writing.

From the 1830s to the 1860s, abolitionists tried to convince other Americans to join their antislavery cause. They often did this through the use of newspaper or magazine editorials similar to the one below.

Discover
- **What words does the writer use to persuade?**
- **How does she express her opinion?**

Slavery is not an issue we women of American can abide any longer. How can we tell our children that we accept the enslavement of another human being on the basis of race? We remind them daily that we are all beloved in God's sight. How can we reconcile that with the indignities we force on slaves? How can we expect our children to treat each other with respect and kindness when they see us abuse and mishandle our workers? Where in our relationships with our slaves is that Golden Rule we teach our children: "Do unto others as you would have them do unto you"? We are not practicing what we preach, and our children witness our dishonesty. As women, as mothers, we should all be ashamed.

Boston/June 20, 1859

Look at the Model

Understand
- **How the writer appeals to a particular audience**
- **How the writer uses examples to persuade**

1. What audience is the writer trying to persuade? ______________________________

____

____

2. List three examples that the writer gives as reasons women can no longer tolerate slavery. ________

____

____

____

____

____

Name ______________________________ Date ______________________

1 Prewriting

Choose Your Topic

Imagine you are the editor of a newspaper in a large city during the historical period you are studying. What city and time period will you use? ______________________________

Citizens of the city are arguing about some important issues. Choose one of those issues to discuss. Write an editorial to get your readership to agree with your point of view on that particular issue. Whatever topic you choose, your editorial must (1) express an opinion and (2) give reasons and examples to support that opinion.

Think about your purpose. Will your editorial inform, persuade, or entertain? Think about your audience. Who will read your editorial? How can you make them share your point of view? Now choose your topic. Write your choice below.

____

Tell what your purpose is: ______________________________

Tell who your audience is: ______________________________

Make a Cluster Diagram

A cluster diagram can help you organize your thinking. For a persuasive paragraph, your opinion should go in the center of the cluster. Around the cluster you can list supporting reasons and examples. Cross out any examples that do not support the opinion or that do not fit with the other examples and reasons.

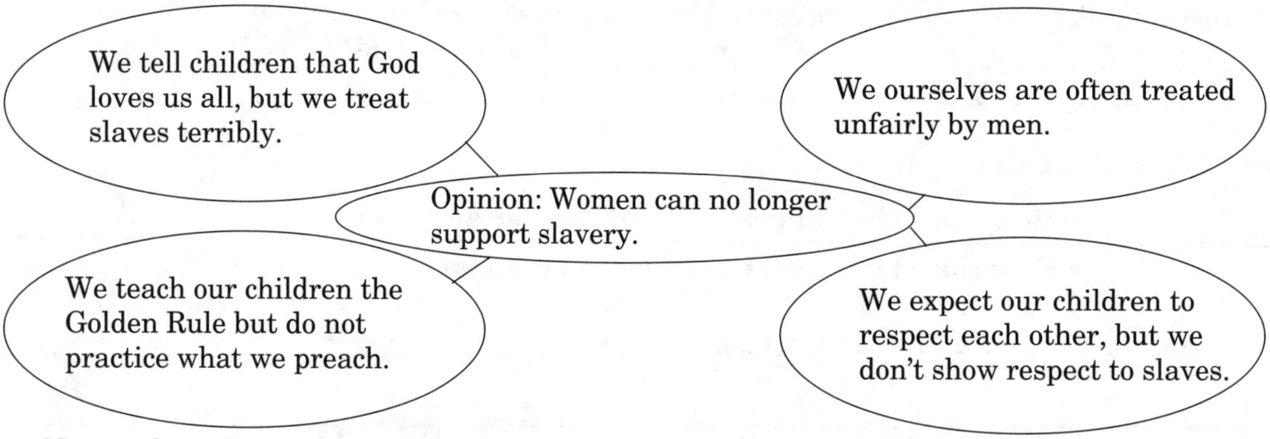

We tell children that God loves us all, but we treat slaves terribly.

We ourselves are often treated unfairly by men.

Opinion: Women can no longer support slavery.

We teach our children the Golden Rule but do not practice what we preach.

We expect our children to respect each other, but we don't show respect to slaves.

Now make a cluster diagram for your topic. Begin by writing your opinion in the center of the cluster. Add reasons and examples that support the opinion. Cross out any reasons that do not fit.

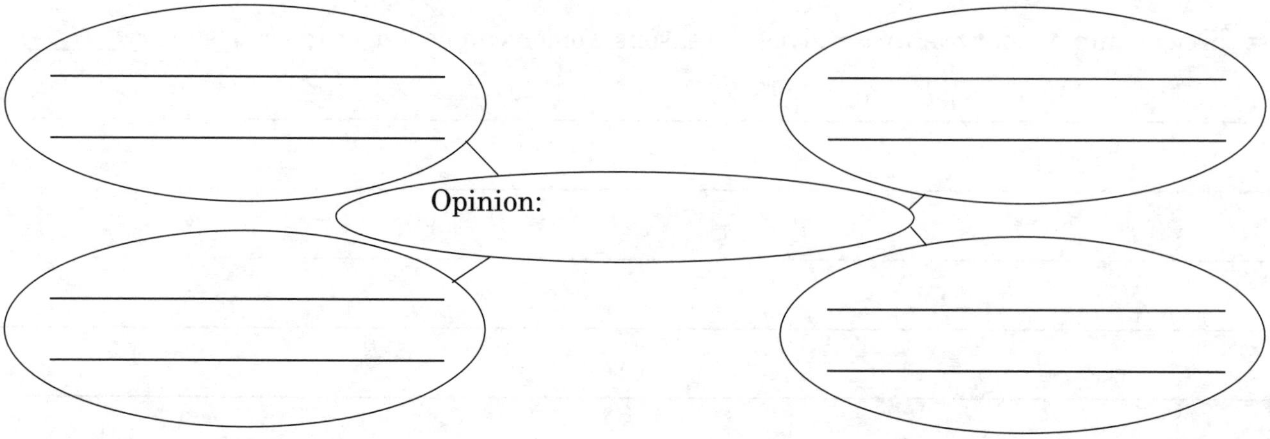

______________________ ______________________

______________________ ______________________

Opinion:

______________________ ______________________

______________________ ______________________

Name ______________________________ Date ____________________

2 Writing

First Draft

Use this space to write a first draft of your editorial. Do not worry about errors in spelling or punctuation. You will have time later to correct those errors. Use your Prewriting cluster to organize your editorial. Use the guidelines on the left as you write your draft.

Write a topic sentence that introduces your topic and gives your opinion. (Keep your audience in mind. Are you using language they will understand?)

Add supporting reasons from your Prewriting cluster diagram. (Think about your purpose. In what order should the reasons be listed to best persuade your audience?)

Use persuasive words such as *should* or *better* to make your point.

End your editorial with a statement that clarifies and sums up your argument.

Name ______________________________ Date ____________________

3 Revising

Talk It Over

Choose a partner. Listen as your partner reads his or her work aloud two times. The first time, listen for the writer's opinion. The second time, try to answer these questions:

1. Am I convinced of the logic of the writer's argument? How could the editorial do a better job of persuading me?
2. Do all the examples and the reasons given support the opinion?

After the second reading, answer the questions for the writer. Then change places. Follow the same steps with your partner.

Vary Sentence Beginnings

You can improve your writing by varying the beginnings of sentences. You can change the order of words in the phrases or add prepositional phrases to keep from making all your sentences look alike. Rewrite these sentences so that the beginnings vary.

We need cheap labor to prop up our sagging economy.
We stand firmly on the side of good and mercy.
We can no longer stand by and watch.

Make the Changes

Reread your first draft. Do your sentence beginnings vary? Think about your partner's comments and suggestions. Make only those changes that improve your editorial. Then copy the revised editorial on a clean sheet of paper.

4 Proofreading

End sentences with the correct punctuation.
We cannot tolerate this. Do you understand?
Read the newspaper. What a problem we have!

Find and correct four punctuation errors in this paragraph. Use these proofreading marks:
[^] insert [⊙] add a period

This is a serious issue Can we survive without this source of inexpensive labor Imagine a South without plantations What a nightmare we face

Proofread your editorial. Be sure you have punctuated sentences correctly. Check for other errors in spelling and punctuation. Then make a final neat copy of your work.

Name ______________________ Date ______________

☆ WRITING WORKSHOP

Comparing and Contrasting

Writers compare two things or ideas to show how they are alike. They contrast two things or ideas to show how they differ.

During periods of great change and reform, comparisons and contrasts can help us see how things changed. For example, around the turn of the century, writers such as Jacob Riis and John Spargo wrote about the painful lives of poor city children. Their work helped lead to laws that improved the lives of these children. This report looks at some changes that took place.

Discover
- **What is being compared and contrasted?**
- **What words are used to compare and contrast?**

> The period of reform saw great improvements in the lives of children. Before the reforms limiting child labor, it was not unusual to see children working 14-hour days in the dark, dangerous factories. According to the 1900 census, over 1.5 million children under the age of 16 were then so employed in the United States. Children were subjected to unsafe and unclean conditions. Some rarely saw the light of day. School, of course, was out of the question.
>
> As the muckrakers brought the issue to the public, certain reforms were made. Children still worked in factors, but laws were passed that restricted the number of hours they could work. Other laws called for children to attend school until age 16. Health and safety regulations were established for factories that employed children. Although the law fixing the minimum age for employment in factories at 16 was not passed until 1938, these early reforms changed the lives of many poor city children.

Look at the Model

Understand
- **How the writer uses comparison to show continuity**
- **How the writer uses contrast to show change**

1. Does this report primarily show comparisons or contrasts?

____

2. How were things still the same after the reforms?

____

3. How were things different after the reforms? List two changes.

____

____

Name ______________________ Date ______________

1 Prewriting

Choose Your Topic

Write a two-paragraph report comparing and contrasting some aspects of life in the United States before and after the period of change. Possible subjects include immigrant life, housing, city government, or women's rights. Whatever topic you choose, your report must tell (1) how things were alike before and after the change and (2) how things were different before and after the change.

Thing about your *purpose*. Will your report inform, persuade, or entertain? Think about your *audience*. Who will read your report? How much do they already know about your topic? Now choose the topic about which you will write. Write your choice below.

____

Tell what your purpose is: ______________________________

Tell who your audience is: ______________________________

Make a Venn Diagram

A Venn diagram is a good way to show comparison and contrast. The area where the ovals intersect is the area of comparison. The other areas are areas of contrast.

unsafe conditions
long hours
no school

Children work
in factories

safety regulations
restricted hours
compulsory school

Before Reform

After Reform

Now make a Venn diagram for your topic. Write the ways things are the same in the center where the ovals intersect. Write the ways things differ in the ovals where they belong.

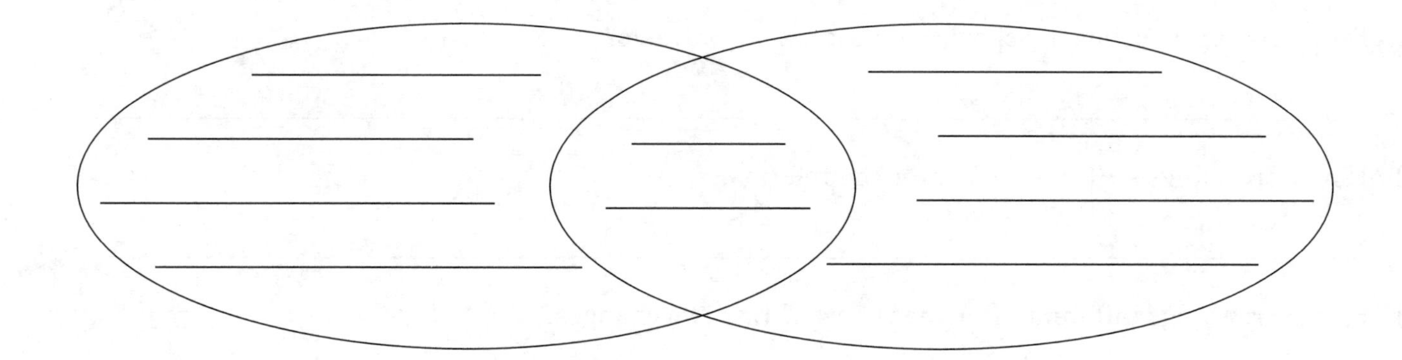

Name ______________________ Date ______________

2 Writing

First Draft

Use this space to write a first draft of your report. Do not worry about errors in spelling or punctuation. You will have time later to correct those errors. Use your Venn diagram to organize your report. Use the guidelines on the left as you write your draft.

Write a topic sentence that introduces your topic.

Use your chart to write sentences that tell about conditions before reform. (Keep your audience in mind. How much do you need to explain?)

Begin a new paragraph. Tell about conditions after reform. (Remember your purpose. Will you concentrate on comparisons or contrasts?)

End with a sentence that sums up your main idea.

Name ______________________________ Date ____________________

3 Revising

Talk It Over

Choose a partner. Listen as your partner reads his or her work aloud two times. The first time, try to tell what is being compared and contrasted. The second time, try to answer these questions:

1. Does the first paragraph tell about life before reform? Does the second tell about life after reform?
2. Are examples given in a logical order?

After the second reading, answer the questions for the writer. Then change places. Follow the same steps with your partner.

Use Transition Words

When you compare and contrast, there are a number of transition words you can use to make your points clearer.

Comparison	**Contrast**
like, just as, too, as well	however, but, whereas, on the other hand

Rewrite these sentences to show a clearer contrast.
Children once carried fifty-pound sacks. Now adults did the heavy lifting.

____

____

Make the Changes

Reread your first draft. Could transition words be added to make your report clearer? Think about your partner's comments and suggestions. Make only those changes that improve your report. Then copy the revised report on a clean sheet of paper.

4 Proofreading

Use a comma between two clauses of a compound sentence.
Jake rose before dawn, and he worked until dark.

Find and correct five punctuation errors in this paragraph. Use these proofreading marks:

Children had always worked but factories changed the kind of work they had to do. The bosses needed labor and children provided a cheap source of it. Once children worked out in the fields and the work was healthy. Now they were stuck inside, and forced to do heavy labor. Reformers revealed these conditions and the situation began to change.

Proofread your report. Be sure you have used commas correctly. Check for other errors in spelling and punctuation. Then make a final neat copy of your work.

Name ______________________________ Date ______________

☆ WRITING WORKSHOP

Cause and Effect

Nothing in history happens without a cause. When one event leads to another, we call the first event the *cause* and the second event the *effect.* Understanding cause and effect is vital to an understanding of history.

For example, wars often have many causes and many effects. To understand why the United States has fought a war, it is important to understand clause and effect. This report tells about a cause of U.S. involvement in World War I.

Discover
- **What is the primary cause discussed, and what is its effect?**
- **What words are used to signal cause-effect relationships?**

When war broke out in Europe in 1914, the United States decided to remain neutral. The issue that profoundly angered U.S. policy-makers and ultimately led to the ending of neutrality was Germany's use of submarine warfare.

In May of 1915, German submarines sank the passenger liner *Lusitania.* When the United States strongly protested, Germany revised its policy on submarine warfare. However, in March of 1916, another passenger ship, the *Sussex,* was destroyed. Because of this, the United States issued an ultimatum, with the effect that Germany once again agreed to restrict its use of submarines.

The last straw may have come when Germany began unrestricted use of submarines again in February of 1917. The United States broke off diplomatic relations that week and formally entered the war in April after Germany attacked U.S. commercial ships. Other factors certainly helped prompt this action, but Germany's use of submarines was a major reason behind our entry into the global conflict.

Look at the Model

Understand
- **How the writer emphasizes cause-effect relationships**
- **What conclusions the writer has drawn about cause and effect**

1. What, according to the writer, is a major cause of the United States' involvement in World War I?

____

____

2. What event was an effect of the sinking of the *Sussex*? ______________________________

____

Name ______________________ Date ______________

1 Prewriting

Choose Your Topic

Write a one- or two-paragraph report explaining the major cause-effect relationship in the historical period you are studying. You might discuss Britain's taxes and the Patriots' responses, alliances before World War I, or the spread of communism after World War II. Whatever topic you choose, your report must (1) draw conclusions about cause and effect and (2) organize these conclusions logically.

Think about your *purpose.* Will your report inform, persuade, or entertain? Think about your *audience.* Who will read your report? Will they agree or disagree with your conclusions? Now choose the topic on which you wish to write. Write your choice below.

____

Tell what your purpose is: ______________________

Tell who your audience is: ______________________

Make a QAD Chart

When you think about cause and effect, you can think in terms of questions, answers, and details. This helps you see what is cause and what is effect.

Topic:	U.S. involvement in World War I
Question:	What caused our involvement?
Answer:	German use of submarines
Details:	sinking of the *Lusitania*
	sinking of the *Sussex*
	sinking of several U.S.-owned commercial ships

Now make a QAD chart for your topic. Include details that support and explain the cause-effect relationship.

Topic:	______________________
Question:	What caused ______________________
Answer:	______________________
Details:	______________________
	______________________
	______________________

Name ______________________ Date ______________

2 Writing

First Draft

Use this space to write a first draft of your report. Do not worry about errors in spelling or punctuation. You will have time later to correct those mistakes. Use your QAD chart to organize your report. Use the guidelines on the left as you write your draft.

Write a topic sentence that introduces your topic and states the major *cause.*

____

____

____

____

Write sentences that tell the *effects* of this cause. (Remember your purpose. Have you included only those effects that have to do with your main idea?)

____

____

____

____

____

____

Use words such as *because, due to,* or *led to* to show transitions from cause to effect. (Think about your audience. Is the language you are using appropriate?)

____

____

____

____

____

____

Finish with a sentence that sums up and draws a conclusion about cause and effect.

____

____

Name ______________________________ Date ____________________

3 Revising

Talk It Over

Choose a partner. Listen as your partner reads his or her work aloud two times. The first time, listen for the primary cause-effect relationship. The second time, try to answer these questions:

1. Are transition words used to move the writing clearly from cause to effect?
2. Do I agree with the conclusion? How might the report be more logically organized?

After the second reading, answer the questions for the writer. Then change places. Follow the same steps with your partner.

Add Vital Details

The logic in a report that shows cause and effect may be hard to find simply because important facts are left out. Read this paragraph.

> Belgium had declared itself neutral. The British were outraged and declared war on the German occupiers of Belgium.

Then draw an arrow to the place where you would add these details to make the transition between cause and effect clearer: Although Belgium was neutral, the Germans invaded Belgium, an ally of Britain, anyway.

Make the Changes

Reread your first draft. Have you left out any vital details? Think about your partner's comments and suggestions. Make only those changes that improve your report. Then copy the revised report on a clean sheet of paper.

4 Proofreading

Use quotation marks around titles of short written works, including short stories, poems, and articles.
"Anthem for Doomed Youth" is a poem about the war by Wilfred Owen.

Use this proofreading mark to add quotation marks where needed in this paragraph.
[❛❜] add quotation marks

> Wilfred Owen and Siegfried Sassoon were English poets, and Alan Seeger was an American. All three wrote about World War I. Strange Meeting is one such poem by Owen. Sassoon is known for the poem called Counter-Attack. Seeger wrote I Have a Rendezvous with Death shortly before being killed in action.

Proofread your report. If you refer to a written work, punctuate it correctly. Check for other errors in spelling and punctuation. Then make a final neat copy of your work.

ANSWER KEYS

CHAPTER QUESTIONS AND REVIEWS

VOLUME 1

Chapter 1 **1:1.** because of its diverse cultures **2.** the movement of someone from his or her homeland to live permanently in a new country **2:1.** includes all the parts of nature that affect a group **2.** because they influence people and history **3:1.** for travel **2.** Interior Plains region has the best grazing land and farmland. **Review I. 1.** c **2.** d **3.** a **4.** e **5.** b **II. 1.** by bringing in a variety of people and cultures **2.** They determine where people live, their work, how people use the land, and provide natural boundaries. **3.** Possible answer: Pacific and Intermountain regions are both mountainous and rugged. Pacific mountains are near sea, while Intermountain region is inland. Pacific region is more populated and has more cities. **4.** Mountains cut the region off on all sides and it lacks water. Land is less expensive. **5.** transportation, irrigation, drinking water, form natural borders **III. 1.** Appalachian Mountains, Atlantic Plain **2.** Interior Plains **IV. 1.** Some obstacles may include wide rivers, the mountains and dry weather of the Plains region. Students may suggest trying to go around the mountains, bring plenty of fresh water to get through the desert, and create some type of float to get across the rivers. **2.** Students' pictures should clearly illustrate the climate of their choice. **V. 1.** Students should refer to the chapter, as well as outside resources, for information on their groups region. **2.** Students may want to observe their environment and list the affects it has on them.

Chapter 2 **1:1.** in pursuit of their prey **2.** As they spread out across the United States, they developed different languages, beliefs, and foods. **2:1.** Anasazi, Pueblo, Iroquois, Miwok, Chumash, Yuma, Navajo, Hopi, Zuñi, Apache, Comanche, Pima, Cherokee, Creek, etc. **2.** used as a model for the U.S. government **3:1.** the Maya **2.** Tenochtitlan was one of the largest cities in the world at that time. **Review I. 1.** d **2.** e **3.** b **4.** c **5.** a **II. 1.** allowed Native Americans to settle in villages **2.** Possible answer: Anasazi build cliff dwellings to save them from attacks. Pueblos grew crops which grow well in the heat and sandy soil. **3.** united under the League of Five Nations **4.** a special underground room where people prayed **5.** a system of numbers, a way of writing using picture symbols, and an accurate calendar **III. 1.** 3, 1, 2 **IV. 1.** Students may point out advantages growing crops, rather than having to hunt for food. **2.** Descriptions may include wealth, huge crowds, advanced buildings, variety of goods and services, religious objects and temples. **V. 1.** Students should include the important aspects of their chosen culture. **2.** Reports should note how Americans adapt to their regions today.

Chapter 3 **1:1.** a series of wars fought over part of the Middle East known as the Holy Land, between Christians and Muslims **2.** set up a school for sea captains that taught navigation **2:1.** a shorter route to the Indies **2.** Spanish soldier/explorers **3:1.** Santo Domingo **2.** built buildings, worked farms, mined gold and silver **Review I. 1.** a **2.** d **3.** c **4.** b **5.** e **II. 1.** introduced products of the Indies to Europe, started a new age of trade and exploration **2.** did not want to pay those who controlled the overland routes **3.** Many were killed or enslaved. **4.** a fountain of youth **5.** a free African conquistador **III.** Christopher Columbus, 1492, Hispaniola and other Caribbean islands. Juan Garrido, 1513, joined Ponce de Leon in Puerto Rico. Juan Ponce de Leon, 1513, Florida. **IV. 1.** Students should remember that the Spanish had better weapons but the Taino were defending their lives. **2.** Students may include seeing new plants and animals. **3.** Students may feel angry because of his cruel treatment of Native Americans. **V. 1.** Cartoon books should contain details about the incident. **2.** Possible answer: space; may think of the earth as a united whole

Chapter 4 **1:1.** a large grant of land offered to Spaniards to settle in North America, including the right to use Native American labor **2.** sugar **2:1** trade in gold and salt **2.** became a major center of learning for religion, medicine, and law; had excellent libraries **3:1.** because the Aztec treated their vassals cruelly **2.** believed Cortés was a god **Review I. 1.** b **2.** c **3.** e **4.** a **5.** d **II. 1.** forced to do hard labor, mistreated, deprived of almost all rights **2.** Native Americans were killed off, mainly through disease, so the Spaniards used enslaved Africans as a source of labor to work the sugar fields. **3.** While in Mecca, Mansa Musa convinced some of the finest builders and scholars to return with him to Timbuktu, and help enlarge the city. **4.** more powerful weapons, Native American allies, disease **5.** a trade of salt and gold between North and West Africa **III.** Ghana, a.d. 500 and 1600, "king of gold", largest army, silent trade. Mali, early 1200s, Mansa Musa, Timbuktu becomes center of learning. Songhai, 1450 and 1600, Askia Muhammad, set up strong and fair government and system of fair taxation **IV. 1.** Students should be aware of the landowner's desire to make money. **2.** Students may answer that Montezuma could help the Aztec Empire stay united. **V. 1.** Students should include facts about each African empire. **2.** Students should list five examples.

Chapter 5 **1:1.** silver **2.** *criollo*: a Spaniard born in New Spain, *mestizo:* part Spanish and part Native American **2:1.** tales of the seven cities of gold **2.** Coronado's fierce attacks on the Zuñi **3:1.** to convert Native Americans to Christianity **2.** a Native American leader who led a rebellion which drove the Spanish out of Santa Fe **4:1.** Africans, Native Americans, Latinos **2.** Native Americans: foods such as potatoes, tomatoes, corn and chocolate; medicines, clothing. Africans: foods such as peanuts, yams, black eyed peas and bananas; music, religious practices, language. **Review I. 1.** e **2.** d **3.** a **4.** b **5.** c **II. 1.** *peninsulares* held all top positions in the government and the church and were very wealthy and powerful **2.** went looking for cities of gold but found only Zuñi villages **3.** gave Native Americans a place to live, protected them from colonists, taught new skills to earn money **4.** took away Native American culture **5.** foods, such as peanuts, yams, black-eyed peas, bananas; music, religious practices; language; customs **III. 1.** *peninsulares* held positions of power in government and church; *criollos* owned land; *mestizos* and some mulattos had skilled jobs in trade and business; Native Americans and African slaves did manual labor **2.** traveled and mapped the borderlands, built missions **3.** language, Roman Catholic religion, foods, and animals **IV. 1.** join: to defend land and culture; refuse: the strength of the Spanish army **2.** Students may show the differences in the three classes they choose by their jobs and the color of their skin. **V. 1.** Artwork may show different points of view. **2.** Students may agree that culture is changing because of immigration.

Chapter 6 **1:1.** tobacco **2.** when the supply of indentured servants could no longer keep up with the labor needed to harvest the tobacco **2:1.** taught colonists how to grow crops, hunt for animals and fish, shared food with them **2.** Salem, Massachusetts **3:1.** Roger Williams **2.** British settlers taking Native American land **Review I. 1.** b **2.** e **3.** a **4.** d **5.** c **II. 1.** colonists were more interested in digging for gold than raising crops or building shelters, supplies ran out, many colonists died of starvation and sickness **2.** Members of the general assembly were elected by colonists and represented their interests. **3.** to have religious freedom **4.** to regain lost lands **5.** by holding town meetings, allowing white male landowners to vote **III. 1.** 90 years **2.** about 10 years **3.** the formation of the Virginia House of Burgesses **IV. 1.** no help: colonists are a threat; help: sympathetic to the newcomers **2.** Students should emphasize the importance of religious freedom. **V. 1.** Students may want to refer to the text for facts on their chosen colony. **2.** Students should recognize the similarities in state legislators with processes such as voting.

Chapter 7 **1:1.** the Hudson River Valley **2.** a Quaker who founded Pennsylvania **2:1.** a high demand for labor due to tobacco, cotton and rice plantations **2.** English debtors **3:1.** winters were long, growing season was short, soil was not fertile **2.** New England **Review I. 1.** b **2.** a **3.** e **4.** d **5.** c **II. 1.** New England: Puritans did not allow religious freedoms. Middle Colonies: people with different faiths and beliefs, allowed religious tolerance **2.** to allow religious freedom for all Christians **3.** wanted Georgia to be equal for all by not allowing slavery, but he lost control and it became like other Southern colonies **4.** New England: infertile soil, farmers grew crops only for their family. Other regions: fertile soil, large farms could grow cash crops **5.** the Southern colonies **III.** *New England:* small farms produce for family consumption; first public schools, strict Puritan religion; whale products, fish, manufactured goods; Boston. *Middle:* large farms that sell crops; many religions, most schools private and religious; crops, some manufactured goods; New York, Philadelphia. *Southern:* plantations that sell a cash crop; Church of England, few schools; tobacco, cotton, rice, indigo; Charleston. **IV. 1.** stay: New York has become home; return: English may discriminate against Dutch **2.** Speeches may emphasize Penn's fair treatment of Native Americans. **V. 1.** Mural should show information from the chapter. **2.** same: to flee persecution, political unrest. different: to get an education, to have higher standard of living.

Chapter 8 **1:1.** grew gardens, worked in fields when needed, cared for farm animals, prepared meals, paid bills, bought supplies, made many household items **2.** ran taverns, worked as shopkeepers, blacksmiths, silversmiths, woodworkers, teachers, tailors, printers, publishers **2:1.** the trip enslaved Africans Americans were forced to take across the Atlantic **2.** less profitable for Northern farmers to clothe and feed slaves throughout the year to work on small seasonal farms **3:1.** the trade between Africa, the West Indies, and Europe **2.** widespread education, self government, independent trade **Review I. 1.** e **2.** b **3.** a **4.** c **5.** d **II. 1.** household and farming chores, made household items, some women worked outside the home in trade and business **2.** greater rights in marriage, more control over property, and laws were passed to protect widows **3.** by breaking their owners tools, attacking their owners, rebelling **4.** no plantations, less need for labor **5.** religious diversity, self-government, growing illegal trade, and education made Americans different; colonists felt less in common with British so less loyal and more in common with each other **III. 1.** foods, tobacco, indigo **2.** Gold Coast, Slave Coast, Gabon, Congo, Angola **IV. 1.** Students should discuss whether they would risk being thrown in jail like Zenger. **2.** Stories may make mention trauma of being torn away from their homes in Africa, terrible conditions on the slave ship, and the horrors of slavery. **V. 1.** Skits should be as descriptive as possible. **2.** Groups should list three similarities and three differences.

Chapter 9 **1:1.** to protect French claims in North America from other European nations **2.** the Mississippi **2:1.** The fur trade was the main source of money. **2.** French did not take Native American land for farming, some French lived with the Native Americans, and there was only a small population of French settlers in New France. **3:1.** to maintain control over the Ohio Valley **2.** France gave up most of its territory in North America. Spain got land west of the Mississippi. British got all territory between 13 colonies and the Mississippi, except New Orleans, and took control of Canada. **Review I. 1.** b **2.** c **3.** e **4.** a **5.** d **II. 1.** gold, riches, a short sea route to Asia **2.** the fur trade **3.** sent wives over for male colonists, offered rewards for marriage and big families, fined men who did not marry, made land available to farmers **4.** did take away Native American land; did not threaten their ways of life, lived among them, spoke their language, married some Native American women; New France had a very small French population **5.** all territory between 13 colonies and the Mississippi, except New Orleans, and Canada **III. 1.** the Mississippi **2.** part of Canada, the entire Mississippi River valley from the 13 British colonies to the Rockies **IV. 1.** agree: fur trade is profitable; disagree: an alliance may force the Huron to fight for the French later (as in the French and Indian War) **2.** Skit should explain the difference between European warfare and the techniques the French and Native Americans used. **V.1.** Murals should clearly depict the event chosen. **2.** Possible differences: official language would be French, the revolution may have never occurred, Native Americans may be better off

Chapter 10 **1:1.** an Ottawa chief who led a war against the British settlers **2.** stated that British settlers could not settle on land between the Appalachians and the Mississippi, and that Native Americans owned the land they lived on **2:1.** a direct tax on all colonists on legal and other documents; colonists protested it strongly **2.** a group of colonists formed to protest the Stamp Act **Review I. 1.** d **2.** c **3.** e **4.** a **5.** b **II. 1.** some had claimed land west of the Appalachians and expected to sell it to small farmers; others wanted to move west to settle new land **2.** the huge debt incurred defending the colonies during the French and Indian War **3.** taxed many imported goods, tightened rules for shippers, made smuggling more difficult **4.** the British Parliament was taxing them directly for the first time and they felt their rights were being violated **5.** sent representatives to the Stamp Act Congress which demanded the act be repealed, staged violent protests, defied it by buying and selling items covered by the act without paying for the required stamps **III. 1.** Proclamation of 1763 **2.** after **IV. 1.** Speeches may point out that Native Americans were being cheated and were losing their lands. **2.** join: must stand up of our rights; not join: too risky to defy the British **V.1.** Students should be able to defend their point of view. **2.** Students should be made aware of taxes that exist today before beginning lists.

Chapter 11 **1:1.** taxed many goods imported from Britain to the colonies **2.** a group of colonial women who opposed the Townshend Acts **2:1.** a song sung by British soldiers to offend the colonists **2.** British soldiers fired into a mob, killing five colonists; caused an uproar in the colonies **3:1.** spread news between the colonies; helped unite them against the British **2.** closed the port of Boston, took away self-rule from Massachusetts, made land west of the Appalachians part of Canada **Review I. 1.** d **2.** c **3.** e **4.** b **5.** a **II. 1.** taxed many goods imported from Britain to the colonies **2.** protested in their newspapers, stopped drinking British tea, demonstrated against the acts, boycotted British goods **3.** tension had built up between the colonists and the British troops **4.** to punish the colonies for the Boston Tea Party **5.** a boycott of all British goods; declared that colonists had the right to govern themselves and that many laws passed since 1763 were illegal **III. 1.** the Boston Massacre **2.** before **IV. 1.** join: must stand up to the British; not join: have to make a living **2.** Students should include all of the facts concerning the Boston Massacre. **V. 1.** Students should present their decision and the arguments that support it. **2.** Charts should show colonial ways of protesting still used (boycott), ways no longer used (Continental Congress), and new ways used today (TV advertisement).

Chapter 12 **1:1.** must go to war with Britain **2.** members of the colonies' militia **2:1.** to get arms and ammunition **2.** convinced many colonists to declare independence from Britain **Review I. 1.** d **2.** c **3.** b **4.** e **5.** a **II. 1.** to find and destroy guns and supplies the colonists had hidden there **2.** the first time colonists had fought for their ideas of freedom **3.** colonists tried to keep the British from leaving Boston but could not; the bloodiest battle of the Revolution **4.** sent a message to King George listing the colonists' complaints **5.** make up a plan for a new government, write a declaration of independence **III. 1.** O **2.** F **3.** O **IV. 1.** Entries should describe the battle. **2.** accept: want to participate in the struggle for freedom; refuse: might be tried for treason **V. 1.** Storyboards should clearly show the chosen event. **2.** Have students explain why the two ideas they wrote down are important to them.

Chapter 13 **1:1.** declaring independence would lead to a war with Britain without any help from the European nations; even if the colonies won, they would not remain united **2.** felt their rights would never be safe if they remained colonies of Britain, hoped for support from other European nations in their war for independence **2:1.** states the reasons why the declaration was written **2.** tells how the British took away the colonists rights **3:1.** colonists who supported independence **2.** 5,000 **Review I. 1.** b **2.** d **3.** e **4.** a **5.** c **II. 1.** felt their rights would never be safe if they remained colonies of Britain, hoped for support from other European nations in their war for independence **2.** it would lead to a long and destructive war ; the colonies would not get help from Britain's enemies; if the colonies won their independence, they would not remain united **3.** everyone had the right to "life, liberty, and the pursuit of happiness;" all men are created equal **4.** colonies are independent states and have a right to be free; they are pledged stay united in the struggle ahead **5.** accused of treason, their property was taken away **III. 1.** the reasons why the Declaration as written **2.** the principles upon which the new nation will be based **3.** the reasons for breaking away from Britain **4.** declares the colonies independent of Britain **IV. 1.** Posters should include details about the Declaration. **2.** join: want freedom; not join: may be more skeptical and point out that slavery would still exist if the British remained in control of the colonies **V. 1.** Students may refer to the chapter to find arguments to support their position. **2.** Students may mention the idea that "all men are created equal" and the right of the people to choose who runs their government.

Chapter 14 1:1. the British; they had more soldiers, a strong navy, and Native American support **2.** to cut New England off from the rest of the colonies **2:1.** it blocked Britain's chances of cutting New England off from the other colonies; showed other European nations that the Americans had a chance to win **2.** sent troops, advisors, and arms to aid the Americans **3:1.** Marquis de Lafayette, Baron von Steuben, Bernardo de Gálvez, Thaddeus Kosciusko, Count Casimir Pulaski **2.** led an army against British posts in West Florida; helped Americans sneak weapons past British forts on the Mississippi; took Pensacola from the British **Review I. Vocabulary. 1.** d **2.** a **3.** e **4.** b **5.** c **II. 1.** Britain—advantages: powerful navy and army, Native Americans allies; disadvantages: some British opposition to the war, distance from war. American—advantages: goal of independence, defending their homes, fighting on familiar ground, good leaders; disadvantages: no navy, small, ill-trained, and ill-equipped fighting force. **2.** military and political experience, calm in a crisis **3.** spread himself too thinly by capturing Philadelphia **4.** gave Americans weapons, supplies, more soldiers; divided Britain's attention, since the British had to fight the French too **5.** African Americans, both free and enslaved, served in the Continental Army. Latinos like Bernardo de Gálvez also fought against the British. **III. 1.** F **2.** O **3.** O **IV. 1.** Students may mention feelings of fear and intimidation at the site of a great fleet of British warships. **2.** join: should try to weaken the British military so they would not threaten the Spanish colonies; not join: increases the threat of the Britain military on Spanish Louisiana. **V. 1.** Skits should include how the town supported the side it was defending. **2.** Students should list a number of reasons, such as humanitarian reasons, to influence a countries way of governing, and economic reasons.

Chapter 15 1:1. state governments had more power than federal government, Congress had only a few powers, Congress could not collect taxes **2.** to discuss changes in the Articles of Confederation **2:1.** a federal system **2.** federalism, representation, counting slaves **3:1.** supporters: federalists; opponents: anti-federalists **2.** Federalists wanted stronger government. Anti-federalists were against a strong central government. **4:1.** Bill of Rights, more amendments **2.** powers that do not belong to the federal government belong to the state and the people **Review I. 1.** c **2.** a **3.** b **4.** e **5.** d **II. 1.** national government depended on states to collect taxes, so it had little money to pay for an army or navy **2.** federal system: limited powers of the national government (this would help protect slavery); slaves count as 3/5: helped give the South a strong position in the House of Representatives. **3.** a Congress with two houses; in House of Representatives, big states would have more votes; in Senate, all states would have two representatives **4.** Constitution gave too much power to the national government; people's freedoms might be taken away; a president could easily become a tyrant **5.** In 1787, only one person in ten could vote. The Constitution allowed slavery and ignored the rights of African Americans, women, and others. Twenty-seven amendments have since been added. Today, all Americans have a say in our democracy. **III.** *Federalism:* delegates who wanted a strong national government and those who wanted to protect states' powers; a federal system of government in which the national and state governments shared power. *Representation:* big and small states; a Congress with two houses—in House of Representatives, big states would have more votes and in Senate, all states would have two representatives. *Counting Slaves:* Southern and Northern states; Each slave was counted as 3/5 of a free person. **IV. 1.** Students may question how the delegates reached a compromise, what their original agenda was, how long the whole process took, and how this will effect the people. **2.** Students may point out that the Constitution still did not protect the rights of minorities, therefore questioning why they should support it. **V. 1.** Reasons given should match the person chosen. **2.** Compromises should solve the problems listed.

Chapter 16 1:1. two **2.** President: veto bills; Supreme Court: declare a law unconstitutional **2:1.** to carry out laws, commander in chief of armed forces, direct foreign policy, propose new laws **2.** Congress: can pass laws over the President's veto, controls federal money, Senate must approve President's appointments, can impeach the President; Supreme Court: makes sure President obeys Constitution, makes sure executive branch follows laws passed by Congress **3:1.** nine **2.** President: appoints justices; Congress can remove them if they do not act properly **4:1.** freedom of speech, religion, and press **2.** the government must follow rules that are the same for everyone **Review I. 1.** d **2.** e **3.** a **4.** c **5.** b **II. 1.** Constitution lists specific types of laws that Congress may and may not pass and reserves certain powers to the states or to the people. **2.** President can propose bills, Congress makes the laws, and the Supreme Court makes sure they are constitutional. **3.** district: bottom of judicial pyramid where most cases start and end; appeals: hears cases appealed from a lower court **4.** federal: case involves a federal law or the U.S. Constitution; state: others **5.** Fifth Amendment: suspect cannot be brought to trial on important charges until a grand jury has found there is suitable evidence; suspect does not have to answer questions if answers would make him/her seem guilty; if a jury finds a suspect not guilty, the suspect cannot be tried again on the same charge; requires "due process" **III. 1.** Words should be accurately defined. **2.** right to freedoms of speech, religion, and press **IV. 1.** Students should support decisions with reasons. **2.** Posters should show how the amendment chosen relates to everyday life. **V. 1.** Section 1: legislative branch, powers, and checks. 2: executive branch, powers, and checks. 3: judicial branch, powers, and checks. 4: some significant amendments in the Constitution. **2.** Students should describe how their life would be different without the freedoms of speech, religion, and press.

Chapter 17 1:1. the people were not united, first loyal to their states; U.S. government had to pay debt for borrowing during revolution; unsure whether democracy would work **2.** Hamilton: wealthy and educated people should run the country, a strong national government. Jefferson: believed the country should be run by rich and poor, states should have more power. **2:1.** many farmers west of the Appalachians rebelled when the U.S. government placed a tax on whiskey **2.** the United States should devote its energies to making itself stronger **3:1.** Both Jefferson and Burr ran for President. No one ran for Vice-President. When the election came in a tie, Burr became Vice-President. **2.** electors must vote separately for President and Vice-President **Review I. 1.** c **2.** d **3.** a **4.** e **5.** b **II. 1.** having a cabinet, leaving office after two terms **2.** some members of Congress took Hamilton's side, others supported Jefferson **3.** thought tax on whiskey was unfair **4.** Democratic Republicans supported the spread of democracy. Federalists worried that the violence might spread to the United States. **5.** Some federalists were angry with Adams for refusing to declare war on France so they split from the party. **III. 1.** Both Jefferson and Burr ran for president and received the same number of electoral votes. It took the House of Representatives voting 36 times before the tie was broken. **2.** People had to vote separately for President and Vice-President. **IV. 1.** Students should list at least five characteristics. **2.** Students should explain their choice. **V 1.** Designs should include the structure of each building. **2.** Lists may include the conflicts still occurring between political parties and U.S. involvement in other countries' wars.

Chapter 18 1:1. set up rules for government in the territories, abolished slavery, guaranteed freedom of religion, trial by jury; set up a way in which the territory could be organized into states **2.** to unite Native Americans to push back the settlers **2:1.** It was a key link between settlers in the Mississippi River valley and markets in the east and in Europe. **2.** to gather information about the new territory, to find a route through the Rocky Mountains to the Pacific Ocean **3:1.** feared Britain might try to win back control of the United States, wanted more land **2.** the United States **Review I. 1.** e **2.** d **3.** b **4.** a **5.** c **II. 1.** Northwest Ordinance, Land Ordinance of 1785 **2.** It was a key link between settlers in the Mississippi River valley and markets in the east and in Europe. **3.** to gather information about the new territory, to find a route through the Rocky Mountains to the Pacific Ocean **4.** badly hurt the U.S. economy **5.** The United States proved it could defend itself and thus gained more respect from the European nations. **III. 1.** before; this law had to be passed as a result of so many people moving west **2.** before; Lewis and Clark were exploring the new territory **IV. 1.** join: defending land against the settlers is worth putting differences between the tribes aside; not join: would not trust them because of previous attacks by other Native Americans **2.** Students may include seeing a number of Native American tribes and the enormous landscape. **V 1.** Story boards should include facts concerning the event. **2.** Students should discuss the outcomes of the United States remaining neutral today before drawing a conclusion.

Chapter 19 **1:1.** Samuel Slater memorized each part of the British factories, then built a cotton mill in the United States. **2.** female workers who lived in a boardinghouse and worked in a factory owned by Francis Cabot Lowell **2:1.** Eli Whitney **2.** needed more slaves to grow more cotton **3:1.** developed their own culture, created strong family bonds, turned to activities that reminded them of their homeland, had strong religious beliefs, fought back **2.** a slave who planned a slave uprising and was caught and executed **Review I. 1.** c **2.** e **3.** b **4.** d **5.** a **II. 1.** Samuel Slater memorized each part of the British factories, then built a cotton mill in the United States. **2.** able to pay them less than male workers **3.** Cotton became an important cash crop. **4.** Northern mills used the cotton that was grown on Southern plantations. **5.** developed their own culture, created strong family bonds, turned to activities that reminded them of their homeland, had strong religious beliefs **III. 1.** parts of Virginia, North and South Carolina, Tennessee, Georgia, Alabama, Mississippi, Louisiana, Arkansas, Texas, Florida, Missouri, Unorganized Territories **2.** Virginia, South Carolina, Georgia, Alabama, Mississippi, Louisiana **3.** Slavery was in greater demand in those areas that grew the most cotton. **IV. 1.** yes: factory work paid better; no: factory conditions were bad **2.** Songs should express a longing for freedom **V. 1.** Mural should show specific details about life in the early 1800s. **2.** Students may want to include inventions like the computer, cars, electric appliances, and satellites.

Chapter 20 **1:1.** a waterway people dig to connect two bodies of water **2.** roads, canals, trails **2:1.** simple shelters **2.** different—East: only white male property owners could vote; West: all white men over the age of 21 could vote same—only white men **3:1.** Sequoyah **2.** the forced removal of Native Americans from their homelands to Indian Territory west of the Mississippi **Review I. 1.** c **2.** e **3.** a **4.** b **5.** d **II. 1.** made transporting goods cheaper and quicker **2.** land had to be cleared, family members had to manage farm themselves **3.** Settlers faced the same hardships and fears, causing them to see each other as equal. **4.** created schools; recorded their history, beliefs, and treaties; printed books and published a newspaper; created a written constitution **5.** President Jackson supported the settlers and urged Congress to pass it. **III. 1.** canals, roads, trails **2.** Paragraphs should summarize the section. **IV. 1.** yes: good land available, more equality; no: have to build new homes, fears of Native Americans and Mexicans using the land as well **2.** Speeches may note that Cherokee helped in War of 1812, hoped to live in peace with white settlers, and had a written constitution. **V. 1.** Students should note what type of transportation could be used, where to settle, and what roads and canals to take. **2.** Students should note how democracy has expanded to include women and minorities.

Chapter 21 **1:1.** led hundreds of U.S. families to settle in Texas **2.** Santa Anna was forced to recognize the independence of Texas. **2:1.** Santa Anna **2.** to treat Mexicans who lived in the areas that had been ceded fairly **3:1.** forced all "foreign" miners, including *californios,* to pay 16 dollars a month **2.** had to pay a tax to mine, faced prejudice and violence from eastern U.S. miners **4:1.** land reviews, discriminatory laws, prohibiting Native Americans as witnesses in court, having to change their culture **2.** law giving married women greater rights over property than women had in other parts of the United States, water rights **Review I. 1.** d **2.** c **3.** b **4.** a **5.** e **II. 1.** Mexico feared the United States would try to annex Texas. **2.** the U.S. annexed Texas, Polk sent troops to the Rio Grande **3.** the gold rush **4.** Land Act of 1851 made land owners have to prove they owned their land; many lost their land while their case was in court **5.** ways of farming and irrigation, property and water rights laws, language **III.** Students may want to refer to the timeline in the chapter for assistance. **IV. 1.** join: gaining independence from Mexico is more important; not join: do not trust U.S. settlers **2.** Students may include the unjust treatment by settlers. **V. 1.** Programs should reflect some events that occurred during the mid-1800s. **2.** Some may include language, food, government, and art.

Chapter 22 **1:1.** Irish: the Great Famine; Germans: to escape from Revolution. **2.** new music, Christmas trees, kindergarten, log cabins, leadership positions in politics, the church, and labor unions **2:1.** to participate in the gold rush **2.** merchants, construction workers, miners, farmers, peddlers **3:1.** party formed by people who disliked immigrants **2.** seemed strange or different; people feared losing their jobs; lowered wages; ethnic and religious prejudice **Review I. 1.** b **2.** d **3.** a **4.** e **5.** c **II. 1.** caused more than 750,000 people in Ireland to die from hunger and disease; many Irish emigrated to the United States **2.** that is where their ships landed; most were too poor to buy land to farm **3.** many revolutions broke out; when they failed, thousands had to escape **4.** California; the gold rush **5.** disliked them; wanted to reduce immigration and expand the waiting period for citizenship **III. 1.** unhealthy **2.** Students should include other hardships faced by immigrants. **IV. 1.** Letters may include a new sense of independence and the harsh working conditions in factories. **2.** Students should keep in mind that everyone who came to the country was an immigrant, despite how long ago it may have been. **V. 1.** Students may want to include questions on why they came, what hardships have they encountered, what opportunities have they found. **2.** Answers will vary according to people in their community and their reasons for coming to the United States.

Chapter 23 **1:1.** marked beginning of an organized movement for women's rights **2.** the right to vote and to have equal citizenship **2:1.** In some states, women gained the right to control their own property, married women had right to keep any money they made by working and could sue in court for the right to their money, and equal rights to custody of their children, and voting rights in some states. **2.** Women chose their group's rulers, voting rights, and all decisions had to be approved by three fourths of all voters and three fourths of all mothers. **3:1.** the imprisonment of and cruelty to mentally ill people **2.** the temperance movement, free public education, education for women **Review I. 1.** b **2.** e **3.** a **4.** d **5.** c **II. 1.** strong opposition from males, religious leaders, other women; politicians could ignore them because they had no vote **2.** all men and women were created equal; men were unjust by refusing the rights and privileges which belong to women as citizens **3.** Between 1820 and 1860, women in some states gained new rights as a result of new laws. The rights of married women to own property were extended. Women gained equal rights to custody of their children and the right to sue in their own name. **4.** New schools were started for women—high schools, colleges (Mount Holyoke), teacher's colleges; Oberlin became the first college to admit both men and women. **5.** the first female doctor in the United States; opened a clinic for poor people **III. 1.** a good generalization **2.** Titles should reflect a good generalization about the speech. **IV. 1.**

join: important to fight for rights; not join: other concerns are more important, afraid of other people's reactions **2.** Letters should note the great influence women held in Seneca society. **V. 1.** Students can use a variety of sources; books, encyclopedias, videos if available. **2.** Students should choose one reform and a plan of action.

Chapter 24 1:1. the American Anti-Slavery Society **2.** Angelina Grimke and her sister Sarah spoke publicly and wrote essays against slavery. Lucretia Mott and Elizabeth Cady Stanton attended a world antislavery convention in London. **2:1.** being beaten, hunted with dogs, shot, sometimes crippled **2.** took slaves and brought them North, stopping at houses of people who were sympathetic to the abolitionist movement **3:1.** participated in the Underground Railroad, spoke and wrote against slavery **2.** held abolitionist meetings, acted as stations for the Underground Railroad, gave African Americans faith in a better future **Review I. 1.** b **2.** e **3.** c **4.** a **5.** d **II. 1.** Earlier movements acted more slowly and quietly. The abolition movement insisted on an immediate end to slavery. **2.** Garrison stirred controversy because of his strong opposition to slavery; took positions that angered other abolitionists such as supporting women's rights and refusing to vote in elections. **3.** Southern slave owners: feared a loss of their slave "property;" Northern business people: often did business with Southern slave owners and feared that abolition would hurt their business interests; some Northern workers: feared freeing the slaves would mean more free workers competing for jobs. **4.** runaways: death or a return to slavery with beatings and even mutilation as punishment; helpers: physical harm, prosecution under fugitive slave laws **5.** Canada: had the right to vote and own property and the right of children to get an education; United States: to help family members or friends escape slavery **III. 1.** Texas, Missouri, Arkansas, Louisiana, Kentucky, Tennessee, Mississippi, Alabama, Florida, Georgia, South and North Carolina, Virginia, Delaware, Maryland **2.** four **3.** Charleston, New Bern, Norfolk, Washington, D.C. **4.** Possible answer: through Charleston; it is the closest station **IV. 1.** Students should remember the risks someone took by hiding slaves. **2.** Students should note that it was highly uncommon for a women to speak out to crowd with men present. **3.** Students can refer to the photos and text in the chapter. **V. 1.** Skit should show details about the person chosen. **2.** Students should imagine how successful these methods would be today.

Chapter 25 1:1. It was just right for plantation farming. **2.** a compromise between the North and the South: (1) two new states entered the Union, Missouri as a slave state and Maine as a free state; (2) Congress drew an imaginary line running westward from Missouri's southern border, and north of that line, Congress forbade slavery completely, except in Missouri. **2:1.** made California the 16th free state and ended the slave trade in the capital, which angered the South; the Fugitive Slave Act of 1850 angered the North **2.** created a Kansas Territory and a Nebraska Territory, and let voters in the two territories decide whether to allow slavery **3:1.** outraged because they felt they could not keep slavery from spreading **2.** outraged by the raid and praise for Brown in the North; some thought about leaving the Union **Review I. 1.** d **2.** a **3.** b **4.** e **5.** c **II. 1.** wanted support for Southern goals in Congress and to keep the free states from becoming too powerful by keeping a balance **2.** Free-Soilers did not want to end slavery everywhere like abolitionists, just keep it from spreading. **3.** advantages: democratic, allowed people who lived in these states to decide; disadvantages: risked expanding slavery, led to open warfare as in Kansas **4.** Fugitive Slave Act; set steep penalties for people who helped fugitive slaves and made it easy for slave catchers to enslave free African Americans **5.** outraged by the raid and praise for Brown in the North; some thought about leaving the Union **III. 1.** Disputes breaking out in the new territory between the North and South. **2.** A solution through compromise was unlikely. Civil war would break out. **IV. 1.** Possible answers: join the crowd, choose less violent protest, do nothing **2.** Possible answer: free Scott—pro: Congress had forbidden slavery in Minnesota; con: "property" rights of slave owners may be lessened. **V. 1.** Students may want to refer to the time line in the chapter. **2.** Students should suggest compromises to solve the problems they identified.

Chapter 26 1:1. South Carolina **2.** Fort Sumter in Charleston, South Carolina **2:1.** the North **2.** an African American regiment in the Union army that fought bravely **3:1.** to capture Richmond, Virginia **2.** both passed draft laws **Review I. 1.** c **2.** a **3.** d **4.** e **5.** b **II. 1.** feared he would try to end slavery everywhere **2.** needed the Fort Sumter to defend Charleston **3.** made clothing and supplies, ran farms and businesses, worked in factories and offices **4.** by holding on until the North grew tired of fighting **5.** lacked good leaders for its army in the East **III. 1.** slavery was wrong; did not want to abolish slavery completely, just keep it from spreading **2.** some served as nurses and soldiers, others took jobs normally done by men **3.** much larger population, most of the nation's factories and railroad lines **IV. 1.** nurses, soldiers, spies, make clothing and supplies, run farms and businesses, work in factories and offices **2.** join: could end slavery completely; not join: the North also had discrimination **V. 1.** Check to ensure entries on timelines are in chronological order. **2.** Answers may include women still not being permitted to fight in wars.

Chapter 27 1:1. Missouri, Kentucky, Maryland, Delaware **2.** weaken the South through loss of slave labor, keep Great Britain and France from coming to the aid of the South **2:1.** halted Lee's invasion of the North, ended the South's best chance to win the war **2.** Grant forced Lee out of Richmond, took the Confederate capital, then caught Lee's army near Appomattox **3:1.** the North **2.** major cities ruined, farms and plantations burned, railroads and factories destroyed. **Review I. 1.** c **2.** e **3.** a **4.** b **5.** d **II. 1.** feared border states might secede **2.** did not free slaves in border states or Union-controlled areas, only areas in rebellion **3.** Union navy took New Orleans, then sailed up Mississippi. Union army under Grant moved south along river, splitting Confederacy by taking Vicksburg. **4.** Confederate capital had fallen, his army was shrinking, to carry on would just mean more deaths **5.** federal government: (1) now clearly supreme over the states; (2) played a larger role in U.S. economy **III. 1.** brought freedom to enslaved African Americans, but it left them without homes or jobs **2.** Congress passed a bill to give free land to farmers and to build railroads. **3.** The North lost the most soldiers, while the South lay in economic ruin. **IV. 1.** support: intended to hurt Confederacy, does not apply to border states; oppose: a step toward ending slavery completely **2.** Students should note Lincoln is confident of the Union's victory and says the war is not in vain, justice will prevail. **3.** Northern: sorrow for a great leader who saved the Union. Southern: less upset because of resentment for the war. **V. 1.** Students should say why they chose that person(s) and why they are being honored. **2.** Possible answers: similar: destruction, loss of life; different: greater loss of life, total global destruction

Chapter 28 1:1. the Freedmen's Bureau **2.** Black Codes, laws that took away their rights **2:1.** 14th and 15th Amendments **2.** vetoed many acts of Congress and interfered with plans for Reconstruction **3:1.** gave a share of crops harvested to land owners as rent **2.** to keep African Americans from voting and otherwise exercising their rights **Review I. 1.** c **2.** e **3.** d **4.** a **5.** b **II. 1.** helped find homes and jobs, reunite separated families, build schools. **2.** The South was divided into five districts ruled by U.S. troops. Before readmittance, Southern states had to ensure that African American males could vote, bar former high Confederate officials from holding office, and approve the 14th Amendment. **3.** new programs brought services to freedmen; overturned Black Codes; approved 14th and 15th Amendments **4.** so that white male Democrats would once more control the South **5.** the North lost interest in the South's problems; Democrats took control of all Southern state governments; U.S. troops pulled out in 1877 **III. 1.** before; Grant became the next President **2.** after; Black Codes keep African Americans from voting in 1866 elections; Congress's new Reconstruction plan was drawn up in 1867 **3.** creation of the Freedmen's Bureau, passage of the 14th Amendment, pullout of U.S. troops **IV. 1.** vote: must exercise new freedom; not vote: frightened for their lives and their families **2.** Editorials may discuss the obstruction of federal law and the injustice to African Americans. **V. 1.** Plans should include who can attend, subjects taught, and school design. **2.** Paragraph should state which government services are necessary even at high cost.

Chapter 29 1:1. passed laws to limit African American voting **2.** to segregate whites and African Americans **2:1.** by publicizing its evils in newspaper articles and in books **2.** education for jobs in industry and farming **3:1.** little money and poor locations **2.** More African American businesses would make things better for all African Americans. **Review I. 1.** c **2.** d **3.** a **4.** e **5.** b **II. 1.** poll taxes, property tests, literacy tests, grandfather clauses, white primary elections **2.** to segregate whites and African Americans **3.** boycotted companies that segregated streetcars; started their own companies **4.** Washington: focus on jobs in industry and farming; DuBois: press for full rights immediately **5.** formed an African American middle class; pushed for civil rights **III. 1.** new restrictive voting laws **2.** segregation in the South lasts 50 years **3.** number of lynchings drop sharply **IV. 1.** Letters may express outrage over the decision to keep segregation. **2.** Washington: supporting a family comes before other issues. DuBois: without rights the ability of African Americans to earn a living is at the mercy of whites. **V. 1.** Possible answers: posters, leaflets, speakers, going door-to-door **2.** Groups should discuss why some people do not vote today.

Chapter 30 1:1. transcontinental railroad; 160 acres of land free to anyone who farmed them for five years **2.** to escape Jim Crow laws; for a better life **2:1.** latinos called *vaqueros* **2.** to take cattle to railroads and then to markets **3:1.** food, way of life **2.** broke up reservations; each family got 160 acres of land, the rest could be sold off; Native Americans lost some 83 million acres. **Review I. 1.** c **2.** e **3.** d **4.** b **5.** a **II. 1.** gave 160 acres to anyone who farmed them for five years **2.** used steel plows to cut the tough sod; used the sod to build houses; farm with less water, drill wells and use windmills to get more water; build fences made out of barbed wire to protect their crops **3.** ranches built near railroads; farmers fenced in land, ending open ranges; more cattle were raised, driving down prices **4.** to protect their lands from U.S. settlers **5.** U.S. government had more soldiers and better weapons; destruction of buffalo herds by white hunters eliminated the Native Americans' chief food supply **III. 1.** F **2.** O **3.** O **4.** F **IV. 1.** rancher: cattle should roam freely over the plains, barbed wire might hurt the cattle. farmer: fences needed to protect crops from being eaten or trampled by free-roaming cattle. **2.** Students may say that too much land has already been lost. **V. 1.** Arguments should weigh the difficulties of life under Jim Crow laws with the hardships of life on the plains. **2.** Students should think of reasons why people move today.

Chapter 31 1:1. Passengers and freight had to change from one line to another less often. **2.** electricity, oil, gasoline **2:1.** became corporations, selling shares in the business to raise money **2.** bought and controlled all parts of the steel production process **3:1.** strong competition for jobs **2.** Haymarket Riot in Chicago **Review I. 1.** e **2.** c **3.** b **4.** a **5.** d **II. 1.** carried goods more quickly and cheaply to wider markets; building of the railroads spurred production **2.** agree: many U.S. inventions **3.** raised money to start mass production by becoming a corporation and selling shares to the public **4.** If a company had no competition, it could drive up prices for its good or service. **5.** low wages, long hours, few job benefits, little job security, dangerous working conditions **III. 1.** factory owner **2.** factory worker **3.** factory owner **4.** factory worker **IV. 1.** no: fear of losing job; yes: more protection in the long run, worth the risk **2.** Choices should be supported logically. **V. 1.** Groups should come up with product, description, and advertisement. **2.** Groups must list five modern inventions and changes made in people's lives.

Chapter 32 1:1. old: from Northern and Western Europe, Protestants; new: from Southern and Eastern Europe, Roman Catholics, Jews or Eastern Orthodox Christians **2.** to fit in, become more Americanized **2:1.** a law that said no Chinese worker could come to the United States for the next ten years **2.** first Hawaii, then the mainland **3:1.** a new law allowing rich people in Mexico to gain large amounts of land **2.** in cities like New York, Philadelphia, and Boston **Review I. 1.** b **2.** e **3.** c **4.** a **5.** d **II. 1.** better conditions in northern and western Europe; in southern and eastern Europe, machines took over farming, peasants were forced off land; pogroms against Jews **2.** felt sense of belonging; felt unwelcome outside their own neighborhoods **3.** unions would not accept most immigrants as members **5.** Mexicans were being squeezed off the land; Puerto Ricans and Cubans were fleeing war and injustice. **III. 1.** Europe: greater poverty, fear of pogroms; United States: poverty, difficult working conditions, prejudice, but also a chance to get ahead **2.** similarities: excitement of arriving in a new land, hard work, difficult living conditions, hostility from native-born Americans; differences: location (East Coast, Midwest cities, West Coast), racial differences made it harder for Asians to assimilate **IV. 1.** Entries may include the difficulties of learning a new language and new customs, and prejudice from other native-born school children. **2.** yes: desire to get re-elected; no: belief that restricting immigration is wrong **V. 1.** Displays should show early and recent immigrants and their contributions. **2.** Discussions on current immigrant situations may mention Haiti.

Chapter 33 1:1. growth of industry; improved transportation and city services **2.** modern transportation, city services, a variety of culture and entertainment **2:1.** unpaved streets, poor sewers, piles of garbage, impure drinking water, epidemics **2.** using a government position for personal profit **3:1.** offered day care and kindergartens, social evenings, classes, meeting rooms, a community theater **2.** Irish and Italian Catholics social groups, church-supported schools, Hebrew Immigrant Aid Society, special newspapers **Review I. 1.** e **2.** d **3.** a **4.** c **5.** b **II. 1.** created a demand for more jobs, attracting more people to cities **2.** creation of subways, cable cars, trolley cars, elevateds **3.** department stores, theaters, restaurants, concert halls, museums, libraries **4.** lived in tenement apartments under very bad conditions with little to eat **5.** reformers who tried to improve city life; Riis: journalist who exposed tenement living conditions; Addams: created Hull House **III. 1.** (a) by 17,883,393 (b) by 52,802,699 **2.** 1890-1900 **IV. 1.** Letters may reflect the struggle of learning another culture. **2.** Students should support their decision. **V. 1.** Ads should attract new residents, businesses, and tourists to the city. **2.** Sentences should clearly explain goals of reform group.

Chapter 34 1:1. Wyoming **2.** to improve working conditions for women by bringing them into labor unions **2:1.** jobs in which workers served or helped others **2.** Candace Thurber Wheeler, Mary Seymour, Henrietta King, Maggie L. Walker, Madame C.J. Walker **3:1.** as domestics or farm laborers **2.** to educate African American women for better jobs **Review I. 1.** b **2.** e **3.** d **4.** a **5.** c **II. 1.** office workers, sales clerks, nurses **2.** clean work, did not require great physical strength **3.** typewriter, telephone **4.** nurses, teaching, business **5.** educated African American women for better jobs **III. 1.** 1881 **2.** before **3.** 24 years **IV. 1.** no: women's suffrage was an extremely radical and new idea; yes: improve the inequalities women had to face **2.** Interviews may cover issues such as full suffrage to many occupations open to women today. **V. 1.** Scenes may show that office jobs were limited for women. **2.** Sentences should note there are greater job opportunities today for women than in the late 1800s.

Chapter 35 1:1. Alaska **2.** The new Hawaiian government did not represent Hawaiians, only Americans. **2:1.** recognized spheres of influence to guarantee equal trading rights in China **2.** The U.S. contributed 5,000 troops to the international force to put down the Boxer Rebellion. **3:1.** reported detailed accounts, sometimes made up, of cruel treatment of the Cubans by the Spanish; when U.S.S. *Maine* exploded, demanded the U.S. government declare war **2.** to protect it from being taken over by another country **Review I. 1.** b **2.** e **3.** a **4.** c **5.** d **II. 1.** to get colonies to serve as army bases; to provide raw materials **2.** to free Cuba from Spain's rule; to protect U.S. businesses in Cuba **3.** wanted a strong Pacific outpost due to concern about Japan's navy **4.** stopped European nations from taking over

China **5.** against: it went against everything the United States advocated; for: a weak Philippino government would be taken over **III. 1.** the Hawaiian Islands; Guam **2.** The Aleutian Islands **3.** Florida **4.** to protect the canal **IV. 1.** with her: it is important to preserve customs and traditions; against her: possibility of greater economic gains **2.** Letters may argue for or against war with Spain. **V. 1.** Students should refer to the chapter to support their countries' discussion. **2.** Students may discuss current situations in which international armies have been involved in other countries.

Chapter 36 1:1. zippers, fiberglass, electric kitchens, calculators, long-distance telephone lines **2.** skyscrapers, reversing the flow of a river in the city **2:1.** not allowed jobs either in building or running the fair; not allowed to use most public restaurants and restrooms **2.** from southern and eastern Europe **3:1.** the right to vote **2.** foreign-language newspapers and clubs **Review I. 1.** c **2.** a **3.** d **4.** e **5.** b **II. 1.** The White City stressed the progress of the future and ignored the problems which were evident in everyday Chicago. **2.** pollution, poor housing, an underpaid working class **3.** to make clear to visitors that African Americans were being ignored or mistreated at the fair, just as in the United States as a whole **4.** At the time of the fair, 40 percent of its citizens were foreign-born. **5.** a belief in ideals expressed in the Declaration of Independence and the Constitution **II.** Possible answers: **1.** fear and resentment of newcomers **2.** make cities more densely populated **IV. 1.** Students might suggest staying away since African Americans are not treated equally with other visitors. **2.** Speeches should include women's contributions to the growth of the nation. **V. 1.** Students should represent as many groups as possible. **2.** Students should discuss current problems and promises facing Americans today.

VOLUME 2

Chapter 1

1:1. making large quantities of goods quickly **2.** Owners did not care about consumers. **2:1.** she demanded laws protecting children who worked **2.** laundries **3:1.** streetlights, improved public transportation **2.** crowded, built close together, cut off light and fresh air **Review I. 1.** e **2.** c **3.** a **4.** b **5.** d **II. 1.** electric light, automatic lubricator, mass production, assembly lines **2.** lowered price of his oil so much that other companies were forced to go out of business **3.** long hours, low wages, poor treatment **4.** Immigrants were hired for "dirty" jobs and African Americans were only hired in laundries. **5.** paved streets, had running water, streetlights, public transportation, reservoirs, sanitation, fire, and police departments **III. 1.** 1880 **2.** Mother Jones **3.** assembly lines **IV. 1.** Have the students refer to the chapter, using some of Carnegie's strategies. **2.** Entries should reflect miserable working conditions that people endured. **V. 1.** Have students refer to chapter for benefits and problems surrounding growth of U.S. industries. **2.** Lists should include five ways cities are better today.

Chapter 2 1:1. people from Southern and Eastern Europe **2.** Jews were forced to live in ghettoes, were not allowed to own land, and they were being massacred in Europe. **2:1.** in cities **2.** let immigrants discuss issues, study English, play sports, and learn about their adopted country **3:1.** jobs that no one else wanted **2.** around 1900 **4:1.** feared immigrants would take jobs away because immigrants worked for lower wages **2.** Their language, physical appearance, clothing, and customs set them apart. **Review I. 1.** b **2.** e **3.** c **4.** a **5.** d **II. 1.** both fled persecution **2.** They had very little skills and did not speak English well. **3.** formed self-help groups **4.** feared immigrants would take jobs away, prejudice **5.** They helped make the United States an urban nation and helped build the economy, especially in the West. **III. 1.** Southern and Eastern Europeans **2.** Northern and Western Europeans **3.** Laws barring Asian immigration, like the Chinese Exclusion Act, caused Asian immigration to be low. **IV. 1.** Student may say they would settle in a neighborhood with people from their own background. **2.** Students should give reasons why immigration should not be limited. **V. 1.** Interviews should include reasons for coming, first impressions of the United States, and special experiences. **2.** Charts should reflect more immigration from Latin America and Asia.

Chapter 3 1:1. laws passed in the South to segregate African Americans in housing, transportation, and other aspects of daily life **2.** discrimination, run-down housing, no coverage by city services **2:1.** head of the Tuskegee Institute; advised African Americans to learn skills so that they could earn a better living **2.** a committee formed to secure equal rights and opportunities for all people **3:1.** over 70 percent of African Americans could read; more students were graduating from schools and moving into professional positions **2.** Carver changed agriculture in the South by telling people to grow crops like peanuts, which made the soil rich. **Review I. 1.** b **2.** d **3.** e **4.** c **5.** a **II. 1.** needed to borrow plows, seeds and homes; had to go into debt to landlord; stuck in a cycle of poverty and debt **2.** segregated in practice but not by law; lived in poor neighborhoods and in run-down housing; often received the lowest paying jobs **3.** took out ads, published studies on African American living conditions, attacked discriminatory laws in the courts **4.** Carver's change in agriculture, Williams's achievements in the medical field, many inventions made by African Americans **5.** ragtime, blues **III.** Washington: believed African Americans should be trained to get better jobs in industry, thought earning a living and buying property were more important than voting. DuBois: believed African Americans should organize to push for civil rights, wanted African Americans to explore their African roots and to develop their own art and literature. **IV. 1.** leave: sharecropping does not pay well enough, Jim Crow laws, civil rights are denied. stay: conditions are not much better in the North, there is still prejudice, rest of the family lives in the South, setting is familiar. **2.** Editorials should stress the strong belief in the vote as a step up in the civil rights movement. **V. 1.** Students should refer to the text and other sources for information. **2.** Students can refer to the text for contributions by African Americans.

Chapter 4 1:1. gave citizenship to all Puerto Ricans who wanted it **2.** in search of a better life **2:1.** a cigar manufacturer who built low-cost housing for his employees **2.** an amendment to Cuba's constitution that allowed the U.S. army to return to Cuba if U.S. interests there were threatened; also gave the United States the right to build and rent a naval base at Guantánamo Bay **3:1.** a group of *nuevomexicanos* that fought to protect their way of life **2.** New Mexico's constitution protected the right to vote, the right of children of Spanish descent to be treated equally in public schools, and it made Spanish as well as English an official language. **Review I. 1.** b **2.** d **3.** a **4.** e **5.** c **II. 1.** Spain lost the Spanish-American war to the United States and was forced to surrender its two colonies, Cuba and Puerto Rico, to the United States. **2.** in search of job opportunities and a better life **3.** the cigar making industry **4.** The United States pressed Cuba to make the Platt Amendment part of their constitution, then granted them independence. **5.** guaranteed all rights of U.S. citizens **III. 1.** F **2.** O **3.** O **4.** F **5.** F **IV. 1.** Students may note both the benefits of Ybor City and the low wages and violence during strikes. **2.** Students should give reasons for their decision. **V. 1.** Answers will vary according to availability of a *bodega* to students or research in the library. **2.** Lists should include information on who the Latino politicians are, what job they fill, and what state they are from.

Chapter 5 1:1. The Haymarket Riot resulted in a number of deaths and injuries, causing people to turn against the Knights. **2.** Wages of skilled workers increased 25 percent and the work day was shortened to 9 hours per day. **2:1.** formed the Japanese-Mexican Labor Association **2.** National Women's Trade Union League **3:1.** young children handling sharp tools, dangerous machinery, ice-covered fire escapes ending 12 feet above ground **2.** limiting women's workday to ten hours **Review I. 1.** c **2.** d **3.** a **4.** e **5.** b **II. 1.** losing their jobs **2.** Skilled workers were harder to replace than unskilled workers, therefore their strike would be more effective. **3.** Illinois government passed laws improving sweatshop conditions. **4.** a raise; also proved that women would join unions **5.** Unions helped to organize workers, strikes helped win their demands, commissions helped to reveal horrible working conditions, and courts helped in the passage of laws protecting workers. **III. 1-3.** Students should provide reasons for their opinions. **IV. 1.** join: must demand better treatment; not join: risking their job is not worth it **2.** Some may include better safety exits, healthier atmosphere, shorter hours. **V. 1.** Students should give reasons for change. **2.** Reports should summarize article about union.

Chapter 6 1:1. exposed corruption in government and business **2.** poverty and misery **2:1.** passed the Sherman Anti-Trust Act, protected workers **2.** child care, English classes, tried to improve poor neighborhoods **3:1.** switchboard operators, office secretaries, maids, cooks, factory workers, a few were professionals **2.** Catt fought to amend states constitutions for women's suffrage. Paul staged parades, protests, and hunger strikes. **Review I. 1.** d **2.** a **3.** b **4.** c **5.** e **II. 1.** exposed corruption in government and big business **2.** initiative, referendum, recall, primary election, changed the way U.S. senators gain office **3.** "bad" trusts that forced competitors out of business **4.** The NAACP was formed to use the law to help African Americans who were treated unfairly. **5.** Women organized, protested, and won public attention in their successful attempt to get the 19th Amendment passed. **III. 1.** 1911 **2.** Southeast **3.** West **IV. 1.** Articles should describe community problems and suggest solutions. **2.** Answers should show understanding of the suffrage issue. **V. 1.** Students should refer to chapter to find information about the person. **2.** Posters should show state reforms and when they were first used.

Chapter 7 1:1. The United States said that Filipinos were not ready to govern themselves. **2.** Filipino civilians **2:1.** kept China from being completely divided by European powers and Japan **2.** because Japan was building up its military and economic power **3:1.** attend segregated schools **2.** Japanese Americans did not have to attend segregated schools but Japan agreed to limit immigration to the United States. **Review I. 1.** d **2.** a **3.** e **4.** b **5.** c **II. 1.** independence for the Phillipines from Spain and the United States **2.** to have influence in East Asia **3.** Japanese and European powers were trying to carve "spheres of influence" in China. **4.** U.S. army rescued foreigners in China. **5.** Californians were prejudiced toward Japanese immigrants. **III. 1.** cause, effect **2.** effect, cause **3.** effect, cause **IV. 1.** Possible answer: to send troops to arrest Aguinaldo, but not to kill or injure any Filipinos **2.** Letters will express Japanese parents' outrage because their children were forced to attend segregated schools. **V. 1.** Try using different colors to show which countries are independent and which ones are colonies. **2.** Answers will vary according to which country and event students choose.

Chapter 8 1:1. Mosquitoes carry yellow fever. **2.** The United States could send its army into Cuba to keep order, and the U.S. had the right to establish a navy base in Cuba. **2:1.** became a one-crop economy **2.** Their culture would vanish and be replaced by that of the mainland United States. **Review I. 1.** b **2.** d **3.** e **4.** a **5.** c **II. 1.** Finley had the idea that yellow fever is transmitted by mosquitoes, and Reed proved that it. **2.** U.S. troops set up temporary government in 1906, put down a sugar revolt in Cuba in 1912 **3.** Cuba's economy boomed; however there became too much sugar on the world market, causing prices to drop and hurting the economy. **4.** Puerto Ricans were able to elect both houses of their legislature. **5.** They were afraid their culture would vanish and be replaced with U.S. culture. **III. 1.** 1898 **2.** Dominican Republic **3.** Haiti **IV. 1.** Answers should reflect an understanding that the Platt Amendment limited Cuba's sovereignty to the benefit of the United States. **2.** Answers should reflect the importance of Rivera to the cause of Puerto Rican independence. **V. 1.** Posters will vary according to students' opinions on the issue. **2.** Arguments should be presented either in favor of or opposed to U.S. control in the Caribbean.

Chapter 9 1:1. to make traveling from coast to coast quicker, safer, and cheaper **2.** disease, bugs, snakes, mud, and miles of swamps, rivers, and mountains **2:1.** the Dominican Republic **2.** substituted "dollars for bullets" by encouraging U.S. businesses to invest in Latin America **3:1.** Veracruz **2.** failed; Villa was not captured **4:1.** to find food, jobs, and safety from the Mexican Revolution **2.** workers that travel from state to state harvesting crops **Review I. 1.** e **2.** a **3.** c **4.** b **5.** d **II. 1.** supported Panamanian rebels' independence from Columbia and then made a deal with the government of Panama to build the canal **2.** "big stick" policy, policed Latin America **3.** to protect U.S. business interests **4.** to protect U.S. property and business, and to capture Villa **5.** migrant farm workers, miners, factory and steel-mill workers **III. 1.** Columbus, New Mexico **2.** San Francisco, Los Angeles, El Centro, Calipatria, Browley, Columbus, Denver, El Paso **IV. 1.** Students should include such difficulties as diseases, animals, and the miles of swamps, rivers, and mountains. **2.** Students should keep in mind the violence and poverty during the Mexican Revolution. **V. 1.** Timelines should have at least three illustrated events. **2.** Presentations should give reasons for the importance of the Panama Canal today.

Chapter 10 1:1. Allies: France, Great Britain, Russia, Belgium, Serbia, Italy, Japan, United States. Central Powers: Germany, Austria-Hungary, Turkey, Bulgaria. **2.** submarine attacks; asked Mexico to join Germany and declare war on the United States. **2:1.** mostly in army kitchens and labor units, but a few fought and became officers **2.** U.S. citizens doubted the loyalty of Mexican Americans; and because of their lack of English skills, many remained at the training centers. **3:1.** African Americans and Mexicans migrated because of the necessity of more labor for the war effort. **2.** the U.S. Senate **Review I. 1.** d **2.** c **3.** a **4.** e **5.** b **II. 1.** The murder of Archduke Francis Ferdinand by a Serb led Austria-Hungary to declare war on Serbia, and then European alliances brought other nations into the war. **2.** Germany tried to get Mexico to declare war on the United States. **3.** African Americans and Latinos often worked as laborers, but some fought in combat positions. **4.** The government took over entire industries, supplies of food and other goods, and controlled prices. **5.** U.S. army helped push the Germans out of France and Belgium. **III. 1.** Allies were closer to the coast, while the Central Powers were mainly inland. **2.** German submarine warfare could have cut off all supplies to the Allies that came from the United States. **IV. 1.** Most students will probably decide against allying with Germany, since the United States is so close to Mexico. **2.** Students should provide reasons for their decision. **V. 1.** Each group should suggest what their country could have done to prevent the war. **2.** Students may want to refer to the text for further assistance.

Chapter 11 1:1. Attorney General Palmer arrested immigrants as communists and deported them. **2.** Italian immigrants that were arrested with little evidence against them and executed in 1927 **2:1.** businesses were booming, suburbs sprung up, auto industry became very important **2.** Native Americans, African Americans, Latinos **3:1.** jazz entertainment, sports, movies **2.** Women were granted more individual freedoms in dress, working conditions, and political rights. **Review I. 1.** d **2.** e **3.** a **4.** b **5.** c **II. 1.** formed unions and went on strike **2.** quotas were imposed and no Asians were allowed in the country; laws were passed like the Emergency Quota Act of 1921 and 1924 **3.** cut taxes for wealthy people in the hope that they would invest in business and create more jobs **4.** cars and electronic appliances such as radios, refrigerators, washing machines, and vacuum cleaners **5.** jazz, sports, movies **III. 1.** Prohibition was not working. **2.** Factories produced more products so they required more electricity. **IV. 1.** Students may want to look for alternative ways for an immigrant to get a job such as, learning English, getting an education, and becoming more Americanized. **2.** Articles should answer *who, what, when, where, why,* and *how.* **V. 1.** Students might need to look at a magazine from the 1920s to help them get ideas. **2.** Groups should list at least four reasons airplanes are important today.

Chapter 12 1:1. the belief that people of African descent should rely on themselves and be proud of their blackness and roots **2.** opened a branch in Harlem, published stories about African American leaders, started the Black Star Line in the hope of developing business ties with African people all over the world **2:1.** James Weldon Johnson, Jean Toomer, Jessie R. Fauset, Claude McKay, Langston Hughes, Zora Neale Hurston **2.** an actor and singer who campaigned for equal rights and was accused of being a communist and forced to live abroad **Review I. 1.** d **2.** e **3.** b **4.** c **5.** a **II. 1.** Whites resented their African

American neighbors and were worried that African Americans would take their jobs. **2.** economic, political, and cultural independence for people of African descent **3.** began a movement to make people of African descent a united people **4.** Harlem was the nation's largest African American community; also New York City was the center of publishing, theater, and music businesses. **5.** racism and prejudice and visions of African American pride **III. 1.** the establishment of the first powerful black nationalist movement **2.** Harlem was the cultural center for all people of African descent in the United States. **IV. 1.** Obituaries should include Garvey's accomplishments. **2.** yes—it is important to speak out for civil rights; no—Robeson had to pay for his bravery by being branded a communist and exiled **V. 1.** Students can refer to the chapter for information on the Harlem Renaissance. **2.** Student may need to refer to outside sources.

Chapter 13 1:1. the stock market crash of October 1929 **2.** settlements of shacks made by the homeless **2:1.** churches: soup kitchens, clothing; National Urban Leagues: food and shelter **2.** farming families from Oklahoma, Arkansas, Kansas, Texas, and Missouri who traveled west to look for work **3:1.** 1929 **2.** cheerleading, started projects to give people jobs such as the Hoover Dam, set up an agency that gave loans to banks, railroads, and insurance companies. **Review I. 1.** e **2.** c **3.** b **4.** a **5.** d **II. 1.** American economy was already weak, farming was depressed due to low prices for crops, millions of workers were paid low wages and could not afford American products **2.** destroyed many families; some husbands who could no longer earn a living left their families; some children left home so their parents would not have to feed them; however, most American families survived the Depression **3.** jobs disappeared, cities did not want to support them with their relief programs **4.** turned large parts of the Plains states into the Dust Bowl, driving many farmers off the land and adding to the unemployment that already existed **5.** He feared government aid to the needy would undermine their independence. Neither Hoover or some of the American people realized how bad the Depression really was. **III. 1.** stock market crash **2.** build the Hoover Dam **IV. 1.** Students should keep in mind that it cost money to travel and that economic conditions in the North were bad. **2.** Some may include questions about jobs, food, homelessness, banks, and solutions. **V. 1.** Skits should show struggles families endured during the Depression. **2.** Some may include aid to the homeless, shelters, and soup kitchens.

Chapter 14 1:1. to provide immediate help to suffering Americans, to improve the economy, and to pass new laws so there were not so many poor people **2.** job program for young men, agency that gave money to states for the needy, National Recovery Administration, building projects program, helped farmers by reducing crops, Tennessee Valley Authority **2:1.** law put millions of people to work building roads, hospitals, schools, airports **2.** felt it made people depend on the government or made the federal government too powerful **3:1.** Frances Perkins, Secretary of Labor **2.** by paying them less and forcing them to live in segregated housing and work in segregated units in the CCC **Review I. 1.** b **2.** e **3.** d **4.** c **5.** a **II. 1.** closed banks for several days to allow for time for Congress to pass a bill to help banks **2.** to provide immediate help to suffering Americans, to improve the economy, and to pass new laws so there were not so many poor people **3.** by paying farmers not to plant as many crops so prices would rise **4.** provided pensions to retired workers, unemployment insurance, and welfare payments to needy or handicapped Americans; improved millions of Americans' lives **5.** early on it allowed discrimination; later it helped young African Americans get an education **III. 1.** Tennessee, Kentucky, Alabama **2.** Alabama, Tennessee **3.** 13 **IV. 1.** Possible answers: It was vital to get the New Deal programs enacted into law, even if discrimination continued; Roosevelt should have fought harder to end discrimination, especially since these were often the poorest groups. **2.** Poster should show how program will help people and contain an explanation. **V. 1.** Students should support their positions. **2.** Students should think of modern communication, such as TV.

Chapter 15 1:1. supplied Allies with war material **2.** the bombing of Pearl Harbor **2:1.** fast and powerful planes and jets, rockets, bombs, atomic bomb **2.** the murder of six million Jews and millions of other civilians in Nazi concentration camps **3:1.** one of the first African American heroes in World War II **2.** developed secret codes to send information to U.S. soldiers on the battlefields **Review I. 1.** e **2.** c **3.** d **4.** b **5.** a **II. 1.** believed Germans were superior and hated Jews, issued laws that discriminated against Jews, arrested many Jews, put Jews in concentration camps and murdered 6 million Jews in the Holocaust **2.** did nothing to stop either Germany or Japan until 1939 in the hope of avoiding war **3.** the bombing of Pearl Harbor by Japan **4.** June 6, 1944, began the largest naval invasion in history **5.** the military remained segregated and African Americans usually were given only low-level, noncombat jobs; but some fought and became officers **III. 1.** Britain and France declared war on Germany. **2.** Germany defeated France. **3.** The United States entered the war. **IV. 1.** Students should take into consideration the defeat of U.S. allies, the threat to the United States, and the millions of people being persecuted. **2.** Entries may include information about the segregation of African Americans or perhaps being promoted to an officer. **V. 1.** Posters should point out why the war is important. **2.** Studies should note boundary differences in Europe and Asia today.

Chapter 16 1:1. Factories had to build equipment for the war, providing jobs and money. **2.** gasoline, meat, butter, shoes, sugar, canned goods **2:1.** There was a labor shortage due to men being drafted or joining the war. **2.** child care and housework **3:1.** victory over enemies abroad and racism at home **2.** sailors attacked Mexican Americans in zoot suits **4:1.** prison camps for Japanese Americans on the west coast **2.** 1988 **Review I. 1.** e **2.** c **3.** d **4.** a **5.** b **II. 1.** Price controls kept prices from rising further. Rationing helped to ensure that all people got a fair share of the available goods. **2.** Families often had to move to new cities and towns to get factory jobs; schools were overcrowded; there were rations, blackouts, and civil-defense drills. **3.** women's pay helped families live better **4.** victory over enemies abroad and over racism at home **5.** surrounded by barbed wire and soldiers, crowded, limited medical care **III. 1.** Women took jobs in factories where only men had been employed. Women worked for the government and were able to support their families. **2.** Discrimination was banned in war industries, and the FEPC was set up. **3.** More women and minorities entered the workforce. **IV. 1.** benefit: earnings helped her family; hardship: still had childcare and housework while holding a job **2.** Students may point out that over 30,000 Japanese American young men entered the military, suffered casualties, and won many medals. Other might say that people need not fight for a country that imprisons them without just cause. **V. 1.** Students should refer to the chapter for items being rationed. **2.** Students might cite problems like day care and having two jobs, outside and inside the home.

Chapter 17 1:1. to establish Communist governments throughout the world **2.** the boundary between independent Western Europe and Soviet-controlled Eastern Europe **2:1.** to prevent the spread of communism **2.** when the Soviet army stopped all land traffic to the western parts of Berlin **3:1.** Communist North Korea invaded South Korea **2.** ended as a draw **4 1.** an invasion of Cuba by Cuban exiles supported by the United States that resulted in failure **2.** so that the Soviet Union could not send more missiles or supplies there **Review I. 1.** c **2.** a **3.** b **4.** e **5.** d **II. 1.** the Soviet Union would spread communism throughout Western Europe **2.** to help Western Europe rebuild so that it would not turn to communism **3.** The Soviet Union occupied part of these countries and set up communist governments while the United States occupied the other parts and set up noncommunist governments. **4.** ended as a draw, costing the United States thousands of dead and wounded soldiers **5.** Cuba was right in the backyard of the United States. **III. 1.** Norway, Great Britain, Denmark, the Netherlands, Belgium, France, Luxembourg, West Germany, Italy, Greece, Turkey **2.** East Germany, Poland, Czechoslovakia, Hungary, Romania, Bulgaria, the Soviet Union **3.**

Estonia Latvia, Lithuania **IV. 1.** Interview might mention how powerful the Soviet Union had become in Europe and that Western Europe was not recovering on its own which created yet more opportunities for Communists to take power. **2.** Some students might say that Kennedy could neither allow Soviet missiles to stay in Cuba nor allow more supplies to enter. Other might point out the risks involved and question whether strong negotiations might have been tried first. **V. 1.** Students should refer to the chapter to find events for their timelines. **2.** Students may be interested in researching the present situation in countries like Bosnia and the current international relations of the United States with countries.

Chapter 18 1:1. gave money to veterans to go to school and gave loans to help start businesses and buy homes **2.** a large increase in birth rates after World War II **2:1.** a senator who, without any proof, accused many people of being Communists **2.** caused many Americans to fear communism **3:1.** *Brown* v. *Board of Education* **2.** arrest of Rosa Parks **Review I. 1.** d **2.** c **3.** e **4.** b **5.** a **II. 1.** Inflation soared, causing many workers to strike. However, conditions improved because people saved money during the war. Consumer spending shot up and replaced government spending. There was an economic boom. During the 1950s, the income of the average American doubled. **2.** The Soviet Union occupied Eastern Europe and tested its first atomic bomb. **3.** Many people, particularly in the movie industry, were blacklisted. **4.** ordered desegregation in all public schools **5.** sparked the Montgomery bus boycott **III. 1.** the Fair Deal **2.** the Soviet Union's takeover of Eastern Europe **3.** *Brown v. Board of Education* decision **IV. 1.** Entries should describe possible reactions of Rosa Parks. **2.** Students should explain why Americans feared communism. **V. 1.** Skits must include discussion of King's nonviolence policy. **2.** Group should list other nonviolent methods to achieve goals.

Chapter 19 1:1. received support from some Democrats and was blocked by conservative Democrats and Republicans **2.** government went to court to back the right of African Americans to vote, proposed a sweeping civil rights bill **2:1.** Job Corps, Head Start, federal aid to education **2.** drained money way; turned Americans against Johnson **3:1.** pulled troops out of Vietnam, established trade with China, went to the Soviet Union, signed treaties slowing down the arms race, supported bills for clean air and water **2.** the Watergate scandal; tapes were stolen from Democratic headquarters by persons in Nixon's election campaign, and he tried to hide the facts **4:1.** a bad economy, inflation, high cost of living, oil shortage, (Carter) American hostages in Iran **2.** Both were blamed for all the wrongs that occurred while they were in office. **Review I. 1.** c **2.** e **3.** b **4.** a **5.** d **II. 1.** to fight poverty, improve education, provide health care for the aged, promote social justice, expand civil rights laws, send astronauts to the moon **2.** new civil rights laws, a war on poverty (Job Corps, Head Start, etc.), federal aid to education, Medicare, Medicaid, federal housing programs **3.** opened trade with China, signed treaties with the Soviet Union to reduce nuclear arms, pulled troops out of Vietnam **4.** high inflation, rising oil prices, a decline in U.S. economy **5.** Iran hostage crisis **III. 1.** effect, cause **2.** cause, effect **3.** effect, cause **IV. 1.** approve: U.S. victory in the "space race," boost to the economy, advances in technology; oppose: too costly, money could be better spent to fight poverty and to improve social welfare **2.** lower use of heat or air conditioning in homes, insulate homes, avoid unnecessary car trips, make factories more efficient **V. 1.** Suggest that the students make a mock front page with a big headline for each event. **2.** race riots, affirmative action, education, poverty

Chapter 20 1:1. If Vietnam fell to communism, its neighbors would topple too. **2.** North Vietnam won in 1975, and South and North Vietnam became one nation. **2:1.** Doves were people against the Vietnam war; hawks were for it. **2.** the Tet offensive and the killings at Kent State University and Jackson State College **3:1.** African Americans, Latinos **2.** Ford granted a limited amnesty to draft evaders, the Vietnam Memorial was completed in 1982, and a memorial honoring the women who served in the war was unveiled in 1993. **Review I. 1.** d **2.** b **3.** e **4.** c **5.** a **II. 1.** The United States feared that if Vietnam fell to communism, then all its neighbors would. The United States tried to avoid this by sending troops to South Vietnam. **2.** The United States sent undercover agents to blow up bridges and to do other damage to North Vietnam. **3.** to turn the fighting over to South Vietnam's army and start bringing U.S. soldiers home **4.** Some Americans criticized the war, others supported it. **5.** The war raised questions about the uses of power. **III. 1.** the Gulf of Tonkin **2.** Cambodia, Laos **3.** 1975 **IV. 1.** Some students may feel that it is a duty to fight for their country. Others may feel that it is wrong to fight in a war they do not believe in. **2.** Students should note the friends' contrast in opinion over the war. **V. 1.** Interviews should describe how the Vietnam War affected someone's life. **2.** Some students may point out the failure in Vietnam; therefore, we should be hesitant to use armed force again in other countries.

Chapter 21 1:1. mass production; made rows of houses with the same plan **2.** whites moved to suburbs; African Americans, Latinos, and immigrants moved to cities **2:1.** united Americans at times of crisis such as the assassination of President Kennedy; built support for civil rights movement; turned some Americans against Vietnam War **2.** mixed tunes from rhythm and blues with amplified guitars of country and western **3:1.** by adopting new types of music, dressing, and hair styles; by dropping out of school and jobs **2.** the difference between generations **Review I. 1.** e **2.** a **3.** b **4.** c **5.** d **II. 1.** the large increase in birth rate after World War II **2.** People and jobs moved out of cities to the suburbs; and large numbers of African Americans, Latinos, and immigrants moved into cities. **3.** only showed two parent families; fathers worked, mothers stayed home, and ethnic groups were always in the background as helpers **4.** had more money to spend, went further in education **5.** political debates, joined civil rights and antiwar movements **III. 1.** couples had saved money during the war; veterans got government loans **2.** less need for human labor; African Americans traveled North in search of work **IV. 1.** Poems or songs might include the reasons for migrating. **2.** Students should tell why they would be involved in that kind of social action. **V. 1.** Skits may include hippies, protests, or growth of suburbs. **2.** Students should state their opinions on attacks on popular music.

Chapter 22 1:1. nonviolently **2.** People felt sympathy for protesters because television aired violent attacks against them. **2:1.** became more violent **2.** White Americans began to show less support for the civil rights movement. **3:1.** Civil rights leaders were unable to agree on some issues like affirmative action. **2.** African Americans ran for President and received other high political offices. **Review I. 1.** e **2.** b **3.** a **4.** d **5.** c **II. 1.** boycotts, sit-ins, marches **2.** violent resistance by the police and civilians **3.** Through nonviolent protest, King was able to secure civil rights and voting rights for African Americans, as well as win the Nobel Peace Prize. **4.** concluded that, "Our nation is moving toward two societies, one black, one white—separate and unequal" **5.** African Americans were getting a stronger voice in government and held high political positions. **III. 1.** Texas **2.** Mississippi **IV. 1.** support: affirmative action secures advancement for those groups being discriminated against. oppose: it is a form of reverse discrimination. **2.** Speeches may point out how far civil rights has come. **V. 1.** Students should refer to the text and/or outside sources for information on the person of their choice. **2.** Have students explain why they have picked the protest.

Chapter 23 1:1. television, film, literature, music, dance, sports **2.** the first African American to play major league baseball **2:1.** branched out into broadcasting, TV production, cosmetics, and hair care **2.** unemployment and incomes lower than other ethnic groups **3:1.** issues affecting African Americans **2.** the Civil Rights Movement's voting drives **Review I. 1.** d **2.** a **3.** e **4.** c **5.** b **II. 1.** through excellence in television, film, literature, music, dance, sports **2.** He opened the way for African Americans to participate in U.S. sports. **3.** JPC, banks, car dealerships, food and beverage companies, insurance companies **4.** Since 1960, African American incomes have grown 15 percent to qualify them as middle class. **5.** More African Americans have been elected to national, state, and local political offices. **III. 1.** Students may want to look at a wide variety of sports before making judgments. **2.** Problems such as health and homelessness may also be considered. **3.** Other actions might be taken to improve African Americans' economic condition. **IV. 1.** no: fighting back would be counterproductive; yes: African Americans have kept quiet for too long. **2.** Paragraphs should tell why the student thinks the person chosen is important. **V. 1.** Students may include current examples of ways in which African Americans are still being treated unjustly. **2.** Discussions should link family and U.S. histories.

Chapter 24 1:1. became better educated and more went to college **2.** paid much less money than men, had a hard time getting loans and credit cards **2:1.** tried to change laws and filed court cases against companies that discriminated against women **2.** a proposed amendment that called for total equality for men and women under the law **3:1.** More women have high political positions. **2.** Women still get paid less, have a harder time advancing in their careers, and have to juggle careers and children. **Review I. 1.** d **2.** a **3.** b **4.** e **5.** c **II. 1.** Today more than half of all women work outside the home, they have moved into jobs that were once considered "men's work," and women's salaries are closer to men's for comparable work. **2.** Job-holding women were dissatisfied with the jobs available and low pay. Homemakers felt confined to their home and family. **3.** The women's liberation movement tried to change people's beliefsfor example, that women are the weaker sex. NOW sought new laws to achieve equality between the sexes. **4.** The ERA died when only 35 of the necessary 38 states had ratified it. **5.** The gap between women's pay and men's pay has narrowed. **III. 1.** O **2.** F **3.** F **4.** O **IV. 1.** yes: women still do not have equal rights and, therefore, need the amendment; no: women already have all the legal protections that they need **2.** Students should indicate whether the person interviewed supports or opposes the women's liberation movement. **V. 1.** Posters should show the significance of women's roles in U.S. society. **2.** Graphs may show the number of women working going up.

Chapter 25 1:1. conditions were very poor **2.** the fight for improved conditions for migrant farmworkers **2:1.** through voting and forming a political party **2.** More Latinos won state and national offices; more rose to high positions in business and education. **3:1.** politics, entertainment, music **2.** feared that U.S. businesses would move factories to Mexico and they would lose their jobs **Review I. 1.** d **2.** a **3.** e **4.** b **5.** c **II. 1.** *Braceros* were paid low wageswhich kept wages low for all farm workers. **2.** won the support of church leaders and people in the Civil Rights Movement; held marches and rallies **3.** pushed for full civil rights for all Latinos **4.** pardoned many illegal immigrants; set fines for businesses that used illegal workers **5.** less illegal immigration to the United States; more Mexicans could afford to buy U.S. products **III. 1.** The U.S. government renews the *bracero* system; César Chávez begins to organize farm workers in California; Congress passes Immigration Reform and Control Act; Canada, Mexico and the United States form a free-trade zone. **IV. 1.** join: take the risk to improve working conditions; refuse: fear of losing job **2.** Students may want to work in groups for this project. **V. 1.** Students should think of persuasive ways to get people to join their unions. **2.** Answers should include union and changes needed.

Chapter 26 1:1. tried to have the government to control the economy; many businesses were taken over; land was redistributed; new health care and literacy programs **2.** members of the upper and middle classes, including many professionals **2:1.** in Miami, especially Little Havana **2.** technical, sales, and administrative support, managerial and professional jobs **Review I. 1.** e **2.** a **3.** b **4.** c **5.** d **II. 1.** Many wealthy people and middle-class professionals lost jobs or property when Castro took control of the economy. **2.** Professionals leaving the island had skills the Cuban economy needed. **3.** Many were blue-collar workers, and Cubans of African ancestry. **4.** became a large city that is home to many multinational businesses and has strong ties to Latin America **5.** the flight of needed professionals; continuing U.S. embargo; breakup of the Soviet Union, Castro's strongest economic backer **III. 1.** Key West **2.** about 200 miles **3.** the naval base at Guantánamo Bay **4.** Guatemala, Florida **5.** Camarioca, Mariel **IV. 1.** stay: ties to homeland and friends are too strong; go: can not live in a country where rights and freedoms were limited **2.** Stories should include reasons why people were fleeing Cuba. **V. 1.** Posters may cite such events as the Camarioca and Mariel boatlifts and the building up of Little Havana, or events covered in Chapter 17. **2.** Groups should present reasons to support their position.

Chapter 27 1:1. low wages, high unemployment, poor living conditions **2.** New York City **2:1.** full civil rights for Puerto Ricans, better living conditions in the *barrios* **2.** spread out across the United States and less concentrated in the New York area **3:1.** dictator of the Dominican Republic from 1930 to 1961 **2.** Northern Manhattan Coalition for Immigrant Rights, Dominican Small Business Association **Review I. 1.** d **2.** a **3.** c **4.** e **5.** b **II. 1.** from a U.S. colony to a commonwealth **2.** Operation Bootstrap invited U.S. factories to the island. **3.** use of only English; political status of Puerto Rico—commonwealth, state, or independent **4.** political unrest, natural disasters, economic uncertainty **5.** Dominicans are one of the nation's fastest-growing immigrant groups **III. 1.** Cuba, Dominican Republic, Haiti, Jamaica, other **2.** 34% **3.** Haiti **4.** Puerto Ricans have U.S. citizenship, therefore they are not considered immigrants. **IV. 1.** just Spanish: important to preserve Puerto Rican traditions; both: can improve the island's economy by creating stronger ties with U.S. businesses **2.** Possible reasons: poor economic conditions, political unrest **V. 1.** Possible events: Puerto Rico—election of Governor Muñoz Marín, change from colony to commonwealth, Operation Bootstrap, "great migration," actions of Young Lords, election of Puerto Rican Representatives to the U.S. Congress; Dominican Republic—assassination of Trujillo, huge damage by hurricane, increasing immigration to the United States **2.** Students should include the effect that statehood, independence, or commonwealth status will have on the people, economy, and politics.

Chapter 28 1:1. to end federal programs for Native Americans or shift them to the states, move Native Americans to reservations **2.** Most opposed termination; many fought to end it. **2:1.** National Indian Youth Council, American Indian Movement (AIM) **2.** Some peoples have taken advantage of resources on their lands, have gone into manufacturing, or have targeted the tourist trade by building resorts and casinos. **Review I. 1.** b **2.** d **3.** a **4.** e **5.** c **II. 1.** to ensure access to natural resources on Native American lands and save money after expenses incurred during World War II **2.** Native Americans lost control of large parts of their reservations as state governments sold or leased land to businesses that wanted resources. **3.** reforms to give Native Americans self-determination on reservations, shape federal policies toward Native Americans, civil rights for Native Americans **4.** (a) cases accusing federal and state governments of treaty violations (b) some won return of lost lands or payment of large sums of money as settlements, or both **5.** Some want to merge into broader U.S. society; Others want to preserve traditional ways of life. **III. 1.** F **2.** O **3.** O **4.** F **IV. 1.** Possible points: fair federal policy toward Native Americans, return of lost reservation lands, better job-training programs for Native Americans, better housing and health care programs on reservations **2.** Poster and slogan should illustrate the protest chosen. **V. 1.** Designs should represent both the Wounded Knee massacre in 1890 and the AIM takeover in 1973. **2.** Action plans may use protests, takeovers, and court cases.

Chapter 29 1:1. permitted immigration from most Asian nations and allowed them to become naturalized citizens **2.** the Immigration Act of 1965 **2:1.** the Exclusion Act of 1882; U.S. officials feared Chinese immigrants were Communists **2.** run-down, crowded, expensive housing; heavy competition for low-paying jobs **3:1.** lost homes and businesses **2.** approved payments to Japanese American internees **4 1.** Los Angeles, New York City **2.** political and economic reasons **Review I. 1.** c **2.** e **3.** a **4.** d **5.** b **II. 1.** the United States eased restrictions on immigration from Asia as it sought allies against the U.S.S.R. **2.** (a) more Asian families have come rather than single men; (b) more have come with the intention of remaining rather than earning money and then returning to their home country **3.** do not know English; heavy competition for jobs **4.** Japan has a booming economy that provides jobs for almost all its citizens who want them. **5.** opening new businesses **III. 1.** changes in immigration from Asia between 1961 and 1990 **2.** increased **3.** Japan **IV. 1.** Letters may cite the proven loyalty of Japanese Americans as demonstrated by their wartime service. Note that citizens of German or Italian descent were not similarly treated, and remind the recipient of the heavy financial losses that the internees endured. **2.** do not come—difficulties learning English, lack of higher paying jobs, prejudice and discrimination; come—political freedoms and better economic opportunities **V. 1.** Storybook may include obstacles and opportunities for immigrants. **2.** Maps will vary depending upon the country each student group researches.

Chapter 30 1:1. the Displaced Persons Act of 1948 **2.** Communist countries did not allow migration; Europe's economy recovered **2:1.** as peddlers, owned clothing shops, worked in auto industry **2.** Islam **Review I. 1.** b **2.** d **3.** e **4.** c **5.** a **II. 1.** accepted many immigrants fleeing from communism; passed Immigration Act of 1965 **2.** Communist countries did not allow migration; Europe's economy recovered **3.** Economic conditions worsened with the fall of communism. **4.** the formation of Israel, continued fighting in Middle East **5.** Many Arab Americans fear that they will face prejudice because of acts of terrorism in the Middle East. **III. 1.** Between 1948 and 1952, about 450,000 displaced persons entered the United States **2.** About 30 percent of displaced persons were Jews who survived the Holocaust. **3.** It brought many immigrants from Asia and Latin America, not Europe. **IV. 1.** support—it is our duty to help displaced persons; oppose—we have no obligation to provide special treatment to these people. **2.** Letters should give reasons for the position chosen. **V. 1.** Speeches and activities should include a wide variety of immigrant groups. **2.** Students should be sure to discuss both sides of the issue before reaching their conclusion.

Chapter 31 1:1. to lower taxes to encourage investment, then businesses could hire more workers **2.** the first woman appointed to the Supreme Court **2:1.** in the Navy, in the House of Representatives in Texas, director of the CIA, from 1981 to 1989 was Reagan's Vice President **2.** wanted to improve U.S. public schools; but said state and local governments should pay for it **3:1.** reduce the national debt, improve U.S. economy, make government active in social programs, improve health care **2.** developing a new health-care plan **Review I. 1.** e **2.** a **3.** d **4.** c **5.** b **II. 1.** cut spending on social programs, cut taxes **2.** They denied needed social programs for the poor. **3.** the growing deficit and sudden recession **4.** new taxes on gasoline and other products, higher taxes for the rich. **5.** universal health care for all Americans regardless of ability to pay; opposed because they thought it would cost too much and limit people's choice of doctors **III. 1.** the economy boomed; had a charming manner; conservative mood of many Americans **2.** did not improve education, spent billions on savings-and-loan problems; there was a bad recession at end of his term **3.** tried to cut spending and raise taxes, proposed a national health care plan **IV. 1.** Students should explain how and why their plans would improve the economy. **2.** Posters should explain why to vote for candidate. **V. 1.** Possible subjects: the attempted assassination of Reagan or Clinton's health care proposal. **2.** Editorials should give reasons for opinion.

Chapter 32 1:1. tried to introduce a free market economy; cut military spending **2.** economy got worse and conflicts broke out **2:1.** Iraq invaded Kuwait and defied Bush's deadline to pull out. The United States and the UN went to war with Iraq. **2.** to help supplies reach Somalis who were starving because of civil war **3:1.** the Contras **2.** to capture Manuel Noriega for making himself dictator of Panama and for his role in the illegal U.S. drug trade **4:1.** when a country buys more goods made in other countries than it receives from selling to those countries **2.** a trade agreement stating that free trade will be enacted in North America **Review I. 1.** b **2.** a **3.** e **4.** c **5.** d **II. 1.** The Soviet economy got progressively worse and conflicts broke out between different groups within the Soviet Union. **2.** Noriega made himself dictator of Panama and was involved in illegal drug trafficking with the United States. **3.** sent in troops **4.** He wanted Aristide back in power but did not want to use force. **5.** Trade agreements have been made with competing nations; NAFTA. **III.** Kuwait; Iraq invades to take over oil supply; U.S. forces drive Iraqi army out of Kuwait. Somalia; Somalis are starving because of civil war; U.S. forces get supplies to Somalis. Panama; Noriega makes himself dictator; U.S. forces invade Panama and capture Noriega. **IV. 1.** Letters may discuss when the United States has used force in the past and decide whether it was successful or not. **2.** support—help U.S. economy; oppose—hurt American businesses and workers **V. 1.** Map should include Panama, Nicaragua, Haiti, Somalia, Kuwait. **2.** Groups should research how past events created a crisis and suggest solutions.

Chapter 33 1:1. the end of the Vietnam War **2.** had little education, mostly fishers; earlier immigrants were mostly well-educated city people who could speak English **2:1.** opened travel agencies, diners, clothing shops **2.** The American family is not as close-knit as the Indian family. **3:1.** economic troubles, violence, political unrest **2.** an immigrant from Bolivia who came in 1964 to teach math in California; named one of the best teachers in the United States; a movie in 1988 *Stand and Deliver* was written about him. **Review I. 1.** c **2.** e **3.** a **4.** b **5.** d **II. 1.** South Vietnam fell to the Communists in 1975, and many Vietnamese fled. **2.** Some American fishers felt the Vietnamese were taking away jobs. **3.** Many educated Indians could not find work in their profession at home and came to the United States to find better job opportunities. **4.** Argentina's "dirty war," economic hard times, violence, political unrest, military takeovers **5.** large cities, such as Los Angeles, Chicago, New York, Miami **III. 1.** over 650,000 **2.** Peru **IV. 1.** Possible answer: I would try to reason with the local fishers. **2.** family may have immigrated because there were no jobs; teen may have trouble adjusting to new environment; U.S. families are not as close knit **3.** Students should list at least four questions and show an understanding of who Escalante is. **V. 1.** Displays will vary according to the group of immigrants that the students chose. **2.** same reasons: religious, political, and economic hardship in home country.

Chapter 34 1:1. ruin soil, destroy trees, kill fish in bodies of water **2.** to enforce laws protecting the environment **2:1.** a minimum amount of money that a person can earn in order to survive **2.** lack of low cost housing, unemployment, mental illness, drug abuse **3:1.** having more accidents, trouble producing good work, families are hurt, children are often neglected, physical abuse can occur **2.** To pay for drugs, addicts often turn to crime. **Review I. 1.** c **2.** a **3.** e **4.** d **5.** b **II. 1.** by creating acid rain, which damages trees, soil, and water, killing animals and contaminating drinking water **2.** cuts down on garbage, keeping landfills from overflowing **3.** government: free or cheap homes to the poor if they fix them up. Private groups: volunteers help the poor build and repair homes they can buy cheaply **4.** costs billions of dollars due to crime, loss of productivity, treatment programs, and deaths **5.** gun control, neighborhood groups policing their area, fighting drug use **III. 1.** EPA, Clean Air Act, Clean Water Act **2.** often women and children, African Americans, and other minority groups **3.** Students should describe the link between crime and drug abuse. **IV. 1.** Answer might deal with loyalty versus protecting society. **2.** Poster art and text should be persuasive in getting people to recycle. **V. 1.** Students should find ways to present each activity in an effective manner. **2.** Students should refer to Chapter 1, compare today's pollution problems, and then imagine future solutions.

Chapter 35 1:1. smaller, much more powerful **2.** computers that are linked together **2:1.** takes X-rays from different angles and creates a single picture **2.** laser surgery, organ transplants, CAT scan, optical fibers **3:1.** can be used more than once **2.** give information about weather, location of natural resources, study pollution, spot forest fires, send telephone calls and live TV broadcasts, give business information **Review I. 1.** c **2.** a **3.** d **4.** e **5.** b **II. 1.**

Computers control machines and through this automation factory jobs are lost, but business will expand and high-paying jobs such as managers, machine repair, and computer programmers will increase. **2.** a worldwide network **3.** people live longer **4.** discoveries about planet and universe; useful inventions; advances in medicine, computers, and communication; useful satellites **5.** Money spent on space program could go to other programs. **III. 1.** 18.2% **2.** 79% increase **3.** between 1982 and 1983 **IV. 1.** Letters may describe benefits of automation and assure workers they will not lose their jobs. **2.** Entries may describe the excitement of being in space. **V. 1.** Students can refer to the chapter for ideas of breakthroughs. **2.** Groups should brainstorm about problems or challenges of new technology before writing.

Chapter 36 **1:1.** immigration **2.** Asians **2:1.** increasing as people live longer **2.** required owners of public places to provide an easy way in **3:1.** Possible examples: restaurants, shops, and neighborhoods representing different ethnic groups; Americans who speak different languages or ways of speaking English **2.** In a melting pot, everyone blends into one culture. In a mosaic, people can keep their identity while still being part of something larger. **Review I. 1.** b **2.** d **3.** a **4.** e **5.** c **II. 1.** Today, Americans come from many countries. **2.** early 1900s: mainly from Southern and Eastern Europe; today: mainly from Latin America and Asia **3.** right to work as they got older **4.** ban on unfair treatment of disabled people in government programs; all disabled students have the right to free public education; owners of public places must provide an easy way in **5.** Old and new immigrants in the United States have not "melted" completely into the population, but have retained their culture and customs, forming many separate pieces in the overall design, as in a mosaic. **III. 1.** 18 years **2.** about 60 years **3.** Age Discrimination in Employment Act of 1967 **IV. 1.** Stories might include differences in ethnic makeup of population. **2.** Some answers may include leaving the restaurant or complaining to the owner. **V. 1.** Students' bulletin boards will vary, but should include a variety of people and backgrounds. **2.** Students should note that in the early 1900s the elderly had a much stronger role than they do today (i.e. in the family).

UNIT TESTS

VOLUME 1

Unit 1 **1.** c **2.** i **3.** g **4.** e **5.** h **6.** b **7.** a **8.** d **9.** j **10.** f **11.** allowed people of many cultures to come to the United States **12.** allowed them to end their nomadic lifestyle and settle in villages **13.** desire for Eastern luxuries without going through Muslim traders **14.** Encomiendas needed workers; Native Americans were beaten and died from European diseases to which they had no immunity. **15.** The deaths of Native Americans caused a shortage of workers. **A.** diversity in the people, climate, and landforms—for example, 59 million immigrants; climates of Arizona and Alaska, landforms of the Rockies and the Plains **B.** spread out across the continent; developed different cultures and languages; discovered farming; settled in villages. **C.** Examples: large plantations, sugar crops, money, and natural resources.

Unit 2 **1.** j **2.** i **3.** d **4.** g **5.** h **6.** b **7.** e **8.** c **9.** a **10.** f **11.** a missionary who converted Native Americans in the Spanish colonies. **12.** Tobacco was shipped to Europe, making money for the settlers; led to the demand for indentured servants, and slavery. **13.** Huge Southern plantations required much labor. The North farms were small due to its weather and poor soil; little need for slave labor. **14.** gave their children African names; introduced African crops; drums and banjos similar to those used in West Africa; dancing **15.** sent "king's daughters" to New France rewarded couples who had large families; punished those who refused to marry; tried to persuade colonists to become farmers **A.** Protect; prevented bad treatment by the colonists, gave them new skills to earn money. Harm: took away Native Americans customs, causing many to rebel. **B.** North Carolina: more varied economy; had a larger number of small farms. South Carolina: mainly large tobacco plantations; slavery and huge rice farms **C.** North: farms were small; the winter was too cold for farmers to work; making it unprofitable to feed and clothe slaves, laws permitted slaves to win their freedom. South: huge plantations with good soil and warm weather; caused demand for labor to be much higher.

Unit 3 **1.** c **2.** e **3.** h **4.** d **5.** i **6.** f **7.** b **8.** g **9.** a **10.** j **11.** The French and Indian War had been costly; people in Britain were complaining about their high taxes and felt colonists should pay for their own protection. **12.** The organized protests, boycotts, hanging dummies as warnings, tar and feathering, refusing to buy stamps, Boston Tea Party, Committees of Correspondence, and letters to King George III and Parliament. **13.** showed that colonists were willing to fight for freedom; would not back down. **14.** All men are created equal; everyone has basic rights of life, liberty, pursuit of happiness; the government's job is to protect those basic rights; if government does not do that, it is people's duty to change the government. **15.** French navy would not allow British ships in to relieve Cornwallis; French and American soldiers surrounded British troops and forced them to surrender. **A.** Letters vary. Possible response: planning boycotts and protests against the British. **B.** Boston Massacre: the British, in a panic, opening fire on colonists. Boston Tea Party: colonists dressed as Native Americans dropping boxes of tea into the harbor. Battles: colonists' determination to win their freedom. **C.** The colonists were angered by all these acts. Captions should show that the colonists felt they should not be taxed because they lacked representation in Parliament.

Unit 4 **1.** d **2.** a **3.** g **4.** j **5.** i **6.** h **7.** e **8.** c **9.** f **10.** b **11.** to allow a slave to be counted as three fifths of a citizenincreased South's representation in Congress; a Congress with two houses, one based on population, the other with an equal number of members from each state balanced power with more populous North; agreement not to ban the importation of slaves for another 20 years; allowed slave trade to continue **12.** executive, judiciary, and legislative **13.** Louisiana Purchase, land from Mexico as a result of the Mexican-American war. **14.** conflicts over slavery **15.** Native Americans, African Americans, Mexican Americans, Chinese **A.** Accept any two: freedom of speech, freedom of religion, due process, right to a trial, no unreasonable search, right to bear arms **B.** invention of cotton gin increased cotton production and slavery, textile factories increased cloth production and women and children were used in the factories, Northern cities grew rapidly. **C.** executive: can veto bills, appoints judges; legislative: may remove President from office, must approve President's appointments and treaties, can pass laws over veto; judicial: can declare laws or President's actions unconstitutional

Unit 5 **1.** d **2.** e **3.** f **4.** i **5.** g **6.** h **7.** c **8.** j **9.** b **10.** a **11.** slavery; opening of the territory west of the Mississippi sharpened the bitter division over slavery between the North and South, helped bring on the Civil War, and dominated Reconstruction policies **12.** to escape political turmoil, famine, and poverty, and to seek political freedom; hoped to find jobs, education, and economic opportunity **13.** goals: suffrage, the right to own property, the right to receive an education, more job opportunities, equality **14.** Garrison, a white New England abolitionist, helped found the movement and spread its cause with his paper *The Liberator.* Douglass, an African American who escaped from slavery, became a leading abolitionist speaker. **15.** because there was almost no other way to earn a living and once they became sharecroppers the cycle of debt kept them there **A.** set up by white abolitionists and free African Americans to help enslaved African Americans escape to the North **B.** Battles may include: Gettysburg, Antietam Creek, Vicksburg, New Orleans, First and Second Bull Run, Fredericksburg, the Seven Days' Battle, Chattanooga, Chancellorsville **C.** Answers may include: Harriet Tubman, Frederick Douglass, James Forten, Sojourner Truth, Henry Highland Garnet

Unit 6 **1.** e **2.** a **3.** i **4.** g **5.** j **6.** h **7.** c **8.** f **9.** d **10.** b **11.** Booker T. Washington and W.E.B. DuBois; had very different ideas about the kind of education and job training their people needed to improve their lives. **12.** enforced racial segregation in transportation, schools, restaurants, hotels, parks, and other public places; made it impossible for African Americans to vote or hold public office in many Southern states. **13.** Farmers: wanted to use the land on the Great Plains for farming and raising crops; believed that the scarce water supplies in most areas should be used to irrigate crops; fenced in their land to keep out cattle. Ranchers: Plains were the place where cattle could graze and be driven to railroad towns, where they would be sent to market; insisted cattle had a right to water in rivers and streams and should not be fenced out. **14.** Most immigrants to the United States came from Southern and Eastern Europe. Before, most immigrants had arrived from Western and Northern Europe. **15.** Women began to work at jobs outside the home as nurses, sales clerks, and office workers. Some also began to enter the professions as doctors, lawyers, and business leaders. **A.** The world map should show these labeled territories: Guam, the Philippines, Cuba, Puerto Rico. It might also include Alaska and Hawaii. **B.** new technology and wealth on display demonstrated the advances being made; large cities grew in size and wealth; libraries, and schools; the overcrowded ethnic neighborhoods where immigrant and African American families lived; low-paying factory jobs barely enabled many workers to survive. **C.** Possible answers: Most new immigrants poor and lacked money to buy farms; forced to move into slum areas in Eastern and Midwestern cities; families lived in tenement apartments, without electricity and often without heat and running water; neighborhoods near jobs; enjoyed friendships of others like themselves who came from the same country and shared the same culture.

VOLUME 2

Unit 1 **1.** c **2.** e **3.** f **4.** h **5.** a **6.** j **7.** d **8.** g **9.** b **10.** I **11.** Unions helped workers organize to protect their rights and improve working conditions. Strikes were sometimes effective in forcing business owners to meet workers' demands. The courts sometimes decided in favor of workers regarding working hours and child labor. **12.** After the United States defeated Spain in the Cuban-Spanish-American War, Cuba became a protectorate of the United States, which granted it independence in 1902. **13.** fought in courts; published ads in the newspapers describing violence against African Americans; fought for laws to end discrimination and segregation. **14.** Immigrants were willing to work for lower wages than American workers. Some Americans hated immigrants because their language, dress, and customs were often different. **15.** the electric light and machines run by electricity, a device that oiled machines while they were running, mass production, assembly lines, the telephone. **A.** Answers might include: hot and dirty conditions in steel mills, unsanitary conditions in meat-packing plants, overworked and tired employees in crowded sweatshops. **B.** Choices will vary, but may include corruption in state and city government, laws that allow citizens to recall officials and introduce legislation, horrible and unhealthy conditions in meat-packing plants, and the unfair practices of big business. Students should make clear why the problem they have chosen was an important flaw in U.S. life. **C.** Answers will vary. For escaping: Jim Crow laws and the cycle of poverty that was formed by sharecropping. Against escaping: face just as much discrimination in the North; would not be much better off economically.

Unit 2 **1.** d **2.** e **3.** c **4.** f **5.** b **6.** j **7.** i **8.** a **9.** h **10.** g **11.** All nations have equal trading rights throughout China. **12.** by owning most of the sugar industry **13.** Roosevelt often used force to impose U.S. policy. Taft's policy was more business oriented. **14.** paid less to do the same job; given the most dangerous jobs; not allowed to join unions; their children had to go to segregated schools. **15.** Germany tried to get Mexico to join in a war against the United States. Germany also sunk a number of U.S. ships. **A.** The Platt Amendment made Cuba a protectorate, allowing it to send U.S. troops there and establish a naval base in Cuba. For Cuba, the Platt was a symbol of its lack of independence, which it had expected after the Cuban Spanish-American War. Students will vary in their views of the Platt Amendment. In favor: important for the United States to have the right to send troops to Cuba in view of Cuba's strategic position in the Caribbean. Opposed: the United States was acting as an imperialist power without regard for the rights of Cubans. **B.** Letters may include such dangers as poisonous snakes, mosquitoes that carried yellow fever and malaria. Also, dangerous and unsanitary conditions throughout the jungles, swamps, rivers, and mountains. **C.** Possible answers: For women job opportunities in factories, as well as, with the government. For African Americans new opportunities in the wartime factories and mills; earned more money than they had before, but often not paid as much as white workers. For Mexicans: new job opportunities throughout the West on railroad lines and in cotton fields, farms, and copper mines.

Unit 3 **1.** c **2.** g **3.** e **4.** f **5.** i **6.** d **7.** h **8.** a **9.** j **10.** b **11.** Jobs were few; wages were low; prices shot up; many Americans blamed "outsiders" for striking, taking jobs and being different. People blamed immigrants for the poor economic conditions. Fear of communism led to the Red Scare in which people who were thought to be communists were persecuted. **12.** African Americans contributed a number of talented artists and writers; famous singers and musicians. **13.** The Great Depression was the worst economic crisis ever, leading to great unemployment. Many in the middle class were wiped out. There was homelessness and starvation for many. Family life was destroyed. People lived on breadlines and government relief. **14.** Some steps President Roosevelt took in the New Deal: the bank holiday, reform acts such as the CCC, WPA, TVA, the social security system and unemployment insurance. **15.** Accept any of the following: Many women went to work during the war and as a result earned money, raised their families standard of living, enjoyed new freedoms, found jobs that they had previously been barred from and experienced a new sense of importance. **A.** Accept any of the following: flappers, jazz musicians, black nationalism. **B.** Answers might include the following: People waiting on breadlines, living in Hoovervilles. **C.** Tragedies mentioned might include the include: Holocaust, internment of Japanese Americans, death marches, Pearl Harbor, atomic bombing of Hiroshima and Nagasaki, huge losses of life in both the military and among civilians, destruction of many cities.

Unit 4 **1.** e **2.** b **3.** a **4.** h **5.** g **6.** i **7.** f **8.** c **9.** d **10.** j **11.** a period of distrust between the United States and the Soviet Union brought on by the Soviet Union's control of its communist governments in Eastern Europe and the U.S. fear of the spread of communism **12.** Wages doubled, there was a shift from military spending to production of consumer goods, more jobs were created, consumer spending increased, and the economy boomed. **13.** to fight poverty, improve education, provide health care for the aged, promote social justice, help unemployed youths find jobs (Job Corps), provide early schooling for poor children (Head Start), pass stronger civil rights laws, provide government housing for poor and middle-class families **14.** Hawks and doves emerged; there was violence on college campuses; the war took money from Great Society programs **15.** African Americans and Latinos moved into the cities, white city dwellers moved to the suburbs, jobs and population shifted to the South and Southwest, older people moved to warmer climates **A.** Answers should cover three of the following: the Truman Doctrine; the Marshall Plan; the Berlin airlift; the creation of NATO; McCarthy and his investigations; blacklists; war in Korea; the Bay of Pigs; the Cuban Missile Crisis. **B.** Answers should include: more jobs created; higher wages; increase in consumer spending; movement of minorities to cities, movement of city dwellers to suburbia; population shift from North and East to South and Southwest; movement of older people to warm climates; affordable "assembly-line" housing; boom in building and buying of houses; baby boom, generation gap, rock 'n' roll; segregated neighborhoods, stronger civil rights laws, voting rights laws, Supreme Court decisions such as the *Brown* v *Board of Education* and Alabama bus desegregation decision; more opportunities for minorities in employment, including sports and entertainment. **C.** Rosa Parks's arrest for not giving up a seat on a bus; the bus boycott; emergence of Dr. Martin Luther King,

Jr. as a leader of the Civil Rights Movement and his idea of nonviolence; boycott lasted 381 days; the 1956 Supreme Court decision outlawing segregation on Alabama buses.

Unit 5 **1.** j **2.** g **3.** d **4.** i **5.** b **6.** h **7.** c **8.** a **9.** f **10.** e **11.** Malcolm X: pride in their African heritage, separate from whites in order to control their own lives. The Black Panthers: programs in black communities to help rebuild their neighborhoods, feed and house poor families, to improve their lives. **12.** He founded the United Farm Workers, the union that gained better working conditions and higher wages for Mexican American farm laborers in the Southwest and California. Chávez's efforts began the movement to gain full civil rights for Latinos in the United States. **13.** In 1980, Cuban dictator Castro allowed Cuban exiles in the United States to go to the port of Mariel to pick up their relatives who wished to leave Cuba. About 125,000 Marielitos left Cuba during the boatlift. **14.** Although Puerto Rico was the wealthiest island in the Caribbean, Puerto Ricans could earn higher wages in the United States and had more opportunities to improve their lives. The low air fares after 1945 also made it cheaper and faster to come to the United States. **15.** increased the production of resources from their lands, have charged larger amounts for those resources, opened factories to manufacture electric appliances and auto parts, produce beautiful silver and turquoise jewelry, run a large ski resort, opened gambling casinos. **A.** In 1948, Congress paid $38 million in damages for losses suffered to Japanese Americans who had been in internment camps during the war. In 1976, President Ford officially admitted that the wartime treatment of Japanese Americans had been wrong. In 1988, Congress passed the Civil Liberties Act that paid $10,000 to all the internees. **B.** The charts will vary in completeness, but should be based on the people whose achievements are discussed in the text. **C.** NOW was founded as a national group whose purpose was to organize "a civil rights movement for American women." It filed court cases to end discrimination against women in the work place. It tried to get laws passed to help women and families. It worked to achieve the feminist goal of equal political, social, and economic rights.

Unit 6 **1.** d **2.** e **3.** a **4.** b **5.** c **6.** i **7.** j **8.** h **9.** f **10.** g **11.** to bring food and supplies to the starving people of the African nation of Somalia. Several million Somalis faced starvation and death as a result of a long civil war. **12.** because of his personal charm; he survived an assassination attempt, which increased his popularity; his ideas reflected the conservative mood of the majority of Americans tired of paying high taxes to support social programs **13.** refugees who fled Vietnam after the Communist takeover at the end of the war; by 1990, over 650,000 Vietnamese settled in the United States **14.** Congress passed the Clean Air Act of 1970, the Clean Water Act of 1972, and also set up the Environmental Protection Agency to enforce these and other laws to curb pollution. Recycling programs to reuse cans, newspapers, plastic, bottles, and other items and cut down on the garbage in landfills became popular in every town and city. **15.** Europeans, Latinos, and Asians came as immigrants; brought their cultures with them during the era of the melting pot as well as the present age of the mosaic. Diversity also includes racial groups and ethnic groups, disabled Americans, and older Americans. **A.** increased the amount of information and the speed with which it can be spread; perform the work once done by large groups of workers in factories and offices; used in schools and colleges as aids to education; are being linked with networks and satellites for a global information highway; computerized robots changed the way cars are manufactured, steel is produced, and businesses and industries operate. **B.** Answers should include many of the world trouble spots discussed in the text, such as Cuba, the Middle East, North Korea, China, the Balkans. **C.** Crime became a serious threat to the safety of Americans. Murders and violent crime especially affected young people, who were often both the victims of crime and those who committed crimes. Murder was the third-leading cause of death for elementary and middle grade children. Gangs grew and profited from the vast sums of money they gained from the drug trade. Drug addicts committed crimes to pay for drugs.

CHAPTER TESTS

VOLUME 1

Chapter 1 **1.** a **2.** c **3.** e **4.** d **5.** b **6.** c **7.** a **8.** d **9.** c **10.** a **A.** Possible answers: the Great Lakes and the rivers provided waterway for trade; fertile plains made farming possible. **B.** Reasons vary by region. Possible answer: coastal plains because of large cities and relatively mild climate.

Chapter 2 **1.** e **2.** c **3.** a **4.** d **5.** b **6.** c **7.** b **8.** d **9.** d **10** b **A.** Possible answers: Trees for canoes, bark for rope, dog hair for blankets. **B.** spread out over the continent, developed farming, settled in villages, developed different languages and religious practices.

Chapter 3 **1.** d **2.** a **3.** e **4.** b **5.** c **6.** a **7.** d **8.** a **9.** d **10.** c **A.** Answers should include: Europeans wished to have access to the riches of the East directly, without having to acquire and pay for them through the Muslims of the Middle East. **B.** Answers might indicate that Europeans were interlopers and oppressors; European oppression was so hard that they would fight the Europeans; European rule was so strong that they would hesitate to oppose them.

Chapter 4 **1.** d **2.** e **3.** a **4.** c **5.** b **6.** b **7.** d **8.** c **9.** d **10.** c **A.** Answer should include large buildings; several universities for religion, law, and medicine, the city's libraries. **B.** Possible answer: Yes: help Cortés because of the cruel way in which the Aztec rulers treated their vassals. No: fear that after he conquered the Aztec, Cortés would treat the vassals as badly as the Aztec did.

Chapter 5 **1.** d **2.** a **3.** b **4.** a **5.** c **6.** c **7.** a **8.** b **9.** d **10.** d **A.** Advantages: given food, clothing, and a place to live; being taught skills. Disadvantages: destruction of their traditional culture; frequent cruelty of the missionaries; being forced to convert to a new religion. **B.** Spanish: the Spanish language, Catholic religion, European foods. African: religious beliefs, music, African words added to Spanish. Native American: medicines; types of clothing; such foods as tomatoes and potatoes.

Chapter 6 **1.** e **2.** c **3.** a **4.** d **5.** b **6.** c **7.** a **8.** a **9.** b **10.** c **A.** Answers should include: the Virginia House of Burgesses, the Mayflower Compact, New England town meetings. **B.** Yes: Native American knowledge of farming and other skills that the settlers could learn; friendship might keep the Native Americans from attacking them. No: Native Americans could not be trusted; could attack at any time.

Chapter 7 **1.** d **2.** a **3.** b **4.** e **5.** c **6.** c **7.** b **8.** a **9.** a **10.** b **A.** New England: farming hard; the soil was rocky and the growing season was short; more people turned to fishing and whaling. Middle Colonies: farming easier because the weather was milder; more people earned a living from trading. South: plantations large; many African American slaves. **B.** The mural should show differences in farming, business, religion, and education.

Chapter 8 **1.** d **2.** e **3.** b **4.** a **5.** c **6.** a **7.** c **8.** a **9.** a **10.** b **A.** Answers include: the diversity of the population, the growth of self-government, the growing trade among the colonies and with other nations, the increase in education. **B.** Similarities: responsible for household, food; clothing, family expenses; some worked outside home. Differences: could not read or write, not able to vote.

Chapter 9 **1.** c **2.** d **3.** e **4.** b **5.** a **6.** a **7.** b **8.** d **9.** c **10.** c **A.** Champlain founded Quebec and explored the St. Lawrence; Joliet and Marquette reached the Mississippi; La Salle claimed Louisiana for the French. **B.** Suggested response: to find husbands, to escape poverty in France, to find adventure in a new land.

Chapter 10 **1.** b **2.** c **3.** d **4.** a **5.** e **6.** a **7.** d **8.** b **9.** a **10.** d **A.** The French and Indian War was expensive for the British; since it benefited the colonists, they should help pay for it. **B.** boycotted British goods, merchants promised not to buy from the British; colonists did not buy goods that were taxed.

Chapter 11 **1.** a **2.** e **3.** c **4.** d **5.** b **6.** b **7.** a **8.** b **9.** d **10.** a **A.** The colonial assemblies protested the acts; claimed they violated the law;

colonists demonstrated in the streets; the Sons of Liberty built a mock tree that seemed to show British officials hanging from it; the Daughters of Liberty boycotted British cloth and tea; Boston Massacre brought to a climax anti-British feeling. **B.** Colonist: Boston Tea Party was a justified expression of colonial anger over the tax on tea. Member of Parliament: It was vandalism that destroyed valuable property.

Chapter 12 **1.** c **2.** d **3.** e **4.** b **5.** a **6.** c **7.** d **8.** d **9.** c **10.** d **A.** Colonists had the advantage of fighting on their own ground, were more flexible in their tactics than the British were, and were dedicated to their cause. The British, far from home, fought with Hessian soldiers who had no investment in the cause. **B.** Suggested response: the British king, a tyrant; had no real right to rule the colonies; since the only good form of government is one elected by the people, the colonies should declare independence.

Chapter 13 **1.** c **2.** e **3.** b **4.** a **5.** d **6.** b **7.** c **8.** b **9.** c **10.** c **A.** Suggested response: the delegates did not trust the British, who did not carry out their promises; the colonists were already fighting the British; to get needed help from France and Spain, they would have to declare independence. **B.** Choices vary. Possible responses: "all men [people] are created equal" and have the same rights especially since many groups are discriminated against; government gets its powers from the "consent of the governed" and may not take away the people's rights.

Chapter 14 **1.** b **2.** d **3.** e **4.** a **5.** c **6.** b **7.** b **8.** d **9.** a **10.** a **A.** The British advantages: large well-trained army and navy. Disadvantages: many British did not support the war, had to supply armed forces that were 3,000 miles away, the Hessians who fought for them did not have any great loyalty to them. Colonial advantages: fighting for freedom on familiar ground with excellent leaders. Disadvantages: colonial officers had little military training; army was small; had a hard time raising money for the army. **B.** It reflected the rivalries among Great Britain, France, and Spain; aid the French gave the Americans in the form of money; help given by the Spanish through Gálvez; help that the Americans had from foreign military men such as von Steuben, Kosciusko, and Lafayette.

Chapter 15 **1.** b **2.** a **3.** d **4.** c **5.** e **6.** c **7.** a **8.** a **9.** d **10.** a **A.** The ad might show that there was no money for a navy; the government couldn't pay its debts; other nations had little respect for the nation, as shown, for example, by Spain's refusal to allow the United States to use the Mississippi by and Britain's failure to remove its soldiers from the Great Lakes region. **B.** Compromises: (1) North and South agreed slaves counted as three-fifths of a free person, a tax put on the slave trade, no laws prohibiting the importation of slaves not to be considered until after 1808. (2) The large and small states satisfied by the creation of a Congress with two houses, one with membership based on population, the other with two members from each state. (3) Power divided between the federal government and the states.

Chapter 16 **1.** c **2.** d **3.** a **4.** e **5.** b **6.** c **7.** c **8.** a **9.** b **10.** a **A.** At the bottom the federal district courts; above them the federal courts of appeal; at the apex the U.S. Supreme Court. **B.** Suggested response: the Topeka system of separate schools not constitutional because it violates the due process provision of the 5th Amendment, which guarantees that all groups of people should be treated equally.

Chapter 17 **1.** b **2.** d **3.** c **4.** a **5.** e **6.** d **7.** a **8.** d **9.** b **10.** c **A.** He set the country on a firm course; set precedents for future Presidents; he showed that people could not defy the government (Whiskey Rebellion); kept out of wars. **B.** Showed that the Constitution could be changed to take care of something that the writers of the Constitution had not foreseen—in this case the possibility of a tie vote for President between Burr and Jefferson.

Chapter 18 **1.** b **2.** c **3.** d **4.** a **5.** e **6.** a **7.** c **8.** a **9.** b **10.** a **A.** Possible responses: the Louisiana Territory remained a possession of France or sold to Britain, the U.S. expanded westward. Other possibilities should be evaluated on the basis of students' understanding of the material. **B.** Suggested response: Lewis and Clark received help from the African American York, the Native American Sacajawea, and other Native Americans.

Chapter 19 **1.** e **2.** d **3.** a **4.** b **5.** c **6.** a **7.** b **8.** a **9.** c **10.** d **A.** The poster should include some of the following: clean rooms, good meals, adult supervision, no work on Sundays, time to go to school, listen to lectures, write poetry. **B.** Students who would join a slave revolt might express the desire to escape the cruelty of the plantation owners, the beatings by overseers, the crude living conditions. Students who would not join might point out the likelihood of the revolt failing and of being severely punished.

Chapter 20 **1.** b **2.** d **3.** a **4.** c **5.** e **6.** d **7.** d **8.** d **9.** d **10.** b **A.** Diary entries may include cruel treatment by the soldiers, lack of food, lack of care for the old or ill. **B.** Many people felt the East was becoming crowded; transportation improved; land was available.

Chapter 21 **1.** c **2.** a **3.** d **4.** e **5.** b **6.** c **7.** d **8.** a **9.** a **10.** c **A.** California's population increased, Spanish-speaking residents and Chinese were discriminated against, unfair laws were passed to keep out foreign miners, *Californios* were driven off lands they had owned. **B.** War was just a way of getting more territory for the United States; it was a scheme to add more slave territory to the nation; the United States really started the war.

Chapter 22 **1.** c **2.** e **3.** a **4.** b **5.** d **6.** c **7.** d **8.** a **9.** c **10.** b **A.** worked on the docks and in factories, built the nation's canals and railroads. **B.** Discrimination might include not being hired, only being hired for "dirty" jobs, verbal and physical attacks.

Chapter 23 **1.** c **2.** a **3.** d **4.** e **5.** b **6.** d **7.** b **8.** b **9.** a **10.** d **A.** Property rights of married women expanded, Seneca Falls Convention began the women's movement, women gradually go more job opportunities, education for women expanded. **B.** Chances would be very slim. Most medical schools only accepted men.

Chapter 24 **1.** c **2.** e **3.** d **4.** a **5.** b **6.** c **7.** b **8.** d **9.** a **10.** c **A.** Abolitionists were sworn to end slavery and to free all enslaved Africans. Moderates worked within the political system, using peaceful means to change existing laws. Militants wanted immediate actions to end slavery and were willing to use violence. **B.** risked: your life, being shot, captured and punished severely or disabled, turned in by someone to collect a reward or arrested by local officials enforcing the fugitive slave laws

Chapter 25 **1.** e **2.** a **3.** c **4.** b **5.** d **6.** b **7.** d **8.** d **9.** d **10.** d **A.** The United States gained territory from Mexico. The new territories were not a part of the Missouri Compromise. Congress had to decide if the new lands were to be slave or free. Compromise of 1850 was the result, but it did not please the North or the South. **B.** Answers should focus on the deep divisions in both political parties over slavery, the growing fervor and strength of the abolitionist movement, and dissatisfaction over the Compromise of 1850.

Chapter 26 **1.** d **2.** a **3.** c **4.** b **5.** e **6.** d **7.** d **8.** c **9.** b **10.** c **A.** Lincoln believed that slavery was wrong, and he opposed its spread into the territories. In the election, all his votes were from states in the North or West. Southerners were sure Lincoln would try to end slavery everywhere. They believed that states' rights meant they could oppose any federal attempt to interfere with slavery. Southern states began to secede from the Union and formed the Confederacy. Lincoln believed the Union had to be preserved, even at the cost of civil war. **B.** Mention should be made that some people felt they were being forced to fight to end slavery. Others resented that the rich could buy their way out of fighting.

Chapter 27 **1.** c **2.** d **3.** a **4.** e **5.** b **6.** b **7.** d **8.** c **9.** b **10.** c **A.** Answers may include: caused great loss of lives and property on both sides, the freedom gained by all African Americans, the legacy of bitterness on both sides, the death and destruction in the nation's most devastating conflict. **B.** Possible answers: feelings of sadness at the loss of the great leader who had headed the nation during its greatest crisis, fears about the nation's future

Chapter 28 **1.** b **2.** d **3.** a **4.** e **5.** c **6.** c **7.** a **8.** b **9.** a **10.** d **A.** Congress passed the 13th Amendment banning slavery, and the 14th and 15th

Amendments granting African Americans citizenship and the right to vote, set up the Freedmen's Bureau to help African Americans acquire education and job training and to find missing family members, when the Southern states passed Black Codes, Congress enacted Reconstruction laws to protect African Americans **B.** Most students should recognize Reconstruction as only a partial success. Most gains by African Americans were lost when U.S. army left the South.

Chapter 29 **1.** c **2.** e **3.** d **4.** b **5.** a **6.** c **7.** c **8.** d **9.** d **10.** a **A.** By organizing boycotts of white businesses, challenging laws in courts, by urging states to protect their civil rights. **B.** Possible points: personalities, their status and appeal to white society, their philosophies about the kind of education and jobs African Americans needed, the pace of progress toward achieving full civil rights.

Chapter 30 **1.** c **2.** d **3.** a **4.** e **5.** b **6.** d **7.** a **8.** a **9.** b **10.** c **A.** The settlers staked out the free land offered them by the Homestead Act and set up farms and ranches there; ignored the rights of Native Americans to these lands; the U.S. army sent force them to move; required to move into areas in their own land set aside as reservations. **B.** The letters may include the difficulty of surviving in a new unsettled area, often isolated and long distances from any town, facing the constant hardships of bad weather, crop failures, and rivalry between ranchers and farmers; the close family ties, the independence and freedom, and the majesty of the landscape made the experience unique.

Chapter 31 **1.** c **2.** a **3.** d **4.** e **5.** b **6.** c **7.** a **8.** b **9.** a **10.** d **A.** Possible answers: the outpouring of new machines and the invention of revolutionary new industrial processes that propelled the U.S. into the period of its greatest growth; become the world's leading economic power. **B.** Yes: the unions' efforts to improve the long hours, low pay, and dangerous working conditions in the new mass-production industries, exploitation of workers from the ranks of newly arrived immigrants, African Americans, Latinos. No: fear of losing job.

Chapter 32 **1.** b **2.** d **3.** a **4.** e **5.** c **6.** d **7.** c **8.** d **9.** a **10.** c **A.** Similarities: escaping poverty, did not speak English on arriving in the United States, faced discrimination. Differences: Europeans settled in cities of the East and Midwest, planned to remain in the United States; most Mexicans settled in the Southwest, planned to return to their native lands. **B.** Answers may include: Most immigrants lived in separate rundown sections; families crowded together in small tenement apartments that lacked running water or electricity; sanitation primitive; immigrant families felt sense of belonging, of sharing hardships in living together, speaking the same language; attending the same church.

Chapter 33 **1.** b **2.** c **3.** e **4.** a **5.** d **6.** b **7.** c **8.** a **9.** c **10.** a **A.** Paved streets made it possible to travel to work on electric-run trolley cars and cable cars. Streetcars carried numerous riders. Elevated trains on tracks above the street and subways that ran underground helped make travel faster and easier. **B.** Answers may include struggle and sacrifice establishing a new life in the United States, ability to work hard, raising a family, eventual success in business.

Chapter 34 **1.** a **2.** c **3.** b **4.** d **5.** e **6.** b **7.** d **8.** d **9.** a **10.** b **A.** The importance given to women's roles as mothers and housewives; men's roles defined as job holders and economic providers for the family; lack of the vote slowed women's efforts to change conditions through political action; the rise of big business brought opportunities in office and service jobs; began to offer employment for women outside the home; opened new careers to them. **B.** Did not require great physical strength; the invention of the telephone switchboard and the typewriter increased the numbers of workers needed in business offices; worked for lower wages, women replaced men; skills and determination to succeed in their work.

Chapter 35 **1.** c **2.** a **3.** d **4.** e **5.** b **6.** c **7.** b **8.** a **9.** d **10.** b **A.** Answers may include: Cuba was only 90 miles south of Florida; U.S. businesses owned tobacco and sugar plantations in Cuba; American trade growing with the island; the United States was interested in building a canal in nearby Central America; Cuban revolution posed a threat to American interests. **B.** Answers may focus on feelings of loyalty to the embattled ruler struggling to keep her island from being taken over by the American planters who controlled Hawaii's economy. The queen's efforts to resist American missionaries who threatened the island's traditional culture and the American sugar plantation owners' plan to overthrow her rallied support among her people, even though she was eventually driven from her throne by these Americans.

Chapter 36 **1.** c **2.** a **3.** d **4.** b **5.** e **6.** a **7.** a **8.** a **9.** d **10.** a **A.** Agree: the modern, technologically advanced city that was evolving. Disagree: the reality of the industrial city with its overcrowded neighborhoods, poverty, settlement houses; immigrant and African American populations that lived in the city's ethnic, segregated neighborhoods. **B.** Possible answers: scant regard most Americans had for Native Americans, who had lost what was once their homeland and now were largely confined to reservations; a negative stereotype of Native Americans in the minds of immigrants and native-born generations alike. There were too few Native Americans left to counter these views, and there were few prominent advocates of their cause in the white community.

VOLUME 2

Chapter 1 **1.** a **2.** c **3.** e **4.** b **5.** d **6.** b **7.** c **8.** b **9.** a **10.** c **A.** Students may describe: electricity made machines more efficient; device which oiled machines while they were still running; assembly lines and mass production allowed products to be made more quickly and cheaply. **B.** Possible examples: improper ventilation; no fireproofing; poor lighting that led to numerous accidents; long working hours; machines that lacked safety devices

Chapter 2 **1.** c **2.** a **3.** b **4.** d **5.** e **6.** c **7.** b **8.** d **9.** a **10.** d **A.** Possible reasons: poverty; limited opportunities in their homelands; for Jews, persecution; pogroms, and anti-Semitism **B.** Entries may include: astonishment at the size of the buildings; noise and crowding of the city; poor housing (which may have been better than back home); pleasure of living in a neighborhood where immigrants from the same country lived; finding work that was hard with low pay and poor working conditions.

Chapter 3 **1.** c **2.** a **3.** b **4.** e **5.** d **6.** a **7.** c **8.** d **9.** a **10.** d **A.** Entries might include: hard work for very little money; poor living conditions; harsh treatment from the landowner; cycle of debt that kept them tied to being sharecroppers **B.** Washington: believed training African Americans in a trade, so they could make economic gains was more important than pressing for civil rights. DuBois: believed in fighting for civil rights immediately.

Chapter 4 **1.** a **2.** e **3.** c **4.** b **5.** d **6.** d **7.** a **8.** b **9.** b **10.** d **A.** Answers may include: pleasure at living in a *barrio,* where Spanish is spoken and where familiar foods; low quality but expensive housing; jobs are not easy to find and most jobs are hard and pay little; education is available, especially the opportunity to learn English **B.** Poster should show that *Las Gorras Blancas* fights for the rights of *nuevomexicanos* against eastern landowners who wanted to deprive them of their land and that this was their opportunity to get back their way of life.

Chapter 5 **1.** d **2.** e **3.** b **4.** a **5.** c **6.** a **7.** c **8.** a **9.** b **10.** a **A.** Haymarket Riot was a clash between striking members of the Knights of Labor and the Chicago police, resulting in several deaths after a bomb was thrown. After the riot, many people turned against the Knights of Labor, and their membership declined. **B.** Students should mention that women organized the National Women's Trade Union League and the Illinois Women's Alliance and Latinos and Japanese formed the Japanese-Mexican Labor Association.

Chapter 6 **1.** d **2.** a **3.** b **4.** e **5.** c **6.** b **7.** a **8.** d **9.** b **10.** c **A.** Methods: drive to get states to allow women to vote, formation of the National American Woman Suffrage Association; parades and demonstrations organized by women such as, Alice Paul **B.** Possible problems: corruption in state and local governments; conditions in the meat-packing industry; evils of big business (all of these showed that the United States was not living up to its ideals.)

Chapter 7 **1.** c **2.** a **3.** d **4.** b **5.** e **6.** b **7.** c **8.** a **9.** a **10.** a **A.** support: he was fighting for Philippine independence and U.S. control of his country was no different from Spanish control; oppose: the Philippines would be better off under U.S. control than they had been under Spanish rule **B.** The United States wanted as much right to trade with China as the European countries. The policy would also help the United States establish a strong presence in China to keep the European powers from taking possession of the Philippines and its other Pacific islands.

Chapter 8 **1.** e **2.** c **3.** d **4.** a **5.** b **6.** d **7.** c **8.** b **9.** a **10.** b **A.** similarities: both were taken over by the United States, neither received immediate independence; Americans took over sugar plantations. differences: Cuba never became part of the United States, whereas Puerto Rico became a commonwealth; Cuba became independent, while Puerto Rico was under U.S. control; Puerto Ricans were able to claim U.S. citizenship. **B.** Finlay: he argued first that yellow fever was carried by a mosquito. Reed: he proved it.

Chapter 9 **1.** c **2.** a **3.** d **4.** e **5.** b **6.** c **7.** c **8.** d **9.** a **10.** c **A.** no right: the United States used the threat of force to get the right to build the canal. right: the whole world benefited from the canal; helped Panamanians who wanted independence from Columbia set up the new nation of Panama. **B.** fight: hope for better conditions if the revolution was successful; leave: avoid the chaos, violence, and poverty in Mexico and have the chance of a better life in the United States.

Chapter 10 **1.** b **2.** a **3.** d **4.** e **5.** c **6.** d **7.** a **8.** b **9.** d **10.** b **A.** The murder of Archduke Francis Ferdinand by a Serb led Austria-Hungary to declare war on Serbia, and then European alliances brought other nations into the war. **B.** Volunteer: the German attacks on U.S. ships; to defeat an aggressive Germany because it threatened countries with which the United States had ties. Not volunteer: despite the abuse the U.S. suffered at the hands of Germany, going to war was not a necessary step.

Chapter 11 **1.** c **2.** d **3.** e **4.** a **5.** b **6.** d **7.** d **8.** c **9.** d **10.** c **A.** The poster could show flappers dancing, entertainment, jazz musicians, cars, suburbs, manufactured goods. **B.** new roads, trucks, larger cities, gas stations, motels and restaurants, busy industries making steel, glass, and rubber to be used for automobiles.

Chapter 12 **1.** a **2.** d **3.** c **4.** e **5.** b **6.** a **7.** d **8.** c **9.** b **10.** a **A.** suggested response: the liveliness and excitement of the nightclub, with African Americans singing, playing music, and dancing, for both an African American and white audience. **B.** suggested response: the many clubs in Harlem; the performers of jazz and composers of classical music; the developing art and literature, murals and other art forms; newspapers; major African American writers of poetry and fiction.

Chapter 13 **1.** c **2.** e **3.** d **4.** b **5.** a **6.** a **7.** d **8.** b **9.** a **10.** c **A.** Answers should include unemployed people, living in sewers, under bridges, and in parks; include lack of money, hunger, crowded breadlines, difficulties in getting relief, and so on. **B.** Headlines might include: Stock Prices Crash, Millions of Dollars Lost, Panic Sets in on Wall Street.

Chapter 14 **1.** d **2.** c **3.** b **4.** a **5.** e **6.** a **7.** d **8.** d **9.** a **10.** c **A.** Answers should include the creation of work programs that resulted in new jobs, the reform of the banking system, help to the poor, better prices for farmers. **B.** The advertisement should emphasize dams on the river to provide electricity and a rebirth of the economy of a region.

Chapter 15 **1.** e **2.** c **3.** b **4.** d **5.** a **6.** d **7.** c **8.** a **9.** a **10.** a **A.** Reports might include a description of U.S. ships that are being bombed, the sailors who are trying to man guns and cannons to repel the attackers. **B.** Posters might show cities being bombed, the death march on Bataan, concentration camp scenes, soldiers who are dying on the beaches at Normandy (D-Day), the aftermath of the atomic bomb attack on Hiroshima and Nagasaki.

Chapter 16 **1.** a **2.** c **3.** d **4.** b **5.** e **6.** d **7.** a **8.** d **9.** a **10.** a **A.** Answers include: the crude accommodations in the camps; the pain of having been singled out by the government as possible traitors; missed being in school with other Americans; loss of jobs by the adults; loss of homes and family possessions. **B.** The posters should show one of the items requested.

Chapter 17 **1.** d **2.** b **3.** e **4.** a **5.** c **6.** c **7.** a **8.** c **9.** b **10.** d **A.** Both were designed to stop the spread of communism. Truman Doctrine gave $400 million in aid to Greece and Turkey; the Marshall Plan gave $12.5 billion in aid to Western Europe to help it recover from World War II. **B.** Americans feared communism spreading to Cuba because the threat was right in their own backyard, as opposed to thousands of miles away.

Chapter 18 **1.** c **2.** a **3.** d **4.** b **5.** e **6.** d **7.** a **8.** b **9.** b **10.** a **A.** Benefits: consumer spending increased; the United States sold many goods to other nations; an economic boom; the GI bill provided veterans with money for education, housing, and business; income doubled; postwar economy provided jobs for millions of women; a baby boom. Problems: inflation, over 5 million workers went on strike for higher wages; 1 million women lost jobs to returning servicemen; segregation. **B.** Americans became afraid of communism, and thought there were spies for the Soviet Union in the United States. Joseph McCarthy accused many of being Communists. Many people in entertainment and teaching lost their jobs.

Chapter 19 **1.** b **2.** d **3.** e **4.** a **5.** c **6.** a **7.** b **8.** a **9.** c **10.** a **A.** approve: he established friendly relations with communist China, a longtime enemy of the United States, and improved relations with the Soviet Union. opposed: he escalated the Vietnam War. **B.** It was feared that if North Vietnam won, communism would spread to the rest of East Asia. It was also felt that a victory for North Vietnam would make China and the Soviet Union more appealing to underdeveloped countries.

Chapter 20 **1.** e **2.** c **3.** b **4.** a **5.** d **6.** b **7.** c **8.** c **9.** d **10.** b **A.** Nixon's plan for ending the war was Vietnamization, or turning the fighting over to the South Vietnamese army and bringing American troops home. **B.** Americans were split on the Vietnam War. There were those who supported the war, called hawks. And those who opposed the war, called doves.

Chapter 21 **1.** c **2.** d **3.** a **4.** e **5.** b **6.** a **7.** b **8.** c **9.** a **10.** d **A.** Possible changes: greater conflict between parents and children, freer lifestyle of the hippies, movement of many middle class people to the suburbs, availability of television, movement of many African Americans and Latinos to Northern cities, popularity of new kinds of music such as rock 'n' roll. **B.** Answers might include toys for the growing number of babies that were born, houses for returning veterans, rock 'n' roll records, and "weird" types of clothing for the many rebellious young people.

Chapter 22 **1.** e **2.** d **3.** a **4.** c **5.** b **6.** c **7.** c **8.** b **9.** d **10.** d **A.** the sit-in, a protest in which people take a seat and refuse to leave; the freedom ride, bus trips to test civil rights laws; protest marches, such as the Birmingham march, the March on Washington, and the Selma to Montgomery march. **B.** Victories: barriers to voting fell, African Americans became better educated, had reached high positions in U.S. society. Problems: equality still not achieved, race riots continue.

Chapter 23 **1.** e **2.** c **3.** a **4.** b **5.** d **6.** c **7.** d **8.** a **9.** d **10.** d **A.** Choices will vary, but students should be accurate in selecting the correct fields and the achievements of their choices. **B.** started businesses such as car dealerships, food and beverage companies, insurance, and banks; increased income; more managers and professionals.

Chapter 24 **1.** b **2.** c **3.** a **4.** e **5.** d **6.** a **7.** d **8.** d **9.** d **10.** d **A.** women elected to serve in Congress, as governors and legislators in states, in local government; Supreme Court justices, U.S. representatives to the United Nations. Serve as role models for many younger women. **B.** Answers should include a reasonable explanation of the accomplishments of the woman chosen and reasons for choosing her.

Chapter 25 **1.** d **2.** c **3.** a **4.** b **5.** e **6.** b **7.** a **8.** c **9.** c **10.** d **A.** Students should back up their choice with factual information about that person and reasons that reflect an understanding of the text. **B.** The map will show California, New Mexico, Arizona, and Colorado.

Chapter 26 **1.** c **2.** d **3.** a **4.** b **5.** e **6.** b **7.** b **8.** b **9.** c **10.** d **A.** Answers may focus on the divided feelings many Cuban Americans have developed. They are proud of their culture and their homeland, but at the same time they have established new lives in the United States. **B.** established successful businesses in Miami and have helped to revitalize the city's economy; in Little Havana, replicated Cuban cultural traditions and made the city into an active center of opposition to Castro; made Miami a center of Latin American trade; attracted multinational corporations to set up headquarters there and invest $1 billion in its economy.

Chapter 27 **1.** d **2.** c **3.** e **4.** a **5.** b **6.** b **7.** d **8.** b **9.** d **10.** b **A.** Answers may include: Although Operation Bootstrap strengthened Puerto Rico's economy, low-cost airfare to the United States attracted many Puerto Ricans who wanted to earn higher wages and find a better life. Though they faced discrimination and started at the bottom of the economic ladder, many Puerto Ricans found opportunities to rebuild their lives and decided to remain in New York City. **B.** Most Dominicans who came to the United States settled in the Washington Heights section of New York City, where they have set up restaurants and other small businesses. Dominican business owners have set up associations and formed groups to help their people handle problems with the city, state, and national governments.

Chapter 28 **1.** e **2.** a **3.** d **4.** c **5.** b **6.** b **7.** a **8.** c **9.** d **10.** b **A.**The U.S. government needed to cut spending and to get supplies of natural resources. The termination policy ended federal programs for Native Americans and shifted them to the states. State governments then sold rights to resources on Native American lands to businesses. Many Native Americans lost their land and had to move off the reservations. Native Americans responded by forming the National Congress of American Indians to fight termination. As a result of their protests, termination ended in the 1960s. **B.** Poverty on reservations led Native Americans to take action. Congress passed a law giving Native Americans full civil rights. The Indian Self Determination and Education Act gave Native Americans a role in shaping reservation programs. Other laws supported Native American culture and protected Native American worship. New economic development programs for reservations were started. Native Americans also scored victories in the courts.

Chapter 29 **1.** b **2.** d **3.** c **4.** e **5.** a **6.** d **7.** a **8.** c **9.** a **10.** a **A.** After World War II, Japanese Americans protested their wartime internment and demanded that the U.S. government apologize and repay them for their suffering. Most Americans came to agree with their viewpoint. President Ford and Congress admitted the U.S. policy toward Japanese Americans had been wrong and that they had, indeed, suffered "a grave injustice." **B.** Answers may focus on the changing patterns of U.S. immigration. During the next century, Asians will compose a larger part of the population. In 2050, it is predicted, they will be 10 percent of the total population, and European immigration will continue to decline.

Chapter 30 **1.** b **2.** e **3.** d **4.** a **5.** c **6.** b **7.** d **8.** c **9.** a **10.** b **A.** Western European nations quickly recovered from the war. Their booming economies provided many new jobs with good wages for their people. Communist governments in Eastern Europe refused to allow their citizens to leave, until communism finally collapsed in 1989 in those nations. **B.** Arab Americans such as Farrah and Haggar have been successful in establishing successful businesses in the clothing industry. They also worked at factory jobs in the automobile industry and built prosperous Arab American neighborhoods in Dearborn and Toledo. However, Arab Americans sometimes face prejudice because of acts of terrorism and unrest in the Middle East.

Chapter 31 **1.** c **2.** a **3.** d **4.** e **5.** b **6.** c **7.** b **8.** b **9.** d **10.** a **A.** Answers include: many Americans tired of having to pay the high taxes required to support the increasing costs of the many social programs; many middle class Americans became conservative in their views; favored cutting back programs that benefited other groups but were paid for by their taxes. **B.** Bush wanted to improve American education, both to help people improve their lives and to make the nation more competitive in the world economy. In this, Bush also was reflecting a long-established goal of the nation and its people.

Chapter 32 **1.** b **2.** a **3.** d **4.** c **5.** e **6.** d **7.** c **8.** a **9.** d **10.** c **A.** The collapse posed a challenge to defense policies and strategic economic and military alliances of the Cold War. As the sole superpower, the United States had to redefine its relations with the former Soviet republics and other Eastern European nations. The United States also turned more to the United Nations now to rally support for actions it took on the international scene. **B.** The first statement: the need of the United States for imported oil and the importance of repelling any threat to its sources. The second statement: the United States has a moral obligation to keep powerful nations from overrunning their neighbors; that it fulfilled this obligation in Operation Desert Storm. Some students may say there is truth in both statements and that they do not necessarily contradict each other.

Chapter 33 **1.** b **2.** e **3.** a **4.** c **5.** d **6.** b **7.** b **8.** b **9.** b **10.** a **A.** Answers should reflect students' understanding of the content about the group chosen. **B.** Escalante's ability to overcome the difficulties he faced in the United States; his drive to learn English and then earn an engineering degree; his decision to pass up high-paying jobs in favor of teaching, where he has taught students, most of whom were poor and Latino; his being named one of the best teachers in the United States; his success story, *Stand and Deliver*.

Chapter 34 **1.** c **2.** e **3.** d **4.** a **5.** b **6.** d **7.** d **8.** d **9.** b **10.** b **A.** Answers should focus on welfare programs, food stamps, special education and job training programs. Opinions on their effectiveness will vary, but should be supported by facts. **B.** The posters should illustrate the consequences of selling drugs such as arrest and jail sentences as well as murder. They should also show the outcome of drug use such as addiction, criminal activity to buy drugs, inability to work, and alienation from family.

Chapter 35 **1.** d **2.** e **3.** a **4.** b **5.** c **6.** c **7.** c **8.** b **9.** b **10.** a **A.** Answers should focus on one of the advances described in the chapter in medicine, computer technology, communications, or space exploration. The effect on Americans' lives should be spelled out as explained in the chapter. **B.** Drawings should show an understanding of the technology of the subject chosen, supported by a clear and accurate explanation in the captions.

Chapter 36 **1.** c **2.** e **3.** a **4.** d **5.** b **6.** d **7.** c **8.** d **9.** d **10.** d **A.** The motto supports the idea of the melting pot, which was the prevalent view of the United States until recently. **B.** The chart should include many of the following: elevators, special parking areas, ramps, flattened curbs, special bathroom facilities, wider aisles, closed captioned TV, hearing amplification devices in theaters, and so on.

ACTIVITY SHEETS

VOLUME 1

Chapter 1 **1.** number of foreign-born people in the United States from 1900 to 1990 **2.** top ten nations to send immigrants in the 1980s **3.** 1930–1940 **4.** go down; because it had been dropping steadily since 1930 **5.** Mexico **6.** Latin America and Asia **7.** yes; immigration has added millions of people from many cultures to the U.S. population.

Chapter 2 Sketches will differ but should reflect an understanding of the chapter.

Chapter 3 **1.** because they sailed beyond the sight of land for many days **2.** promised them riches; kept the distance traveled secret **3.** that his crew might throw him overboard **4.** 33 days **5.** October 12, 1492 **6.** took possession of the island **7.** as less than his own **8.** Sample answer: conflicts over land ownership, efforts to force Native Americans to become servants, efforts to convert Native Americans to Christianity

Chapter 4 **1.** Ghana, Mali, Songhai **2.** gold, salt **3.** Routes will vary. Mansa Musa headed overland to Cairo and then onto Mecca.

Chapter 5 **1.** amount of silver exports from Spain's American mines **2.** years in which exports were recorded **3.** tons of silver taken out of the Americas **4.** 1561–1570 **5.** 1591–1600 **6.** go down; because they had been dropping since 1601–1610

Chapter 6 The dates for the randomly arranged events are 1619, 1620, 1588, 1635, 1628, 1675, 1587, 1607, 1619, 1609–1610, 1647. Students should organize these in correct sequential order in the time box that follows.

Chapter 7 **1.** Massachusetts, Virginia **2.** Massachusetts, Virginia **3.** Southern colonies **4.** Georgia **5.** not founded until 1733 **6.** enslaved Africans increased the population greatly **7.** immigration

Chapter 8 **1.** View A **2.** View D **3.** Sample words: horrible; air or sunlight; lie side by side in a cramped, unhealthy space.

Chapter 9 **Causes:** France and Great Britain were rivals in Europe; both wanted land in the Americas. Many Native Americans feared British settlers would take their lands so they joined the French. **Effects:** France gave up most of its North American territory; Spain got French territory west of the Mississippi; Britain got all territory between British colonies and the Mississippi and Canada.

Chapter 10 **1.** 70 years **2.** buyer **3.** helped; gave England a market in which to sell its goods **4.** probably not; because New England had to import so many items **5.** 1760–1770 **6.** colonial boycott of Stamp Act **7.** try to limit colonial exports (which had risen) and increase colonial imports (which dropped) **8.** keep the boycott going because it was successful

Chapter 11 Postcard and message should reflect adventure of the trip to Philadelphia.

Chapter 12 **Chart:** March 1775; Henry urges the colonists to protect their freedom, even it means war. Battle of Lexington. Colonists try to block British entry into Concord. Battle of Ticonderoga. Second Continental Congress begins; May 1775. June 1775; Colonists show their resolve in the bloodiest battle of the Revolution. January 1776; Many colonists are convinced that the colonies should become independent. Rhode Island declares independence. **Summary:** By May of 1776, the colonists were fighting the British and moving closer to independence.

Chapter 13 Student responses will differ but should reflect an understanding of the arguments for and against the Declaration of Independence.

Chapter 14 **1.** Washington led Continental Army. Hays took husband's place at a cannon. Lafayette led combined American and French forces. Armistead spied on British for Lafayette. Steuben trained American soldiers. Gálvez led Spanish troops against the British in the South. Kosciusko built forts on Hudson River. Pulaski led Pennsylvania Germans in many battles. **2.** Students should give an adequate reason for their choice. **3.** Stamp should honor the person chosen.

Chapter 15 **1.** Delaware **2.** Rhode Island **3.** New Hampshire **4.** Rhode Island, Virginia, New Hampshire, New York **5.** Rhode Island, North Carolina **6.** It ranked last in population so it would have the least representatives in the House. **7.** Henry objected to the power given to the national government. **8.** Probably. Ratification came by only a ten-vote margin.

Chapter 16 **1.** F **2.** B **3.** S **4.** F **5.** F **6.** S **7.** F **8.** S **9.** F **10.** B

Chapter 17 Check that news stories answer *who, what, where, when, why* and *how?*

Chapter 18 **1.** Key was expressing his joy and relief that the Americans had defeated the British at Baltimore. **2.** It expressed great pride in the U.S. flag and what it stood for. **3.** It is still a symbol of people's pride in the United States.

Chapter 19 **1.** enslaved African Americans **2.** to emphasize the suffering of enslaved African Americans **3.** the woes of slavery **4.** to seize enslaved African Americans out of bondage; to give them the joys of freedom **5.** Letters might thank George for writing against slavery.

Chapter 20 **1.** six months **2.** plains, mountains, Columbia River **3.** disease, death **4.** (a) a belief in liberty and independence (b) July 4 **5.** no house to live in during the winter **6.** Students might note the land and freedom mentioned in the text.

Chapter 21 **Texas Rebellion:** What/rebellion of Texans against Mexico; Who/American settlers and some *tejanos* against Mexico; Where/in Texas; When/1835–1836; Why/many Americans wanted Texas to become part of the United States and some *tejanos* wanted independence from Mexico. **Mexican War:** What/war over control of Mexican borderlands; Who/United States and Mexico; Where/in Mexico and southwestern part of the United States; When/1846–1848; Why/United States wanted Texas, California, and Nuevo Mexico

Chapter 22 **1.** because he is no scholar; did not spend enough time in the schoolroom **2.** likes it better than ever; thinks it is a grand handsome city **3.** many Irish people in New York **4.** Some have become rich; others have become big in politics. **5.** many jobs, pay is good **6.** The number of Irish Catholics will help preserve their culture. **7.** Students should mention the economic hardships in Ireland. They might also have Pat's mother express relief that her son is safe among other Irish immigrants.

Chapter 23 **1.** from 6 AM until 8:15 PM (about 14 hours) **2.** ancient history, poetry, calisthenics, chorus (singing) **3.** Students report on infractions. **4.** that it is very strict **5.** as pleasant **6.** Sample answer: similarities/subjects studied, silent study halls, gym class; differences/tightly ordered day, required prayer, advice sessions from the head of the school

Chapter 24 **1.** by use of the words "Ladies Department" **2.** that white women and enslaved African American women are united by their gender (they are "sisters") **3.** a life of woe **4.** because a white man can tear away her children **5.** wisdom of complete freedom from slavery **6.** probably; picture shows an African American woman in chains

Chapter 25 **1.** to free the slaves **2.** "No man sent me here; it was my own prompting and that of my Maker, or that of the Devil—whichever you please to [think]." **3.** "Do unto others as you would have them do unto you." **4.** because enslaved African Americans had no one to help them; because the slave states would never see the subject of slavery in its true light **5.** that the issue will be settled; the struggle will not end with his death **6.** It pushed the North and South even farther apart.

Chapter 26 **1.** 13.2 million **2.** 1,500,000 square miles **3.** North had larger population and size. **4.** larger manufacturing output, greater production of iron, more miles of railroad tracks **5.** $269.9 million **6.** The North would win. **7.** most knew how to ride and shoot; many of best officers in U.S. Army came from the South; white Southerners were fighting for a way of life; only had to hold out to win (i.e., wage a successful defensive war) **8.** Some students may say that Northern advantages would eventually wear down the South. Others may say that a well-fought defensive war would wear down the North.

Chapter 27 **1.** areas of Confederate states not held by Union troops **2.** free states of the Union, border states loyal to the union, Confederate areas held by the Union **3.** yes; because border states still had the right to hold onto their slaves **4.** to weaken the South by encouraging enslaved African Americans to flee; to discourage foreign nations from helping the South; to give Northerners a new reasons for fighting the war

Chapter 28 **1.** white-hate groups such as the Ku Klux Klan **2.** former enslaved African Americans **3.** a return to white control of the South **4.** the standing figures **5.** by the words "this is a white man's government"; by the threats of death (skull and crossbones) to suppress African Americans **6.** that African Americans are losing their rights **7.** opposes them **8.** Negative caricatures of the thuglike figures versus the sympathetic treatment of the African American family

Chapter 29 Additional similarities: racial background, occupation, ideas on business ownership. Additional differences: ideas on education, ideas on equal opportunity, pace of change. Entries in each category should reflect information in the text.

Chapter 30 **1.** central part of present-day United States **2.** north **3.** west, east **4.** Texas **5.** Cheyenne **6.** Ellsworth and Abilene

Chapter 31 **1.** Sample answer: Work Stoppages, 1881–1900. **2.** 1890 **3.** go up or stay roughly the same; work stoppages had stayed between 1,000–1,800 ever since 1885 **4.** formation of unions such as the AFL, poor working conditions during early growth of industry

Chapter 32 **1.** China, Japan **2.** (c) 50 percent **3.** Chinese Exclusion Act of 1882 **4.** 1901–1910 **5.** Hawaii, California **6.** (a) India, (b) Korea, Philippines, Vietnam **7.** 1981–1990 **8.** Sample answer: Asian immigrants have come to the United States since the 1800s, with the largest number arriving in recent times.

Chapter 33 **1.** dark rooms, unlit stairs, lack of fresh air, disease **2.** many die **3.** fouler and darker **4.** Answers might reflect a tenement-dweller's sense of hopelessness or determination to survive. **5.** Riis wrote descriptions to shock the middle class into helping. Addams started settlement houses that offered schooling, day care, and other activities to improve life. Immigrants formed organizations to create a sense of community.

Chapter 34 **1.** Wyoming, Idaho, Utah **2.** 15 **3.** West **4.** The frontier made women more independent. By giving women the vote, territories such as Wyoming attracted more women, making statehood possible.

Chapter 35 **1.** (a) Uncle Sam (b) the United States **2.** Cuba, Puerto Rico, Hawaii, Aguinaldo (Philippines) **3.** (a) a belt (b) use it on Aguinaldo/Philippines **4.** that it is a childish rebellion **5.** drawing Aguinaldo as a child, showing Aguinaldo thumbing his nose at the United States, the self-assured portrayal of Uncle Sam **6.** also as children **7.** All three figures were independence leaders. They would disagree with this cartoon's presumption that their nations could not govern themselves or that Uncle Sam "knows what's best" for them.

Chapter 36 Letters should comment on the new things at the fair.

VOLUME 2

Chapter 1 **1. a)** 3.4 **b)** 6.7 **2.** Correct number of symbols for the graphs: Iron: 1870, 1.5; 1880, 3.4; 1890, 8.1; 1900, 12.3. Railroad track: 1870, 2.1; 1880, 3.7; 1890, 6.7; 1900, 7.7. **3.** Both graphs show strong increases, meaning iron production grew as did the miles of railroad track constructed.

Chapter 2 **1.** immigration to the United States **2.** 1890 to 1939 **3.** Italy **4.** 5 percent **5.** Mexico **6.** 6.8 percent **7.** "Other"

Chapter 3 Postcard should represent a Northern city in the early 1900s. The message should contain adequate reasons for the stated opinions.

Chapter 4 Picture and caption should correctly represent events in the chapter.

Chapter 5 Sample answers: Knights of Labor: 1869; all workers; Haymarket Riot. AFL: 1886; Samuel Gompers. Women's Alliance: 1888; women workers in a variety of trades. Japanese-Mexican Labor Association: 1903; Japanese and Mexican farm workers in California; successful sugar-beet strike. NWTUL: 1903; women from different trades and social classes; Mary Kenney O'Sullivan. ILGWU: garment workers; the Great Uprising of 1909.

Chapter 6 **1.** $45 million **2.** invest in other businesses **3.** gas companies, railroads, banks, steel companies **4.** railroads **5.** It could limit competitor's access to railroads or cut it off completely by charging high rates. Without access to transportation, competitors would be driven out of business. **6.** If Standard Oil controls transportation, it will set rates as it wishes, driving competitors out of business. Then it would be free to raise the prices of its own products, leaving the American public to pay higher prices.

Chapter 7 Correct chronological order and dates for events: 1895, Japan defeats China; 1897, Aguinaldo becomes leader of Philippine independence movement; 1898, U.S. troops capture Manila; 1899, United States calls for Open Door policy; 1900, Boxer Rebellion breaks out; 1902, U.S. troops capture Aguinaldo; 1905, Japan defeats Russia; 1906, San Francisco segregates Japanese schoolchildren. Picture and caption should correctly describe the event.

Chapter 8 Sample answers: **1.** Thousands died of the disease throughout Cuba and Latin America each year. During the Cuban-Spanish-American War, more U.S. soldiers died of yellow fever than died in battle. **2.** The Platt Amendment written into the Cuban constitution gave the United States the right to take military action in that nation. **3.** Sugar prices rose from 6.5 cents a pound to 22.5 cents. Sugar was planted everywhere in Cuba. Cuban landowners and sugar-mill owners grew rich. **4.** The U.S. President would appoint the island's governor and members of the upper house of the legislature. The U.S. Congress could overrule any Puerto Rican laws. **5.** Puerto Rico gave strong support to the United States during World War I.

Chapter 9 Captions should reflect understanding of the big stick policy. **1.** President Theodore Roosevelt **2.** looks like Roosevelt; is carrying a club labeled "Big Stick," one of Roosevelt's phrases **3.** the Caribbean Sea and nations in and around it **4.** Dominican Republic [Santo Domingo], Cuba, Mexico, Panama **5.** Roosevelt saw the Caribbean as an area that the United States could dominate. **6.** Dominican Republic [Santo Domingo]:sending U.S. warships to collect taxes and pay that nation's European debts; Cuba: sending U.S. troops to put down a rebellion; Mexico: U.S. seizure of Veracruz to keep supplies from reaching President Huerta; Panama: aid to Panamanian rebels so United States could build the Panama Canal.

Chapter 10 **When:** 1914–1918, U.S. entered in 1917. **Where:** in Europe; **Who:** Allies: France, Great Britain, Belgium, Serbia, Russia, Italy, Japan, United States, and others against Central Powers: Germany, Austria-Hungary, Ottoman Empire [Turkey] and Bulgaria. **Why:** Archduke Francis Ferdinand, next in line to be emperor of Austria-Hungary, was shot by a Serb rebel. Austria-Hungary declared war on Serbia. The European system of alliances led other countries to war.

Chapter 11 **1.** 1900–1920 and 1920–1940 **2.** from what regions immigrants came to the United States **3.** 3% **4.** the Americas **5.** eastern and southern Europe **6.** laws limiting immigration such as the Emergency Quota Act of 1921 and the Immigration Act of 1924 **7.** Paragraphs should summarize graphs.

Chapter 12 **1.** November 13, 1922 **2.** *The New York Times* **3.** lynching **4.** 3,436 **5.** tensions between whites and African Americans as African Americans moved north in the Great Migration; actions of the KKK **6.** There was an anti-lynching bill before the U.S. Senate at that time. **7.** It asked readers to let their senators know they wanted the bill passed. It also asked readers for contributions.

Chapter 13 Sample answers: Bank Depositors: bank closings, loss of savings. African Americans: jobless rate 50% in 1932, double the national average. Workers in U.S. businesses: a quarter of workforce unemployed. Mexican Americans: repatriation. Stock Market Investors: stock market crash. Farmers of the Great Plains: dust bowl.

Chapter 14 **1.** Great Depression **2.** 12.5 million **3.** decreased **4.** by 7 million **5.** Students should describe the slow drop in unemployment from 1915 to 1925 during the Roaring Twenties, the sharp increase in the 1930s during the Great Depression, the gradual decrease from 1933 to 1940 during the New Deal, and the sharp decrease to the lowest level in 40 years during World War II.

Chapter 15 Sample answers: **A.** In 1941, Japan staged an attack on the United States naval base at Pearl Harbor in Hawaii. (3) **B.** The Allies sent a huge fighting force across the English Channel to France on D-Day, June 6, 1944. (4) **C.** Adolph Hitler and the Nazi party came to power in 1933 by promising to lead Germany out of an economic depression. (1) **D.** The decision by the United States to drop atomic bombs on Hiroshima and Nagasaki brought the war with Japan to an end in 1945. (5) **E.** In 1938, France and England gave in to Hitler's demands and let Germany seize western Czechoslovakia. (2)

Chapter 16 **1.** south-central Idaho **2.** semi-desert with flat prairies **3.** the evacuees themselves **4.** possibly lack of privacy; isolation from the rest of the world **5.** because the Japanese had been interned as security threats and now they were being asked to join the army

Chapter 17 **1.** organization of the UN **2.** six **3.** General Assembly; it is centrally located in the diagram and other branches flow out of it or report to it **4.** International Court of Justice **5.** Economic and Social Council **6.** Secretariat **7.** Security Council

Chapter 18 **1.** early December 1955 in Montgomery, Alabama **2.** Rosa Parks **3.** African Americans in Montgomery **4.** to boycott the

Montgomery buses **5.** The company might lose enough money to force it to change its policies. **6.** In late 1956, the U.S. Supreme Court barred segregation on Alabama buses and the boycott ended as African Americans rode the Montgomery buses and sat wherever they wished.

Chapter 19 Sample answers: John F. Kennedy: Dem; 1961–1963; space race with Soviet Union [Bay of Pigs and Cuban Missile Crisis in Chapter 17]; New Frontier, civil rights; assassinated. Lyndon B. Johnson: Dem; 1963–1969; Vietnam War; Great Society, war on poverty, civil rights; chose not to run for reelection. Richard M. Nixon: Rep; 1969–1974; improved relations with Soviet Union and China, pulled U.S. troops out of Vietnam; tried to decrease federal spending; resigned. Gerald R. Ford: Rep; 1974–1977; oil crisis; high inflation and economic stagnation; lost reelection. Jimmy Carter: Dem; 1977-1981; Camp David Treaty, Iran Hostage Crisis; energy crisis; lost reelection.

Chapter 20 **1.** African American soldier **2.** Vietnam; because of the label on the box **3.** reading a letter from his parents **4.** the African American struggle to win civil rights **5.** African American soldiers are fighting for freedom for other peoples even though they are denied many freedoms at home.

Chapter 21 Sample answers: **1.** love of talking, listening to "top-tune" radio, 30-minute telephone calls, and use of slang **2.** revolutionaries **3.** Vietnam War **4.** "We shall overcome our parents' misunderstanding of us." "We will dress and act differently [from our parents]." **5.** both loved music, especially rock; both were different from their parents **6.** To get students started, you might have them brainstorm what sets teenagers in the 1990s apart from older age groups.

Chapter 22 **1.** Portland, San Francisco, Watts/Los Angeles, Tucson **2.** Grenada, Louisville, Nashville, Atlanta, Americus, Tampa, Washington D.C. **3.** Milwaukee, Chicago, Pontiac, Detroit, Rochester **4.** eastern part of U.S. **5.** Paragraphs will vary. Between 1965-1968, 24 major riots took place across the nation. In 14 of these riots, people died. Many riots took place in the cities of the Northeast.

Chapter 23 You may need to ask students to brainstorm about how the Civil Rights Movement has changed their lives before they begin writing their letters.

Chapter 24 Student responses should show an understanding of the arguments for and against the ERA.

Chapter 25 Obituaries should use information on the activity sheet and in the text.

Chapter 26 **1.** the geographic distribution of people of Cuban ancestry **2.** Florida and New Jersey **3.** 674,000; 85,000 **4.** the South **5.** Sample response: Although Cuban Americans live in states throughout the nation, the largest concentration live in the South and in some states in the East such as New Jersey and New York.

Chapter 27 Postcard and message should reflect information in the text.

Chapter 28 **1.** Mexico **2.** Bolivia **3.** 1,959,000 **4.** 13,388,000 **5.** Sample response: Large numbers of Native Americans still live throughout the Americas, and in several nations they account for the majority of the population.

Chapter 29 **1.** 1,505,000 **2.** in the United States (52.4%) **3.** Southeast Asian, South Asian **4.** Chinese, Filipino, Korean, Southeast Asian **5.** Sample answer: The large number of foreign-born Southeast Asians and South Asians shows that many immigrants have arrived from this region in the 1980s.

Chapter 30 **1.** 1961–1970 55,540; 1971–1980 170,700; 1981–1990 332,800 **2.** Afghanistan **3.** Iran **4.** Middle Eastern immigration has steadily increased. **5.** It will probably increase in the future. **6.** The growing number of Muslim immigrants increases the practice of Islam in the United States. (You might remind students that many African Americans also practice Islam, a faith spread into Africa by Muslim conquerors and traders.)

Chapter 31 Additional similarities: racial background, occupation, ideas on business ownership. Additional differences: ideas on education, ideas on equal opportunity, pace of change. Entries in each category should reflect information in the text.

Chapter 32 Check diagrams for correct information on the foreign policy crisis.

Chapter 33 **1.** German, Irish, English, African **2.** Asia **3.** Table 1: Many people trace their ancestry to Mexico. Table 2: Large numbers of immigrants arrived from Mexico, the Dominican Republic, and El Salvador. **4.** Generalizations will vary. As a tip, tell students to use the word "diverse" or "diversity" in the their generalizations.

Chapter 34 Charts will differ but should reflect understanding of the chapter material.

Chapter 35 Students can use ideas from the chapter or their imaginations to create their pictures.

Chapter 36 **1.** 244,780,659 **2.** The average American was a European male teenager. He lived in a rural area in a house of at least six people. **3.** The average American is a 33-year-old woman of German ancestry. She lives in a city in an apartment or condo with one or two other people. **4.** It will probably become more diverse. A comparison of the two sets of figures shows that the United States has had a pattern of increased diversity. The rate of growth among Latinos and Asians/Pacific Islands also promise to make the nation more diverse.